S0-BEH-428

VoiceXML

VoiceXML: Strategies and Techniques for Effective Voice Application Development with VoiceXML 2.0

Chetan Sharma
Jeff Kunins

Wiley Computer Publishing

John Wiley & Sons, Inc.

NEW YORK · CHICHESTER · WEINHEIM · BRISBANE · SINGAPORE · TORONTO

Publisher: Robert Ipsen
Editor: Carol Long
Assistant Editor: Adaobi Obi
Managing Editor: Geraldine Fahey
Associate New Media Editor: Brian Snapp
Text Design & Composition: North Market Street Graphics

Designations used by companies to distinguish their products are often claimed as trademarks. In all instances where John Wiley & Sons, Inc., is aware of a claim, the product names appear in initial capital or all capital letters. Readers, however, should contact the appropriate companies for more complete information regarding trademarks and registration.

This book is printed on acid-free paper.

Copyright © 2002 by Cheta Sharma and Jeff Kunins. All rights reserved.

Published by John Wiley & Sons, Inc., New York.

Published simultaneously in Canada.

No part of this publication may be reproduced, stored in a retrieval system or transmitted in any form or by any means, electronic, mechanical, photocopying, recording, scanning or otherwise, except as permitted under Sections 107 or 108 of the 1976 United States Copyright Act, without either the prior written permission of the Publisher, or authorization through payment of the appropriate per-copy fee to the Copyright Clearance Center, 222 Rosewood Drive, Danvers, MA 01923, (978) 750-8400, fax (978) 750-4744. Requests to the Publisher for permission should be addressed to the Permissions Department, John Wiley & Sons, Inc., 605 Third Avenue, New York, NY 10158-0012, (212) 850-6011, fax (212) 850-6008, E-Mail: PERMREQ @ WILEY.COM.

This publication is designed to provide accurate and authoritative information in regard to the subject matter covered. It is sold with the understanding that the publisher is not engaged in professional services. If professional advice or other expert assistance is required, the services of a competent professional person should be sought.

On file with the Library of Congress

ISBN: 0471-41893-5

Printed in the United States of America.

10 9 8 7 6 5 4 3 2 1

*Dedicated to the fond memories and life of
Shri YagyaDatta Sharma.*

—CHETAN

*To Karina — my unexpected partner in life's
adventures for whose presence and union
I thank God every day.*

—JEFF

Professional Developer's Guide Series

Other titles in the series:

GPRS and 3G Wireless Applications by Christoffer Andersson,
ISBN: 0-471-41405-0

Constructing Intelligent Agents Using Java by Joseph P. Bigus and
Jennifer Bigus, ISBN: 0-47139601-X

Advanced Palm Programming by Steve Mann and Ray Rischpater,
ISBN 0-471-39087-9

WAP Servlets by John L. Cook, III, ISBN: 0-471-39307-X

Java 2 Micro Edition, by Eric Giguere. ISBN: 0-471-39065-8

Scripting XML and WMI for Microsoft (r) SQL Server(tm) 2000,
by Tobias Martinsson ISBN: 0-471-39951-5

Contents

Acknowledgments

VoiceXML: *Strategies and Techniques for Effective Voice Application Development* would not have happened without the help from the following fine individuals. I am forever indebted to:

Margaret Hendrey for considering and encouraging the project since its inception,

Staff at John Wiley & Sons for their help, attention to detail, continuous feedback, and support throughout the length of this project,

Jeff Kunins, my co-author, for his friendship, support, and enthusiasm for this project,

Eswar Eluri and Hari Kanangi for building the field services application, for technical review of the manuscript, for our endless conversations on the future of voice Web, and for their excitement and support for this project,

Michel Gaultier, Lisa Davis, and Tod Knight for reviewing the manuscript and making helpful suggestions at short notice,

Scott Williamson for his support and encouragement of my extra-curricular activities,

My parents Dr. C. L. Sharma, Prem L. Sharma, Dropadi Sharma, and family members Rahul, Aditya, Deepti, for their encouragement and support throughout my life

My wife Sarla whose endless love, immense patience, good humor, constant encouragement, and dedicated support is a blessing for which I am thankful every moment.

This project owes its successful completion to these people.

Chetan Sharma

Special thanks to the entire Voice Technology and Design team at Tellme Networks, including and especially Dr. Lisa Stifelman, Dr. Barry Arons, Dr. Bruce Buntchuh, and Matt Marx, without whose knowledge and expertise this book would not have been possible. Additional thanks to Matt Oshry, Ross Fubini, and Tom Thai for their permission to liberally borrow from their code examples on Tellme Studio, and to David Weiden and Andy Scott for their support of me taking the time to work on this book.

Jeff Kunins

Introduction

No one would disagree that 2001 has been an extremely challenging year for the technology industry. The dizzying acrobatics of the Internet explosion of 1998 and 1999 truly brought Silicon Valley's excitement and relentless pursuit of innovation into the broadest public arena for the first time. As soccer moms feverishly opened E*Trade accounts and words like *IPO* and *disaggregation* entered the common vernacular, most of us in the industry found ourselves living the dichotomy of both living (and spending with) the hype and waiting for the other shoe to drop. In the year since the initial Microsoft antitrust ruling precipitated the bursting bubble, the landscape of technology emergence and adoption has hastily returned to its more traditional shape and contours.

The name of the game for technology buyers and corporate decision makers in the latter half of 2001 and moving on toward 2002 is cost reduction and demonstrated return on investment. CIOs are under fierce pressure to deliver results that rapidly and materially trim the bottom line while retaining or increasing revenues and customer satisfaction. Solutions that don't satisfy this critical rubric are unlikely to be funded in the short term, while those that do well are to be aggressively adopted.

Voice recognition technology, and the emerging VoiceXML open standard, is a bold standout in this arena. U.S. companies spend more than $30 billion annually on the simple task of answering the phone for customer service. Through a combination of live agents and various automated systems, this massive cost center has been a necessary cost of doing business since well before the rise of toll-free phone service in the early 1970s.

The basic premise is simple: Companies need to answer the phone, and customers expect to get great service all the time, but it's simply cost-prohibitive to have enough live people available 24 hours a day to provide that service. For large call centers, every single percent of their incoming calls that they can automate with self-service solutions can easily drive hundreds of thousands or even millions of dollars in cost savings every year.

Over the past thirty years, a steady stream of technologies has evolved to attack this problem and help businesses deliver strong customer service on a reasonable budget. Unfortunately, touch-tone interactive voice response (IVR)—the primary technology used to provide automated self-service over the phone—is plagued with a variety of problems, not the least of which is that people tend to simply hate it. *USA Today* has ranked touch-tone systems among the top 10 most annoying things in modern life, and satirists of popular culture such as *Seinfeld* and *The Simpsons* have repeatedly commented on how these systems are a ubiquitous—and maddening—piece of everyday life.

The primary reason why traditional touch-tone IVR applications are so despised is simply that people like to use the phone *for talking*. Pushing arbitrary sequences of digits on the phone to navigate painfully designed, hard-to-understand menu trees is slow and confusing, not to mention dangerous in today's world of explosive mobile phone adoption. Voice recognition technology has come of age in the past three to five years, and it is now absolutely possible to build dramatically better self-service solutions for the telephone that allow callers to get what they want simply by using their own voices. While in some cases there is simply no substitute for a live customer service agent, the vast majority of common tasks can be automated in a way that gives people convenient access to the information and services they want without ever waiting on hold.

However, all has not been solved overnight. Traditional IVR and voice recognition platforms have remained proprietary, complex, and isolated from the open standards–based revolution that the Web development paradigm has almost unilaterally brought to corporate information technology. This has severely limited adoption of voice recognition technology to date, and has retained a world where the call centers and Web development resources within most corporations have remained separate groups that are isolated from—if not politically at odds with—one another.

VoiceXML is an emerging open standard that brings the Web development paradigm to the IVR and voice recognition market, which means that existing Hypertext Transfer Protocol (HTTP) gateways to enterprise services and data built using technologies like Secure Socket Layer (SSL) and cookies can be seamlessly extended to the phone. VoiceXML has rapidly received almost unilateral adoption and support from all corners of the voice technology industry. As of August 2001, more than a dozen companies and 15,000 developers have actively announced VoiceXML-compatible products and have begun developing VoiceXML applications.

In this book, we aim to provide a strong survey of the history and business context of VoiceXML, as well as a practical programming resource for professional VoiceXML developers.

How This Book Is Organized

VoiceXML: Strategies and Techniques for Effective Voice Application Development with VoiceXML 2.0 is organized into 15 chapters in five sections, as well as five appendixes with additional information. As with most technologies, successfully building VoiceXML applications and a voice strategy for your company requires a working understanding of the market trends, history, and corollary technologies surrounding VoiceXML and the voice applications space at large.

While it is certainly possible to use just the reference portions of this book as a directed search tool when building applications, we strongly recommend that developers read the chapters sequentially to build a reasonable foundation upon which to grow specific skills in VoiceXML programming. Particularly for developers involved in efforts, either on their own or at their company, to formulate a comprehensive voice strategy and understand how VoiceXML fits in, the nonprogramming chapters throughout the book are critical reading.

The sections and chapters of the book are as follows.

Section 1: Introduction and Context Setting

This first section sets the backdrop against which VoiceXML has emerged and the corollary market trends that make VoiceXML relevant to business today.

- **Chapter 1: "Pervasive Computing and Voice."** The convergence of computing and the communications industry is bringing us close to the promise of pervasive computing: access to any information, anytime, anywhere. It is becoming clear that the value gained by a multichannel strategy and implementation (online, wireless, voice, broadband, etc.) is enormous. Due to various breakthroughs and the standardization of technology in the past few years, voice-based Internet access to applications and services is becoming not only popular but also critical to enterprises. In this chapter we will take a look at the pervasive computing model and how voice fits into the big picture.

- **Chapter 2: "Speech Recognition and Synthesis—The Basics."** Before we jump into the details of VoiceXML, it is important for us to understand the basics of speech recognition and synthesis—the elements that make the implementation of Net access using VoiceXML possible and so powerful. In this chapter, we discuss the various underlying technological components that make up speech recognition (speech to text) and speech synthesis (text to speech).

- **Chapter 3: "The Birth of VoiceXML: Bringing the Web Development Paradigm to the Phone."** The global impact and universal penetration of the Web was predominantly driven by the simplicity of the open Hypertext Markup Language (HTML) standard. The Web development paradigm brought vendor and network independence to distributed applications, and drastically reduced the cost and skills required to quickly deliver powerful solutions. VoiceXML is an emerging open standard that brings the Web development paradigm to the IVR market, which means that existing HTTP gateways to enterprise services and data built using technologies like SSL and cookies can be seamlessly extended to the phone. In this chapter, we cover the specific history and emergence of the VoiceXML standard, as well as its rapid industry adoption.

- **Chapter 4: "VoiceXML for the Enterprise: Deployment Challenges and the Rise of Voice Application Networks."** In theory, VoiceXML makes it as easy to build and deploy enterprise-class voice applications as it has been for traditional Web-based applications. While this is true from a pure application development perspective, in practice, designing great voice applications and deploying the requisite telephony and voice recognition infrastructure in a scalable and reliable fashion is dramatically more complex and demands rare and specialized skills. Voice Application Networks are a network-based solution that help enterprises bridge this gap and rapidly capitalize on the benefits of VoiceXML and great voice applications.

Section 2: Developing VoiceXML Applications

This section contains the core reference material on the VoiceXML programming language and provides a practical, step-by-step guide for developers to get started working with VoiceXML.

- **Chapter 5: "Setting Up a VoiceXML Development Environment."** In this chapter, we cover various development tools and environments available to developers to help them start building VoiceXML applications. Like HTML, Extensible Markup Language (XML), and Wireless Markup Language (WML), VoiceXML files are also text files, so you can use your favorite text editor (VI, emacs, Wordpad, etc.) to write your VoiceXML documents. However, it's better to take advantage of the free tools available on the Internet as they not only allow you to build sample applications, but also to test and in some cases host your applications. The available tools can be divided into two basic categories: Web-based tools and software development toolkits.

- **Chapter 6: "VoiceXML Programming."** In this chapter we will get introduced to the basics of VoiceXML programming language and how you can go about creating the building blocks of your VoiceXML application or service.

- **Chapter 7: "VoiceXML Reference."** This chapter provides a detailed reference with code examples on each element in the VoiceXML language (including VoiceXML 2.0).

- **Chapter 8: "VoiceXML Grammars and Speech Synthesis Markup Language (SSML)."** In speech applications, grammars define acceptable user utterances at various prompts and states of an application or service. This chapter provides a tutorial and reference guide for the new World Wide Web Consortium (W3C)-standardized vendor-independent XML and Backus-Naur (BNF) grammar definition format, as well as for SSML, which makes it possible to specify articulation, prosody, and other criteria to text-to-speech engines in a vendor-independent way.

Section 3: Advanced VoiceXML Topics

Given the fundamentals of programming with VoiceXML, these chapters explore some related and critical topics to consider when building large-scale, production applications.

- **Chapter 9: "Dynamic VoiceXML: Generating Voice Applications from Server-Side Data."** As discussed in previous chapters, the true power of VoiceXML goes far beyond the details of the language itself; rather, it is in the fact that VoiceXML extends the Web paradigm for application development to the phone. In this chapter, we will briefly recap how traditional Web applications are built using server-side logic to dynamically generate HTML markup, and then walk through a series of simple examples that demonstrate using analogous techniques to create powerful VoiceXML applications that fully inherit any existing Web-based infrastructure you may have in place.

■ **Chapter 10: "VoiceXML Security."** As has been stated and demonstrated throughout this book, one of the primary advantages of developing voice applications using VoiceXML is how expertise, infrastructure, tools, and solutions can be directly inherited from traditional Web development. Security is no exception. While there are a few security areas unique to voice applications (most notably the telephone network itself), by and large the number one takeaway is that VoiceXML security works just like Web security, and that companies that have taken the necessary steps to make secure transactions ranging from online commerce to online stock trading available via the Web should be extremely confident that they can safely extend these services to the phone. This chapter walks through the critical security issues developers and companies should consider when evaluating VoiceXML technology vendors and their own implementations.

Section 4: Designing Successful Voice Solutions

One of the key messages repeated throughout this book is that VoiceXML programming is only one (and in many ways the least challenging) component of delivering successful voice solutions. In this section, we survey the design and application life cycle factors developers must consider to achieve successful results.

■ **Chapter 11: "The Voice Application Life Cycle."** As with any programming language, learning to write VoiceXML code is just one of the many components that are essential to designing, developing, deploying, and operating a successful world-class application. All successful software development projects, whether they are customer-facing services or shrink-wrapped packaged products, are the result of carefully executing against all states of a detailed development life cycle. Voice applications are anything but an exception to this, and while several of the high-level stages of the voice application life cycle are similar to those for other kinds of services, there are many critical details that are unique to doing voice well.

■ **Chapter 12: "Designing an Effective Voice User Interface (VUI)."** As emphasized throughout this book, VUI design is the most critical element of the development process and it needs to be taken into account right at the start of the project. VUI emphasis and attention need to continue throughout the length of the project, even long after the application or service is officially launched. In this chapter we discuss the guiding principles and best practices of voice user interface design. A specific field service application is used to illustrate key examples.

■ **Chapter 13: "Building an Application: A Case Study."** In this chapter, the full details of the field service case study application are presented, including complete VoiceXML and data model source code listing.

Section 5: Strategy and Futures

Now that we've presented the historical context and working technological framework within which VoiceXML applications are built, we conclude with some commentary on future directions for voice technologies and a rubric for business managers to consider when evaluating their voice strategy.

■ **Chapter 14: "The Future of Voice/VoiceXML Solutions."** The past several years have been instrumental in promoting the role of voice solutions in the computing ecosystem. The improvement in speech technologies and progress with standards such as VoiceXML, Session Initiation Protocol, etc., has laid the groundwork for future innovation in design and development of applications and services. Voice is the most commonly used interface modality, and as we continue to get over the hurdles of making user interfaces better, voice-enabled access is going to become more and more pervasive. We will move from simple text to speech and speech recognition to multimodal machine translation–based applications and services. There are no doubt some serious challenges, but, as in the past, we will continue to develop new ways to accentuate progress through relentless innovation, standardization, and paying attention to the user experience every step of the way.

■ **Chapter 15: "The Final Word—Strategy, Applications, and Conclusions."** VoiceXML-enabled solutions have started to replace traditional IVR systems because they are proving to be more cost-effective and efficient. VoiceXML also improves time to market for voice solutions and increases flexibility in deploying at multiple locations. In this final chapter, we will take a look at various elements to consider while implementing your voice strategy, look at some of the players in this emerging field, review some of the applications and vertical sectors that are adopting voice-enabling technology right now, and conclude with a summary.

Appendixes

■ **Appendix A: "VoiceXML Tips and Tricks."** In this appendix we present a series of common questions and answers from VoiceXML developers. All of these come from real questions submitted by developers to Tellme Networks and other public forums.

Additionally, Appendixes B to D provide a list of acronyms, books, magazine and journal articles, white papers, reports, and conference proceedings in case you want to explore voice applications further. The Useful URLs section lists some useful Web sites and URLs of companies listed in the book.

Who Should Read This Book

Our intention in this book is to provide a fairly broad survey of the technologies and issues developers and business managers should consider when beginning to explore

VoiceXML, while at the same time providing sufficient technical detail to make a useful reference manual for professional VoiceXML programmers.

While we recommend that all readers proceed sequentially from start to finish, developers looking to immediately become productive VoiceXML code writers may focus on Sections 2, 3, and 4.

Business managers who are looking to understand VoiceXML in the context of the traditional IVR market so that they can make effective strategic decisions should focus on Sections 1 and 5.

Tools You Will Need

There are no special tools or software required to work with this book, although Chapter 5 provides developers with significant detail on how to set up a VoiceXML programming environment.

What's on the CD-ROM/Disk/Web Site

The companion CD contains a wealth of information. Software toolkits for developing voice applications discussed in Chapter 5 are available on the CD, including toolkits from IBM, Nuance, Motorola, and University of California, Berkeley. Additionally, there are several white papers and data sheets on the CD from leading voice vendors, including Tellme Networks.

Enjoy!

In summary, we hope that you find *VoiceXML: Strategies and Techniques for Effective Voice Application Development with VoiceXML 2.0* both an informative survey of the overall voice technology market and a practical reference for enterprise VoiceXML development that you will turn to repeatedly when building powerful, robust solutions that help your company improve customer service quality while reducing costs and complexity. Every effort has been made to keep the content accurate. We apologize for any inaccuracies that might have inadvertently sneaked in.

We are very much interested in learning about your thoughts as to how you found this book useful, your suggestions, and advice for future work. Please feel free to contact us at *chetan@ieee.org* and *jeff@tellme.com*.

Happy reading and best wishes.

## CHAPTER 1

Pervasive Computing and Voice

We live in interesting times. The rate at which innovations and ideas are being conceptualized, implemented, and introduced in the market is phenomenal. The convergence of the computing and communications industries is bringing us close to the promise of pervasive computing: access to any information anytime, anywhere, from any device. It is becoming clear that the value gained by a multichannel strategy and implementation (online, wireless, voice, broadband, etc.) is enormous. This allows businesses to keep in touch with their customers and partners and efficiently take the pulse of their fast-moving enterprises. It also allows consumers to have information at their fingertips (literally!).

Due to various breakthroughs and to the standardization of technology in the past few years, voice-based Net access to applications and services is becoming not only popular but also critical to enterprises. It helps them gain a competitive advantage and extend consumer brands, and also directly affects their bottom line. In this chapter we will take a look at the pervasive computing model and how voice fits into the big picture. We will also look at the market drivers of the voice Internet technology sector.

The Pervasive Computing Model

Lou Gerstner, CEO of IBM, has defined pervasive computing as a billion people interacting with a million e-businesses with a trillion devices interconnected.

E-business is all about establishing better and more efficient relationships among consumers, producers, and partners. The transactions that make up e-business involve the buying and selling of goods among businesses (B2B, e.g., Onvia.com); between businesses and consumers (B2C, e.g., Amazon.com); and among consumers (C2C, e.g., Ebay). The first generation of e-business services moved the traditional client-server applications to a Web-centric model where one could get connected to any networked computer using a simple Web interface, which could reside on any computer. The powerful underlying principle of the next phase of e-business metamorphosis is *any information, anytime, anywhere, any device*. This is the promise of the next information revolution, and the Internet is at the core of this incredible electronic boom.

During the last decade, a swift transition has been made from a client-server computing model to an Internet-centric model. The advantages were obvious: no need to be tied to proprietary user interfaces and technologies. In the Internet-centric world, using a browser, one could connect to applications and services like never before. This simple concept has revolutionized the computing industry and has led to enormous innovation and growth. Though Internet-centric computing is still evolving, it has two key drawbacks:

1. **Lack of mobility.** One still has to be tied to the physical network to access information.

2. **Use of a single type of access device.** d computers are the only way to access information.

The convergence of the computing and communications industries has rapidly blurred the lines between the devices produced by each industry. Phones and personal data assistants (PDAs) now possess the power and sophistication of desktops. This, coupled with an astonishing surge in the number of mobile subscribers worldwide, is fueling the tremendous momentum of pervasive computing. Nokia estimates that there will be more than 1 billion mobile subscribers worldwide by 2002. Similarly, there has been a surge of solutions in the voice-enabled applications and services space. Interactive TV (iTV) and broadband are also experiencing growth in Europe and North America. Additionally, there is a strong desire to make both narrowband and broadband devices (phones, PDAs, autoPCs, webpads, iTVs, others) capable of accessing Internet.

It is the interlinking and interfacing of various technologies working in concert that makes the vision of pervasive computing a reality. And voice-based solutions are at the center of it. (Figure 1.1 gives a glimpse into the pervasive computing ecosystem.) If you think about it, telephones (wireless and wireline) are the most pervasive devices in the world (approximately 1.3 billion, increasing to 4.9 billion worldwide by 2005 [Source: Telsurf Networks]) and are within reach of the most consumers. So extension of Net content to such devices makes sense. There is no special hardware required on the user side and yet one can take advantage of the convenience and ubiquity of using a simple technological device—**"the telephone"**.

Let's go a little deeper into the pervasive computing concept with the help of an example. Figure 1.2 depicts a representative pervasive computing model. The legacy and back-end information is being accessed by different channels of information: autoPC, wireless phone, wireless PDA, online desktop, voice, and interactive TV. It is the same information, but it is being presented to the user based on the device being used. It becomes very critical to present information based on user preferences and device capabilities to customize the user experience for the given channel. In this example, the network and browser technology used by the end device are different, but the user doesn't have to worry about that. Table 1.1 provides a summary of the various network and browser markup languages used in the example being discussed.

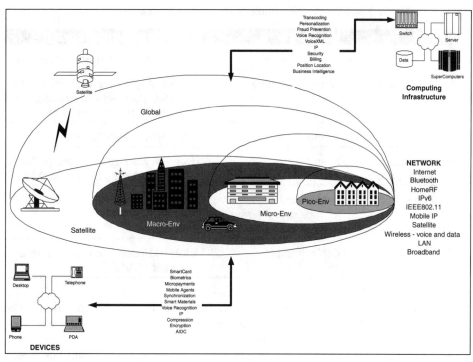

Figure 1.1 The pervasive computing ecosystem.

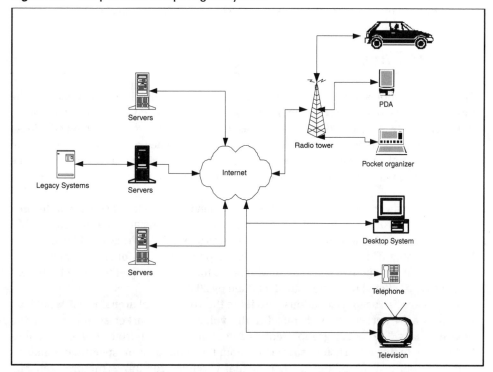

Figure 1.2 The pervasive computing model.

Table 1.1   Network and Browser Technology for Various Devices

DEVICE	NETWORK	BROWSER TECHNOLOGY
AutoPC	Wireless, satellite	Compact HTML (CHTML), VoiceXML
Wireless phone	Wireless, satellite	Wireless Application Protocol (WAP), cHTML, Handheld Device Markup Language (HDML), VoiceXML
PDA	Wireless, satellite	WAP, cHTML, WebClipping
Desktop systems, Network Appliances	Internet	Hypertext Markup Language (HTML), Extensible Markup Language (XML)
Telephone	Cable, wireless, satellite, Voice over Internet Protocol (VoIP)	VoiceXML
Television	Cable, Internet	Advanced Television Enhancement Format (ATVEF)

With the standardization of the VoiceXML specification and the improvement in speech recognition accuracy, voice is becoming a popular device input choice for consumers. It is simple and convenient, and of course pervasive.

In this section, we have reviewed the pervasive computing model and how voice-based information access fits into the picture. In the next section, we will take a look at some key market drivers for the growth of the voice solutions industry.

Market Drivers

Speech recognition applications are not very new to us. We are all very familiar with the interactive voice response (IVR) applications that we have encountered over the years. For example, "Welcome to Bank of America. Our options have recently changed. Please listen to all the options very carefully. Please press 1 for checking account," and so on sound very familiar. Almost any enterprise that has a customer care center has some form of IVR application that functions to guide users to the information they might be looking for.

In the past several years, there has been a tremendous amount of activity in the area of voice access of Net information. According to Allied Business Intelligence (ABI), there are close to 4 million fixed voice portal users in North America and 15.9 million in Western Europe. This number is expected to jump to 17 million for North America and 60 million for Europe by 2005. The total market for voice commerce-related business revenues is predicted to be close to $50 billion by 2005.

Also, there has been tremendous activity in the voice portal arena. Frost & Sullivan estimates a 54 percent growth rate for the voice portal market segment over the next six years. The Kelsey group predicts $5 billion in voice portal services revenues by 2005, including advertising, subscriber bounties, and location-specific commerce, with an additional $7 billion in incremental revenues for infrastructure (see Figure 1.3).

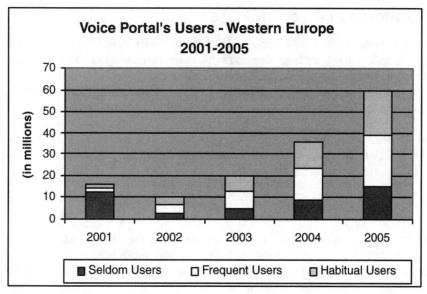

Figure 1.3   Voice portal users—Western Europe, 2001–2005.

(Source: The Kelsey Group.)

Research by International Data Corporation (IDC) and Dain Rauscher Wessels indicates that speech recognition software to speech-enable enterprise applications has the opportunity to capture as much as 10 percent of the $100 billion (by 2005) enterprise application market (see Figure 1.4). Needless to say, this represents a huge business opportunity.

Now let's take a look at the market drivers for this industry.

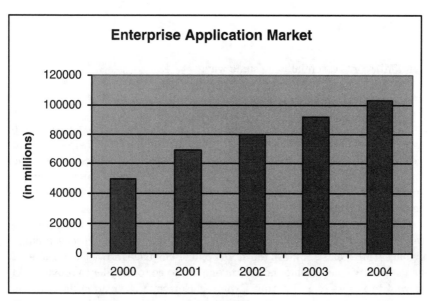

Figure 1.4   Size of enterprise application market.

(Source: IDC.)

New Standards and Technologies

Short Message Service (SMS), WAP, and iMode (in Japan) were introduced to the wireless industry in that order. They helped energize the consumers, and hence the industry, to varying degrees. Similarly, simple HTML helped galvanize the Internet as we know it today. Windows jump-started the PC industry. Every now and then, there comes an agreed-upon, widely adopted standard or enhancement in a technology that starts a tidal wave in the industry by enhancing performance, by reducing costs at least a factor of 10, or by allowing for applications and services that were not easily attainable before. XML, VoiceXML (which is based on XML), and speech recognition are such new standards and technologies for the voice industry.

XML

Extensible Markup Language (XML) is the programming language that has allowed content and application providers to publish richly structured information over the Internet. Over the past couple of years, XML has evolved into the next-generation e-business markup language. It was created to overcome the limitations of HTML's restricted tag set and semantics and derived from pre-Web Standard Generalized Markup Language (SGML). From the early days of static HTML content, applications rapidly started to serve dynamic on-the-fly created interactive HTML content. HTML does a good job at formatting and presenting the content but lacks the ability to apply meaning to the content. That's where XML's value can be realized. XML makes the data smart, meaning it can be extracted to be used in other applications and in providing other services across partner extranets or the consumer Internet.

For example, to italicize text in HTML, you use the <I> tag. This tag instructs the browser where to start italicizing the text. The ending tag </I> tells where to end the italics.

```
<I>Badminton</I>
```

Markup in XML works essentially the same way:

```
<Racquet Sports>Badminton</Racquet Sports>
```

Unlike in HTML, with XML you can create your own elements to describe exactly what you want the data to mean. The document type definition (DTD) helps standardize the structure of the XML documents that can be exchanged with others. DTDs define the rules for the elements that can be used in XML file and their valid values. Extensible Style Language (XSL), the style standard for XML, specifies the presentation and appearance of XML documents.

The same XML document can be transformed into a variety of formats using XSL, the language that controls the presentation aspects of data. As things stand today, multiple markup languages (MLs) exist. Some of the more popular languages are listed in Table 1.2.

HTML developers will appreciate the efforts one has to go to in order to provide content to different browsers (e.g., Internet Explorer, Netscape Navigator). Imagine the conundrum, then, if one has to format the content for multiple microbrowsers, each

Table 1.2 Markup Languages

MARKUP LANGUAGE	PROPOSED BY	COMMENTS
Web Clipping	Palm	Proprietary format based on HTML.
VoiceXML	IBM, Lucent, Motorola, Nokia	Based on XML; used mainly for creating content to be accessed by voice phones.
Compact HTML	Microsoft, Ericsson	Based on HTML.
cHTML (iMode)	NTT DoCoMo	Based on HTML; primarily popular in Japan, although NTT DoCoMo has made significant investments in Europe and the U.S. to spread iMode adoption.

having its own markup language. Fortunately, by design, XML provides a solution for that very problem. Using style sheets, as shown in Figure 1.5, the same content can be displayed in a variety of formats that are applicable for different browsers and devices. This way, a single content source can be used to publish content in different formats [Wireless Markup Language (WML), HTML, VoiceXML, cHTML, etc.) not matching with] instead of keeping multiple content sources based on markup language formats.

VoiceXML

VoiceXML is an XML-based markup language for distributed voice applications, much as HTML is a language for distributed visual applications. The establishment of a VoiceXML forum to standardize a voice markup language is probably the single largest reason for the growth in the interest and market potential of voice-based applications and services. VoiceXML is designed for creating audio dialogues that feature synthe-sized speech, digitized audio, recognition of spoken and dual-tone multifrequency (DTMF) key input, recording of spoken input, telephony, and mixed interactive con-versations. The goal is to provide voice access and interactive voice responses (for example, by telephone, wireless phone, PDA, desktop, kiosks, etc.) to Net-based con-tent and applications. VoiceXML brings the power of Web development and content delivery to voice response applications and frees the authors and designers of such applications from low-level programming and resource management. It enables inte-gration of voice services with data services using the familiar Internet-centric para-digm, and it gives users the power to seamlessly transition between applications. Document servers provide the dialogues, which can be external to the browser imple-mentation platform.

Let's consider a simple dialogue interaction to demonstrate the power of VoiceXML. Table 1.3 compares the user interaction of traditional IVR dialing versus VoiceXML dial-ing. The number of transaction steps is reduced significantly (especially for experi-enced users). This promotes information interaction using natural voice. More importantly, interactive voice applications can be built using VoiceXML with significant ease by leveraging your current investments and talent.

Table 1.3 An Example to Illustrate Differences in IVR and VoiceXML Dialing

TRADITIONAL IVR DIALING	VOICEXML DIALING
"Welcome to Mutual Bank. Please enter your five-digit account number."	"Welcome to Mutual Bank. Please enter your five-digit account number."
1-2-3-4-5	*1-2-3-4-5*
"You can access your checking or savings account, transfer funds, or have a statement e-mailed, mailed, or faxed to you. Please choose from the following options:	"You can say checking, savings, transfer funds. To have a statement sent to you, say e-mail, postal mail, or fax."
"Press 1 for checking accounts.	*"E-mail."*
"Press 2 for savings accounts.	"Your bank statement will be e-mailed to you."
"Press 3 for transfer of funds.	
"Press 4 to have a statement e-mailed to you.	*"Checking."*
"Press 5 to have a statement mailed to you.	"Your checking account balance is $10,000 as of September 5, 2001."
"Press 6 to have a statement faxed to you.	
"Press 7 to repeat.	
"Press 8 to quit."	
4	
"Your bank statement will be e-mailed to you."	
"You can access your checking or savings account, transfer funds, or have a statement e-mailed, mailed, or faxed to you.	
"Please choose from the following options:	
"Press 1 for checking accounts.	
"Press 2 for savings accounts.	
"Press 3 for transfer of funds.	
"Press 4 to have a statement e-mailed to you.	
"Press 5 to have a statement mailed to you.	
"Press 6 to have a statement faxed to you.	
"Press 7 to repeat.	
"Press 8 to quit."	

TRADITIONAL IVR DIALING	VOICEXML DIALING
1	
"Your checking account balance is $10,000 as of September 5, 2001."	

The sample VoiceXML code for the application in Table 1.3 is as follows:

```
<?xml version="1.0"?>
<vxml version="2.0">
        <form id="login" dtmf="true">
                <field name="account_holder_name" type="digits">
                <dtmf src="builtin:dtmf/digits"/>
                        <prompt>
                                Welcome to <emp> Mutual Bank</imp>
                                Please enter your five digit account
                                number
                                <break size="small"/>
```

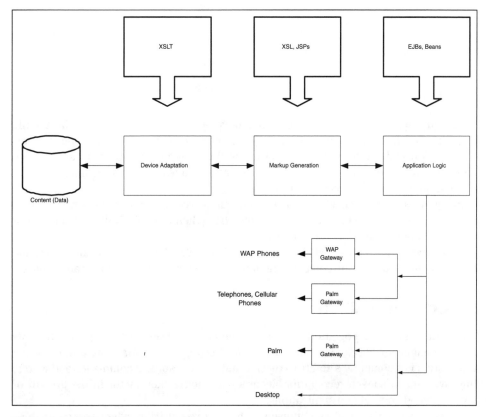

Figure 1.5 XML content processing.

```
                                </prompt>
                        </field>
                        <filled>
                                <submit next="servlet/verifyaccount"/>
                        </filled>
                        <filled>
                                <submit next="/servlet/login"/>
                        </filled>
                        <field name="options">

                                <prompt>
                                        You can access your checking or savings
                                        account,transfer funds, have a
                                        statement e-mailed, mailed, or faxed
                                        to you.
                                        <emp> Please say your option </emp>
                                </prompt>
                                <grammar>
                                        checking [account]|savings [account]|
                                        transfer [funds]|e-mail [statement]|
                                        mail[statement]|fax [statement]
                                </grammar>
                        </field>
                        <filled>
                                <submit next="/servlet/options"/>
                        </filled>
                </form>
        </vxml>
```

As you can gather, VoiceXML allows Web developers to use their existing Java, XML, and Web development skills to design and implement interactive voice applications. They no longer have to learn the proprietary IVR programming languages. This also allows them to keep a single point of maintenance for business function and thus lays a foundation for consistent customer experience.

Early on, several companies launched consumer voice portals based on VoiceXML (see Table 1.4). This has helped promote and strengthen the VoiceXML movement. For more information, see Chapters 3 and 4.

Throughout this book we will be discussing VoiceXML's history, its specifications, and how it can be used to create compelling and revenue-generating applications and services.

Speech Recognition

The value of speech recognition software, equipment, and services is expected to grow to $22.6 billion by 2003, according to *Speech Recognition Update Magazine*. Speech recognition is a computer's ability to receive and process spoken commands and words. Improvement in speech recognition accuracy is another key factor in the growth of voice-enabled content and applications.

Speech recognition is often confused with *voice recognition*, which is a computer's

Table 1.4   Consumer Voice Portals

VENDOR	SERVICE ACCESS	APPLICATIONS
Tellme Networks	www.tellme.com 1-800-555-TELL #121 from any AT&T wireless phone	Airlines, announcements, blackjack, driving directions, extensions, horoscopes, hotels, lotteries, movies, news, phone booths, restaurants, shopping, ski reports, soap operas, sports, stock quotes, rental cars, taxis, traffic, wakeup calls
BeVocal	www.bevocal.com 1-800-4-BVOCAL	Business finder, driving directions, flight information, horoscopes, lotteries, news, sports, stock quotes, traffic, TV dramas, weather
HeyAnita	www.heyanita.com 1-800-44-ANITA	Stock Quotes, Flight Tracking, Weather, Traffic, News, Sports, Horoscopes, Email Reader.

ability to recognize a specific voice or speaker and is used for security and authentication purposes. Speech recognition systems essentially have two main functions: to understand the words being spoken and then convert them into text for further use, and to convert text to speech for the purposes of information access. It allows a convenient and natural way to use voice as an input mechanism (and is thus interactive). The three basic components of speech recognition are:

1. **Capture and preprocessing.** Speech is an analog signal and it needs to be captured and converted into digital format (spectral representation and segmentation). Once the speech is captured, computer algorithms analyze acoustic signals and recognize common sound patterns called *phonemes*. Any language can be broken down into phonemes including the sounds of the individual letters and their pairings, such as *ao* and *sh*. Words, phrases, and sentences can be represented digitally as sequences of these phonemes.

2. **Recognition and feature extraction.** Once the speech signal is segmented, phoneme probability (i.e., the probability that a particular phoneme represents what was spoken) is calculated. Based on this statistical analysis, words are reconstructed by matching the phonetic sounds to the lexical database. Complex neural network programs are being used to accurately predict the sequence of the words that make up a conversation or a sentence.

3. **Communication with other application software and hardware.** After speech input has been identified, it is communicated to the application software or speech-aware applications for further processing.

We will discuss the basics of speech recognition in more detail in Chapter 2.

Competition

Enterprises are constantly looking for ways to differentiate themselves from both traditional and nontraditional competitors. Voice-based applications and services provide another channel to connect with customers, partners, and employees. By offering them yet another way to connect to the enterprise, it might help in keeping users when churn rates run high and the competition is only a click or a call away. By offering these services early in the life cycle of a technology, enterprises can attract early adopters and can learn from and adapt to user behavior before the competition does.

Voice also enables enterprises to reach a new key segment that is often left out—users with disabilities. Voice empowers these users to purposefully derive benefit from their natural voice interaction with Net applications and services.

The Internet and the Wireless Revolution

The past decade has been incredible from a technology point of view. With the convergence of computing and the communications industry, we have dramatically enhanced the way we collaborate, share, and disseminate information. Memory, power, and processing costs are dropping rapidly. Because of that, it is increasingly becoming possible to realize the pervasive computing vision of access to any data anywhere, any time. According to NUA, which provides online source for information on Internet demographics and trends analysis, five new users accessed the Internet every second in 2000. Users around the world are getting familiar with interacting with Net-based content using devices of different forms and functionalities.

Similarly, the numbers for wireless usage and wireless Internet adoption are going through the roof. Japan's NTT DoCoMo recently became the world's largest Internet service provider (ISP), ahead of AOL.

In addition to server-based speech recognition, there is now device-based speech recognition, which allows for much-improved user interfaces and navigation. In the future, using multimodal browsing, we will be able to interact with an application using both keypad and speech as inputs simultaneously. For example, in the WAP example in Figure 1.6, it takes at least three clicks to go to the required menu item to access the 401K balance. Using speech recognition on the phone, it is possible to navigate directly to the Balance menu item. This feature is especially handy when operating the phone in a hands-free mode.

The Need to Streamline Enterprise Processes and Procedures

Companies are always looking for ways to decrease cost of doing business. As they adopt each new wave of technology, enterprises have to find ways to integrate their existing processes and infrastructure with new technologies to truly take advantage of various innovations and ideas. Not only does voice-based access to corporate information, applications, and services increase efficiency, productivity, and brand awareness

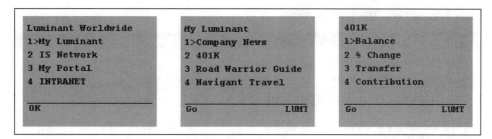

Figure 1.6 WAP portal.

among consumers, partners, and employees alike, but converting call center applications into automated voice-based applications can have a direct effect on the bottom line. According to SpeechWorks (Figure 1.7), there is a cost reduction of approximately 90 percent when automated speech-enabled applications are used.

Consumer Awareness and Demand

Speech recognition is fast becoming a mass-market, self-service option that satisfies and is, in fact, preferred by the vast majority of users over other options including human operators, touch-tone systems, and the Web. Nuance, a leader in speech technology, has conducted a survey on the favorability of speech-enabled applications (see Table 1.5). More and more users are becoming familiar with these applications and are willing to pay for them.

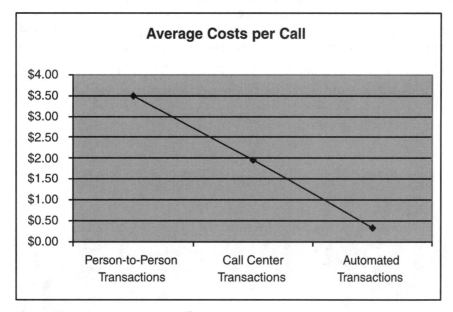

Figure 1.7 Average costs per call.
(Source: Speech Works.)

Table 1.5 Speech Survey by Nuance

STATEMENT	2000 SCORECARD RATING 4 OR 5
I like the freedom to use the system whenever, wherever I want.	78% (4.28)
This is a system I feel comfortable with.	75% (4.05)
I like speaking my responses better than pushing buttons.	68% (3.89)
This system is really fast to use.	65% (3.82)
The fact that the system exists tells me that the company cares about giving customers and employees what they want and need.	65% (3.82)
This system understands what I say.	64% (3.76)
I feel in control when I'm using the system.	62% (3.69)
I can always get what I want from the system.	60% (3.64)

Numbers in parentheses are mean ratings on a five-point scale, where 5 is "fits the way I feel perfectly" and 1 is "does not fit the way I feel."

In this chapter, we have looked at the pervasive computing model and analyzed the market drivers behind voice applications and services. Some industry experts predict that voice-based access will be as big as the Web. It is clear that, however big the market may be, voice-based Net access is here to stay. In the next chapter, we will take a look at how speech recognition works and also get familiar with the associated terminology.

## CHAPTER 2

Speech Recognition and Synthesis—The Basics

In Chapter 1 we discussed the importance of voice technologies in the pervasive computing ecosystem. We also reviewed the key market drivers for the voice technology market. Before we jump into the details of VoiceXML, it is important for us to understand the basics of speech recognition and synthesis—the elements that make the implementation of Net access using VoiceXML possible and so powerful. In the following sections, we will learn about the various components that make up speech recognition (speech to text) and speech synthesis (text to speech).

Speech Recognition

Automatic speech recognition (ASR) is a technology that allows a machine to understand human speech. Over the years, human speech interactions have become more sophisticated. Over the past 30 years, through much research and development, speech recognition accuracy has increased tremendously; processor costs have gone down dramatically; and, with the advent of the Internet and VoiceXML, there has been a general enthusiasm for voice-based solutions among the business community and consumers alike. Figure 2.1 and Table 2.1 show a cursory relationship of cost versus complexity for various speech recognition technologies. Touch-tone is not a true speech recognition technology; with most touch-tone applications today, one could either press the telephone buttons or say the numbers. From touch-tone technology, we graduated to computer or interactive voice response (IVR) directed dialogue interaction. During 2000, VoiceXML gathered significant momentum and support within the industry to become industry's de facto standard for voice access to content on the Internet. (For more on the historical evolution of VoiceXML, please refer to Chapter 3.) Due to the way the technology and standards are evolving, we should see a tighter integration of natural language understanding (NLU) and multimodal browsing with speech recognition by

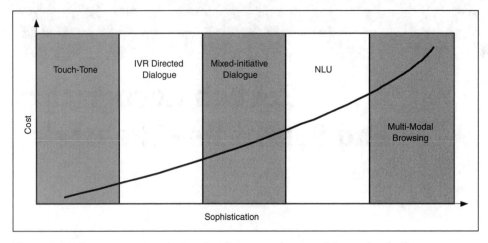

Figure 2.1 Cost versus complexity of various speech recognition technologies.

2003. NLU refers to a more conversational style of speech interaction (as would be used in conversing with a person). Multimodal browsing means that your input and output mechanisms for interactions might involve a combination of different modalities such as speech, text, video, and/or graphics. In the example given in Table 2.1, the user says into the phone, "Show me the weather forecast," and the server returns the information back to the Wireless Application Protocol (WAP) display on the phone. The server could

Table 2.1 Speech Recognition Technologies

TECHNOLOGY	COMPUTER-USER INTERACTION
Touch-tone	C: Press 1 for airline reservations.
IVR directed dialogue	C: Would you like to look for airline reservations or schedules?
	U: Airline reservations.
Mixed-initiative dialogue	C: Would you like to look for airline reservations or schedules?
	U: I want to fly from Boston to New York tomorrow morning.
NLU	C: United Airlines. How may I help you?
	U: Could you please book me a first-class seat from Seattle to Hong Kong? I want an early morning flight leaving the day after tomorrow.
	C: Done. Have a nice trip.
Multimodal browsing	U: Show me the weather forecast.
	C: (Returns information over the phone.)

very well deliver the information via both channels—text to speech and speech to text—depending on user preferences and device and network capabilities.

Let's dissect a basic speech recognition interaction. (Figure 2.2 outlines the primary steps involved.) The whole process works as follows:

Step 1. User input. The user says a word or phrase (or a combination of words and phrases) using an input device such as a telephone or wireless phone. The system captures the speech (in its analog form) in the form of an acoustic signal.

Step 2. Digitization. The analog speech signal is converted into a digital signal so the computer can further process it. The conversation process takes into account the acoustic properties of the human ear.

Step 3. Phonetic breakdown. The speech recognition software breaks down the digital signal into basic components of speech—consonant or vowel sounds.

Phonemes are the single distinctive speech sound of a language—its primary unit. Phonemes combine to form syllables and the syllables combine to form words. Each phoneme is distinguished by its own unique pattern in the spectrogram. For voiced phonemes, the signature involves large concentrations of energy called *formants;* within each formant, and typically across all active formants, there is a characteristic waxing and waning of energy in all frequencies, which is the most salient feature of human voice.

Spectrograms help analyze speech. Speech consists of vibrations produced in the vocal tract. The vibrations themselves can be represented by speech wave-

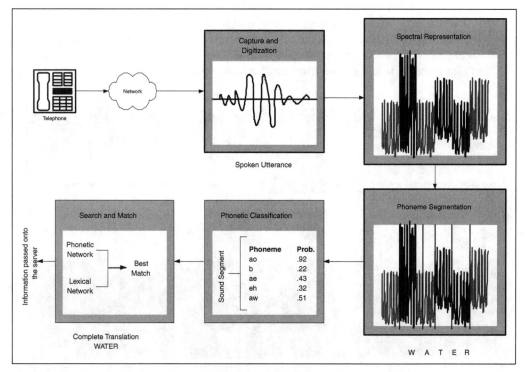

Figure 2.2 Automatic speech recognition process for the word *water.*

forms. Though it is not possible to distinguish phonemes in a waveform, if the waveform is chopped into frequency components, it can be viewed as the spectrogram. The vertical axis represents frequencies up to 8,000 Hz and the horizontal axis shows positive time toward the right. Colors represent the most important acoustic peaks for a given time frame. Figure 2.3 shows the waveform and spectrogram of the word *important*.

Changing the phoneme of a word changes its meaning. For example, the difference between *fat* and *vat* is a single sound, but changing the sound changes the meaning of the word. Similarly, the same language could be phonematically different in different regions. For example, the word *schedule* in American English is represented as S K EH D UW L, while in the United Kingdom, it is SH EH D YUW L. The English language has approximately 38 phonemes (about one-third are consonant phonemes, with the rest being vowel phonemes).

Step 4. Statistical modeling. The system then tries to match these sounds to their phonetic representations. A *dictionary* is the phonetic representation of words that are used by the recognition engine to recognize speech. For example, *the* can be pronounced *thee* as well as *thuh*.

Step 5. Matching. The ASR application then tries to match the possible phonetic representations to words or phrases defined in the grammar of that application. For example, in a travel application, the user might say "second class" to reserve a seat in economy class. But if the words *second class* haven't been defined as acceptable synonym for *economy class*, the application will not be able to accept the utterance.

Language modeling technology is also used to increase accuracy by comparing recognized sounds to a list of usage rules or constraints to determine the probability of one sound following another. The system then returns the *n*-best list based on word or phrase matches to the spoken utterance and associated confidence scores. The recog-

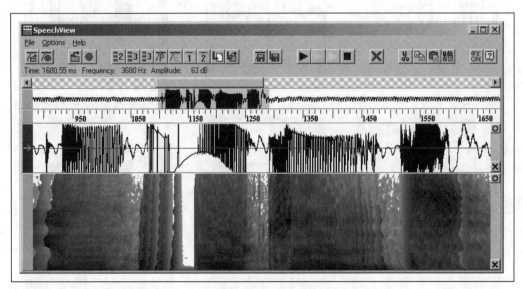

Figure 2.3 Waveform and spectrogram for the word *important*.

nizers, which are made up of ASR and language modeling technology, can be either hardware or software solutions depending upon the methodology in use. One of the most commonly used recognizer models is the Hidden Markov Model (HMM), which is a digital signal processing (DSP)-based mathematical model that describes a complex system in terms of a finite set of possible system states, with statistical information representing the probability of each possible transition from one state to another.

HMMs are used to predict hidden sequences based on external observations of the system, such as the acoustic information collected from a microphone. HMMs are widely used and are considered to be an essential strategy for implementing accurate and fast recognizers.

Speaker Dependence versus Speaker Independence

Speech recognition can be speaker dependent or independent. For speaker-dependent applications, the system is trained to recognize a user by his or her voice. For applications such as dictation or speaker verification, the system first creates a voice fingerprint database based on some initial sessions (typically the user recites a series of phrases or sentences to cover a wide range of phonetic representation).

Speaker-independent applications are those for which system training is not required and are designed for use by a larger set of users. In such applications, the user is generally guided by system prompts and the applications are quite generic in nature. The commonly used banking, travel, and customer service applications that use interactive voice response fall under this category. The system must take into consideration the wide variations in possible responses from the user and account for foreign accents, dialectical differences, and speech impairments. This is generally done by defining a set grammar for the application so as to elicit a correct response from the user. A majority of the VoiceXML applications run on top of speaker-independent voice-recognition platforms.

Continuous versus Discrete Input

You might be most familiar with discrete voice input applications such as telephone credit card applications, where you say the credit card number, one digit at a time, with pauses and beeps in between the utterances. The same applies for an application that might request you to say your Social Security number or identification number. However, with the advent of continuous speech processing (CSP) technology, it is possible to allow the user to say digits or words in a continuous mode (unbroken string of utterance), eliminating the need to wait for beeps and pauses between utterances. With CSP, there is an improvement in the performance, accuracy, and scalability—and hence cost savings—of running a voice application.

CSP is generally done on a DSP board to offload the central processing unit (CPU) of the intensive operations. This way preprocessed data (voice) can be fed directly to the server (processor).

Word Spotting

Word spotting is a technique used by some applications to give the user an impression of continuous speech processing. In this method, certain words are recognized from a continuous stream of words to make sense of what the user is trying to convey. This makes the interaction with the system look more natural and responsive. For example, if the user says, "Please look up my account balance," the system will key in on *account balance* and will do a query to the database to fetch the user's account balance.

Grammars and Vocabularies

One of the most important aspects of any speech application is its grammar and vocabulary. A properly designed grammar is absolutely critical to the voice user interface of any speech application.

A *grammar* is the union of words and phrases comprising the expected range of input and output for the application. It basically defines what an application needs to listen for from the user at every step. For example, in our banking application in Chapter 1, the following grammar was used to direct the user:

```
<grammar type="x-ref">

    checking [account]|savings [account]|transfer
    [funds]|e-mail [statement]|mail [statement]|
    fax [statement]

</grammar>
```

In this example, the user has to select from six available options, each of which can be communicated two different ways (to have a statement e-mailed, the user could say "e-mail statement" or just "e-mail"; both inputs would be acceptable). Similarly, if in a travel application the system prompts, "Please say the departure city or airport," the user needs to pick from the list of cities and/or airports that the application is designed for. The system should be able to account for nuances and variations in the utterances. And if the user picks something that is not defined in the grammar, then the application should help guide the user to the correct choices (by reprompting) or enable the user to connect to a human operator or exit the application.

A *vocabulary* is the list of words used in a given application. Various vendors have defined reusable components by vertical markets such as brokerage, health care, customer care, field services, etc. These vocabularies contain all the words and phrases that a user would possibly speak. Figure 2.4 provides an example of predefined grammars available from Nuance with the V-Builder toolkit. (V-Builder, which is also available on the CD that accompanies this book, will be discussed in more detail in Chapter 5.) In this example, commonly used words and phrases, such as names of airlines or airports and digits (dates, credit card numbers, etc.), are already defined and can be used by different applications.

Active Vocabulary

Active vocabulary is the set of phrases that can be recognized at any given moment. An embedded application can have an active vocabulary as small as several words or as large as several thousand. An application can also add words to or subtract words from its active vocabulary. In VoiceXML, this is controlled by scoping, which will be discussed in Chapter 6.

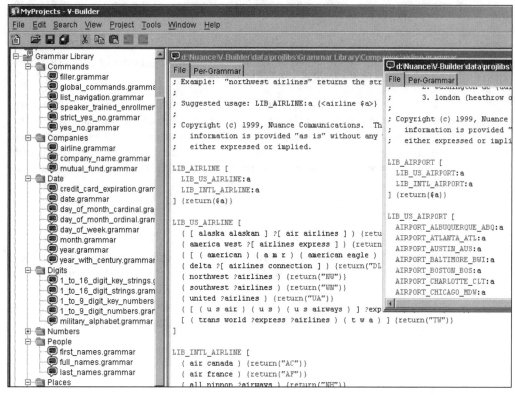

Figure 2.4 Grammar example.

Total Vocabulary

Total vocabulary is the complete set of phrases that are ever recognized by a given speech application or recognition system. This vocabulary can include words that are not in the active vocabulary at any particular moment during execution.

NLU

Natural language understanding (NLU) is considered to be an important step forward for speech-based applications. As mentioned earlier in this chapter, NLU supports conversational dialogue that is unstructured in nature, meaning the system does not constrain the user with a noticeable predefined grammar. Consider the following example:

System: *Welcome to United Bank. How can I help you, Jacob?*

User: *How is my Fidelity account doing these days?*

System: *The price of the Fidelity Magellan is $90. What else can I do for you?*

User: *I would like to buy some more.*

System: *How many shares of Fidelity Magellan would you like to buy?*

User: *Hmm, let's say 200.*

System:	*Buying 200 shares of Fidelity Magellan at the total cost of $18,000. Please confirm.*
User:	*I changed my mind. Please make that 300 and that's my final answer.*
System:	*Transaction complete. You just bought 300 shares of Fidelity Magellan at the total cost of $27,000. Goodbye.*

In this example, the user is conversing with the system as if it is a human. Also, the conversation is unstructured, without any noticeable set of constrained grammars. However, the system is able to make sense of various utterances. A commonly used example and a test for NLU applications is to understand and correctly distinguish between *Wright, write,* and *right* in the utterance, "Ask Mr. Wright to write a letter to give the right directions."

Barge-In

Barge-in refers to the application feature that allows the user to interrupt or override a spoken prompt or dialogue. The recognizer keeps a channel open to listen to the caller while speaking the next prompt or providing feedback. This feature greatly enhances the usability of speech applications because it allows experienced users to skip to the part they really want to interact with, thus shortening the time they spend with the application.

Multiple Language Support

In a few years, the majority of Net users will be non-English speaking and most Net content will not be in English, so, it is becoming increasingly important for corporations—especially global ones—to focus on multilingual support for their call center and Net applications. Even in the United States, there is a huge Hispanic and Asian population, while Canada boasts substantial French demographics. Similarly, in some countries in Europe and Asia, natives might converse in up to five or six different languages. Given this scenario, it makes sense to prepare and offer multilingual prompts (just as you would offer multilingual human agents on the other side of the phones). For example, the name Richard Jean can be pronounced as *Richart Jeeen* or *Reeshard Jon.* This requires support for two pronunciations of the same phrases. The system might also be required to switch between two languages in real time. Applications can also be set up to automatically recognize the language of the caller and switch accordingly. This enhances customer service and strengthens loyalty.

Voice Verification

Various corporations and carriers that provide biometric authentication for services have used voice printing for user identification and authentication. First, the user's voice is fingerprinted and stored; subsequent user interactions are compared to the print for verification and authentication.

Speech Synthesis

Speech synthesis (see Figure 2.5), which is synonymous with text-to-speech (TTS) synthesis technology, is a system's ability to convert text into audible speech. Some of the key areas of TTS applications include converting e-mail or fax information into voice and, more recently, converting any Web (or, for that matter, application) content and data into voice. The application spectrum for such applications can range from simple consumer applications like weather and stock quotes to automatically summarized business intelligence reports of legacy databases in real time. As the synthesized speech comes to sound more like the human voice, TTS will be used for a variety of applications such as the reading of books and large amounts of text and data.

Prosody

Prosody is a significant factor in the perception of natural TTS. *Prosody* refers to intonation (or pitch patterns) and rhythm, which convey a variety of syntactic, semantic, and discourse information about an utterance, as well as information about the speaker's emotional state.

The phonetic correlation of pitch is *fundamental frequency*, the frequency at which the vocal cords vibrate. In a parametric (concatenative or rule-based) approach, fundamental frequency is a separate parameter that can be easily manipulated. In a nonparametric scheme, fundamental frequency can only be manipulated by modifying the waveform directly. Due to the particular signal processing techniques involved, however, waveforms can only be modified within a very restrictive set of limits; otherwise, spurious artifacts occur that significantly deteriorate speech quality. Similar considerations apply to durational adjustments. The inherent problems of controlling pitch and duration in a waveform concatenation system are serious obstacles that must be overcome if this approach is ever to produce truly human-sounding speech. Inappropriate prosody is a more serious liability as TTS is extended into new arenas, including dialogue systems, which critically rely on natural prosody.

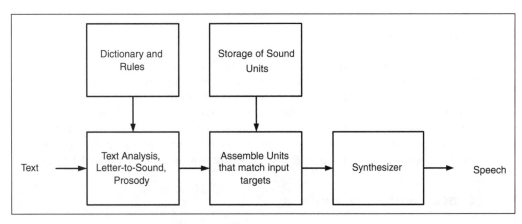

Figure 2.5 The speech synthesis process.

To overcome the difficulties of manipulating prosody in a waveform concatenation scheme, some researchers have attempted to avoid the problem altogether by extracting increasingly larger units from a wider and wider range of prosodic contexts. Such systems tend to be very large in comparison with more constrained concatenation schemes, and their size will only grow combinatorially as more units are added to capture different speaking styles, emotions, and prosodic effects more generally. In the next section we will take a look at various TTS techniques.

Text-to-Speech Methods

Speech synthesis techniques primarily fall under the following three categories:

1. Articulatory synthesis
2. Formant synthesis
3. Concatenative synthesis

Let's discuss each one of these in more detail.

Articulatory Synthesis

Articulatory synthesis uses computational biomechanical models of speech production, such as models of the glottis (which generates periodic and aspiration excitation) and the moving vocal tract. The tongue, which pushes air from the oral cavity, articulates a sound by striking the hard palate, the soft palate, or the teeth, thus changing the direction of the air passing through the oral cavity. The lips, which work in concert with the tongue, also aid in this process called *articulation*. Ideally, an articulatory synthesizer would be controlled by simulated muscle actions of the articulators, such as the tongue, the lips, and the glottis. It would solve time-dependent, three-dimensional differential equations to compute the synthetic speech output. However, this requires complex computation and results in sound that is perceived as unnatural. More understanding and research are required for this technique to become acceptable for consumer applications.

Formant Synthesis

Formant synthesis uses a set of rules for controlling an audio waveform that simulates human speech. This creates a true machine-generated speech that more often than not sounds like a robot. Most of the TTS applications use this form of synthesis in voice applications. Formant synthesis generates speech that is highly intelligible, but not completely natural-sounding. However, it has the advantage of a low memory footprint and only moderate computational requirements. Formant synthesis is also widely used for relaying feedback to the user (for example, repeating the user's speech input).

Concatenative Synthesis

In a concatenative approach, stored speech units originally extracted from natural speech are pieced together to produce the speech output. For example, to give a customer a total account value, the system will store and concatenate the following string of words:

"Your+total+account+balance+is+five+thousand+three+hundred+forty+nine+
dollars+and+twenty+six+cents."

for

"Your total account balance is $5349.26."

Because of the large number of factors that can influence the properties of speech segments in natural speech, many different kinds of units from a variety of contexts are typically stored in today's systems. Systems differ widely as to the number, size, and type of units that are stored. A separate set of units must be stored for every voice in each language.

The speech units may be stored either as raw waveforms or as sets of parameters derived from the waveforms. Although parameter values take less space, the current trend in concatenative synthesis is toward waveform concatenation, which has been developed in large part with the goal of producing more human-sounding voice quality than earlier TTS systems. When an utterance is being synthesized, units are selected from the unit database, concatenated, and modified to reflect prosodic (i.e., intonational and durational) properties of the utterance. Selecting the best units to reconstruct a particular utterance is a complex and difficult task on which much research is still being conducted.

This technique is good for systems requiring small vocabularies. Elementary units (i.e., speech segments) are, for example, phonemes (individual vowels or consonants) or phone-to-phone transitions (diphones) that encompass the second half of one phone plus the first half of the next phone (e.g., a vowel-to-consonant transition). Some concatenative synthesizers use so-called demisyllables (i.e., half-syllables or syllable-to-syllable transitions that are recorded either from the beginning of the sound to its center point or from the center point to the end of the sound), in effect, applying the diphone method to the time scale of syllables. (A *diphone* represents the transition between two phonemes and is a unit of acoustic data comprising two phonemes recorded from the center point of one phoneme to the center point of the next phoneme.) Concatenative synthesis itself then strings together (concatenates) units selected from the voice database, and, after optional decoding, outputs the resulting speech signal. Because concatenative systems use snippets of recorded speech, they have the highest potential for sounding natural. In order to understand why this goal was, until recently, hard to achieve and what has changed in the last few years, we need to take a closer look.

Figure 2.3 shows a typical concatenative TTS block diagram. The first block is the message text analysis module that takes ASCII message text and converts it to a series of phonetic symbols and prosody (fundamental frequency, duration, and amplitude) targets. The text analysis module actually consists of a series of modules with separate, but in many cases intertwined, functions. Input text is first analyzed and nonalphabetic symbols and abbreviations are expanded into full words. For example, in the sentence,

"Dr. Kay lives at 5201 Peak Dr."

the first *Dr.* is transcribed as *Doctor,* while the second is transcribed as *Drive.* Next, *5201* is expanded to *five two oh one.* Then, a syntactic parser (recognizing the part of speech for each word in the sentence) is used to label the text. The text module has two main components: a text normalization component and a text-parsing component. The text normalization rules read the input text into a stream of the delta utterance representation and spell out any abbreviations, acronyms, digits and similar items. For example, *St. John St.* becomes *Saint John Street, 1 oz.* becomes *one ounce, $500 million* becomes *five hundred million dollars,* and *Dr. Williamson Dr.* becomes *Doctor Williamson Drive.* However, users can override the treatment of particular items by including them in the special words dictionary. The text normalization rules determine when the end of a sentence has been reached, and add a sentence unit to the delta, as exemplified below for the English sentence *Dr. Smith is 43:*

sentence: |sent | |

inp: |D|r|'.'| '|S|m|i|t|h|' '|i|s|' '|4| |'|3 |.|

text: |d|o|c|t|o|r|' '|S|m|i|t|h|' '|i|s|' '|f|o|r|t|y|'|t|h|r|e|e|.|

The vertical bars (sync marks) coordinate the streams at relevant points. All vertical bars in the same column represent the same sync mark. The delta resulting from text normalization for the sentence is sent to the text parsing rules for linguistic processing. The text parsing rules parse the delta produced by the text normalization rules into intonational phrases, words, morphs, syllables, syllable nuclei, dialect-universal phonemes (called *diaphonemes*), and dialect-specific phones, all of which are represented in separate streams of the delta.

In Figure 2.5, the second block assembles the various units together to create natural-sounding speech. This information is then fed into the synthesizer to generate the speech waveform for the user. One of the key functions of synthesis is to assemble the correct string of phones with the help of a pronunciation dictionary. Thus, for our example sentence (*Dr. Kay lives at 5201 Peak Dr.*), the verb *lives* is distinguished from the noun *lives.* Similarly, in the sentence *Write a letter to Mr. Wright to give him the right directions,* the synthesis of *write, Wright,* and *right* is clearly distinguished. If the dictionary lookup fails, general letter-to-sound rules are used. Finally, with punctuated text and syntactic and phonological information available, a prosody module predicts sentence phrasing and word accents and from those generates targets, for example, for fundamental frequency, phoneme duration, and amplitude. In the last few years, TTS systems have become much more natural-sounding, as is evident from voice portal, banking, customer service, and travel applications used by companies such as BeVocal, Tellme Networks, AT&T, Bank of America, Delta Airlines, and United Airlines. It is becoming increasingly difficult for the users to distinguish between a recorded synthesis and live speakers.

Unit selection synthesis is affected by several key factors. One important aspect is the ever increasing processing power and storage capacity of servers. This has a direct effect on the size of the voice inventory storage. Where early concatenative synthesizers used very few (mostly one) prototypical units for each class of inventory elements, we can now easily afford to store many such units. Other important aspects include the fact that efficient search techniques are now available that allow searching of potentially millions of available sound units in real time for the optimal sequence that makes up a target utterance. Finally, we now have automatic labelers that speed up labeling a voice database phonetically and prosodically.

Evaluating Synthesis

The three key factors that determine the success of synthesized speech are:

1. **Intelligibility:** The degree to which the listener understands what is being said. It can be measured by comparing the number of phonemes produced by an application versus the number of phonemes correctly identified by the user.

2. **Naturalness:** The degree to which the listener thinks the synthesized voice sounds like human speech. Its measure is more subjective than that of intelligibility, but equally important.

3. **Pleasantness:** The degree to which the listener enjoys or tolerates a voice.

The degree to which any application or service needs to be designed for intelligibility, naturalness, and pleasantness depends on the user, the task, and the application context.

To sum up, the speech interaction model can be represented by Figure 2.6. The model is organized into five distinct layers: context, control, language, speech, and perfor-

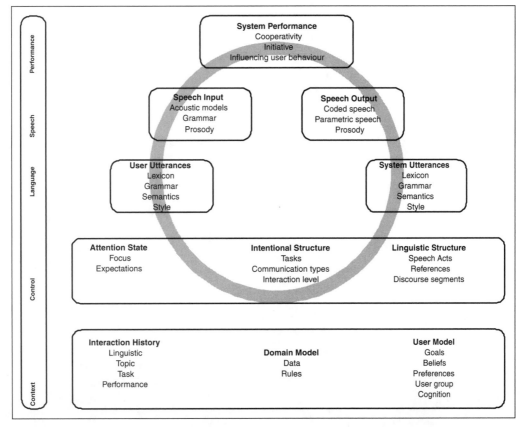

Figure 2.6 Speech Interaction model.

(Source: Bernsen, Dybkjær, and Dybkjær, *Designing Interactive Speech Systems: From First Ideas to User Testing,* Springer-Verlag, 1998.)

mance. The circle connecting the top four layers indicates the overall processing flow among various elements, from speech input and output to system performance. The strength of this model is that it draws its concepts from different disciplines such as linguistics, computer science, and cognitive science. For more details on the model, please consult Chapter 2 of the referenced text.

In this chapter we have discussed the key elements of speech recognition (ASR) and speech synthesis (TTS). We have also reviewed various techniques and definitions that are widely used when discussing voice-based applications and technologies. Speech technologies are a well-researched area that has a long history and excellent literature available for further study. In-depth coverage of speech technology is beyond the scope of this book; however, we have provided an exhaustive list of references toward the end of this book for anyone who is interested in learning more about the field.

In the next chapter we will look at the historical evolution of VoiceXML and why this new standard is going to change the way we think about and implement voice-based solutions.

## CHAPTER 3

The Birth of VoiceXML: Bringing the Web Development Paradigm to the Phone

The global impact and universal penetration of the Web have predominantly been driven by the simplicity of the open Hypertext Markup Language (HTML) standard. The Web development paradigm brought vendor and network independence to distributed applications, and drastically reduced the cost and skills required to quickly deliver powerful solutions. VoiceXML is an emerging open standard that brings the Web development paradigm to the interactive voice response (IVR) market, which means that existing Hypertext Transfer Protocol (HTTP) gateways to enterprise services and data built using technologies such as Secure Socket Layer (SSL) and cookies can be seamlessly extended to the phone. VoiceXML has rapidly received almost universal adoption and support from all corners of the voice technology industry: as of September 2001, more than 20 companies and 15,000 developers have actively announced VoiceXML-compatible products and have begun developing VoiceXML applications.

Historical Roots of VoiceXML

VoiceXML has not spontaneously leaped into existence from the proverbial Zeus' brow. The concept that a simple text-based markup language could be used to describe the conversation flow of automated voice applications has been around at least since 1994 and the earliest days of the Web (see Figure 3.1). Speech scientists in the labs at companies like AT&T and IBM explored this arena while most of the world (and all commercial deployments) focused on traditional low-level proprietary application programming interfaces (APIs) for developing voice applications. The key objection to early voice markup languages was their incompleteness—while simple conversations for basic IVR systems could be modeled, these languages lacked the robustness and expressiveness to represent the complexity of most real-world commercial voice applications.

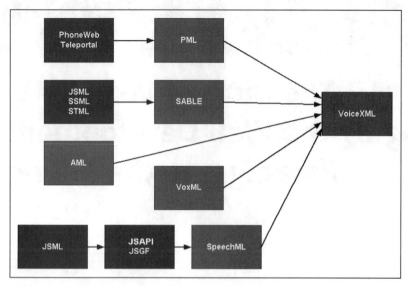

Figure 3.1 Evolution of VoiceXML since 1994.

As a result, two parallel tracks emerged that would ultimately result in both the birth of VoiceXML and a thriving market for commercially deployed enterprise voice applications. On the one hand, budding voice recognition vendors such as Nuance Communications (NASDAQ: NUAN) and SpeechWorks International (NASDAQ: SPWX) aggressively leveraged Moore's Law improvements in computing power to bring some of the first truly commercially viable solutions for speaker-independent voice recognition to market. Each company rigorously evangelized the potential business benefits of great voice applications to enterprise customers, and ultimately secured flagship accounts in key verticals such as airlines and financial services. These applications were built using traditional low-level APIs that exercised tremendous control over the underlying subtleties of the recognition systems, and the new voice recognition infrastructure was deployed as an add-on to traditional IVR platforms such as Periphonics and Intervoice.

At the end of the day, the results were extremely encouraging—given the right expertise, attention, and infrastructure, voice applications were absolutely a success. Callers were thrilled to use high-quality systems using only their voices, and as a result companies could save tens of millions of dollars each year in reduced call center costs. For example, United Airlines (a SpeechWorks customer) increased the automation rate of calls for routine flight departure and arrival information from less than 40 percent to more than 97 percent when it replaced touch-tone IVR with a carefully designed voice recognition application. Other early adopters, such as Charles Schwab, American Airlines, and Federal Express, have enjoyed similar results.

The challenge, however, is that building these systems was still enormously complicated and allowed no integration with the Internet technologies into which the same customers were simultaneously investing hundreds of millions of dollars. There was virtually no separation between application development and tuning the underlying telecommunications and voice recognition infrastructure, and solutions had to be deployed using the massive and cumbersome equipment of the traditional IVR world rather than the more efficient distributed architectures of Web-based systems.

Luckily, the desire to merge the benefits and ubiquity of voice applications with the power and flexibility of Internet technologies continued to grow in the background as these first commercial successes set the stage for a forthcoming explosion.

The Internet Backdrop

By the spring of 1999, the Web had undeniably permeated all but the most conservative of companies. This penetration of Internet technologies ran far deeper than Web access from the corporate desktop and a booming holiday season for Web retailers; in addition, corporate information technology (IT) had, by and large, embraced the fundamental shift from islands of client-server computing to a rich ecosystem of distributed services based on the interoperability, simplicity, and flexibility of open networks and Internet standards.

All told, U.S. companies alone invested $80 billion in Internet infrastructure in 2000 and, despite the dot-com backlash, investment is projected to continue explosive growth and reach nearly $200 billion by 2005 (Source: Cahners In-Stat). Companies made these choices seeking the following key benefits:

- **Extended customer reach and remote access.** Household Internet penetration within the United States reached a critical inflection point in 1998, as popular demand for e-mail and Web access finally exploded and began to approach universality. As Web sites such as Yahoo! and Amazon.com paved the way, everyday consumers began to make the cognitive shift from "I wonder if `<blah>` is on the Web?" to "*Everything* is on the Web . . . I just need to dig around and find it." From true consumer-facing applications such as commerce and communications to enterprise portal services such as sales force automation and business-to-business (B2B) exchanges, offering Web-based access to products and services rapidly became a societal mandate.

- **Simplified development process.** Internet technologies are, by and large, architecturally clean and extremely easy to develop applications with. This cleanliness derives from good abstraction between each layer of the technology stack. Developers can specialize in the requisite skill sets for mastering each layer, and, at the highest level, application developers can focus on interface design without being bogged down by the complexities of issues such as networking, legacy systems integration, and transactional components. HTML is an extremely simple text-based markup language for describing visual interfaces; virtually anyone can quickly learn and begin using it. With the advent of off-the-shelf Web servers or (better yet) outsourced hosting services, both the barriers to entry and time to market for Web publishing rapidly dropped to nearly zero.

- **Interoperability in a multivendor environment.** In the client-server world, a few open and de facto standards such as open database connectivity (ODBC) helped companies choose components from a diverse set of vendors when building comprehensive solutions. However, the number of effective standards and hence the breadth of available choices was actually quite slim. Typically, large organizations would pick their horse and run with it; while this strategy proved very lucrative for vendors such as Microsoft and Oracle, the real-world challenges of integrating solutions across vendor lines was an ongoing pain point for customers and end users alike. At the core of the Internet development paradigm is a commitment to open standards, and the past few years have seen an unprecedented proliferation of widely adopted technology standards such as Dynamic Host Configuration Protocol (DHCP), HTTP, HTML, Lightweight Directory Access Protocol (LDAP), SSL, Transmission Control Protocol/Internet Protocol (TCP/IP), X.509 certificates, and Extensible Markup Language (XML). Open standards drive innovation and healthy industry competition while maximizing customer choices.

- **Flexibility of distributed systems.** The combination of standards-based development and the broad connectivity of previously disparate corporate networks dramatically increased customers' options and flexibility with regard to how and where each component of their systems resides. It became not only possible, but fiscally and operationally prudent, to begin outsourcing large portions of IT infrastructure. Applications could be developed and tested in house, then deployed and managed in remote distributed data centers that provided world-class reliability and redundancy without sacrificing real-time control over applications and data.

The Telephony Backdrop

Alongside this proliferation of new technologies and expanded services on the Internet side, the traditional call center and telephony worlds began to experience a similar, but initially disjointed, series of pressures and shifts that would help set the stage for the emergence of VoiceXML.

- **Explosion of consumer wireless adoption.** By 2002, wireless phones are expected to eclipse traditional landline phone usage (Source: Cahners In-Stat). While the United States still significantly lags Europe and the Pacific Rim, the global adoption curve of wireless phones from 1995 to 2000 has been, and continues to be, staggering. Wireless technology, and specifically wireless phones, has permeated virtually all aspects of life and popular culture; in many demographics and locales, consumer wireless adoption actually far outpaces Internet connectivity. This rapid adoption rate has opened up vast new markets for equipment, infrastructure, and value-added services. By contrast, it has also provoked tough public policy issues regarding safety (talking while driving) and health (allegations linking prolonged wireless phone use with brain cancer).

- **Consolidation of nationwide toll-free service pricing.** AT&T invented the concept of nationwide toll-free service in 1980, making it possible for companies to offer a single nationwide number that customers could access without fear of expensive long-distance telephone charges. Toll-free numbers have become the backbone of customer service in the United States, driving more than 30 billion calls each year. The basic concept behind toll-free service is simple—companies pay the telephone company a per-minute rate on behalf of their customers so callers don't have to pay anything. Traditionally, these rates had been on the order of $.08 per minute for reasonably large customers. In addition, the regulatory structure was such that toll-free service rates were significantly different for long distance, inter-LATA (crossing Local Access and Transport Areas [LATAs], also known as local long distance), and intra-LATA (e.g., truly local) calls. By the late 1990s, the combination of corporate price pressure and massively increased bandwidth on the telecom carriers' networks led to a complete consolidation of toll-free service pricing at lower rates. As of August 2001, the largest customers pay as little as $.03 per minute for flat-rate toll-free service across North America. In addition to the obvious cost savings, this shift also dislocated some companies (e.g., Telera) that explicitly tried to make money on the arbitrage between intra-LATA and other toll-free service rates.

■ **Increased bandwidth in the fiber plant.** The famed Moore's Law posits that the amount of computing power (measured in instructions per second) that can be purchased for a given amount of money doubles every 18 months. This rate has remained relatively constant over the past 20 years, and the only technology observed to be advancing at an even greater rate is the bandwidth of optical fiber networks (see Figure 3.2). In the past few years, new technologies such as dense wave multiplexing continuously deliver remarkable improvements in this arena. As of August 2001, the economic and product benefits of these advances have only begun to trickle into the market as carriers invest deeply in laying new conduits and preparing to light up additional capacity on demand. However, it is more than likely that this blinding progress is a harbinger of further radical changes in the price—and hence the entire market structure—of voice and data transport.

■ **New competition in local and long-distance markets.** The United States Telecommunications Act of 1996 marked the first major overhaul of U.S. telecommunications law in over 60 years. One of the most prominent stipulations of the Act was to reopen both the local and long-distance telephone service markets to broader competition after the divestiture of AT&T in 1984. The seven Regional Bell Operating Companies (RBOCs, also known as Local Exchange Carriers [LECs]), new Competitive Local Exchange Carriers (CLECs), and the various long distance and international service providers (AT&T, Sprint, MCI, etc.) are now all able to compete in the local, long-distance, and data markets. While telecommunications is still a strictly regulated industry and there are substantial legal and regulatory stipulations that must be met for a given company to cross over the line and offer service in new markets, the ability of companies to aggressively compete for an increasing share of residential and corporate services has sparked a price and brand loyalty war in addition to a raft of new market entrants such as Qwest and Level 3 and large-scale consolidations such as Verizon Communications.

■ **Adoption of computer-telephony integration (CTI) middleware solutions.** Over the past 30 years, companies that operate large call centers have adopted a host of technology solutions all focused on improving operational and cost efficiencies while improving customer service quality. Solutions for intelligent call distribution and queuing, load balancing, reporting, touch-tone IVR, and even voice recognition are available from a large number of vendors.

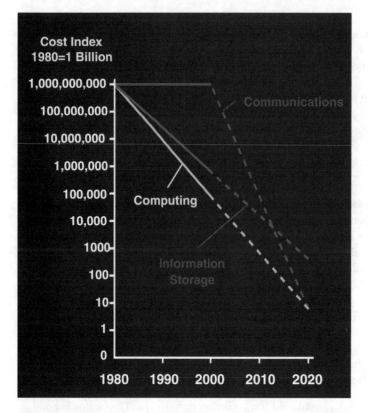

Figure 3.2 Comparison of Moore's Law and advances in optical fiber density.

(Source: Level3 Communications.)

As discussed previously, one of the key challenges faced by call center managers has traditionally been that all of these systems are extremely complicated, very proprietary, and difficult to manage individually, let alone as an integrated whole. Beginning in the early 1990s, companies such as Genesys (now owned by Alcatel) and GeoTel (now owned by Cisco Systems) emerged to offer comprehensive middleware solutions for CTI. These products help abstract away the vast differences in APIs, features, and reporting options offered by different vendors' solutions, giving call center managers a consolidated view and executive management dashboard for managing the resources of many separate facilities. By the late 1990s, many *Fortune 500* and other companies had embraced this powerful technology. While these solutions offer strong direct benefits, they still are themselves proprietary technologies, and are extremely expensive and difficult to deploy. A key consequence of this is that, as new solutions such as VoiceXML come to fruition, integration with this key segment of installed-base infrastructure is an absolute must.

■ **Broad availability of mature voice recognition.** As discussed in detail earlier in this chapter and in Chapter 2, the late 1990s marked the first major commercial deployments of voice recognition technology. From a call center perspective, the unqualified success of applications such as United Airlines flight information and Charles Schwab voice-enabled stock trading quickly made the case that, given the right attention and care, voice recognition was ready for prime time. As stated earlier, the key challenge to broad adoption lay in making it easier and more cost-effective to rapidly build and deploy successful voice applications. All of these factors quietly paved the path for the emergence of VoiceXML.

The VoiceXML Forum Emerges/VoiceXML 1.0

In March 1999, voice technology leaders at AT&T, Lucent Technologies, and Motorola came together to launch an industry consortium called the VoiceXML Forum. Each of these companies had considerable resources invested in voice technology, including some of the aforementioned seminal efforts to produce a simple text-based markup language for voice applications. Specifically, the stated goal of the VoiceXML Forum was to author and evangelize an Internet-based open standard to make the resources of the World Wide Web accessible by telephone.

VoiceXML is designed for creating audio dialogs that feature synthesized speech, digitized audio, recognition of spoken and DTMF key input, recording of spoken input, telephony, and mixed-initiative conversations. Its major goal is to bring the advantages of web-based development and content delivery to interactive voice response applications.

VoiceXML 1.0 Specification

The VoiceXML 0.9 specification was released in August 1999, followed in March 2000 by the much more complete VoiceXML 1.0 specification. At a high level, VoiceXML provides a simple declarative mechanism for specifying the voice user interface of sophisticated interactive voice response applications. VoiceXML has the following key characteristics:

- **XML-based language.** VoiceXML is an XML-based language. All VoiceXML applications are well-formed XML, and XML parsers can validate VoiceXML documents for syntactic correctness.

- **Web application semantics.** To the greatest extent possible, VoiceXML inherits the conventions of HTML and the traditional Web development paradigm. VoiceXML documents are retrieved from traditional Web servers using HTTP, and VoiceXML natively supports JavaScript (ECMAScript) for client-side application logic. The greatest benefit of this is familiarity and reuse; companies that have already deeply invested in understanding the Web development paradigm and used it to solve tough problems like security, personalization, and performance can reuse these solutions when extending their applications to the phone. For example, technologies such as cookies, SSL, HTTP caching headers, and streaming media all apply directly to VoiceXML applications, and analogously to their HTML counterparts.

- **Call control semantics.** VoiceXML supports a basic set of traditional telephony and call control mechanisms. Directly within the language, VoiceXML supports bridged and nonbridged call transfers (including the ability to listen for key phrases or touch-tone input while on a call transfer to take back control of the call), recording audio from the user, and forcibly disconnecting the call. In addition, VoiceXML platforms are free to implement powerful features such as outbound notifications that proactively place a call to a specific user and immediately place the user within a VoiceXML application. Future versions of VoiceXML will include even richer call control features such as conference calling and integration with Voice over IP standards such as Session Initiation Protocol (SIP). Chapter 14 provides more details about the future of VoiceXML and voice technologies.

■ **Spoken input and DTMF.** VoiceXML applications can listen and respond both to spoken and dual-tone multifrequency (DTMF, or touch-tone) input. This means that VoiceXML applications are not required to use voice recognition; any traditional touch-tone IVR application can easily be ported to VoiceXML.

■ **Directed and mixed-initiative dialogues.** VoiceXML supports both directed and mixed-initiative dialogues. Directed dialogue is the traditional way to design and author voice applications. This simply means that the automated system asks a series of specific questions that must be answered in order. This scheme maximizes accuracy and usability by making it very clear to callers what they can and cannot do at any given point in the application, though more experienced users may desire a more streamlined way to get what they want quickly. Mixed-initiative dialogue allows applications to ask for several pieces of information at once. If the caller provides all the information, he or she proceeds immediately to the next part of the application; otherwise, the system will intelligently ask the caller just for the missing pieces until all information has been collected. Mixed-initiative dialogue is a promising technique, but is easily abused and can quickly result in disastrous applications that do not succeed in automating a significant percentage of calls. Chapters 11 and 12 discuss effective voice user interface design techniques in more detail.

In early 2001, the VoiceXML Forum began transitioning ownership of VoiceXML to the World Wide Web Consortium (W3C) and produced the first working draft of VoiceXML 2.0. As of this writing, VoiceXML platform vendors are aggressively implementing the key additions and clarifications of VoiceXML 2.0, including vendor-independent XML grammars. Chapters 5 through 8 cover the specifics of the VoiceXML language and VoiceXML programming in more detail. Table 3.1 briefly summarizes the history of VoiceXML.

Consumer Voice Portals Demonstrate What's Possible

One of the key challenges VoiceXML would have to meet in the marketplace was the aforementioned richness and expressiveness. While companies such as Nuance and SpeechWorks had clearly proved that it was possible to design and deploy commercial-

Table 3.1 History of VoiceXML

DATE	EVENT
March 1999	VoiceXML Forum is founded by AT&T, Lucent Technologies, and Motorola (IBM later becomes a fourth core member).
August 1999	VoiceXML Forum releases VoiceXML 0.9 specification. Total membership grows to 44 companies.
March 2000	VoiceXML Forum releases VoiceXML 1.0 specification. Total membership grows to 79 companies.
April 2000	Tellme Networks launches U.S.-wide beta of 1-800-555-TELL, the first commercially deployed applications written in VoiceXML.
May 2000	VoiceXML Forum submits VoiceXML 1.0 specification to the W3C standards body, with the intention to transition ownership of the standard to the W3C. A key addition to VoiceXML 1.0 is the full integration of ECMAScript (JavaScript), to add richer application logic control and more parallelism with traditional Web applications.
June 2000	Tellme Networks launches Tellme Studio, the first open resource and community for professional VoiceXML developers.
December 2000	W3C Voice Browser Working Group releases draft specification for vendor-independent XML grammars, to be incorporated into future versions of the VoiceXML standard.
January 2001	VoiceXML Forum launches premier issue of the *VoiceXML Review* e-zine.
February 2001	ShopTalk Networks launches 1-800-SHOPTALK (powered by Tellme Networks), the first commercially available voice commerce applications written in VoiceXML.
February 2001	SpeechWorks International and Carnegie Mellon University announce Open Source VoiceXML Browser project.
February 2001	Cisco and OpenWave announce commitment to VoiceXML technology; these are the first Global 1000 companies other than the founding VoiceXML Forum members to publicly commit to VoiceXML as part of their core strategy for voice and call center technology.
March 2001	Tellme Networks announces that *Fortune 500* and other companies have committed to purchase over 1 billion minutes in traffic to VoiceXML applications on the Tellme Voice Application Network.
March 2001	Voxeo launches Voxeo Designer 2.0, the first what you see is what you get (WYSIWYG) developer tool for VoiceXML developers.

continues

Table 3.1 *(Continued)*

DATE	EVENT
March 2001	AT&T Wireless (16 million subscribers) and Qwest (1 million subscribers) both announce commitments to launch comprehensive consumer voice portal services written in VoiceXML, powered by Tellme Networks and BeVocal, respectively.
March 2001	VoiceXML Forum celebrates 2-year anniversary and hosts first annual user group meeting. Total membership rises to 420 companies. Total number of worldwide VoiceXML developers is estimated at 15,000. Total number of commercial VoiceXML platforms available is estimated at 12.
Fall 2001	W3C and VoiceXML Forum formally working under the intention to transition VoiceXML to the W3C, and produce a complete working draft of the VoiceXML 2.0 specification including vendor-independent XML grammars. Multiple vendors including BeVocal and Tellme Networks have already produced complete implementations of VoiceXML 2.0 for their W3C-member customers. Tellme Networks alone handles more than 10 million phone calls to VoiceXML 2.0 applications.
September 2001	AT&T 1-800-555-1212 (toll-free directory assistance) becomes the first top 5 U.S. 800# to be built entirely by VoiceXML (powered by Tellme Networks).
September 2001	Tellme Networks launches first V.IP-based access to VoiceXML development through Tellme Studio.

grade voice applications, it was not at all clear that a simple markup language could deliver sufficient functionality and flexibility to do the same. Additional key challenges included performance, security, and, fundamentally, whether the new specification would gain enough industry momentum to avoid the swift death that would otherwise surely await it. Chapter 10 specifically deals with security issues in VoiceXML deployments.

In the spring of 2000, a series of events happened that would catalyze the whirlwind of activity and adoption of VoiceXML technology and the Web development paradigm for voice applications over the following year. This trend continues to accelerate today. Most of this activity revolved around what would come to be known in the press as voice portals.

The term *voice portal* is somewhat elusive, similar to its Web counterpart. For the purposes of this book, we'll define a voice portal as an automated service that allows callers to get self-service access to a wide and diverse range of information, entertainment, and/or communications services from any telephone using only voice. Note that this definition is independent of business model, pricing, quality, or the specific set of available applications. However, to qualify as a voice portal a service must offer a significant number of diverse applications. Table 3.2 gives details on significant voice portals available as of August 2001.

Table 3.2 Consumer Voice Portals

SERVICE	LAUNCH DATE	BUSINESS MODEL	APPLICATIONS
1-800-555-TELL (Tellme Networks)	April 2000	Free to consumers; advertising and sponsorships	Airlines,announcements, blackjack, driving directions, extensions, horoscopes, hotels, lotteries, movies, news, phone booths, restaurants, shopping, ski reports, soap operas, sports, stock quotes, rental cars, taxis, traffic, wakeup calls
AOL By Phone (AOL, acquired from Quack)	October 2000	$4.95/month for AOL subscribers	E-mail (AOL only), news, shopping, sports, finance, weather, stock quotes
AT&T Wireless (powered by Tellme Networks)	June 2001	Free to subscribers; drives additional wireless minutes revenue	AT&T branded versions of most 1-800-555-TELL applications, plus communications applications such as e-mail reading and voice-activated dialing
BeVocal	June 2000	Free to consumers; advertising and sponsorships	Business finder, driving directions, flight information, horoscopes, lotteries, news, sports, stock quotes, traffic, TV dramas, weather
HeyAnita	October 2000	Free to consumers; advertising and sponsorships	Cool tools, contacts, flight tracker, horoscopes, lotteries, message center, newsroom, sports, stock portfolios, TV dish, weather

continues

Table 3.2 *(Continued)*

SERVICE	LAUNCH DATE	BUSINESS MODEL	APPLICATIONS
Portico (General Magic)	July 1998	$9.95/month + $.15/minute; discounts for frequent users	Long-distance calling, news, personal toll-free numbers, stock quotes, synchronization of calendars/contacts, Web portals
Qwest (powered by BeVocal)	March 2001	Free to subscribers; drives additional wireless minutes revenue	Qwest branded versions of most BeVocal applications, plus communications applications such as e-mail reading and voice-activated dialing
Yahoo! by Phone (Yahoo!)	October 2000	$4.95/month for Yahoo! members	E-mail, voice mail, stock quotes, weather, sports, news

Roots of the Voice Portal: General Magic's Portico

In July 1998, General Magic launched a landmark service that would be the progenitor of the voice portals that would achieve broad consumer mind share in the spring of 2000. General Magic's Portico service was truly revolutionary—using only their voices, callers could get access to a number of powerful personal communications services including e-mail, voice mail, and calendar appointments. Subscribers could also access the services through the Web, making Portico the template for both future voice portals and later efforts in the unified messaging arena.

However, as with many revolutionary technologies, adoption and success are as intimately paired with societal timing as they are with being first. Portico had many great features, and ultimately earned General Magic some foundation patents on crafting certain types of personality-rich automated voice interfaces. That said, the world was not quite ready to embrace voice portals at that time—particularly those that hinged on expensive subscription and usage fees. The Web itself would have to become more fully intertwined in daily life for the majority of the population before consumers could begin to understand and appreciate the value of voice portal services. Additionally, a broader set of diverse applications, a more streamlined user interface, and a more reasonable price point would also have to enrich the offering to make broad consumer adoption more likely.

Voice Portals Emerge: "HeyAnita . . . Tellme, and BeVocal about It!"

Throughout 1999, a series of new companies were founded amid the height of the Internet startup balloon, all focused on the idea of uniting the ubiquity of the telephone with the power of the Internet. As discussed earlier, by this time the world (or at least the United States) appeared ready for a next-generation set of consumer services that took the best of what people had come to expect from the Web and extended it to be available from any ordinary telephone at any time.

Nearly a dozen companies were founded, including BeVocal, HeyAnita, Quack, Telsurf, and VocalPoint; for a variety of reasons, Tellme Networks clearly stood out as the early leader in the press and with consumer mind share. In April 2000, Tellme Networks launched the public beta of its 1-800-555-TELL consumer voice portal. From any phone at any time, consumers could use their own voices to get free access to more than a dozen information and entertainment services including airlines, horoscopes, news, movies, and restaurants. While the advertising- and sponsorship-driven business model was inherently suspect to many, the appeal and instant popularity of the service both with consumers across the country and with press leaders including *The Wall Street Journal's* Walt Mossberg and CBS's Bryant Gumble was clear. By September 2000, at least three major consumer voice portals were collectively driving millions of weekly calls in the United States, the technology press had almost universally begun discussing the emerging voice portal market, and even major consumer publications, such as *Fortune* and *Time*, had latched onto the importance of this new trend.

VoiceXML was tightly, if not universally, adopted within this mix. The two leading companies offering voice portals, BeVocal and Tellme Networks, both built their platforms and applications using VoiceXML. The fact that these voice portals were clearly some of the most sophisticated voice applications ever commercially deployed was immediate and strong validation for the standing concerns about the flexibility and expressiveness of VoiceXML. Clearly, it was possible to develop and deliver very powerful voice applications using this new language, and the stage was set to open this Web development paradigm for voice applications to the broader developer community.

VoiceXML Developer Communities Arise

A primary goal of VoiceXML is to make building voice applications as easy as developing Web applications. However, voice applications inherently require specific and more complex infrastructure above and beyond that dictated by traditional Web applications. In both worlds a Web server is required to host and deliver the actual application logic. It is the browser that is more complicated when dealing with voice. For HTML applications, end users install Web browser software (e.g., Microsoft Internet Explorer 5.1) on their home personal computers (PCs). The browser knows how to talk to Web servers via HTTP over the Internet to retrieve HTML documents and graphics, and then knows how to render or display these on the screen so the user can interact with the applica-

Table 3.3 Editors of the VoiceXML Specification in the W3C

NAME	COMPANY
Pete Danielsen	Lucent Technologies
Jim Ferrans	Motorola
Andrew Hunt	SpeechWorks International
Bruce Lucas	IBM
Scott McGlashan, Chair	Pipebeach AB
Ken Rehor	Nuance Communications
Steph Tryphonas	Tellme Networks

tion. For VoiceXML applications, this same paradigm completely applies; however, the browser is a much more complicated piece of infrastructure.

In the case of VoiceXML, the user places a phone call using an ordinary phone (which of course has no browser software within it) to some service provider that is essentially running a collection of VoiceXML browsers. The VoiceXML browser has hardware and software that enables it to automatically answer the telephone and manage the call, just like traditional IVR systems. Depending on the phone number dialed by the caller, the VoiceXML browser can then start working on the caller's behalf. The VoiceXML browser interacts with a Web server hosting a particular application exactly like Internet Explorer interacts with Web servers; it makes HTTP requests for specific VoiceXML documents and audio files, it posts data it collects from the caller back to the Web server over HTTP, etc. The key difference is that in the case of VoiceXML, rendering the application consists of playing a series of audio files over the phone line, then recording whatever the caller says in response, then passing that recording through voice recognition software to get a result and reacting appropriately.

The end result of this is that while building VoiceXML applications is extremely straightforward and completely leverages all of the existing infrastructure put in place for traditional Web applications, actually delivering VoiceXML applications to callers requires a good deal more. So, the question in early 2000 was how to initiate a vibrant VoiceXML developer community and make it possible for any Web developer to immediately start exploring the possibilities of VoiceXML technology and next-generation voice applications. The answer was free Web-based VoiceXML developer sites.

In June 2000, Tellme Networks launched Tellme Studio, the first open Web-based toolkit and community for VoiceXML developers. In addition to a large set of traditional developer community resources such as tutorials, code examples, and newsgroups, Tellme Studio provided a unique new capability—developers could simply enter the Uniform Resource Locator (URL) into a VoiceXML application they'd written and immediately call a testing phone number to test it out over the phone. Further, they could launch a debugging window and see a real-time trace of their application code while they tested it over the phone. It was that simple. With zero hardware or software to download or install, anyone could immediately become a VoiceXML developer and begin developing applications. Furthermore, grassroots developers could instantly publish their VoiceXML applications through the 1-800-555-TELL voice portal simply by clicking a checkbox on a Web page.

This concept proved very powerful, and by August 2001 more than 15,000 developers had registered to develop VoiceXML applications at Tellme Studio and other sites offering similar capabilities from BeVocal, HeyAnita, VoiceGenie, Voxeo, and Telera. As of this writing, all of these VoiceXML developer communities are available free of charge. To date, each company clearly recognizes the value of investing resources into stimulating the early developer community for a new technology. Chapter 5 provides more detail on choosing and beginning to utilize a VoiceXML developer environment.

Wireless Carrier Adoption and Business Models versus Technology

It is important to distinguish business models from technology. Free consumer voice portals are clearly not a profitable venture in the short term; most of the leading companies that deliver voice portals recognize this and fully focus their revenue-generating

Table 3.4   VoiceXML Platform Vendors as of August 2001

VENDOR	TYPE
BeVocal	Software and hardware to be installed in carrier networks
Carnegie Mellon University	Open source toolkit (through SpeechWorks International)
General Magic	Network-based, Premises-based software and hardware
HeyAnita	Network-based
iConverse	Premises-based software
IBM	Premises-based software and hardware
Lucent Technologies	Premises-based software and hardware
Pipebeach AB	Network-based
Motorola	Premises-based software
Nuance Communications	Premises-based software
SpeechWorks International	Premises-based software
Telera	Software and hardware to be installed in carrier networks
Tellme Networks	Network-based
VoiceGenie	Premises-based software and hardware
Voxeo	Network-based (licenses Nuance platform)

efforts on the enormous enterprise market for voice applications. However, voice portals have been instrumental in rising consumer and industry awareness of how rich and powerful voice applications can be. Without them, it is doubtful that the voice application industry would have achieved the level of momentum and visibility it currently enjoys.

A specific example of this is wireless carriers. The carriers seriously considered deployments of voice portal services in 1998 with the advent of Portico. Bell South actually ran a Portico-powered trial for an extended period of time. However, adoption was ultimately minimal for the aforementioned reasons. With the advent of next-generation voice portals and broader consumer interest and demand for these services, interest from the carriers began to turn a corner. As of March 2001, all of the major carriers within the United States, and most of the carriers in Europe and the Pacific Rim, were actively considering full-blown voice portal rollouts as a value-added service to their subscribers. Beginning in the fall of 2000, active voice portal trials were under way from Bell South (powered by Tellme), Qwest (powered by BeVocal), and Sprint PCS (powered by both Tellme and BeVocal). In March 2001, the first major commitments from wireless carriers to fully deploy voice portal services were announced—AT&T Wireless's 16 million subscribers would receive a branded service powered by Tellme Networks, and Qwest's additional 1 million subscribers would get a similar offering powered by BeVocal. Both of these services added communications applications such as e-mail reading and voice-activated dialing to the existing suites of applications offered through existing voice portals. While the ultimate commercial success of these endeavors for the carriers remains to be seen, they represent a clear step forward and further validation for the voice application market.

The W3C and VoiceXML 2.0

Rarely has a new standard seen such broad and swift adoption by the industry at large as has VoiceXML. In a little over a year, virtually every company working on voice technology has embraced VoiceXML and is committed to the open standards approach for the evolution of the standard. There are more than a dozen VoiceXML platforms commercially available today in a variety of form factors (see Tables 3.3 and 3.4), and customers can choose from standalone software, integrated hardware/software suites, outsourced voice infrastructure services, and even an open source toolkit.

Moving forward, the evolution of the VoiceXML standard is under the auspices of the W3C. The W3C is the same standards body that is responsible for key Web standards such as HTML and LDAP. With the progress on VoiceXML 2.0 and adoption by the enterprise market growing rapidly, the short- and long-term future for the standard and for voice applications in general appears bright, even against the dark background of the challenging economic landscape of 2001.

VoiceXML for the Enterprise: Deployment Challenges and the Rise of Voice Application Networks

In theory, VoiceXML makes it as easy to build and deploy enterprise-class voice applications as it has been with traditional Web-based applications. While this is true from a pure application development perspective-authoring VoiceXML code that seamlessly integrates with existing Hypertext Transfer Protocol (HTTP) interfaces to middleware and back-end systems is analogous to authoring Hypertext Markup Language (HTML)—in practice, designing great voice applications and deploying the requisite telephony and voice recognition infrastructure in a scalable and reliable fashion is dramatically more complex and demands rare and specialized skills. Voice Application Networks are a network-based solution that help enterprises bridge this gap and rapidly capitalize on the benefits of VoiceXML and great voice applications.

Infrastructure Requirements for Deploying Voice Applications

Typically, enterprises deploying voice applications are looking to provide automated self-service for some set of tasks and to make that service available through a free (e.g., 1-800), local toll, or pay-per-call (e.g., 1-900) phone number on the public switched telephone network (PSTN)—in other words, to make their automated infrastructure answer a normal phone line so anyone from any phone can call in at any time to access the application. Recent advances in Voice over Internet Protocol (VoIP) technology through next-generation carriers (e.g., Level 3) and value-added VoIP providers (e.g., iBasis) have begun to expand the options companies have to choose from, making it possible to push the Internet Protocol (IP)-PSTN interface point further away; however, at the end of the day companies must still deal with provisioning a specific number of actual phone lines from a PSTN carrier (e.g., AT&T, MCI, Qwest, Sprint, etc.).

In order to put together a complete on-premises system for production-class voice applications, many additional pieces must be procured, installed, configured, and integrated.[1] These can be summarized as follows:

1. **Provision of telecom capacity.** As described earlier, telecom capacity must be provisioned. Typically, capacity is provisioned in 24-phone-line bundles known as T1s. Twenty-eight T1s can be aggregated into a DS3 (672 phone lines). Typically, provisioning new T1s or DS3s from leading carriers takes 3 to 4 months, even for *Fortune 500* companies. DS3s are typically priced as a monthly lease fee.

2. **Provision of specific phone numbers.** If the company is delivering a new service that needs to be available through a new phone number(s), then these new numbers must be provisioned. If a particular (e.g., vanity) number is desired, the search can take months; if any number is acceptable, or if an existing number is already in place, then this step is trivial. For 1-800 numbers, pricing is typically a small per-month fee in addition to the telecom capacity.

3. **PBX.** A Private Branch Exchange (PBX) is a physical set of boxes that performs switching functionality and handles incoming and outgoing calls. Most medium- to large-sized businesses have PBXs for their internal office phone systems. For large call center applications, PBXs are typically enhanced with Automatic Call Distribution (ACD) software that facilitates flexible rules-based routing of calls to various components of their overall deployment. For example, the PBX may be configured to route calls directly to one of 257 operator desks if one is available and staffed, and to route all other calls (up to the total amount of capacity provisioned on the system) to the local interactive voice response (IVR) until an agent is available. PBXs are typically priced as hardware, per-port licensing fees for each physical phone line to be provisioned, and 18 percent annual maintenance.

4. **Voice Response Units (VRUs) (IVR hardware).** VRUs (interactive voice response systems) are another physical set of boxes that connect via phone lines to PBXs (or directly to the PSTN) and are responsible for processing all automated phone calls. Traditional VRUs embed vendor-specific, proprietary IVR platforms that support various related software components such as automatic speech recognition (ASR), text to speech (TTS), and modules for back-end systems integration. IVR applications are authored using vendor-specific graphical user interface (GUI) tools and/or scripting languages. These application scripts are physically loaded onto the hardware, and communicate at run time with back-end systems. Companies looking to build applications using VoiceXML and open standards must purchase VRUs from a vendor that has expanded its on-board platform to include/support a VoiceXML interpreter and at least one ASR and TTS engine. VRUs are typically priced as hardware, per-port fees, and 18 percent annual maintenance.

5. **ASR.** ASR is voice recognition software. Most leading IVR/VRU platforms have the capability to support each of the leading ASR engines. This ASR software

---

[1]In this list, and throughout this book, readers are generally assumed to be more familiar with Internet technologies than call center and telephony technologies. More detail is presented on the challenges and specifics of telephony systems, while more general familiarity with Internet infrastructure and Web-based systems is assumed.

must be installed and configured on each VRU (and often on additional separate personal computer [PC] hardware). ASR is typically priced per port with 18 percent annual maintenance.

6. **TTS.** TTS software generates natural-sounding speech in real time from any arbitrary text. IVR and ASR applications typically use TTS technology to present very dynamic data that cannot be prerecorded and to save money by not having to prerecord all necessary prompts in each application. TTS software is also installed and configured on each VRU. TTS is typically priced per port with 18 percent annual maintenance.

7. **VoiceXML interpreter.** Typically, ASR and TTS platforms expose low-level, proprietary C, C++, or Java application programming interfaces (APIs) for building applications. VoiceXML interpreter software encapsulates these lower-level APIs and enables application developers to author in VoiceXML. The VoiceXML interpreter is also responsible for all Internet communications with Web servers that host VoiceXML applications. VoiceXML interpreter software must be installed and configured on each VRU and must integrate with the ASR and TTS software. A VoiceXML interpreter must be purchased that supports and integrates with the specific VRU, ASR, and TTS solutions being used. VoiceXML interpreters are typically priced per port with 18 percent annual maintenance.

8. **Call center integration.** Most large call centers have invested deeply in computer-telephony integration (CTI) middleware systems that make it possible to cleanly administer and operate large numbers of geographically distributed PBXs, ACDs, VRUs, and physical agents. For example, the CTI middleware can give the call center manager a centralized view of all real-time traffic on the network and essentially remote control of each unit on the system to dynamically move traffic between physical centers. CTI systems are also used to coordinate data collected during an IVR/VRU session and live agents, facilitating a screen pop on a specific agent's desktop when a call is transferred to him or her that contains information and context already collected from the caller during the automated portion of the call. For each new VRU added to the system, additional hardware (often called *gateways*) and per-port licenses must be purchased to connect the system to the CTI infrastructure. Each VRU must be connected to and configured for interacting with the CTI system, and each application must have custom logic written to take advantage of CTI capabilities such as screen pops.

9. **Operations staff.** Dedicated operations staff with specific expertise in telecom and IVR systems must be hired to install, manage, and maintain all on-premises infrastructure. Assuming that a company already has 24/7 operations staff coverage for maintaining all critical information technology (IT) systems, typically one dedicated staff person is required for each 500 ports of VRU/IVR.

10. **Speech science staff.** As outlined in detail later in this chapter, voice recognition software does not perform optimally out of the box. In order to achieve production-quality results from voice applications, it is typically necessary to pay significant ongoing attention to the low-level configuration of the system. This is similar to requiring a database administrator (DBA) for a large enterprise data-

base system such as Oracle. Deploying the same applications with a specially trained, expert DBA can easily achieve 1000 times better performance than without one. However, there are orders of magnitude more trained Oracle DBAs in the world than qualified speech scientists. Over time the number of qualified speech scientists will undoubtedly grow rapidly; in the meantime companies must search hard to hire this rare expertise in-house.

11. **Design and building of shared application components.** Many companies are looking to deploy comprehensive voice solutions that provide callers with a wide range of choices. For example, an airline may wish to allow callers to look up flight arrival and departure information and find lost luggage, as well as provide driving directions to the nearest airport and real-time weather conditions in cities customers are traveling to. Companies that build applications in house must build everything from the ground up or license shrink-wrapped prebuilt application components. As of August 2001, few options are available for licensing shrink-wrapped applications for on-premises systems.

12. **Design and building of application-specific application components.** All application-specific VoiceXML and back-end integration must be authored.

13. **Deployment of applications on local Web infrastructure.** VoiceXML applications must be deployed on company's existing Web infrastructure. If a Web infrastructure does not exist, it must be procured and deployed as well.

Challenges of Achieving Optimal Voice Recognition Performance

Speaking is the most natural form of human communication, so it is natural to assume that building great voice applications would be at least as easy as designing a Web site. However, it turns out that crafting a voice interface that is easy to use and pleasing to customers is actually difficult. Great voice applications help companies deliver exceptional customer service at reasonable costs, but great voice applications are rare because they are very hard to build and deploy successfully. Companies without core competencies in voice user interface (UI) design, speech science, and audio production will find it difficult to deliver on their own voice applications that callers enjoy and that deliver the expected benefits.

Conversations Are Different than Touch-Tone or Web Pages

Even if voice recognition technology were perfect (which it isn't), designing voice applications would remain fundamentally harder than building Web sites or touch-tone IVR. Consider the following issues:

- **Speaking is slower than reading.** Just think about how much time it takes to read a grocery list out loud versus quickly reading it in print or on a Web page. On the phone, options have to be listed one at a time, and that gets frustrating very quickly. Tasks such as choosing from long lists or listening to long passages of audio (e.g., reading e-mail) will always be harder on the phone, and will require creative solutions that keep the caller engaged. By contrast, Web pages can display hundreds of choices at the same time.

- **People quickly forget what they just heard.** On a Web page, people can carefully browse through screens and menus to find the exact option they're looking for. On the phone, however, information is gone as soon as it's been given, and callers have to remember everything because they can't see the choices any more. Consider what happens when people call 411; without a pencil and paper ready, people often forget the phone number they just heard in the few seconds it takes to hang up the phone and start dialing.

- **It's not clear what you can't say.** Web pages and touch-tone IVR applications are *bounded.* There are a fixed number of links to click or keys to press, and people can't move their mouse beyond the edge of the screen. Conversations are *unbounded* because someone can say anything in response to a given question or prompt. Even if voice recognition were perfect, people would still need to be carefully guided through the available options so they could quickly find what they were looking for without being frustrated. Minute differences in the way prompts and menus are structured have a dramatic impact on customer satisfaction, because callers need to be gently and clearly directed to say the right things, and apologetically led back on track when they get lost or confused.

Recognition Quality Depends upon Specialized Design and Tuning

Voice recognition is demonstrably mature enough for mission-critical applications, and production applications successfully automate hard tasks such as driving directions and stock trading. However, recognizing human speech is still an enormously complex computational task that relies on applying sophisticated heuristic techniques to massive statistical data models in real time. Voice recognition software out of the box does not perform adequately, and applications require specialized design and tuning by qualified experts to be successful. Consider the following issues:

- **People will always say unexpected things.** People are accustomed to having real conversations over the phone; they immediately assume voice applications can understand whatever they say, and can quickly get frustrated when their expectations aren't met. Even applications that prompt callers to choose from a short menu can consistently get hundreds of distinct responses. Voice applications can only understand the specific things they're trained for—similar to the situation when people first bring their phrasebooks to a foreign country. As with people, voice applications do their best to match what they're hearing with the phrases they know, and can easily mistake similar-sounding words for ones that are actually in their list. Depending on the situation, this can quickly lead to a frustrating experience. For example, consider a simple menu of keywords that includes *movies* and *restaurants.* Callers who say *moving* without knowing that it is not a valid choice are likely to consistently get thrown into *movies* and be very frustrated. For this reason, applications must use clear, concise prompting to guide callers to say the right things, and must use data from large amounts of real-world usability testing to take into account the unexpected things people tend to say. Minute shifts in prompt wording or the underlying grammars can have dramatic effects on usability, and ultimately the automation rate and return on investment (ROI) of voice applications.

■ **Grammars must be tuned.** As just stated, voice recognition technology works by comparing what the caller said to a specific list of expected choices. These *grammars* are required to make it computationally feasible to do speaker-independent voice recognition in real time. Large grammars, such as the 10,000+ companies on U.S. stock exchanges, can work very well in production today. Achieving this requires careful attention by both application designers and speech scientists tuning the underlying recognition engine. For example, *Pfizer* and *Fiserv* sound almost identical; the underlying grammar must be tuned to know which choice is more commonly selected, and the application must be carefully crafted to help callers get back on track when the system makes a mistake.

■ **People pronounce the same words differently.** Pronunciations for words and phrases can vary widely across regions of a given country. Proper names further complicate the matter—consider, for example, how to pronounce *Qantas Airways* or *Worcester Court*. Voice recognition engines rely on built-in dictionaries that specify each of the ways callers may say each word and common phrase. If a grammar includes a word that isn't in the dictionary, the recognition engine must guess how it is supposed to be pronounced. While this can work reasonably well, the system is likely to make mistakes or miss common alternative pronunciations. Especially because voice recognition is rapidly being deployed in new industries for new applications, it's critical to ensure that all relevant pronunciations are in the dictionaries—otherwise, recognition quality and automation rates can suffer significantly.

■ **Acoustic models must be continually refined.** Voice recognizers use acoustic models to decide whether a caller has said something that matches a given grammar. Acoustic models are essentially a mathematical representation of how a wide variety of people sound when they say each of the building blocks of words (e.g., *buh* or *ing*). Acoustic models are built by analyzing millions of diverse recordings of real people actually speaking over the telephone. The more data that is used to train these acoustic models, the better recognition quality becomes, particularly when the data is collected under real-world conditions using the same hardware and software. In addition, it is critical to ensure that the voice recognition software has been adequately trained on all of the words and phrases that make up the grammars for a particular application.

■ **Noisy environments are problematic.** Phone conversations—particularly on mobile phones—often contain a lot of background noise. This noise can be ambient sound (e.g., wind, cars honking), ambient conversation (e.g., other tables in a restaurant), side speech (e.g., "Kids, I said stop it!"), or unintended sounds (e.g., a cough or sneeze). Consider how difficult it is sometimes even for real people to distinguish the actual conversation from background noise; the problem is compounded for voice recognition engines because they have far less intelligent context about how to differentiate sounds and speakers' voices from one another. Voice applications and voice recognition platforms must be carefully designed to accommodate and minimize the difficulties presented by background noise.

■ **Hundreds of thousands of calls must be transcribed by hand.** In order to compile the necessary data to address most of the problems just listed, it is necessary to manually compare what callers actually say with what the voice recognition software thought they said. Very large numbers of calls must be manually transcribed in this fashion, so that speech scientists can analyze the data and determine how accurately each grammar in an application is performing. This is a very labor-intensive process, but it is critical to give designers the information they need to make the adjustments to call flows, grammars, prompts, pronunciation dictionaries, and acoustic models that are necessary to achieve the expected benefits of great voice applications.

Audio Production Dramatically Impacts Customer Satisfaction

Automated voice applications allow companies to use distinctive voice talent and professional sound design to consistently convey the full, unique richness of their brand identity and customer service philosophy. This opportunity directly translates to customer satisfaction and can make the difference when customers are selecting whom to do business with.

■ **People love applications that sound natural and feel good.** People simply appreciate and respond more favorably to applications that sound professional, engaging, and personable. This is true for live operators, and is doubly true for automated systems. Poor recording quality, bad music, and robotic-sounding synthesized speech are some of the key reasons why people tend to hate traditional IVR systems so viscerally. By contrast, companies can use a combination of natural-sounding prompts, well-crafted interface design, and creative musical effects to deliver a very compelling experience that callers enjoy and positively associate with the company's brand and commitment to customer service.

■ **Crafting the optimal voice and sound is an art.** Voice talent and sound engineering are an extensive industry in their own right; the American Federation of Television and Radio Artists (AFTRA) union talent contracts alone total more than $1 billion annually. Crafting the optimal audio experience for voice applications is a new and unique art form that demands specific field experience and talent. Creative challenges include choosing the right voice talent (e.g., the optimal voice for stock trading is useless for selling children's games). One of the greatest technical challenges is properly designing and recording prompts for concatenative speech. Concatenative speech is a technique whereby short bits of prerecorded audio are quickly played in sequence to form longer phrases and sentences. Concatenative speech makes it possible for voice applications to sound very human and natural, even when delivering dynamic data such as stock prices or flight information. Without great concatenative speech, applications must resort to robotic-sounding synthesized speech for dynamic data, because prerecording all possible combinations is prohibitively expensive. For example, there are nearly 10 million potential U.S. phone numbers, whereas concatenative speech can be used to deliver outstanding phone number playback with only 1800 prompts.[2] In addition, applications are not static, and new prompts often must be recorded on a moment's notice. It is necessary to have the infrastructure and methodology in place to record new prompts at any time and in different cities, so that they sound indistinguishable from other recordings.

- **Delivering world-class quality at reasonable costs is challenging.** Voice talent, studio time, and editing facilities are all expensive. While there are some economies of scale here, most of the expense is human-intensive and does not inherently drop with volume. Companies must have processes, techniques, and relationships in place to maximize quality at reasonable costs.

The Rise of Voice Application Networks

Voice Application Networks are network-based (outsourced) solutions for rapidly deploying voice applications, typically powered by open standards including VoiceXML. Similar to how network-based voice mail has almost universally replaced on-premises voice mail in residential homes and many businesses, Voice Application Networks enable companies to deploy sophisticated voice applications without having to purchase or administer any voice recognition or telephony-specific infrastructure. They also typically give companies seamless access to a variety of prebuilt applications that can be easily customized and linked in to unique applications built and hosted locally.

Overview of Voice Application Networks

Voice Application Networks typically provide the following set of services:

- **Network-based voice infrastructure.** This includes large deployments of VRUs, ASR, TTS, VoiceXML interpreters, etc. that are preprovisioned with massive telecom and Internet capacity, as well as many preprovisioned phone numbers that are instantly assignable to a particular new customer's application. Typically, these systems are deployed in geographically redundant locations to boost scalability, reliability, and disaster recovery.

- **In-house voice technology expertise.** This includes resident teams of speech scientists, phoneticians, linguists, transcriptionists, audio designers, audio producers, etc. that continually work to optimize performance of voice applications across the network, as well as work on a professional services basis with indi-

---

[2]People tend to say U.S. phone numbers as groups of two and three digits (e.g., *four -one five, five -five five, seven two six three*). In addition, the area code and exchange portions of U.S. phone numbers never start with a 0 or 1.

vidual customers to craft world-class applications that delight callers and maximize automation rates.

■ **VoiceXML platform.** A scalable, VoiceXML-based platform must be provided for building and deploying voice applications, including all necessary integration with ASR, TTS, etc. This could be custom-designed for the specific Voice Application Network provider or licensed from a third party. The key factor is that all lower-level components are architecturally isolated from the developer, and applications are strictly built using VoiceXML and other Internet standards.

■ **Advanced network services.** There must be prebuilt deployments of value-added services such as CTI integration, outbound notifications, and personalization that make it easy for application developers to instantly take advantage of these capabilities through standards-based APIs.

■ **Platform SDK.** This includes development tools, testing facilities that do not require the installation of any on-premises hardware, SDK documentation, and libraries of prebuilt modular components such as grammars, audio, and other examples.

■ **Enterprise-ready modular application suites.** This refers to higher-level customizable application suites tailored to meet the requirements of specific industries, such as airlines and financial services. These application suites typically require some level of customer-specific integration with back-end systems or content feeds, but make common tasks like driving directions, flight status information, and weather reports able to be deployed quickly and cost-effectively because the costs to build and operate the systems are leveraged across many customers.

■ **Management and reporting tools.** These are tools that enable customers to remotely access report information about the usage and performance of their applications. These tools must enforce the necessary security and provide the requisite flexibility to satisfy the needs of enterprise customers who are entrusting mission-critical services to a network provider.

■ **Professional services.** In addition to voice application design and speech science, there must be a comprehensive systems-integrator-style professional services offering that enables customers to choose their level of involvement and obtain a complete solution regardless of their internal level of resourcing and expertise.

Specific Advantages of Voice Application Networks

Voice Application Network providers (see Table 4.1) seek to provide several key advantages to their customers relative to on-premises solutions. Clearly these advantages are most potent when compared to traditional proprietary IVR platforms; newer on-premises platforms that do support VoiceXML inherently provide some of these as well.

■ **Time to market.** Customers can deploy instantly on preprovisioned infrastructures, use standards-based development to fully leverage existing Internet

Table 4.1 Voice Application Network Providers as of September 2001

VENDOR	VOICEXML SUPPORT	MARKET CAP /FUNDING	KEY CUSTOMERS	HEADQUARTERS
BeVocal	Yes	$47 million	Qwest Wireless	Sunnyvale, CA
General Magic	Yes	$57 million (public)	GM OnStar	Sunnyvale, CA
HeyAnita	Yes	~$30 million	Sprint PCS	Los Angeles, CA
Net-by-Tel	No	$21 million	OfficeDepot, Firestone MasterCare, ValPac Coupons	Boca Raton, FL
Telera	Yes	$110 million	Ariba, Covad, Sears	Campbell, CA
Tellme Networks	Yes	$238 million	AT&T Wireless, AT&T 1-800-555-1212, two of the top US airlines, two of the top US brokerages, HomeStore	Mountain View, CA Brussels, Belgium
Voxeo	Yes	$30 million	25+ small	Scotts Valley, CA

investments, and obtain seamless access to libraries of prebuilt applications and components. They can also begin to develop and rapidly prototype instantly without having to purchase, download, provision, or install any hardware or software.

■ **Operational simplicity.** Voice Application Networks eliminate the expense and guesswork of provisioning, allowing customers to scale on demand and pay only for the capacity they use. By leveraging a diverse application base and integration with carrier backbones, Voice Application Networks can maximize year-round port utilization and maintain a healthy overhead of excess capacity amortized across the network. This can be an important cost savings because most commercially deployed voice applications are quite "spiky"—much of their traffic is concentrated in a small period. With on-premises systems, customers must purchase and preprovision for the maximum amount of capacity they will ever need. The more spiky the application, the less cost-efficient this becomes. In addition, on-premises voice infrastructure is a large capital investment that occupies large amounts of physical data center space. For example, when upgrading to a new version of VRUs, it is typically necessary to bring in forklifts to remove existing equipment and install new hardware to support new functionality such as ASR and VoiceXML.

■ **Economies of quality and scale.** Voice applications running on a shared network benefit from unique economies of scale and improved recognition quality. The fundamental costs of transport, hardware, software licensing, and network bandwidth drop sharply with volume, and voice recognition systematically improves with each new application on the network. Each voice application running on the network improves overall performance by providing more tuning data with which speech recognition can be improved considerably. The more applications are sharing network resources, the more accurate speech recognition becomes.

■ **Leveraged voice expertise.** Voice Application Network providers unite centralized teams of the requisite voice expertise for designing world-class voice applications and optimizing voice recognition platform performance. Companies can work with experienced Voice Application Network providers to obtain the benefits of this staff without having to recruit, hire, or maintain these critical resources.

Deploying with Voice Application Networks

In comparison to on-premises systems, companies that choose to deploy using Voice Application Networks must go through a similar set of steps.

1. **Designing and building of application-specific components.** Same as Infrastructure Requirements for Deploying Voice Applications above.

2. **Licensing and linking in of shared application components.** Shared components available from the Voice Application Network provider must be licensed and linked in by the customer. This effort can be trivial or fairly involved, depending on the sophistication of the component and to what extent the component requires specific integration with each company's back-end systems. For example, an application such as driving directions is almost identical across customers and uses a shared data feed; similarly to the way any Web site can trivially embed MapQuest or Expedia directions within the site using simple APIs, a voice application can easily link to a shared driving directions module with virtually no custom work. By contrast, a voice-activated stock trading application is likely to be more like a user interface shell with stubbed-out semantics for the underlying transaction processing. Since every company's trading platform is very different, a substantial amount of custom integration work is required. That said, this work is still dramatically less than building the entire application from scratch, and savings of hundreds of thousands of dollars and months in deployment time can easily be realized.

3. **Deploying applications on local Web infrastructure.** Same as Infrastructure Requirements for Deploying Voice Applications above.

4. **Transferring vanity 1-800 numbers to the Voice Application Network's routing plan (optional).** If the company already has provisioned a specific 1-800 (or other) phone number for the application, the number must be transferred to the Voice Application Network's routing plan so that the network can answer the calls on the customer's behalf. This is typically a straightforward process, and can be completed quickly and at low cost.

Criteria for Evaluating Voice Application Network Providers

As we have seen, Voice Application Networks have the potential to greatly improve companies' ability to rapidly and cost-effectively deploy VoiceXML applications. Successful voice application deployments critically hinge on choosing a vendor with world-class voice expertise and a proven ability to answer millions of calls to sophisticated applications with carrier-grade reliability and performance. Customers should strongly consider these criteria when evaluating Voice Application Network providers.

Voice Application Networks must demonstrate competency in six key areas:

1. **A scalable and reliable platform** ensures that the Voice Application Network provides the carrier-grade performance and availability to satisfy the needs of enterprise customers.

2. **Rich and robust application interfaces** enable the creation of full-featured products and services that meet and exceed caller expectations.

3. **Enterprise-ready application solutions** supplement the core underlying power of the Voice Application Network and deliver prebuilt and tested functionality for the most demanding enterprise applications.

4. **Experience in delivering voice applications** is a key requirement for Voice Application Network providers, ensuring the best usability and customer experience.

5. **A complete suite of development tools and services** assists enterprises in deploying complex voice application solutions.

6. **Corporate health and financial solvency** ensures that the vendor has the strategy and resources to remain in business for the long term.

Scalable and Reliable Platform

Companies that entrust mission-critical applications to a network-based provider must be extremely confident and contractually assured that callers will receive exceptional service at all times, and that additional capacity can be quickly provisioned to meet even explosive demand. Vendors that rely on substandard infrastructure or are unable to demonstrate proven reliability and performance are far less likely to meet expectations. To be successful, Voice Application Networks must deliver on key platform functionality and network performance, including:

- **Scalability** through a well-designed architecture capable of increasing capacity on short notice and as the vendor increases its contractual commitments.

- **Reliability** of telephony infrastructure combined with carrier-grade connectivity to the PSTN.

- **A standards-based architecture including VoiceXML** that ensures companies can fully leverage their existing Internet investments and can retain portability of their application should they choose to switch providers in the future.

- **Exceptional voice application performance,** giving companies the comfort of knowing that their application will run smoothly and efficiently regardless of the number of callers it serves.

- **Effective capacity planning and management,** ensuring that the Voice Application Network can effectively balance the needs of the many customers choosing it for deployment and ensuring that all telephone calls are handled appropriately even in times of unusually high load.

- **Strong security policies** that ensure the integrity and safety of customer data and services.

Currently, there are no officially sanctioned metrics or benchmarks for evaluating VoiceXML interpreter performance. However, it is definitely the case that large companies that are actively building VoiceXML-based solutions are considering performance when evaluating potential vendors.

The distributed nature of VoiceXML, which allows application logic to be cleanly separated from the underlying speech and telephony infrastructure, is one of its greatest strengths. It revolutionizes the IVR market by making network-based IVR practical and cost-effective. However, this same characteristic presents significant technology hurdles that VoiceXML platform vendors must solve in order to guarantee reliable performance at scale.

Table 4.2 presents a few key metrics that make sense to consider when evaluating VoiceXML platforms for either on-premises or network-based deployments. These are not in any way meant to be exhaustive; rather, they are indicative of the kinds of tests companies should consider.

It is important to note that many of these critical performance metrics are not entirely specific to the VoiceXML interpreter, but also involve the relevant subsystems that are required for actually rendering a VoiceXML application, such as voice recognition, audio processing, etc.

Rich, Robust Application Interfaces

As discussed earlier, advanced network services such as notifications and call center integration are critical for most enterprise voice application deployments. Voice Application Networks that do not provide these capabilities are limited in the scope of applications they can successfully service. That said, developers building on-premises systems from scratch must additionally license or build and integrate such functionality into their infrastructures, so Voice Application Networks that do perform well here have a distinct time to market and ROI advantage. In addition, it is important that these advanced network services be exposed through open standards-based interfaces that are flexible and extensible over time and that integrate well with VoiceXML. Examples of important advanced network services include:

- **Initiation of outbound calls** that provide businesses with another avenue to reach, influence, and inform potential customers

- **Robust call transfer capability,** including the ability to dynamically set caller identification data

Table 4.2 Sample Evaluatory Performance Metrics for VoiceXML
Metric*

PERFORMANCE METRICS FOR ALL VOICEXML PLATFORMS
Port density-number of simultaneous inbound/outbound ports per unit rack space
Time to begin playing a prompt of several standardized sizes, both first time and subsequent times in a session (ms)
Recognition time for standardized static grammars of various sizes/complexities (ms)
Recognition time for standardized dynamic grammars of various sizes/complexities (ms)
Recognition time for utterances matching application scope grammars of standardized size (ms)
Inter-state execution time for forms/event handlers within the same document (ms)
Inter-state execution time for forms/event handlers in new documents, discounting Web server response time (ms)
Execution time for standardized blocks of cmaScript (ms)
Processing time for standardized blocks of recorded audio (ms)
Performance variations for calls in progress when a single given call enters a JavaScript loop
ADDITIONAL PERFORMANCE METRICS FOR VOICE APPLICATION NETWORKS
Packet loss metrics from customer Web servers to vendor network (%)
Latency from customer Web servers to vendor network (ms)
Consistently available IP bandwidth from customer Web servers to vendor network (Mbit/s)
Number of simultaneous audio streams without audio breakup
Bandwidth consumed for standardized use of standardized applications of various complexities (measuring cache performance)
Latency in reflecting changes to application content (measuring cache performance)
Number of simultaneous `<record>` posts without performance degradation of other calls

*All metrics should be considered under normal (~50%) and stressed (~80+%) capacity levels.

- ■ **Call center integration** with leading CTI platforms such as Cisco ICM and Genesys to support intelligent call routing, queuing, and facilitating agent screen pops, or providing other relevant session-related information that further personalizes the caller experience

- ■ **Personalization services,** such as the ability to better distinguish between valid and invalid Caller ID information as reported by the telephone network

Enterprise-Ready Solutions

As described earlier, rich libraries of application components and industry-focused solutions can potentially help companies deliver richer and more comprehensive service offerings much more quickly and at dramatically lower costs. Voice Application Network providers should provide a strong offering in this arena that delivers the core features and functionality companies require to deploy compelling voice applications as quickly as possible to their customers. Common examples of such application suites include:

- **Airline solutions.** These enable airlines to offer reservations booking, flight information and notification, baggage tracking, etc.

- **Banking solutions.** These enable consumer banks to deliver telephone banking services, ATM and branch locators, etc.

- **Brokerage solutions.** These enable retail brokerages to bring telephone trading functionality and outbound notifications such as portfolio movements and breaking news to traders anytime, anywhere from any telephone.

- **Government solutions.** These enable government agencies to deliver powerful self-service access to information and services for all citizens, and not just those who have Internet access. This especially can help agencies rapidly implement their Section 508 compliance.

- **Insurance solutions.** These enable insurance providers to let their customers locate health care providers and insurance agents, manage their accounts, etc.

- **Retail solutions.** These enable retailers to deliver order status, store locators, voice-activated commerce, etc.

- **Service provider solutions.** These enable service providers to rapidly add value-added voice services such as stock quotes, weather, directory assistance, voice-activated dialing, e-mail reading, movies, etc.

Voice Application Experience

Cost savings from voice applications are a direct result of an application's ability to successfully automate customer service tasks that previously required live agents. Vendors without core competencies in voice UI design, speech science, and audio production will consistently fail to build applications that callers enjoy and that deliver the expected benefits. Voice Application Network providers should demonstrate competencies and technologies, including:

- **A strong focus on the customer experience,** including detailed studies of user interactions with telephone services as well as codified design standards and principles

- **Quality in-house voice experience** capable of bringing years of design, development, and research familiarity to help solve the problems of enterprise customers

- **An optimized platform** for delivering world-class voice applications at tremendous scale

- **Sophisticated recognition tuning tools,** ensuring that enterprise customers have the necessary tools to analyze application performance

- **World-class audio design and production** that leverage the knowledge and experience of in-house audio experts as well as the unique pressures of generating audio presentation for voice applications

- **Proven design methodology** for architecting, developing, and usability testing high-quality voice applications running on the network

Development Tools and Services

Building compelling voice applications is analogous to constructing good Web sites. Both require solid design expertise, artistic input, markup language coding tools, deployment facilities, and occasional developer technical support. Voice application networks that make design and development easy offer a number of tools and services, including:

- **Powerful development tools,** including the ability to write code, debug applications, look up documentation, and more

- **Cost-effective professional services** that assist in the design and development of complex voice applications

- **Quality audio production facilities and expertise** that help give applications an excellent sound and feel, satisfying users and extending a business's brand identity

- **Valuable developer technical support,** lending voice application developers a helping hand when needed

Corporate Health and Financial Solvency

In today's challenging economic environment, businesses of all sizes are under relentless pressure to reduce significant costs while retaining service quality. Voice applications can save companies millions of dollars in call center equipment and operator expenses. Though building and deploying voice applications requires little to no upfront capital investment, it does demand a firm technology commitment to the voice application network vendor of choice. In the process, enterprise customers must be assured that the vendor exhibits the following traits of a long-term, viable company, rather than a fly-by-night startup or inexperienced organization:

- **Active and strong leadership** in voice application network design and development

- **Adequate funding** to build, run, and promote voice application networks and applications

- **An experienced management team** that understands the requirements of enterprise customers and has a proven track record of delivering quality products on time

Summary

Based upon anecdotal measurements from analysts, *Fortune 500,* and other companies actively evaluating Voice Application Network providers in mid-2001, Figure 4.1 summarizes the current state of the market relative to these evaluation criteria.

Pricing Models for Voice Application Networks

Voice Application Network providers use a variety of pricing models, but a few key components and options stand out.

Voice application network providers earn usage fees as enterprises and service providers use their Voice Application Network. They also earn application licensing and professional services fees for use of their Industry Solutions and custom application development. This business model is a clear win with strong demonstrable ROI for its customers. Enterprises save money relative to live operators whenever their customers' calls are answered by their voice application network provider, and service providers drive revenue when their subscribers use these applications. In addition, customers are able to minimize their up-front capital costs by using the provider's existing network and applications.

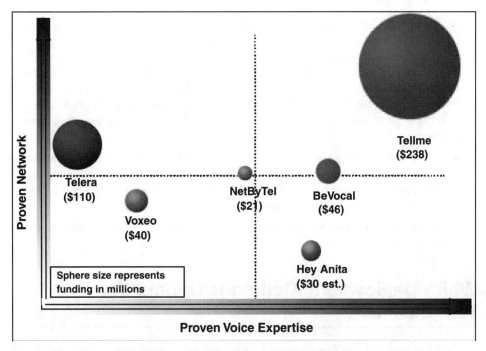

Figure 4.1 Voice application network provider market, August 2001.

■ **Transport and platform.** A key characteristic of most Voice Application Network providers is that they offer (if not require) bundled pricing for telecom transport and the actual voice application platform. It is often also possible for customers to retain their direct billing relationship with their telecom carrier, and to pay the provider directly only for platform usage. In either case, telecom is billed on a standard per-minute rate. There are typically significant discounts for volume and up-front commitments. For platform usage, providers typically offer some combination of the following three options:

■ *Per minute*—This is a strictly usage-based fee that allows customers to pay specifically for the capacity they use. There is typically some notion of normal capacity for forecasting purposes, with the ability to pay extra for dynamic bursting above this capacity at any time.

■ *Per port per month*—This involves a license rental fee that is paid per month for some forecasted number of ports. Dynamic bursting is typically still available.

■ *Per port*—Some providers allow customers to fully purchase all ports, just as if they were deploying them on premises. This carries a higher up-front price tag, and essentially represents customers purchasing their own hardware outright.

In addition to these fees, customers also typically pay industry standard rates for the various types of call transfers that are available. For example, a customer using voice-activated dialing may wish to keep the platform on the line while choosing from a local restaurant directory, so that he or she can easily press ** and return to the application. This requires keeping an extra phone line in use for the duration of the call, and these costs are simply passed on to the customer.

■ **Application licensing.** Voice Application Networks that offer prebuilt application suites typically charge a monthly or annual license fee for usage of these applications, in addition to passing on requisite fees for content feeds, etc. These fees typically include application maintenance, and sometimes grant the customer the right to continue licensing the application in the future—even if the customer chooses to switch to an alternate provider for transport and platform in the future. This option provides an even lower-risk solution for prospective customers.

■ **Advanced network services.** Advanced network services such as notifications and call center integration are typically priced with a modest initial setup fee plus a per-transaction or data dip fee. For example, a company may pay $.02 for every outbound notification generated.

■ **Professional services.** Industry-standard day rates for custom development work apply.

Which Deployment Method Is Optimal for Your Business?

As has been presented in this chapter, Voice Application Networks offer a broad and compelling value proposition, and make it possible for companies to rapidly build and deploy high-quality VoiceXML applications in a scalable environment with minimal up-front costs. That said, each company must actively evaluate its expertise, resources, schedule, and other corporate factors to determine which option makes the most sense for its situation.

For most companies and most situations, the advantages of working with a strong Voice Application Network provider tend to outweigh the inherent challenges of choosing any outsourced solution for any IT project. The choice is the most complex for companies that meet most or all of the following criteria:

- **Extremely large deployments.** It is certainly true that renting infrastructure from a pure cash-flow perspective ultimately costs more than buying given sufficient volume. Companies looking to deploy very large systems (e.g., more than 5,000 ports) that will have good average port utilization and that are not very spiky should certainly look hard at all available options, and make their decision based upon factors beyond absolute price.

- **Existing in-house voice expertise.** Companies that already have, or are willing to hire, in-house voice expertise are better positioned to succeed with on-premises deployments. Again, this only tends to be cost-effective for truly massive deployments of many applications.

- **Existing telecom expertise.** Carriers and large call centers with deep expertise in managing and provisioning telecom have less to gain directly from a network-based solution. That said, Voice Application Networks have the added benefit of providing network-based overflow capacity and "queuing in the cloud," which can be a strong complement to premises-based call center infrastructure and can further slash costs.

This concludes our introduction to the market context and industry background for VoiceXML technology. In the remaining chapters, we will investigate VoiceXML application development in detail.

Setting Up a VoiceXML Development Environment

In the previous four chapters, we introduced the world of VoiceXML and discussed speech technology fundamentals in recognition and synthesis. In this chapter, we will go over various development tools and environments available to developers to start building VoiceXML applications. Like Hypertext Markup Language (HTML), Extensible Markup Language (XML), and Wireless Markup Language (WML), VoiceXML files are also text files; so you can use your favorite text editor (vi, emacs, Wordpad, etc.) to write your VoiceXML pages. However, it is better to take advantage of the free tools available on the Internet, as they allow you not only to build sample applications, but also to test and in some cases host your applications as well. The available tools can be divided into two basic categories: Web-based tools and software development toolkits (SDKs). Web-based tools such as BeVocal, Tellme, and VoiceGenie allow you to build, test, log, and run your applications online for no cost. These vendors have also provided numerous tutorials and examples, which will help you in getting a jump start. (For commercial application hosting, please contact these companies directly.) SDKs, on the other hand, offer self-contained offline development environments, which allow you to use your personal computer (PC) or desktop to work on your applications. You can use microphones and headphones to interact with your application. Some of the SDKs, such as the one available from Voxeo, provide a visual design tool as well. The tools discussed in this chapter are listed in Tables 5.1 and 5.2.

Web-Based Tools

In this section we will review the Web-based tools such as BeVocal Café, Tellme Studio, and VoiceGenie's developer's workshop.

Table 5.1   Web-Based Tools

TOOL	COMPANY	URL AVAILABLE
BeVocal Café	BeVocal, Inc.	developers.bevocal.com
Tellme Studio	Tellme Networks, Inc.	studio.tellme.com
VoiceGenie Developer Workshop	VoiceGenie Technologies, Inc.	developer.voicegenie.com

Table 5.2   Software Development Toolkits

TOOL	COMPANY	URL AVAILABLE
WebSphere Voice Server SDK	IBM	www.ibm.com/software/speech
V-Builder	Nuance Communications, Inc.	developer.nuance.com
Voxeo Community	Voxeo Corporation	community.voxeo.com
Mobile ADK	Motorola, Inc.	mix.motorola.com
Covigo Studio	Covigo	www.covigo.com

BeVocal Café

BeVocal Café, by BeVocal, Inc., is a Web-based hosted VoiceXML development platform (Figure 5.1) that allows quick development and testing of VoiceXML-based applications. The platform includes the following tools:

- **File management,** for uploading VoiceXML, grammar, and audio files. BeVocal also provides a library of reusable VoiceXML components such as SpeechObjects, audio clips, and grammars.

- **Vocal scripter,** a Web-based tool that allows you to interact with an application in a chat mode. This way, the vocal scripter disassociates the application from the recognition aspects and allows users to test their VoiceXML code. Voice scripter can run in either batch or interactive mode. In batch mode, the user either provides a Uniform Resource Locator (URL) or updates a text file (only the .txt extension is accepted) containing inputs for running the VoiceXML application.

- **Log browser,** for call trace log viewing. The browser displays call activity for a given specified time period. Logs provide an excellent way to understand the inner workings of a VoiceXML application, including speech recognition.

- **Trace tool,** for tracing and debugging of applications in real time. This tool allows you to trace several active calls at any given instant.

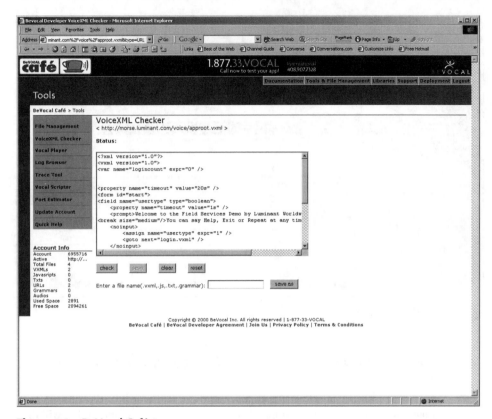

Figure 5.1 BeVocal Café.

■ **Port estimator,** for estimating the number of ports necessary to support a required level of service and users (concurrent).

In addition to all these tools, the site has a VoiceXML tutorial, a reference guide, samples, grammar references, frequently asked questions (FAQs), and an audio library. To test VoiceXML applications from a live touch-tone phone, developers can dial 1-800-33-VOCAL and use their user ID and personal identification number (PIN) to test their applications.

Tellme Studio

Tellme Studio (Figure 5.2) is another widely used Web-based application development platform. Developers can develop, test, debug, and publish their applications to the Tellme platform. The tools available at studio.tellme.com are:

■ **Flexible URL and Scratchpad-based development,** where you can either enter a URL to an existing VoiceXML application or just type some VoiceXML right in the web page.

■ **A grammar checker,** to check for grammar errors.

Figure 5.2   Tellme Studio.

- **A VoiceXML checker,** which can be used for checking the syntax of your VoiceXML code.

- **A grammar phrase checker,** which allows you to test words and phrases against your grammar to determine if they will be recognized and which will display the returned value if the words and phrases are recognized.

- **A grammar phrase generator,** which displays phrases your grammar is capable of recognizing. You can view all phrases your grammar can recognize, or just generate a random sampling.

- **A dual-tone multifrequency (DTMF) generator,** which allows you to generate DTMF (touch-tone) equivalents for a list of words and check for conflicts.

- **A debug log,** which allows you to view log files in real time or from an archive.

- **A record by phone option,** which allows you to record prompts or audio files with just your telephone. Once you have finished recording your prompts, the audio files are e-mailed to you.

- **A VoiceXML Terminal** tool, which allows you to test your application or service by specifying the application as an URL or in the scratchpad and simulating the user response by entering valid user responses from an active grammar.

- **Libraries** of existing components such as VoiceXML code examples, Audio files for commonly used sounds such as "GoodBye," "Help," "Go Back," etc., and library of useful grammars such as Yes/No, Credit Card, and Date/Time commands. In addition there are some audio and perl tools available.

- **The MyExtensions section,** which allows developers to access their applications through 1-800-555-TELL. Callers just say "Extentions," and then dial the right extension.

■ **Voice over IP (VoIP) Access,** which allows developers to use any SIP- and RTP-compatible VoIP phone to build and test VoiceXML applications.

In addition to these tools, there are several tutorials, references, white papers, articles, and sample code documents to help you out with various aspects of voice application development.

VoiceGenie Developer Workshop

VoiceGenie also provides Web-based testing environment, as shown in Figure 5.3. The available tools are a VoiceXML validator, a call log explorer, an audio converter, an extension manager, and several tutorials, white papers, and FAQs. VoiceGenie also has an offline testing tool, Genietracer, which can help verify and test VoiceXML code.

In addition to tools from BeVocal, Tellme, and VoiceGenie, similar toolkits are available from HeyAnita, Informio, etc. If you want your applications to be hosted directly with these vendors, i.e., to be able to access your application via a separate toll-free or regular number, you can contact these companies' sales and support departments directly.

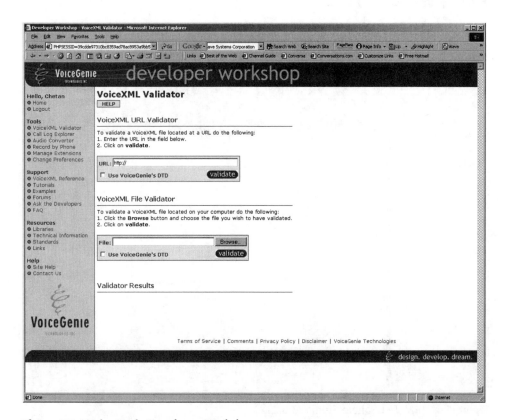

Figure 5.3 VoiceGenie Developer Workshop.

Software Development Kits

We will be discussing the following toolkits in this section: WebSphere Voice Server SDK from IBM, V-Builder from Nuance Communications, Voxeo Community from Voxeo Communications, Mobile ADK from Motorola, and Covigo Studio from Covigo.

WebSphere Voice Server SDK

IBM has been in the voice products and services business for over 30 years with its interactive voice response (IVR) line of products. As a natural extension of its voice software product line and WebSphere application development platform, IBM has rolled out WebSphere Voice Server. Voice Server SDK is available for download from IBM's Web site (see Table 5.2). This toolkit ties in with WebSphere Studio (see Figure 5.4), IBM's suite of tools that brings all aspects of Web site development into a common interface. The voice server SDK is available on the companion CD with this book.

Let's look at how you can go about exploring WebSphere Voice Server SDK. You could use WebSphere Studio's VoiceXML editor or any regular text editor to author VoiceXML program files, although Studio's VoiceXML editor makes it much more convenient to write and test your applications.

Editing VoiceXML Files

Studio helps ensure that your VoiceXML files will be syntactically correct. This VoiceXML editor is a built-in editor for VoiceXML files. It includes a code assist feature

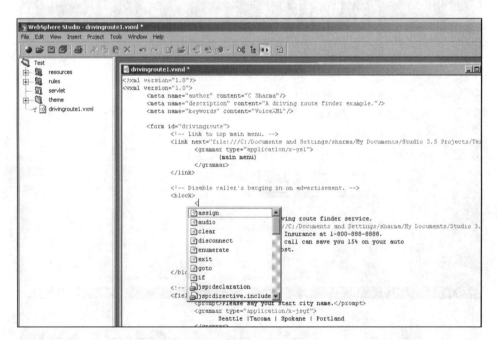

Figure 5.4   IBM WebSphere Studio (3.5.2).

to guide you as you add or change code and tags. This feature is the default editor for files with .vxml and .jsv extensions (VoiceXML files). Whether you add a new VoiceXML file to your project, import or copy an existing one, or create one with the Studio wizards, you can edit it with the default VoiceXML editor. You can also edit VoiceXML files with any other editor you have registered for files with these extensions. This section only discusses Studio's default VoiceXML editor.

Creating a New VoiceXML File

You can create a new VoiceXML file using the Studio Blank.vxml template and add it to your project the same way you create other files—from either the File or Insert main menu choice. This new file will contain the basic VoiceXML version 1.0 tags to get you started, such as `<vxml></vxml>`, `<form></form>`, and `<block></block>`.

To create a new file, in any Studio view:

- Select the project or folder where you want the file to reside.
- From the main menu, select File →New (or select Insert → File).
- On the Create New tab of the Insert File dialogue, select Blank.vxml.
- Rename the file and click OK.

The file is placed in the selected folder and checked out for you.

Editing a VoiceXML File

Studio's default VoiceXML editor allows you to edit and modify the VoiceXML source in a textual mode. The VoiceXML editor includes many of the helpful functions available with other Studio editors.

If your VoiceXML file needs to link to other files in the Studio project, you can create links using the Copy As function. (You cannot, however, paste the results of the Copy As markup function into a VoiceXML file.) You can change the look and format of the text source to your own preference. The Options dialogue gives you choices for changing:

- The color of code elements such as tags, comments, attributes, values, and text
- The font family and font size
- The case for tags (upper or lower)
- Indentations and word wrap

The Options dialogue also includes choices specific to VoiceXML, such as:

- Default end-of-line code
- Default file extension for VoiceXML files
- The code page to use for character encoding
- Whether or not to check the syntax when you save the file

With syntax checking turned on, Studio will not save your file if the VoiceXML syntax is incorrect. It highlights the syntax problems so that you can correct them. Syntax checking is turned on by default. To change your VoiceXML editor options in the VoiceXML editor, right-click to open the context menu, select Source Edit Options, change the look and format on the Edit Source tab, and, to change the VoiceXML-specific options, click the VoiceXML tab and click OK.

To apply your formatting changes, in the VoiceXML editor, right-click to open the context menu and select Format Source.

Getting Assistance with VoiceXML Code

In addition to syntax checking, the VoiceXML editor provides coding assistance. As you edit your VoiceXML files in the Studio VoiceXML editor, you can display and choose from a list of the valid elements for the exact place you are in your code. Depending on the context, the list will contain VoiceXML tags, attributes, or values. The list might also contain Java Server Pages (JSP) tags for inserting beans and connecting to databases. When the Websphere application server processes pages with JSP tags, it returns the data from the beans and databases to the VoiceXML browser for formatting.

You can invoke the list of valid elements by typing a new opening tag character (<) or a space within a tag. For example:

- If you type a space within the `<vxml>` tag (for example, `<vxml >`), the list will contain the elements `<application>`, `<base>`, `<lang>`, and `<version>`.

- If you type a space within a tag that already has a version defined, such as `<vxml version=2.0">`, the list will just contain the elements `<application>`, `<base>`, and `<lang>`.

- If you type an opening bracket (<) between two tags, such as between `<vxml version=2.0">` and `</vxml>`, the selection list will include all other valid tags. When you select one of the tags, both the beginning and ending tag for that selection are inserted in place. For instance, if you select form from the list, the editor inserts `<form></form>`. If your focus is within a tag (between the opening and closing brackets), you can also invoke the code assist feature from the Context menu.

You can also get assistance with VoiceXML code by right-clicking on Context and selecting Code Assist.

Speech Grammars (.gram Files)

In its VoiceXML specification, the VoiceXML forum defines a speech grammar as part of VoiceXML. A speech grammar can specify a set of utterances that a user may speak to perform an action or supply information, or it can provide a corresponding string value or set of attribute-value pairs to describe an information or action.

VoiceXML includes the `<grammar>` element to specify an inline grammar or an external grammar. When you choose to create VoiceXML files in the Studio Database and JavaBean wizard, you can associate a speech grammar with any of the fields on your input page. You can specify an inline grammar by choosing the grammar type or an external grammar by providing the Uniform Resource Indicator (URI) to the grammar file (.gram) in your project.

A .gram file might contain the following set of valid utterances for a field:

```
#JSGF V1.0;
grammar ex_1_2;
public <restaurant> = italian|american|mexican|nothing;
```

Testing Your Work

Once your VoiceXML files are ready, you have two options to run your programs: either invoke Speech Browser from Studio or invoke a DOS prompt to run Voice Server from command line. For the latter, go to the installation directory, which contains the binaries-vsaudio and vstext. Running vsaudio allows you to interact with your application using headphones and microphones. *vstext* allows you to interact with the application in a text (command line) mode. Voice Server also launches a DTMF simulator (as shown in Figure 5.5) and can be used if the application needs DTMF input.

The WebSphere Studio and Voice Server development environment is really useful if you are looking at developing code for multiple channels and devices, namely HTML, XML, WML, Handheld Device Markup Language (HDML)

IBM's Transcoding Tool

IBM has extended its WebSphere Transcoding Publishing (WTP) tool to do HTML-to-VoiceXML transcoding. Due to complexity and importance of voice user interface (VUI) design, it is not advisable to use transcoders for a complete application design and implementation. However, WTP can be used for converting small, well-defined and -contained HTML content from existing pages hosting dynamic information/data such as stock quotes, weather updates, sports scores, phone numbers, etc. for use within a VoiceXML application. Figure 5.6 shows the transcoding process to VoiceXML. To make sure usability of the application is not compromised, an annotation step is introduced to modify the HTML document by clipping sections and inserting new content depending on the design of the application.

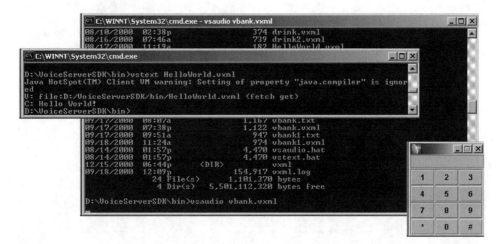

Figure 5.5   Running IBM Voice Server on DOS command line.

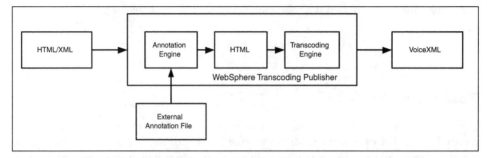

Figure 5.6   IBM HTML-to-VoiceXML transcoding tool.

The annotation instructions can be internal or external. In internal annotation, the instructions reside within the HTML file itself, while in the case of external annotation, they reside in a separate file and are applied at runtime. IBM's WebSphere Studio's editor allows for internal annotations to be built visually.

V-Builder

V-Builder is an excellent VoiceXML integrated development tool available from Nuance, a leader in the voice solutions market. In this section we will view the tool through the eyes of an application. The tool comes with a set of predesigned dialogues, grammars, prompts, and SpeechObjects, to allow for fast application development and testing. We will discuss these elements in more detail in Chapters 6 and 7. Figures 5.7 and 5.8 give

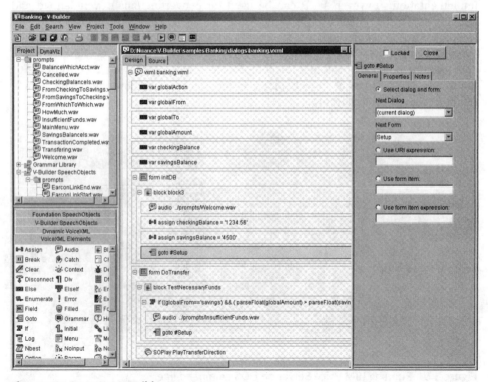

Figure 5.7   Nuance V-Builder.

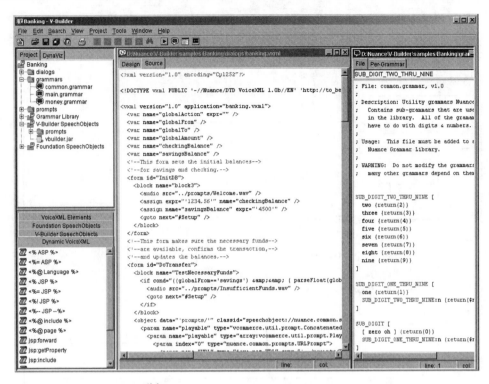

Figure 5.8 Nuance V-Builder.

a view of the development environment. The left side of the tool contains all the design elements, namely dialogues, grammars, prompts, VoiceXML elements, V-Builder Speech-Objects, and Foundation SpeechObjects. You can drag and drop the elements into the design palette in the center and configure the properties of these elements by right-clicking on the elements in the palette and editing the properties on the right-side palette.

Before getting into the steps involved in creating an application, let's discuss our application briefly. The basic call flow diagram of an insurance application is shown in Figure 5.9. It is always a good idea to draw such a flow diagram before you start writing VoiceXML code to guide your design and testing. In this application, the user is first greeted with a welcome message and then requested to choose from four available types of insurances: health, life, auto, and flood (starting point and main menu). If the user picks one of these, the system thanks the user and brings the user back to the main menu. If there is some error (poor speech recognition, wrong choice, or no utterance), system will play a help message and bring the user back to the main menu or starting point. If the user says *help* or *cancel* anytime during the conversation, a help message is played and the user is directed to the starting point.

Let's look at the steps required to design this application using V-Builder.

Getting Started

First, create a project called insurance, and in the new project, create a new dialog called insurance.vxml. (For detailed instructions, please refer Nuance V-Builder Tutorial available with the Nuance software package on the companion CD.) Now, from the

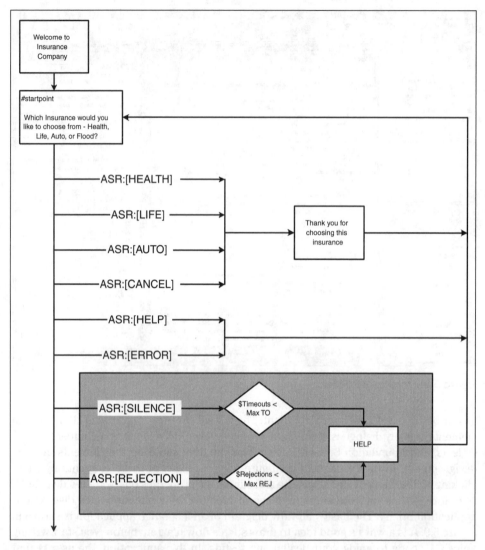

Figure 5.9 Insurance application call flow.

VoiceXML elements on the bottom left palette, drag the `<var>` element and drop it just after the `<vxml>` tag. Select the inserted `<var>` element and change the property (Value) to be choice (becomes a global variable). Edit the value of id property of the `<form>` element to welcome. Next, insert three new forms (drag and drop from the VoiceXML palette) and name the id property to be selectInsurance, matchedInsurance, and unmatchedInsurance, respectively.

The Welcome Form

Now, insert a SOPlay SpeechObject (Nuance V-Builder SpeechObjects Pack is required for this to work) in the welcome form (drag and drop from the Speectobjects palette).

Click on the object so that the property sheet is viewable on the right side. Click on the value field of the playable property. Here you can create and record a new prompt file named welcome.wav with the transcription, *Welcome to the Insurance Company*. Now, drag and drop a <block> element from the VoiceXML palette underneath the SOPlay box and then drop a <goto> element into this block box. Customize the goto by selecting insurance.vxml from the next dialog pull-down list and selectInsurance from the next form pull-down menu.

The selectInsurance Form

Drag-and-drop a *SOChooseOne* element from the SpeechObjects palette into the select-Insurance form. Edit its *SOKey* property to *SOChooseInsurance*. Select the dropped instance, so that a property sheet window displays its attributes, and click the Value cell of the *initialPrompt* property to open the playable editor dialog. Now, select and remove the item 0 (a default prompt that comes with every new instance of an *SOChooseOne*). Here you can create a prompt, "Which insurance would you like to choose from—health, life, auto, or flood?" (create file pinsurance.wav). In the property sheet of the *SOChooseInsurance* object, click the value cell of the grammar property to open the grammar editor. Then you can use this editor to specify the grammar that recognizes the user's response to the pinsurance.wav prompt.

Drag a <block> element from VoiceXML palette and drop it in the *selectInsurance* form, just below the *SOChooseOne* box. Then drag and drop an <assign> element from the same palette into this <block> element. Now, set the value cell of its name property to choice and the value of the expr property to =SOChoiceCity.choice. Next, drag and drop an <if> element into the block box (after the <assign> element). The value cell of the <if> element should now read:

```
choice=='health'||choice=='life'||choice=='auto'||choice=='flood'
```

Now, drag and drop a <goto> element inside the <if> box. Set the Next dialog to insurance.vxml and Next form to *matchedInsurance*. Next, customize *SOChooseInsurance* so that the transition to the *unmatchedInsurance* form occurs after the *SOChooseInsurance*'s grammar runs into a recognition error. Select the *SOChooseInsurance* box and set *maxErrorCount* to 1. Now, to catch error conditions, drag a <catch> element from the VoiceXML palette, drop it inside the *selectInsurance* form, and set the event property to *error.semantic.vcommerce.so.MaxErrorsExceededException*. Next, insert a <goto> element inside the catch box and direct the control to unmatchedInsurance form within the insurance.vxml dialog.

At this point, most of the work for this application is done. All you have to do is customize the *unmatchedInsurance* and *matchedInsurance* forms. The structure is pretty similar to the *selectInsurance* form except for the prompts spoken back to the user. For *unmatchedInsurance*, name the .wav file to be unknown.wav and store the transcription "Sorry, your choice is not available." For *matchedInsurance*, name the file to be minsurance.wav with the transcription "Thanks for choosing this insurance."

Figure 5.10 shows the design and source palettes for this application. The VoiceXML source code is automatically created from the design process.

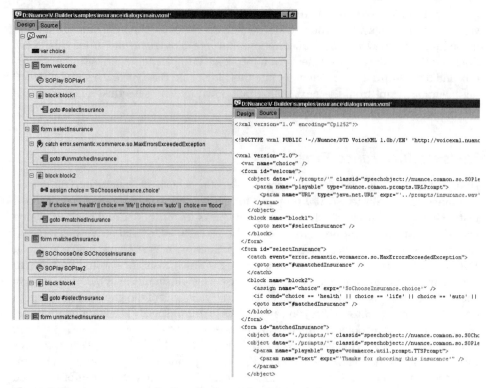

Figure 5.10 Insurance application design and source palette.

Summary

You could make this application more sophisticated by extending the interaction and application past the matchedInsurance step, providing tapered dialogues so that users are helped based on how they interact with the application (we will talk more about tapering dialogs in Chapter 12). There are several other examples that come with the V-Builder toolkit and are explained in the V-Builder tutorial (available on the CD).

Computer-human interaction for this application might sound something like this:

C: *Which insurance would you like to choose from—health, life, auto, or flood?*

H: *(Silence)*

C: *Which insurance would you like to choose from—health, life, auto, or flood?*

H: *Earthquake.*

C: *Sorry, your choice is not available. Which insurance would you like to choose from—health, life, auto, or flood?*

H: *Flood.*

C: *Thanks for choosing this insurance.*

V-Builder allows developers to very quickly build, test, and deploy VoiceXML applications and services. Nuance also has several other voice products—voice server, optimizer, and grammar builder. More information is available on its developer site (see Table 5.2).

Voxeo Community

Voxeo's Designer tool (see Figure 5.11) is somewhat analogous to tools such as Microsoft FrontPage, NetObjects Fusion, or Dreamweaver. It is used for visually designing HTML pages and allows the Web developer to focus on look and feel rather than syntax.

Voxeo Designer delivers the same benefit for phone markup languages. You can use the designer to visually design phone applications, and it will automatically generate the VoiceXML or CallXML markup (Voxeo's proprietary markup language) for you. This allows a voice application developer to focus on important issues like usability and functionality without having to worry about syntax.

Some of the features of the designer tool are:

- Visual application design using flowcharts
- Full round-trip, bidirectional development
- Element/attribute syntax validation
- File Transfer Protocol (FTP) and HTTP support for file read and write
- Full VoiceXML 1.0 Tag support (beta)
- 100 percent Pure Java integrated development environment (IDE) (runs on any Java Virtual Machine)

It enables users to leverage simple flowchart techniques to create VoiceXML applications.

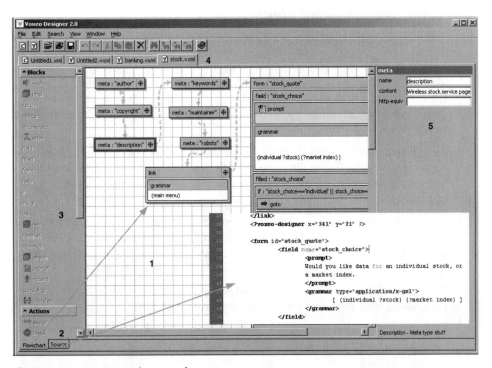

Figure 5.11 Voxeo Designer tool.

Screen Layout

The screen is divided into the following palette sections: Grid (design and source), Element, Blocks, Actions, and Events.

The Grid area is used to lay out your application. It will be the palette upon which you draw the visual description of your phone-based application. This is where you will see the visual view of your application. The blue lines in this view represent the default flow of the user through the application. The green lines represent links you have created between elements using <goto> elements and may be manipulated by dragging their control points (the icons shaped like a target.)

The Element palette area is where the various components of VoiceXML are represented. You may click on any one of them to add an element of that type to your document. See the following text for information on what the various object types are for.

These Element palette objects provide access to VoiceXML elements that will alter the flow of your application and are the main building blocks of your application. You will use these objects to generate and respond to events. Please refer to the VoiceXML documentation for a full listing of the properties for these objects and the events they are capable of firing.

The tabs across the top of the application window give you access to all the files you may have open in the Voxeo Designer at once.

The tabs across the bottom of the application window allow you to switch between the visual design view (Block diagram) and the source code view (Source) of your applications.

Application Development Steps

Let's review some basic steps in creating and testing a new application with the designer tool.

1. To add elements to your application, click the button in the Element palette for the element you wish to add. This will add an instance of the element to whatever block or event element you have selected, or to the top level of the application if you have no block selected.

2. To delete elements, select them and press the Delete key or choose the Edit menu and then the Delete menu item. Note that if you delete a parent object (a block or an event object, for example), you will also delete the children of that object.

3. Most applications you create in the Voxeo Designer will contain many blocks. Blocks are container objects that allow you to group a number of other elements. Voxeo Designer 2.0 allows you to create nested blocks by selecting an existing block and clicking the Block button on the Element palette.

4. To reorder elements in a block (thus affecting the order in which they will be processed), drag them up or down within that block.

5. To visually collapse a block in the block diagram view, double-click its title bar.

6. The properties for each element may be accessed and manipulated by right-clicking the element.

7. To establish a link between an element such as a goto and another block or element, drag the target handle on the goto to the block to which you wish the flow to continue.

8. To change a link between blocks, drag from the target handle to the block you wish to change the link to.

9. If you select the Source tab at the bottom of the application window, you will be able to directly manipulate the VoiceXML that Voxeo Designer 2.0 is creating. Any changes you make in this view will be reflected back into the visual editor when you switch tabs.

10. If you introduce an error into the XML file while editing it in source view, you will not be able to switch back to the block diagram view until you fix the error.

11. If you open an XML file with errors in it, you may not see the entire file rendered out visually in the block diagram view.

Voxeo's Designer SDK is available on the accompanying CD.

Motorola Mobile ADK

Motorola Mobile ADK for Voice Simulator 3.0 (see Figure 5.12) is a toolkit to develop, debug, and test voice applications using its VoiceXML simulator. Developers can interact and test their VoiceXML applications using the interactive simulator available with the toolkit. Like IBM and Nuance, Motorola also has a voice server product bundled into its voice solutions offerings, which includes hardware configuration as well.

The Covigo Platform

Covigo provides a software platform that enables enterprises to build and deploy mobile applications. The Covigo Platform is a leading mobile applications platform that enables enterprises to build integrated voice and data applications, from the ground up or as extensions to existing applications, using visual modeling. Based on a user-centric process modeling approach, the Platform separates user interaction workflow from presentation design and data source integration. The Platform integrates seamlessly with data sources (databases, XML feeds, application data formats, etc.) and works across different mobile channels (mobile phones, Short Message Service [SMS]-enabled devices, personal data assistants [PDAs], and voice-only telephones).

The Covigo Platform consists of the following components: Covigo Studio, a rapid development environment; Covigo Engine, for serving applications; Covigo Insight, a reporting and analysis tool that helps in deployment; and Covigo Console, a management tool that allows for the remote administration of deployed applications.

Development of a Voice Application Using Covigo Studio

Covigo Studio is a Java-based tool that supports telephony language and platform choices as plug-in components. The environment supports application development for VoiceXML, Compact HTML (cHTML), HTML, HDML, and WML.

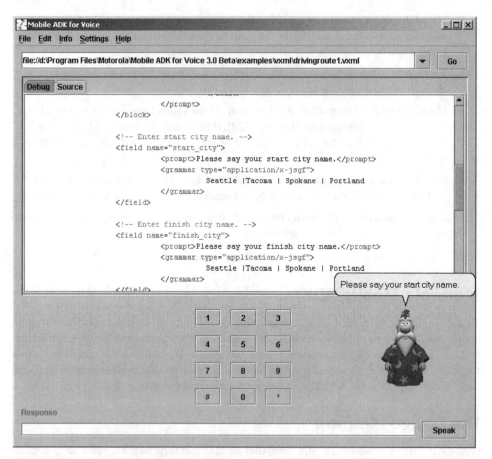

Figure 5.12 Motorola Mobile ADK toolkit.

In fact, one application can support multiple access devices, with the Covigo logic controlling device detection and multichannel rendering, interaction workflow, session management, and back-end integration. To make integration as flexible as possible, you can drag and drop adaptors to external data sources such as HTML, XML, Enterprise Java Beans (EJB), JSP, voice objects, or Customer-Relationship Management (CRM) tools to connect voice applications to existing databases, Web applications, and enterprise systems.

As an example of how you can develop an application using Covigo Studio, let's go through the structure of a currency conversion application that can be used by telephone, WAP-enabled phone, PDA, or PC. The program lets users speak or type in a currency conversion and will respond with the equivalent in any of seven currencies through either voice or data display.

Covigo Studio is organized into three separate workspaces, allowing application flow, presentation, and integration to be performed simultaneously by specialized developers. Figure 5.13 shows the application flow workspace, where each node in the application flow represents an application state, while the arcs represent possible transitions between states. States with little square inserts at the upper left represent a dia-

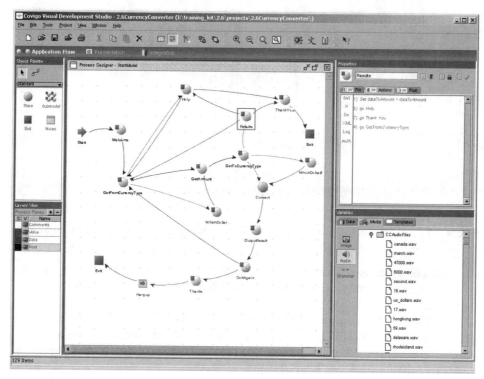

Figure 5.13   Covigo Studio application flow workspace.

log with the user or other interaction. The selected box (Results) on the display high-lights a selected state and the box in the lower right shows the audio files used within the application. States and transitions can have various actions, which cause the appli-cation to conditionally branch to other paths, set model objects, parse XML files, exe-cute methods, log data, or authenticate a user. Application logic is implemented within the Properties panel, as shown in Figures 5.14*a* and 5.14*b*. Figure 5.14*a* shows the actions for a particular state. The state will first set two model objects to HTTP responses, and then try to take the go Results, go WhichDollar2, and go Convert condi-tional branches in sequential order, transitioning to a particular state if the conditions for that branch are met. Figure 5.14*b* shows the if condition for the go Results branch.

Note the disassociation from any specific application language. The application is modeled as logical nodes and transitions in an abstract state machine, with the actual translation to specific languages or XML vocabularies performed as needed for any sup-ported platform and device type.

Presentation elements on the left side of Figure 5.15 contain all the user interface functionality needed to create a voice application. Users drag and drop presentation ele-ments (`<play>`, `<input>`, `<menu>`, `<break>`, `<import>`, or `<confirm>`) and spec-ify the corresponding grammar, audio, error, and help files or commands to associate with those elements. During run time, the appropriate VoiceXML is rendered.

The template shown in Figure 5.15 is a Covigo rapid voice template. A corresponding Covigo rapid data template enables the quick creation of data applications that render

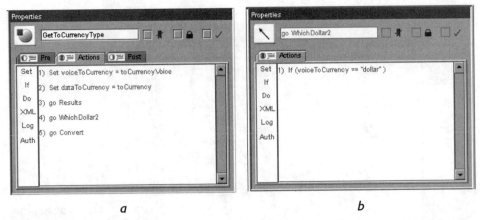

Figure 5.14   *a:* Actions for a particular state. *b:* A conditional expression in Covigo Studio.

the appropriate markup language for different devices and browsers. If a new platform, type of device, or even language is necessary, it is a simple matter to incorporate support for it.

In addition to the Covigo rapid templates, developers can use Extensible Style Language Transformation (XSLT) stylesheets or device-specific markup language templates to customize a presentation for a particular device. They then specify the appropriate rendering rules for rendering templates during run time.

Finally, the integration workspace (shown in Figure 5.16) is where you specify your

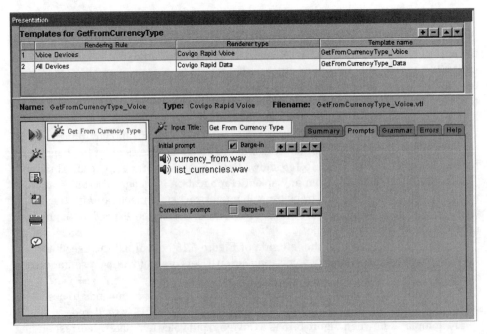

Figure 5.15   The presentation workspace.

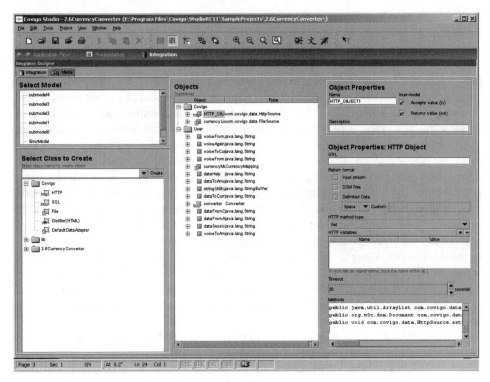

Figure 5.16 The Covigo Studio integration workspace.

adaptors to external data sources such as HTML, XML, EJB, JSP, voice objects, or CRM tools to connect applications to existing databases, Web applications, and enterprise systems.

After applications are created in Covigo Studio, they are deployed onto Covigo Engine, a robust and secure runtime environment for executing and managing applications. At run time, the voice applications render VoiceXML to Covigo Engine, which connects users through voice gateways to enterprises' back-end systems. In addition, developers can integrate and reuse existing voice objects from leading speech recognition vendors.

The Covigo Platform enables developers to build integrated voice and data applications. With Covigo Studio, developers have a single, unified environment for creating integrated voice and wireless data applications. The software is available for download through Covigo's Web site at *www.covigo.com*.

Setting Up an End-to-End VoiceXML Environment

So far we have discussed development environment and development toolkits. When it comes to implementation, deployment, and testing of an end-to-end system, it is a different story. Web-based development environments allow you to have your applications hosted right away and available for interaction and testing. However, if you are looking to set up a voice-based solution within your enterprise, you will have to look at the hardware requirements for a voice server to interact with Voice over Internet Protocol (VoIP), Private Branch Exchanges (PBXs), or the public switched telephone network (PSTN). In this section we will briefly review the end-to-end architecture required for voice solutions and options available to developers if they would like to set up their own application and services environment. If you have a small business and don't want to invest in the hardware, networks, and operations of voice applications, you might want to talk with voice application network providers such as Tellme or Telera.

Figure 5.17 shows an end-to-end configuration for a VoiceXML application. The Web application server serves the VoiceXML content through a voice server, VoIP gateway, and PSTN to the telephone. The voice server has the text to speech (TTS), automatic speech recognition (ASR), and H.323 telephony components along with a VoiceXML browser. The VoIP gateway has the voice interface card (VIC) along with VoIP software and H.323 telephony components that help interface with the PSTN. If you are going to be working on installing an end-to-end environment, your hardware setup will depend on which voice server and VoIP gateway you decide to work with. For most of the solutions coming out now, VoIP and H.323 components are available in one router or gateway (e.g., CISCO 2621). Table 5.3 provides some sample configurations and system requirements.

Figure 5.18 illustrates the end-to-end call flow for VoiceXML applications.

The VoIP gateway and H.323 gatekeeper are responsible for translating data received over ISDN PRI T1 lines into the appropriate packetized formation and routing calls to an available H.323 terminal endpoint or VoiceXML browser in the IP network using the call distribution scheme. After the VoIP gateway receives an incoming message, the called number for that dial peer is translated into the browser's alias—using the appropriate transition rule. (VoIP dial peers have one-to-one correspondence with each VoiceXML browser.) The VoIP gateway then requests the IP address and port number of the VoiceXML browser from the H.323 gatekeeper. If the VoiceXML browser is still handling

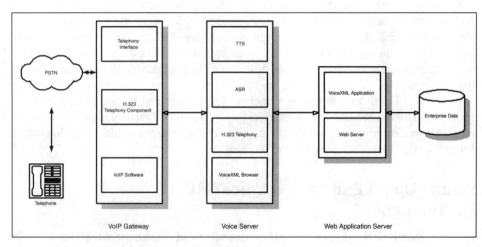

Figure 5.17 End-to-end system architecture.

Table 5.3 Hardware Configurations for Voice Server Solutions

VENDOR	TELEPHONY HARDWARE REQUIREMENTS
IBM—WebSphere Voice Server	Windows NT, Cisco 2600 (IOS version 12.1.5 XM) /H.323v2
Motorola—Voice Developer Gateway/Mya Vx500 (high-end)	Integrated hardware and software reference system Windows NT, Dialogic Telephony Interface Card Cisco IP Switch (for Mya Vx500)
Nuance—Voice Web Server	Windows NT, native audio Windows NT, Dialogic D240 and D300 Intel Solaris 2.7, NMS AG4000 Sparc Solaris 2.7, NMS AG4000
Dialogic	Integrated hardware and software reference system Windows NT, D120, D240, D480, D600 (depending on the configuration and port requirements)

the previous transactions, the gatekeeper will reject the call until the browser becomes available.

Newsgroups

In addition to the resources mentioned in this chapter, there are several newsgroups available where you can ask questions on tools, language, and hardware configuration. Table 5.4 lists some of these newsgroups.

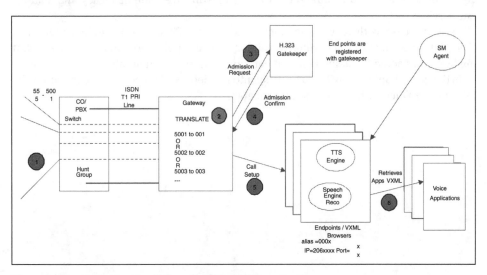

Figure 5.18 End-to-end call flow for VoiceXML applications.

Table 5.4   VoiceXML Newsgroups

VENDOR	NEWSGROUPS
BeVocal	cafe.bevocal.bugs
	cafe.bevocal.feedback
	cafe.bevocal.grammars
	cafe.bevocal.tools
	cafe.bevocal.vxml
Tellme	tellme.sharing.vxml
	tellme.vxml
	tellme.vxml.grammars
	tellme.vxml.interface-design
VoiceGenie	
HeyAnita	heyanita.public.vxml
IBM	ibm.software.websphere.voice-server.voice-server
	ibm.software.websphere.voice-server.sdk
	ibm.software.websphere.voice-server.rdc

In this chapter we have reviewed various Web-based and software development toolkits that will enable you to get started with developing VoiceXML applications and services. Depending on your level of interest and commitment, current infrastructure, and project requirements, you could choose any of these tools. Web-based tools are great to get you off the ground quickly, including testing and running your application live. SDKs provide a more robust development environment and are a better bet if you are planning to host the voice server and VoIP gateways on your own premises and your voice applications need to interact with your existing Web and/or legacy applications and services.

As is the case with new technologies, there are differences in implementation of VoiceXML specifications according to vendor, so your application built with one toolkit might require some tweaking before it can run flawlessly with another.

In the next chapter we will start getting into the details of VoiceXML specifications by introducing VoiceXML programming concepts.

## CHAPTER 6

VoiceXML Programming

In the preceding chapter we reviewed development and testing tools available to developers. We also looked at various hosting and end-to-end development platforms. Armed with this information, you can choose your development platform and get started with learning and developing in VoiceXML. In this chapter we will introduce the basics of the VoiceXML programming language and how you can go about creating the building blocks of your VoiceXML application or service.

The VoiceXML Language: High-Level Concepts

Depending on whether you're approaching VoiceXML from the perspective of a traditional Web developer or a traditional Interactive Voice Response (IVR) developer, the best way to wrap your head around this new programming language differs somewhat. While most of this book focuses on traditional Web developers extending their expertise to the phone, the aim of this chapter is to help all developers internalize a complete (and hopefully useful) framework for thinking about VoiceXML programming.

Declarative, Procedural, Event-Driven, Oh My!

The first thing to come to terms with and accept is that, quite simply, VoiceXML is not very "clean" from a programming language purist's perspective. This is neither good nor bad (though some could certainly argue this point); but it is true. VoiceXML is designed from the ground up as a *practical tool* with which to build sophisticated interactive voice applications that completely leverage the Web development paradigm and the billions of dollars worth of infrastructure, expertise, and other investments companies have made in this area since the mid-1990s.

VoiceXML, an XML-based language, combines elements (pun intended) from several key types of programming languages in common use today. On the surface, this can seem arbitrary or confusing; in practice, all elements of the language's design have been painstakingly assembled to make the art of developing voice applications using Web technologies practical and efficient.

VoiceXML includes components from the following traditional language types (of course, many programming languages—including the ones used as archetypal examples below—are themselves combinations and not "purely" one type versus another):

- **Declarative (for example, "HTML").** At the simplest level, VoiceXML (as expressed via XML documents) applications simply describe a relative static sequence of user interactions, just like HTML Web pages. VoiceXML applications describe a series of "forms," each of which has several "fields" in it for users to "fill out." Once the user "fills out" all the forms in a given document, he or she "submits" the collected information back to the Web server, which processes the information and responds with yet another set of forms. The conversation continues until either the user or the system hangs up the phone, and then we're done. Interpretation of these declarative elements proceeds linearly through a document, and the layout is the moral equivalent of the familiar "what you see is what you get" (WYSIWYG) of HTML. Rather than using HTML's elements to describe laying out text, pictures, and form fields within tables of specific sizes and colors, VoiceXML has elements to play audio prompts in a particular sequence and then "listen" for the caller to respond in a particular way before submitting the "forms" back to the server for processing.

- **Procedural (for example, "JavaScript/ECMAScript").** As it turns out, using a purely declarative language for interactive applications (just like for HTML) doesn't give developers all of the flexibility they typically want. Most notably, Web developers demand a reasonable amount of choice regarding how to break up their applications into "client" and "server" portions. Depending on the application, they sometimes want to avoid round-trips to the server after every minuscule user interaction. As a result, VoiceXML includes full support for, and integration with, the ECMAScript (popularly known as JavaScript) scripting language. Just like in HTML, ECMAScript integration makes it possible to use a full range of dynamic variables, procedures, and functions within the context of a single VoiceXML document to perform a significant amount of data processing "on the client." As it turns out, VoiceXML applications tend to rely on client-side ECMAScript far more than HTML applications do because voice applications (and common programming techniques for building them) simply tend to have more use for it. For example, a very common task in voice applications is to play a slightly different greeting prompt each time a user calls the application. Rather than using server-side script to randomly insert a different URL to a different audio file in the dynamically rendered VoiceXML, it's common to use client-side ECMAScript to generate a random number and play the appropriate audio file (for example, "welcome1.wav" vs. "welcome2.wav"). While it's almost always possible to achieve the same result via either client- or server-side script, professional VoiceXML developers tend to use a healthy mix of the two.

■ **Event-driven (for example, "Microsoft Windows programming").** Another practical fact that VoiceXML has to deal with is that interactive voice applications are almost always nonlinear, and developers need a way to "trap" various events and respond accordingly. This includes things like "listening" for high-level global commands (for example, "goodbye"), as well as things like run-time errors and the caller simply hanging up the phone in the middle of the conversation. Most of these scenarios could be handled declaratively by putting explicit elements in every interaction state within the application to handle every possible event. In practice, this would result in extremely unmanageable code, because in almost all cases there is a high degree of commonality in responses to common "high-level" events. As a result, VoiceXML includes a fairly extensive event model whereby developers can define a nested series of well-scoped event handlers for standard (and custom) events. This is, of course, similar to the "onClick" and other such events trappable via ECMAScript in HTML, but on a much richer and extensible scale. While this adds a tremendous amount of flexibility to the language and can greatly minimize the number of lines of code required to implement a particular application, it also makes things more complicated. It's critical for VoiceXML developers to understand the event model, and carefully consider how their application will react when any given event is "fired" at any particular time.

■ **Object-oriented (for example, "C++, ECMAScript (sort of)").** VoiceXML essentially fits into the same category of "sorta kinda but not really" object-oriented languages as ECMAScript, ECMAScript-based manipulation of the XML Document Object Model (DOM), Microsoft Visual Basic, and other fourth-generation (4G) client-server languages common before the rise of the Web. Scattered throughout the language, VoiceXML includes a handful of constructs where "objects" have a series of "properties" that can be inspected and manipulated. For example, the variable that contains the result of every successful recognition in a given field always has a set of "shadow variables" that contain additional information about the recognition, and are referenced using "dot" notation analogous to referencing the properties of an object (for example, person$.confidence). This is, once again, very similar to HTML and the HTML DOM. However, as of VoiceXML 2.0, the VoiceXML DOM is significantly less extensive than that for HTML.

It's Just a Conversation
("No, It's a State Machine")

At the end of the day, the number one thing to keep in mind when learning VoiceXML is that "it's just a conversation." VoiceXML is simply one possible syntax for describing a conversation between an automated system and a "live" caller. Of course, the caller doesn't really have to be "live" at all—the caller could easily be another VoiceXML application (for example, a testing harness) programmed to simulate a live caller. The point is that the application exhaustively describes the behavior of an automated system in response to audio (spoken and/or touch-tone) input from an unpredictable caller.

The VoiceXML language is simply an attempt to give developers all the tools they need to express this conversational interface: (1) using Web technologies and Internet standards and (2) using the fewest possible lines of code in a manageable and maintainable way.

So, when developing VoiceXML applications, the mental model to use is literally that of a conversation, where the automated system always speaks first. Technically, you could build an application where the system didn't say anything to get the conversation going, but in practice this is neither a good match for voice recognition technology nor socially representative of how (to the best of our knowledge) any human culture tends to use the telephone. Without exception (there are certainly some exceptions, but for all intents and purposes this is true), telephone conversations proceed as follows:

1. Caller dials telephone number.

2. Phone rings zero or more times.

3. Recipient answers phone, and says something to initiate the conversation.[1]

4. Caller responds.

5. This back-and-forth dialogue continues responsively (sometimes with one party interrupting or "barging in" on the other) for a while. . . .[2]

6. Either the caller or recipient hangs up the phone.

7. The other party hangs up the phone.

8. One or both parties may do something "offline" to note what just happened during the conversation.

9. Both parties go along their merry way until their next phone conversation with someone, at which point the process starts over.

When human beings are participating on both sides of the call "just to talk," this of course means there are a virtually infinite number of possible conversations. However, there are many situations—even where both parties are real people—where the interaction is more "scripted" and one of the parties is essentially playing the role of a "service provider."[3] The service provider's job is to offer a (typically very constrained) set of information and/or services and to (one way or another) guide the conversation toward closure. In this case, closure means ending the call after having delivered some of the available information/transactions and/or making it clear that other party is looking for something the service provider can't currently deliver.

It is these scripted or semiscripted interactions that VoiceXML is designed to address. In the United States alone, companies spend more than $30 billion each year just "answering the phone." This money is spent on a combination of people and technology to play the role of "service provider" for the millions of phone calls people make

---

[1]Or they never answer the phone (it's busy, they just don't answer before the caller runs out of patience, or the phone line is down), and the caller hangs up and proceeds to step 8.

[2]It's interesting to note that, as per the previous section, unexpected "events" can happen along the way such as the phone line mysteriously disconnects, a raucous unexpected background noise on one side or the other disturbs the conversation, a "call waiting" notification arrives, etc.

[3]It's important to note that the "service provider" can be either the recipient (for example, David calls his bank looking for current mortgage rates) or the caller (AT&T calls you during dinner for the twelfth consecutive day offering you better long-distance rates).

every day to their banks, airlines, schools, real estate agents, credit card providers, and other companies.

Whether it's traditional touch-tone IVR, traditional speech recognition platforms, or VoiceXML, it all comes down to the same basic paradigm—interactive voice applications are a *finite state machine* that defines how an automated service provider should behave in response to any given input from the other party. Most of the time, this means guiding a human being through a fairly limited set of available services, and working to get them what they're looking for (or make it clear that it's not available) and get them off the phone as quickly as possible.

So, as with most programming languages, learning VoiceXML's syntax is by far the easiest step. Developers (especially Web developers not used to thinking in this way) will rapidly gain proficiency in VoiceXML and avoid unnecessary headaches if they take the time up front to really plan out the conversational flow of their applications. Understand the language's basic constructs for declarative dialog flow and event handling, and then take the time to explicitly and exhaustively map out a given application's flow *before writing a single line of code* (Microsoft Visio or another flowcharting tool is the common way to do this). We'll discuss this a bit more from the user experience angle in Chapter 10, "Voice Application Lifecycle," but this is critical even from a pure programming perspective.

Now that we've set the context, let's begin taking a look at actual VoiceXML syntax and features.

Architectural Model

Before we begin discussing the specifics of the programming language, let's quickly review the architectural model of VoiceXML. As discussed earlier, the conversation begins when a telephone call is initiated. This can either be a person making an inbound call to a specific phone number that is "hooked up" to an automated VoiceXML-powered application or an outbound call proactively generated that dials a particular caller and immediately connects them to a VoiceXML application. Once a call is connected over the phone network,[4] the VoiceXML Infrastructure acts as a "browser" and begins making a series of HTTP requests to a traditional Web server for VoiceXML, audio, grammar, and ECMAScript documents.

The Web server (just like for traditional HTML applications) can generate these documents in any way it wishes—including complex transactions with various backend systems—but ultimately responds with these simple documents over HTTP. Once retrieved, the actual VoiceXML "interpreter" within the VoiceXML Infrastructure executes the VoiceXML application and engages in a conversation with the end user (see Figure 6.1). Along the way, the conversation may include various round-trips back to the Web server, where information that's been collected from the user is POSTed back for further processing and the Web server responds with a new round of VoiceXML and other documents.

All software and resources necessary to "execute" or "interpret" a particular

---

[4]The "phone network" could either be a landline or wireless call on the traditional Public Switched Telephone Network (PSTN), a next-generation Voice over IP (VoIP) connection to an IP service provider.

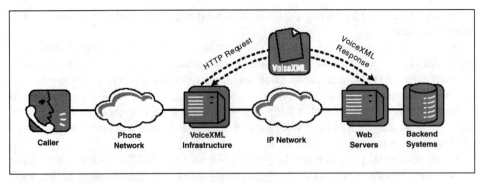

Figure 6.1 The VoiceXML architectural model.

VoiceXML application—such as voice recognition, computer-generated text-to-speech, ECMAScript execution, etc.—are embedded within the VoiceXML infrastructure, just as a traditional HTML Web browser embeds the software necessary to display different fonts, image formats, and interactive forms with radio buttons and text fields.

Scope of VoiceXML

So, once again just as with HTML, the VoiceXML language is explicitly only used to describe the user interface of voice applications. All other components (and even some of these) are actually covered by other related standards (for example, ECMAScript), or are completely independent of the VoiceXML language itself (for example, Web and application server platforms, backend data integration, voice recognition engines, etc.). At the highest level, the scope of VoiceXML includes:

1. Playing audio (both prerecorded and synthesized text to speech).

2. Listening to and recognizing audio (speech and touch-tone).

3. Form processing and a scoped client-side scripting, event, and variable model to facilitate dialog flow and optimize application design.

4. Subdialogs and basic HTTP semantics for document transitions, caching, and passing data back to the server.

5. Basic telephony control (call transfers, ANI).

6. Miscellaneous features (such as recording audio for offline use and runtime-settable properties.)

Anatomy of a VoiceXML Application

In the following sections, we'll build up an understanding of VoiceXML programming by examining each of these capabilities in turn. For now, let's outline the high-level structure of any VoiceXML document. Each document contains four basic components:

1. **Application Declaration.** The first line of any VoiceXML document uses the `<vxml>` element to declare the:

    a. *Version* of the VoiceXML language being used (for example, version="2.0").

    b. *Language and locale* covered by this document (for example, xml:lang= "us-en" for U.S. English).

    c. *Application root document* (*optional*), if any (for example, application= http://myserver/root.vxml). The application root document is a way for applications that contain multiple VoiceXML documents (especially dynamically generated ones) to easily share context and data between them. We'll discuss this in more detail below under variable scoping, but essentially all VoiceXML documents that share the same application root document share a common "application scope" context for variables, grammars, scripts, and event handlers.

2. **"Document Scope" Variables, Grammars, Scripts, and Event Handlers (optional).** After the application declaration, the document may (optionally) declare a set of variables, grammars, scripts, and/or event handlers that have "document scope." This means that they're active and available throughout the rest of the document. For example, you could define a global grammar and event handler for the word "goodbye" here using the `<link>` element. Rather than adding a copy of the "goodbye" grammar (and the code to respond to it) to every form in the document, you can do this at the top and have it handled in one place.

3. **Forms, Fields, and Transitions.** Every VoiceXML application contains at least one "form," each of which may contain zero or more "fields." Forms typically consist of playing some audio to the user (for example, a prompt), listening for a response (that is, filling out one or more fields), and transitioning to the next form or document based on the result. Forms are not required to play audio or contain any fields, but they must explicitly transition to the next form or document. Document execution begins with the first form in a document and proceeds according to the specified transitions until no transition is specified or a `<disconnect/>` transition ends the call.[5] There are several kinds of forms, fields, and transitions:

    a. **Directed Forms and Menus.** Directed forms and menus are the basic building blocks of VoiceXML applications that developers tend to use the vast majority of time. Simply put, they (optionally) do some up-front processing, then (optionally) play a series of audio prompts, and then (optionally) listen for the user to respond and transition to another form based on their response. These forms typically have zero or one field in them, and collect a response to (at most) one question. Because almost all processing has to take place within a form, some forms simply act as "containers" for some processing and a transition.

    b. **Mixed-Initiative Forms.** Mixed-initiative forms are a more complex version of the same basic concept. Mixed-initiative forms contain multiple fields, and

---

[5]`<disconnect/>` actually throws a *telephone.disconnect.hangup* event, which developers can "catch" to perform some post-hangup call processing such as to POST some final data back to the Web server. This is the moral equivalent of step 8 from the "it's just a conversation" section earlier.

a prompt structure that allows users to "fill out" the form in whatever order they wish. The application "listens" for responses to all of the fields at once (that is, all grammars are active), and then cycles through each unanswered field in sequence until they're all complete.

c. **Intradocument Transitions.** Just as HTML documents can include "anchors" that can be used to link to a specific section of the document, VoiceXML forms can transition to other places (that is, other forms) within the same document, using the same "#" URL notation as with HTML (for example, `<goto next="#menu_2"/>`).

d. **Interdocument Transitions and POSTing.** Just as forms in HTML documents have a "submit" button that POSTS all of the fields that the user "filled out" back to the Web server, VoiceXML forms can transition in the same way.

e. **Subdialog Transitions.** Unlike HTML, VoiceXML also includes the notion of a "subdialog"—similar to a "gosub" in old-time BASIC or a function call in a procedural language. We'll discuss the flexible variable and data-passing options for subdialogs in more detail later, but generally speaking they're a way for VoiceXML forms to "take a detour" and get something else done (for example, ask the users to authenticate themselves, etc.), then "come back where you left off" along with the chance to pass some data back and forth along the way.

As with any programming language, there is typically more than one way to skin the proverbial cat. Crafting effective VoiceXML applications that are optimized for performance, manageability, and extensibility is a product of mastering the various options that are available to implement a particular task, and making conscious, explicit choices when designing your applications.

Playing Audio

Playing audio to the caller[6] to deliver some sort of information is the simplest use for VoiceXML. VoiceXML supports playing both prerecorded audio files and synthesized TTS speech. Let's take a look at the proverbial "Hello World" application as a departure point for further examples.

```
1  <?xml version="1.0"?>
2  <vxml version="2.0">
3    <form>
4      <block>
5        <audio>Hello world.</audio>
6      </block>
7    </form>
8  </vxml>
```

[6]We often use the words "caller" and "end user" interchangeably. As discussed earlier, the end user is not necessarily "the caller" because the VoiceXML application may actually be executed as the result of an automated outbound call. However, for the purposes of VoiceXML, inbound and outbound calls are the same—how the call originates is exogenous to the language.

This simple application declares itself as a VoiceXML 2.0 application[7] using the default language for the platform it's running on, with no application root document other than itself. It then has a single form that does nothing other than play some synthesized TTS audio. No transition is specified, so execution ends immediately and the phone call ends.[8] Since no information is being collected from the user in this form, a simple <block> of content (in this case, playing the audio) is used rather than any <field>s.

A quick note on synthesized TTS—as we've discussed in Chapters 3, 4, and will again in Chapter 11, audio quality is one of the most critical factors for building successful VoiceXML applications. While VoiceXML provides support for synthesized TTS (including a fairly rich set of elements for directing the timbre and prosody of synthesized speech, discussed in detail in Chapter 8), the bottom line is that TTS technology (as of August 2001) remains staggeringly poor. It is highly recommended to avoid using TTS in commercially deployed VoiceXML applications to the greatest extent possible and to employ (internally or through vendors) qualified experts to design and produce the audio for any commercially deployed voice applications you develop.

Let's look at an improved version of "Hello World" that references pre-recorded audio in addition to the TTS:

```
1 <?xml version="1.0"?>
2 <vxml version="2.0">
3   <form>
4     <block>
5       <audio src="http://myserver/hello.wav">Hello world.</audio>
6     </block>
7   </form>
8 </vxml>
```

By adding the *src* attribute to the <audio> element, we are able to specify a URL to a prerecorded audio file somewhere in the world. In this case, the plain text now serves the same role as the *alt* attribute on the <img> element in HTML for displaying images. If the VoiceXML interpreter can successfully fetch and play the specified audio URL, then it will go ahead and play it over the phone. Otherwise (for example, if the server doesn't exist, the file that's returned is in an unplayable format, etc.), the interpreter falls back and uses TTS to play the specified text instead. If no TTS text was specified (for example, <audio src="http://myserver/crash_effect.wav" />) and the URL fails to load properly, then an error is thrown (see later section for error handling). For this reason, it's often good practice for sound effects to use at least a blank space as the TTS equivalent (for example, <audio src="http://myserver/crash_effect.wav"> </audio>), just in case an audio file happens to disappear or misfire in production.

That said, it's very useful to, wherever possible, to include meaningful alternate TTS text for all of your audio prompts. This makes code more readable, and more impor-

---

[7]As VoiceXML is an Extensible Markup Language (XML)–based language, line 1 of any VoiceXML application must start with <?xml version="1.0"?>. It may also optionally include a link to a standard XML <DOCTYPE> element definition, which can point to a specific VoiceXML document type definition (DTD) that the interpreter should use when executing this application.
[8]The VoiceXML 2.0 standard does not specify what happens when no transition is provided; it merely states that execution terminates. Most commercial VoiceXML implementations implicitly do a <disconnect/> when no transition is specified.

tantly several VoiceXML platforms include a set of debugging and/or "chat mode" tools that enable you to interact with your voice application visually rather than always on the phone. Having good TTS equivalents can be of great help when debugging.

As a final point, it's important to note that the VoiceXML 2.0 specification does not prescribe the exact list of audio formats that platforms must support, just as HTML does not legislate the list of supported image formats. This cleanly separates the VoiceXML standard from audio format standards, and allows VoiceXML platforms to independently innovate and evolve along with common market practices for that technology. However, VoiceXML does state that platforms must support *at least* the most basic and commonly used formats. See Chapter 7 under <audio> and <record> for details.

Listening to and Recognizing Audio

Of course, few (if any) VoiceXML applications solely involve playing a static message and hanging up the phone. The primary purpose for VoiceXML is to facilitate a conversation between the caller and an automated system, in order to exchange information and/or perform services on the caller's behalf, without the need for a live operator.

VoiceXML provides the ability to recognize both spoken and touch-tone input from the caller and to transition accordingly. Both of these depend on grammars, as described in Chapters 2 to 4, 8, and 11. Grammars are the "phrasebook" that exhaustively tells the VoiceXML platform what the list of expected spoken and/or touch-tone responses from the caller is. Similar to audio, the VoiceXML standard does not prescribe the complete list of grammar formats that platforms must support. Rather, it requires that all platforms support at least one of two vendor-independent formats; they are free to support as many additional formats as they see fit, using standard Multipurpose Internet Mail Extensions (MIME) types to distinguish between them. Chapter 8 covers the vendor-independent formats in detail.

VoiceXML provides three syntactic ways to add recognition to an application: menus, fields, and links.

Menus: Front Desk, Anyone?

The VoiceXML <menu> element is a convenient shorthand for simple forms that contain a single field (for example, ask a single question) and then immediately transition to another form. In practice, they are rarely used because they limit flexibility without actually being significantly fewer lines of code than a normal <form> with a single <field>.

Here is an example of a simple application that uses <menu> to ask a top-level questio, and then transition to another set of applications based on the caller's choice:

```
<?xml version="1.0"?>
<vxml version="2.0">
  <menu id="main_menu" dtmf="true">
    <!-- dtmf="true" means that choices in the menu automatically
         have their touch-tone equivalents (1, 2, etc.) available
         as well
    -->
```

```
      <prompt>
        <audio>Would you like customer service, technical support,
              or the front desk?</audio>
      </prompt>
      <choice next="cust_svc.vxml">customer service</choice>
      <choice next="tech_support.vxml">technical support</choice>
      <choice next="front_desk.vxml">front desk</choice>
      <choice event="event.myapp.goodbye" dtmf="9">goodbye</choice>
      <!-- the "event" attribute throws this event rather
           than transitioning to a particular URL, and the
           "dtmf" attribute overrides the sequential dtmf
           behavior of the menu and explicitly makes "9"
           the touch-tone equivalent for this option -->

      <catch event="noinput nomatch">
        <audio>I'm sorry. I didn't catch that.</audio>
        <reprompt />
      </catch>
    </menu>
</vxml>
```

The <menu> element literally takes the place of a <form>; it is a child of the <vxml> element, and any transition to a new form can equivalently go to a menu. The structure of a menu is very straightforward:

1. **Menu Header.** The <menu> element itself, which names it (so other forms can transition to it) and optionally selects some top-level behaviors such as enabling a sequential set of touch-tone equivalents (for example, press "1" for the first option, "2" for the second, etc.) for the menu.

2. **Prompt.** The <prompt> element is used to play some audio to the caller. For a menu, this prompt must actually inform the caller of what the options are. (It doesn't syntactically have to, but otherwise how will the caller know what to say?)

3. **Choices.** The menu includes one or more options via the <choice> element. Each of these presents a "grammar fragment" (a sort of shorthand "minigrammar") to recognize, and something to do if the caller chooses that option. Choices can either jump to another form (via a URL) or throw an event.

4. **Event Handlers.** While not required, menus can include local event handlers, as well (see later in this chapter for more details on events). For example, the most common events in VoiceXML applications are "nomatch" (if the caller says something unexpected and not in the grammar) and "noinput" (if the caller doesn't respond at all). VoiceXML platforms are required to have "built-in" system-level event handlers for these events that give a standard response such as "I'm sorry, but I didn't hear you" and then replay the previous <prompt>. However, as with all events in VoiceXML, developers are free (and encouraged) to write their own event handlers to give a custom response. As we'll discuss later, event handlers are hierarchical and inherited from higher-level scopes, so it's very easy to define application-level standard event handlers and then override them as necessary in exceptional cases.

Fields: The Bread and Butter

Fields within forms are the bread and butter of VoiceXML applications. The vast majority of VoiceXML applications you (and all other developers) are likely to write employ a relatively straightforward series of forms, each containing one or more fields, complemented by a healthy set of hierarchically defined global and locally overridden event handlers.

As we've discussed earlier, VoiceXML supports the concept of both "directed" forms (basically forms with a single field that ask a single question, or several fields that are visited and "filled out" sequentially) and "mixed-initiative" forms (more complex forms that theoretically allow callers to seamlessly answer a series of questions in whichever order they choose). That said, as we've discussed in Chapters 3 and 4 (and will cover in more detail in Chapters 11 and 12), effective voice user interface design is an extremely subtle and challenging art. Mixed-initiative forms are by no means a panacea for voice application design, and can easily add more complexity and usability problems to your applications if not employed as part of a conscious UI plan crafted by an experienced voice user interface designer.

Directed Forms Asking a Single Question

Here is our front desk menu example given previously in this chapter, reimplemented using form/field syntax:

```
<?xml version="1.0"?>
<vxml version="2.0">
  <form id="main_menu" scope="dialog">
    <!-- scope="dialog" means that grammars for this form
         are only active (only have scope) for this form.
         Alternatively, scope="document" gives the grammars
         document scope and makes them active in all forms
         in this document. If this document was an
         application root for other documents, then
         the form's grammars would be given application scope
         and be active in all documents within the application.
    -->
    <field name="menu_choice">
      <grammar src="g_fdesk.xml"
      type="application/grammar+xml" />
      <!-- this loads in the grammar from an external URL -->

      <prompt>
        <audio>Would you like customer service, technical support,
            or the front desk?</audio>
      </prompt>

      <filled>
        <if cond="menu_choice == 'goodbye'">
          <throw event="event.myapp.goodbye" />
          <!-- this throws the custom event -->
        <else />
          <audio>Okay, now transferring you to <value
```

```
            expr="menu_choice" /></audio>
        <goto expr="menu_choice + '.vxml'" />
        <!-- By using ECMAScript expressions, it's possible to
            insert dynamic data into TTS audio and transitions.
            In this case, the one line of code works for
            all three main options because the grammar
            return value can be used to compute the filename
            we wish to transition to. -->
      </if>
    </filled>

    <catch event="noinput nomatch">
      <audio>I'm sorry. I didn't catch that.</audio>
      <reprompt />
    </catch>
  </field>
 </form>
</vxml>
```

As we discussed before, this is scarcely more complicated than the <menu> version, but its structure immediately places dramatically richer functionality at our disposal. From a pure functionality perspective, the only enhancement added to this version (so far) is delivering some confirmation audio right in the form before transitioning the caller away to the next piece of the application. Among other things, this has the immediate advantage of delivering verbal confirmation to the caller—even if the transition fails for some reason (for example, Web server mysteriously eaten by a mongoose). This of course is just the beginning. As we'll discuss later in this chapter, VoiceXML's robustness as a voice application development language is centered on what's called the *Form Interpretation Algorithm* (FIA). The FIA is the underlying set of rules that governs transitions and behavior within and across fields, forms, documents, and applications. For now we're implicitly covering the basic and fairly intuitive portions of the FIA (for example, start with the first form in a document and the first form in a field, execute pretty sequentially, and transition to the next specified URL as we come to it). Later, we'll cover the FIA in more detail.

As with menus, forms and fields follow a fairly straightforward structure:

1. **Form Header.** The <form> element itself, which names it (so other forms can transition to it) and optionally selects some top-level behaviors.

2. **Event Handlers and Grammars.** While not required, forms can specify form-scope event handlers and/or grammars that apply to all <field>s and <block>s within the form.

3. **Execution Blocks.** The <block> element can be used to include a set of executable content (for example, ECMAScript logic, variable manipulation, playing some static audio prompts, etc.) either before any <field>s or interspersed among them.

4. **Fields.** Forms may include zero or more <field>s, prompting callers with questions and attempting to recognize their answer(s). As with menus, fields specify prompts, grammars (the list of available choices), and transitions (based on the result of the caller's choices). However, fields are far richer than menus. Fields allow developers to specify any number of built-in, inline, or external (by URL)

grammars. Similarly, fields heavily use the VoiceXML event model and FIA, allowing developers to flexibly handle the wide variety of common conversational situations that occur (for example, need to confirm the caller's choice, distinguish between ambiguous choices, offer context-sensitive help, etc.). A "field variable" is set (based on the "name" attribute of the `<field>`) to the result of any successfully matched grammar, and the `<filled>` element within the field allows the developer to inspect, manipulate, and react to its contents. In "directed" forms, fields (if there's more than one) essentially act independently and are "filled out" sequentially. In "mixed-initiative" forms, some more complex FIA structures are employed to allow a more intertwined execution flow. In either case, at the end of the day the final field to be filled in a form must (of course) ultimately either transition to the next form or `<disconnect/>` the phone call.

Asking Multiple Questions—Directed and Mixed Initiative

Now that we've covered the simplest forms, let's look at two examples of an application that ask a couple of questions in sequence. We'll present the same scenario (querying the caller for their social security number and date of birth), both as a "directed" and "mixed-initiative" conversation.

First, the directed dialog version:

```
<?xml version="1.0"?>
<vxml version="2.0">

  <catch event="noinput nomatch" count="1">
    <audio>I'm sorry, I didn't catch that. </audio>
    <reprompt />
  </catch>

  <catch event="noinput nomatch" count="2">
    <audio>I'm having a hard time understanding. </audio>
    <reprompt />
  </catch>

  <!-- these are document scope event handlers that will be
       active for all forms in the document. More on this
       later in this chapter, but essentially event handlers
       are inherited 'as if by copy' from the next-highest
       scope where they were defined. They can always
       be overridden locally. The "count" attribute
       specifies to the FIA when to use a particular
       event handler. In this example, the first
       handler will be used the first time (in a given
       field) that either "noinput" or "nomatch" is
       thrown. The second handler will be used for the
       second (and all subsequent) times within that
       field (unless a "count='3'" was specified locally). -->
```

```
<form id="dob_menu">
  <!-- as we mentioned in the previous example, scope="dialog"
       isn't necessary to specify; it's the default. -->

  <field name="dob" type="date">
    <!-- type='date' relies on a standard date grammar
         that all VoiceXML platforms are required to
         support. See Chapter 7 for the complete list -->

    <prompt>
      <audio>What is your birth date? Please include the month,
             day, and year. </audio>
    </prompt>

    <filled>
      <if cond="dob.indexOf('?')+1">
        <audio>You didn't say the full date.</audio>
        <clear namelist="dob" />
        <!-- the date grammar returns question marks in the
             missing parts of the date if the caller gives
             an incomplete answer. If so, clear the
             field's variable (part of FIA processing)
             so they'll be reprompted to try again.
             This is *not* good UI design, but a
             functional example. -->
      <else />
        <audio>Great. You said
               <value expr="dob.slice(4,6)" />,
               <value expr="dob.slice(6,8)" />,
               <value expr="dob.slice(0,2)" />,
               <value expr="dob.slice(2,4)" />.
               <!-- it would be much better to use a library
                    of ECMAScript functions and pre-recorded
                    audio to replay this information well.
                    Some VoiceXML platforms provide these -->
        </audio>
      </if>
    </filled>
  </field>

  <!-- once the first field has been successfully filled (which
       means that its 'name=' variable has been filled by a
       successful recognition), the FIA will automatically
       transition to the next field. This proceeds sequentially
       until all fields are filled and/or a field explicitly
       transitions out of the form. (More details and exceptions
       later in this Chapter -->

  <field name="ssn" type="digits">
    <!-- type='digits' is another intrinsic grammar -->
```

```
      <prompt>
        <audio>What is your Social Security Number? </audio>
      </prompt>

      <filled>
        <audio>Great. You said <value expr="ssn" /> </audio>
        <!-- once again, this is *not* good UI design -->

        <submit next="process.jsp" namelist="dob ssn" />
        <!-- this transitions to the next form, but does this
             by going to a URL triggering a dynamic, server-side
             script. The "namelist" attribute provides a list
             of variables to include on the HTTP request. By
             default the GET method is used, and the data is included
             on the querystring (e.g. process.jsp?dob=04261974&
             ssn=104622833). The "method='post'" attribute can
             be used to POST the data instead. -->
      </filled>
    </field>
  </form>
</vxml>
```

In this example, we've introduced a few concepts to slightly broaden the palette of discussion. As with all of the examples in this chapter, we've tried to incorporate a significant portion of the commentary directly inline with the code for easy reading. That said, it's worth taking a moment here to recap some of the additional functionality we're now playing with:

- **Scoped Event Handlers.** More on this later, but we're trying to steadily increase your intuitive familiarity with how these behave.

- **Built-in Grammars.** VoiceXML platforms are required to support some common grammars like dates and numbers and to return the results in a consistent way. See Chapter 7 for a complete listing.

- **Conditionals and ECMAScript Expressions.** Both in TTS audio and in evaluating the results of a successful recognition (the <if> element), standard ECMAScript expressions are a very powerful tool for producing flexible, manageable VoiceXML applications. While it would (in most cases) be possible to go back to the Web server after every recognition and do all application logic there, in practice most developers find it very useful to use round-trips to the server only when necessary for POSTing a complete set of collected data that needs to trigger some backend transaction, be stored in a database, etc.

- **Submitting Data Back to the Web Server.** Once the caller has successfully "filled out" both fields in the form, the <submit> element is used to send the data back to the server for processing. The server will respond with another VoiceXML document, which will probably continue the conversation and give the caller access to additional services.

Now let's take a look at this same example as a "mixed-initiative" conversation, where (in theory) the caller is prompted (and allowed) to answer the questions either all at once or in whichever order he or she chooses. So, instead of having a conversation that looks like:

```
Service: What is your birth date? Please include the month, Day, and
         year.
Caller:  June 20.
Service: You didn't say the full date. What is your birth date? Please
         include the month, day, and year.

Caller:  June 20, 1958.
Service: Great. You said 06/20/1958. What is your Social Security
         Number?

Caller:  101-44-4938.
Service: Great. You said 101-44-4938.
         (and so on)
```

. . . we wind up with a conversation that looks like:

```
Service: What is your birth date and Social Security Number?
Caller:  101-44-4938.
Service: Got your SSN. What is your birth date?
         Please include the month, day, and year.
Caller:  June 20, 1958.
Service: Got your birthdate. In summary, you said that you were
         born on 06/20/1958, and your Social Security Number is
         101-44-4938.
         (and so on)
```

To do this, VoiceXML provides a couple of additional concepts:

- **Subgrammars and "MultiSlot" Grammars.** As we discussed earlier, the VoiceXML language itself doesn't legislate the list of specific grammar formats that are available. It does require platforms to *at least* support the vendor-independent XML or BNF grammar format. "Subgrammars" and "multislot" grammars are a notion that aren't yet included in the vendor-independent grammar format, but are a part of other formats in common use today such as Nuance Communications' Grammar Specification Language (GSL) format. While a detailed exploration of multislot grammars is beyond the scope of this book, the basic concept is simple. A *subgrammar* is an isolated grammar fragment (for example, a list of airport codes) that is given a specific name and can be referenced by other grammars as a shortcut or component within them. Multislot grammars are a specific use of subgrammars that allows developers to express situations where the caller is expected and allowed to answer one or more questions simultaneously. The grammar for each question is represented by a subgrammar, and the result for each question populates a named "slot" within the top-level grammar. After recognition completes, the developer can examine which slots have (or have not) been filled and react accordingly. Mixed-initiative forms in VoiceXML are essentially a programmatic convenience for working with multislot grammars to build these kinds of conversational interfaces.

■ **The <initial> Element.** The <initial> element is another form item (like fields and blocks) that can be included in a form. It's especially used for mixed-initiative forms, and is always placed *before* any fields in the form. The key behavioral difference between <initial> and <field> is that as soon as *any* slot in the top-level form grammar has been matched, its "name" variable is set and the FIA will not revisit it (won't replay its prompts) again unless the developer explicitly clears that variable somewhere along the way. In addition, <initial> elements can't contain a <filled> handler; all processing of what the caller said takes place in the individual fields within the form.

So, in summary, mixed-initiative is essentially a way to first prompt the caller to answer multiple questions at once, have a grammar construct that allows this to happen, and then fall back on directed dialogue (if needed) that sequentially walks the caller through any questions they neglected to answer in their original response.

Let's take a look at the code for our scenario, implemented using mixed-initiative:

```
<?xml version="1.0"?>
<vxml version="2.0">

  <catch event="noinput nomatch" count="1">
    <audio>I'm sorry, I didn't catch that. </audio>
    <reprompt />
  </catch>

  <catch event="noinput nomatch" count="2">
    <audio>I'm having a hard time understanding. </audio>
    <reprompt />
  </catch>

  <form id="dob_menu">
      <grammar type="application/x-gsl">
        <![CDATA[
        [
        ( ?(i was born on) Dates:x ) { <dob_slot $x> }
        ( ?(my ssn is) SSNs:x ) { <ssn_slot $x> }
        ( Dates:x ?(and) SSNs:y ) { <dob_slot $x> <ssn_slot $y> }
        ( SSNs:x ?(and) Dates:y ) { <ssn_slot $x> <dob_slot $y> }
        ]

      SSNs [
          [(one oh one four four four nine three eight)]
          {return(101444938)}
      ]
      Dates [
          [(june twentieth nineteen fifty eight)]
          {return(19580620)}
      ]
      ]]>
      </grammar>
```

```
<!-- this grammar defines some "sub-grammars". These are not
     actually active at this moment because they're merely
     defining labels that can be referenced in other grammars
     down the line. The built-in platform grammars cannot be
     used as sub-grammars, and the vendor-independent XML
     Grammar format for VoiceXML does not yet support sub-
     grammars, so the Nuance GSL format is being used instead.
     While it's technically possible to build mixed-initiative
     forms without sub-grammars, it is more academic than
     practical. For brevity and clarity, only one option is
     being included in each of these grammars. In reality, you
     would build the complete grammars using the various
     pattern-matching rules available, store them in a
     separate file, and include them here by URL reference
     rather than inline. -->


<!-- this grammar also defines the actual top-level grammar
     for the form that references the sub-grammars.
     This grammar allows the caller to say either
     their ssn, their dob, or both, as well as some
     surrounding contextual sentence structure.
     The directed version of this example could
     have also included the contextual sentence structure,
     if you were building your own grammars and sub-grammars
     rather than referencing the basic built-in ones. -->


<initial name="try_both">
<!-- the "initial" element is is the defining characteristic
     of a mixed-initiative form. It usually prompts the caller
     for the whole top-level grammar at once, and then
     the other fields are only used to "fall back" on directed
     conversation if the caller fails to answer all of the
     questions (also called grammar "slots") at once. -->
  <prompt>
    <audio>What is your birth date and Social Security
           Number? </audio>
  </prompt>
  <catch event="nomatch noinput" count="2">
    <!-- this overrides the "count=2" event handler. -->
    <audio>sorry, i didn't catch that.</audio>
    <assign name="try_both" expr="true"/>
    <!-- this assigns the "init" form variable to true,
         causing the FIA to skip it on the next pass and fall
         through to the next field in the form. Each of these
         in turn check to see if their "slot" has been
         "filled" yet, and if not prompt the caller
         accordingly. -->
    <reprompt/>
  </catch>
</initial>
```

```
<field name="dob" slot="dob_slot">
  <!-- the "slot" attribute associates this field with a
       particular slot in the form-level grammar. If the
       slot has been filled, it populates the field "name"
       variable. As introduced above, when the "name" variable
       for a given form element (field, block, or initial) is
       non-NULL, then the FIA assumes it's been "filled",
       skips over that form element, and continues evaluating
       the next one in sequential order. -->
  <grammar src="builtin:grammar/date"/>
  <!-- this URL syntax is equivalent to using the "type"
       attribute for the field -->

  <prompt>
    <audio>What is your birth date? Please include the month,
           day, and year. </audio>
  </prompt>

  <filled>
    <if cond="dob.indexOf('?')+1">
      <audio>You didn't say the full date.</audio>
      <clear namelist="dob" />
      <!-- the date grammar returns question marks in the
           missing parts of the date if the caller gives
           an incomplete answer. If so, clear the
           field's variable (part of FIA processing)
           so they'll be reprompted to try again.
           This is *not* good UI design, but a
           functional example. -->
    <else />
      <audio>Got your date of birth.</audio>
    </if>
  </filled>
</field>

<field name="ssn" slot="ssn_slot">
  <grammar src="builtin:grammar/digits"/>

  <prompt>
    <audio>What is your Social Security Number? </audio>
  </prompt>
  <filled>
    <audio>Got your s s n.</audio>
  </filled>
</field>

<block name="process">
  <audio>In summary, you said that you were born on
           <value expr="dob.slice(4,6)" />,
           <value expr="dob.slice(6,8)" />,
```

```
                    <value expr="dob.slice(0,2)" />,
                    <value expr="dob.slice(2,4)" />,
             and your social security number is
                    <value expr="ssn" />
        </audio>
        <submit next="process.jsp" namelist="dob ssn" />
      </block>
    </form>
</vxml>
```

For more information about multislot grammars and subgrammars, please see the documentation for the particular grammar format that you're using (and make sure that your VoiceXML platform supports it).

Links: "Global" Handlers for Universal Commands

Now that we've covered how forms, fields, and grammars interact, the notion of "links" in VoiceXML is a very straightforward thing to add. As you might imagine, a very common thing developers want to do in VoiceXML applications is add some measure of "universal commands" that are always available, and always behave in the same way.

It would certainly be possible—though by no means practical—to write the grammar for these commands, save it to a separate file, reference it in every form in every document in your application, and then write the proper logic in every field of every form of every document to react in the right way if the caller actually says one of these things. With this in mind, VoiceXML has support for the notion of "links."

VoiceXML links (defined by the <link> element) are very simple—they define a grammar and either an event to throw or a URL to transition to; if the caller ever says something to match the link's grammar, control is whisked away from the current field and the specified transition or event is executed. Links can be specified at any scope (from an application root document down through within an individual field), and their grammars are only active within the scope where the link is specified.

Links that fire events are a particularly good way to handle universal commands, because the flexible and hierarchical event model (see later in this chapter for detail, but you're probably already getting the picture) make it easy to specify global event handlers at the application level, and then override them locally when and if needed.

Let's look at a simple example of using links within a single document application; the general concept extends easily to more complex applications.

```
<?xml version="1.0"?>
<vxml version="2.0">

  <link event="event.myapp.chocolate">
    <grammar type="application/x-gsl">
      [chocolate]
    </grammar>
  </link>
```

```
<catch event="event.myapp.chocolate">
  <audio>You said chocolate!!! Goodbye.</audio>
  <disconnect />
</catch>
<!-- this defines a document-scope link for the word "chocolate".
     In any field in this document, if the caller says "chocolate"
     the event will fire, and this document-scope event handler
     will execute, unless a local one overrides it. -->

<catch event="noinput nomatch">
  <audio>I'm sorry, I didn't catch that. </audio>
  <reprompt />
</catch>

<form id="dob_menu">
<field name="dob" type="date">
  <prompt>
    <audio>What is your birth date? Please include the month,
           day, and year. </audio>
  </prompt>

  <filled>
    <if cond="dob.indexOf('?')+1">
      <audio>You didn't say the full date.</audio>
      <clear namelist="dob" />
    <else />
      <audio>Great. You said
             <value expr="dob.slice(4,6)" />,
             <value expr="dob.slice(6,8)" />,
             <value expr="dob.slice(0,2)" />,
             <value expr="dob.slice(2,4)" />.
      </audio>
    </if>
  </filled>
</field>

<field name="ssn" type="digits">
  <prompt>
    <audio>What is your Social Security Number? </audio>
  </prompt>

  <filled>
    <audio>Great. You said <value expr="ssn" /> </audio>
    <submit next="process.jsp" namelist="dob ssn" />
  </filled>
</field>
</form>
</vxml>
```

That's really all there is to it. Using links (and associated event handlers) throughout applications is a flexible technique commonly used by professional VoiceXML developers.

Form Processing: Scoping, the FIA, Event Handlers, and Scripting

Now that we've explored the basics (and along the way we've actually introduced most of the more complex topics as well), let's explicitly cover the details of the Form Interpretation Algorithm (FIA), the event model, and scoping.

Scoping

We've already discussed the notion of scoping in VoiceXML—scoped variables, scoped event handlers, and scoped grammars. As with other programming languages, scoping provides a powerful hierarchical framework for writing "clean" code that maximizes reuse and modularity while minimizing "hacky" techniques like pasting redundant copies of the same code over and over (that all need to be modified individually), managing all data in a global variable namespace, etc.

The VoiceXML scoping hierarchy cleanly follows the document hierarchy, and behaves quite intuitively. The key principles to internalize are that:

- **Each Scope Defines a New and Unique Context.** Each time a new document, form, etc. is entered, then a "clean slate" new context is established. This context can define its own local variables, event handlers, grammars, etc., and the context of all other scopes (besides its direct chain of parents) is inactive and unavailable while in that scope.

- **Variables Are Inherited "By Reference."** As in many languages, variables are directly inherited "by reference" from the chain of parent scopes. For example, if the application root document defines a variable named "user_status," then that variable will be accessible and directly modifiable from any block, field, form, document, etc. within the application. If a scope (for example, a form) defines a local variable with the same name as an existing one in a parental scope, then the local name takes precedence when referencing it. To reference the parental variable, append the name to the scope name itself in "object-like" notation. For example:

```
<vxml version="2.0">
  <var name="usr_status" expr="document stat" />
  <!-- this defines a document scope variable -->
  <form name="test">
    <var name="usr_status" expr="form stat" />
    <!-- this defines a form scope variable with
         the same name -->
    <block>
      <var name="usr_status" expr="anonymous stat" />
      <audio>
        <value expr="usr_status" />
        <!-- this says the local anonymous one -->
        <value expr="dialog.usr_status" />
```

```
        <!-- this says the form one -->
        <value expr="document.usr_status" />
        <!-- this says the document one -->
      </audio>
    </block>
  </form>
</vxml>
```

- **Event Handlers, Links, and Grammars Are Inherited "As If By Copy."**
  When a new context is entered (for example, a form or field), then all of the
  event handlers, links, and grammars from the chain of direct parent scopes
  behave as if they were literally "copied and pasted" into the local scope. For
  event handlers, the "innermost" scope wins (for example, a local handler for
  "noinput" overrides document or application one, a local handler for "error.tele-
  phone" overrides a document one for "error").

- **Contexts Are Re-Initialized on Re-Entry.** Once you leave a context (for
  example, via a `<goto>` or `<submit>`), the context is destroyed and re-
  initialized if you ever re-enter that context—with two exceptions:

  1. The context of the direct chain of parents (for example, application[‡] document[‡]
     form[‡] field[‡] event handler) is always maintained until an explicit transition
     breaks the chain. For example, if an event handler within a field does a `<goto>`
     to another document, then only the application scope remains active and the
     others are destroyed. By contrast, while moving from field to field within a
     form, the current application, document, and form context remain intact.

  2. When using the `<subdialog>` element, the complete current context
     (including the application context) is *temporarily* disabled and effectively
     "pushed on the stack." An entirely new context (from the application context
     on down) is initialized to execute the subdialog. When the subdialog returns,
     its complete context is destroyed, the previous application context is
     restored ("popped off the stack"), and execution resumes at the place where
     the subdialog was originally triggered.

Given this framework, Table 6.1 outlines the scopes and Figure 6.2 shows their
nested structure.

Form Interpretation Algorithm (FIA)

Now that we've repeatedly hinted at various pieces of the FIA, let's complete the picture. As described earlier, the FIA is the core underlying process that VoiceXML
platforms/interpreters continually use to direct the execution flow of VoiceXML applications. It governs—without exception—this execution flow.

Before we outline the FIA, it's necessary to define a few terms and cover some additional basic concepts:

- **Active Grammar Set.** This is the set of grammars that are currently "in scope"
  at any given point where the application is "listening" for input (i.e., the "input
  collection phase"). As described earlier, this can include locally defined grammars, as well as grammars defined by a higher-level parental scope—including

Table 6.1 Variable Scopes

SCOPE	DEFINITION
Session	Items at session scope are omnipresent across the entire phone call (the "session" for VoiceXML applications)—across all applications, documents, forms, etc. In VoiceXML, the session scope is not under the direct control of the programmer. Rather, the underlying platform/interpreter predefines some global behaviors and values at session scope, most of which can be overridden by the application developer at lower scopes. The things defined at session scope are: ■ **Session Variables.** Some global, read-only variables exist at session scope, to provide the developer with information such as the Automatic Numbering Information (ANI) (loosely "Caller ID" of the current caller), etc. See Chapter 7 for a complete list. Session variables are read-only, must *always* be referenced with the "session." Naming prefix, and new ones cannot be created. ■ **Universal Commands/Event Handlers.** VoiceXML platforms are required to define session-level event handlers for common events such as `<noinput>` (the caller doesn't say anything) and `<nomatch>` (the caller says something unexpected). Similarly, platforms must provide a session-level `<link>` (and associated event handler) for the grammar "help," and may provide other default links that are active at session scope. These universal behaviors are to help prevent developers from writing code that systematically breaks due to unhandled events. Developers can turn off these behaviors (at any scope) by setting the "universals" property via the `<property>` element. Similarly, in all cases developers are able to locally override the session-level event handlers as desired. Commonly, developers will override these behaviors at application scope, and then further override them locally as needed for desired special-case behavior. See Chapter 7 for a complete listing of default grammars and event handlers.
Application	Application scope is active for all documents that share the same application root document, as declared in the "application" attribute of the `<vxml>` element for the document. Variables, event handlers, links, and scripts can be declared at application scope by declaring them as a direct child of the `<vxml>` element in the application root document shared by other documents in the application. In addition, VoiceXML defines a small set of platform-defined, read-only application scope variables, which developers can reference. Mostly, these are used to inspect the last successful speech recognition event in the application (see the confidence score associated with it, etc.). See Chapter 7 for a complete listing.
Document	Document scope applies to all forms, fields, etc. within the current document. Document scope grammars, scripts, event handlers, variables, and links are defined as a direct child of the `<vxml>` element in a given document.

continues

Table 6.1 *(Continued)*

SCOPE	DEFINITION
Dialog	Each dialog (`<form>` or `<menu>`) has a dialog scope that exists while the user is visiting that dialog, and that is visible to the element of that dialog. Dialog scope grammars, scripts, event handlers, variables, and links are declared as direct children of the `<form>` (or `<menu>`) element. In addition, each form element within the form (`<field>`s, `<block>`s, `<subdialog>`s, or `<record>`s) automatically defines a dialog scope variable whose name is determined by the "name" attribute of the form element (for example, `<field name="some_variable">`). As such, this "form item variable" can be referenced within all other form items in the form because they share the same dialog scope.
(Anonymous)	Each `<block>`, `<filled>`, and `<catch>` element defines a new anonymous scope to contain variables and scripts declared in that element. Links and grammars cannot be defined within an anonymous scope.

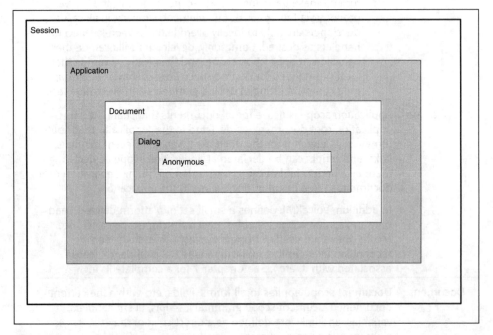

Figure 6.2 Variable scopes.

peer forms within a document who explicitly marked their grammars to have document scope via the "scoping" attribute.

- **Utterance.** Colloquially, voice application developers use the term "utterance" to refer to either to the actual recording of a caller's response to a given prompt or to the voice recognition engine's text-based interpretation of what they said. For the purposes of the FIA, an utterance is slightly different—here, an utterance is the name of the exact grammar being matched, as well as a list of all slots in that grammar (for multislot grammars used in mixed initiative forms) and the recognizer's interpretation of the caller's response matched against each slot. For example, "Grammar *abc* was matched, and the slot values are *dob_slot=19701022* and *ssn_slot=101444938*."

- **Execute.** This is the notion of sequentially executing a series of "executable content" instructions, such as variable declarations, ECMAScript statements, playing audio, <goto> transitions, etc. When entering a block of executable content, execution proceeds sequentially unless interrupted by an event or an explicit transition. If an event is thrown, execution is aborted and the appropriate event handler is executed. If an explicit transition (for example, <goto>) is encountered, then the transition occurs immediately and the remainder of the executable content in the block is ignored (again, this works just like many other programming languages).

- **Form item "cond" attribute.** In addition to a "name" variable, all form items (fields, blocks, etc.) have an optional "cond" attribute. This attribute specifies an ECMAScript expression that must evaluate to "true" in order for the form item to be selected and executed on each successive pass of the FIA through the form. VoiceXML developers don't tend to use this capability very often, but in advanced cases it can be very useful. If not specified, it defaults to "true."

Given this framework, here is the complete VoiceXML 2.0 Form Interpretation Algorithm:

```
// COPIED VERBATIM FROM VOICEXML 2.0 SPECIFICATION, WITH THE
// EXCEPTION OF SOME ADDITIONAL COMMENTARY EXPLICITLY NOTED
// WITH "AUTHOR:"

// Initialization Phase
//

foreach ( <var> and form item variable, in document order )
    Declare the variable, initializing it to the value of
    the "expr" attribute, if any, or else to undefined.

foreach ( field item )
    // AUTHOR: this means form items that are <field>s

    Declare a prompt counter and set it to 1.
    // AUTHOR: prompt counters are implicit internal counters that
```

```
    // govern the behavior of event handlers via the "count"
    // attribute described above

if ( there is an initial item )
    // AUTHOR: an <initial> form item
    Declare a prompt counter and set it to 1.

if ( user entered form by speaking to its
      grammar while in a different form )
{
    Enter the main loop below, but start in
    the process phase, not the select phase:
    we already have a collection to process.
}

//
// Main Loop: select next form item and execute it.
//

while ( true )
{
    //
    // Select Phase: choose a form item to visit.
    //

    if ( the last main loop iteration ended
            with a <goto nextitem> )
        // AUTHOR: the "nextitem" attribute on <goto> is a special
        // version of "next" that allows explicit transitions
        // to another form item within the same form, rather
        // than to another form or document //
      Select that next form item.

    else if (there is a form item with an
            unsatisfied guard condition )
        // AUTHOR: form item's "guard condition" is unsatisfied when
        // *both* its "cond" expression evaluates to true
        // *and* its form item variable is NULL.
        Select the first such form item in document order.

    else
        Do an <exit/> -- the form is full and specified no transition.

    //
    // Collect Phase: execute the selected form item.
    //
    // Queue up prompts for the form item.

    unless ( the last loop iteration ended with
            a catch that had no <reprompt> )
    {
        Select the appropriate prompts for the form item.
```

```
        Queue the selected prompts for play prior to
        the next collect operation.

        Increment the form item's prompt counter.
    }


    // Activate grammars for the form item.

    if ( the form item is modal )
        Set the active grammar set to the form item grammars,
        if any. (Note that some form items, e.g. <block>,
        cannot have any grammars).
    else
        Set the active grammar set to the form item
        grammars and any grammars scoped to the form,
        the current document, the application root
        document, and then elements up the <subdialog>
        call chain.
        // AUTHOR: this also includes any session-level grammars
        // that are currently active according to the currently
        // scoped setting of the "universals" property


    // Execute the form item.

    if ( a <field> was selected )
        Collect an utterance or an event from the user.
    else if ( a <record> was chosen )
        Collect an utterance (with a name/value pair
        for the recorded bytes) or event from the user.
    else if ( an <object> was chosen )
        Execute the object, setting the <object>'s
        form item variable to the returned ECMAScript value.
    else if ( a <subdialog> was chosen )
        Execute the subdialog, setting the <subdialog>'s
        form item variable to the returned ECMAScript value.
    else if ( a <transfer> was chosen )
        Do the transfer, and (if wait is true) set the
        <transfer> form item variable to the returned
        result status indicator.
    else if ( the <initial> was chosen )
        Collect an utterance or an event from the user.
    else if ( a <block> was chosen )
    {
        Set the block's form item variable to the defined value.
        // AUTHOR: the specified value, if any. Otherwise NULL.
        Execute the block's executable context.
    }


    //
    // Process Phase: process the resulting utterance or event.
    //
```

```
// Process an event.
if ( the form item execution resulted in an event )
{
    Find the appropriate catch for the event
    starting in the scope of the current form item.
    Execute the catch (this may leave the FIA).

    continue
}


// Must have an utterance: process ones from outside grammars.

if ( the utterance matched a grammar from outside the form )
{
    if ( the grammar belongs to a <link> element )
       Execute that link's goto or throw.

    if ( the grammar belongs to a menu's <choice> element )
       Execute the choice's goto or throw, leaving the FIA.

    // The grammar belongs to another form (or menu).

    Transition to that form (or menu), carrying the utterance
    to the other form (or menu)'s FIA.
}


// Process an utterance spoken to a grammar from this form.
// First copy utterance slot values into corresponding
// form item variables.

// AUTHOR: Important to note that this implicitly *satisfies*
// the "guard condition" for this form item, so on the next
// iteration of the FIA it will not be re-entered *unless*
// the developer explicitly clears the form item variable
// along the way.

Clear all "just_filled" flags.
// AUTHOR: another internal flag that keeps track of whether a
// given field has just been filled on this pass through the FIA
foreach ( slot in the user's utterance )
{
    if ( the slot corresponds to a field item )
    {
        Copy the slot value into the field item's
        form item variable.

        Set this field item's "just_filled" flag.
    }
}

// Set <initial> form item variable if any field items are filled.
```

```
            if ( any field item variable is set as a result of the user utterance
        )
                Set the <initial> form item variable.

        // Next execute any <filled> actions triggered by this utterance.

        foreach ( <filled> action in document order )
        {
                // Determine the form item variables the <filled> applies to.

                N = the <filled>'s "namelist" attribute.
                // AUTHOR: as an additional shortcut, <filled> handlers can
                // be placed directly at the <form> level, and use the
                // "namelist" attribute to apply "as if by copy" to multiple
                // fields within the same form

                if ( N equals "" )
                {
                    if ( the <filled> is a child of a form item )
                        N = the form item's form item variable name.
                    else if ( the <filled> is a child of a form )
                        N = the form item variable names of all the field
                            items in that form.
                }

                // Is the <filled> triggered?

                if ( any form item variable in the set N was "just_filled"
                        AND  (   the <filled> mode is "all"
                                    AND all variables in N are filled
                              OR the <filled> mode is "any"
                                    AND any variables in N are filled))

                        Execute the <filled> action.
                        // AUTHOR: the "mode" attribute on <filled> is another
                        // optimization, allowing developers to specify that
                        // the <filled> element should only be executed if
                        // "all" versus "any" of the fields specified in
                        // the "namelist" attribute have been "just filled"

                    If an event is thrown during the execution of a <filled>,
                    event handler selection starts in the scope of the <filled>,
                    which could be a form item or the form itself.
                }
        }
```

Once you've taken the time to fully digest the FIA and all of the basic techniques we've discussed so far in this chapter, you're set with a fairly complete understanding of what VoiceXML has to offer and how to use its capabilities to achieve your application goals.

In the rest of this chapter, we'll attempt to flesh out the remaining key features and techniques we haven't covered yet.

Event Handlers

We've already covered most of what there is to know about event handlers. Here, we'll simply recap their behavior and flesh out a few remaining points.

- **Events are handled using the <catch> and <throw> elements.** Use the <catch> element to define event handlers, and the <throw> element to explicitly throw standard (for example, "noinput") or custom (for example, *event.myapp.status_change*) events. Additionally, the <link> and <choice> elements can be used to throw events.

- **Events can be thrown at any time.** Events can be thrown at any time during execution, and when they occur execution immediately transitions to the appropriate event handler.

- **Event handlers are scoped hierarchically and inherited "as if by copy."** Event handlers can be defined at any scope, and inherit downward through all of their children's scopes. When an event is fired in a given context (for example, a field), the nearest scope that has a defined handler for the event is used.

- **Event names are themselves hierarchical, and can be handled accordingly.** The namespace for events is itself hierarchical, using the familiar "object-like" dotted notation. As with the scope hierarchy, the nearest matching handler will be used for a particular event. For example, a handler for "*event.myapp.status*" will catch "*event.myapp.status*," "*event.myapp.status.failure*," and "*event.myapp.status.failure.503*."

- **VoiceXML platforms automatically throw a predefined set of standard events.** VoiceXML platforms are required to throw a set of predefined events, including "*nomatch*" (caller said something unexpected), "*noinput*" (caller said nothing), "*help*" (caller said "help"), telephony call status, and errors (see next point). Platforms are also required to have default session-scope handlers for each of these events, so that developers are not strictly required to write their own handlers for events that they do not explicitly throw. That said, developers are strongly encouraged to provide custom handlers for all of these events. See Chapter 7 for a complete list of standard events.

- **Errors in VoiceXML are simply events.** All runtime VoiceXML errors—from poor syntax to underlying system failures—result in throwing the "error" event.[9] To be more precise, all error events are really "error.*something*," . . . , but as described earlier, a more general handler for "error" will catch all of these.

- **Useful shortcuts are <noinput>, <nomatch>, <error>, and <help>.** VoiceXML has defined these elements as convenient shortcuts for <catch event="noinput">, et al.

- **Additional flexibility from event and message variables.** When executing an event handler (which defines a local anonymous scope), two special platform

---

[9]Errors throw the "error" event wherever possible, of course. There are certainly extreme cases where the VoiceXML platform/interpreter itself may fail and simply drop the session. As with any operating system (and VoiceXML interpreters are essentially an operating system), one measure of a great platform is one that rarely fails in this way.

variables are created at this scope. "_event" contains the full name of the event that was actually thrown—this is useful when catching a generic event (for example, "error") and trying to differentiate between the various more detailed events (for example, *error.badfetch.404*) that may have been thrown. Similarly, the "_message" variable contains additional text related to the event. Developers can explicitly specify this message using the "message" or "message-expr" attribute on `<throw>` (for example, `<throw event="myapp.status .unauthorized" message="invalid password or user id">`). For platform-defined events (for example, errors, nomatch, telephony, etc.), VoiceXML platforms can specify whatever they wish. If not specified, value of message is ECMAScript undefined.

Finally, let's take a look at how to fully exploit ECMAScript scripting in VoiceXML.

Scripting

As we've discussed earlier, VoiceXML fully supports ECMAScript integration, and most professional VoiceXML developers heavily rely on this "client-side" ECMAScript to build sophisticated applications.

Scripts can be declared using the `<script>` element at any scope from application down through anonymous, and strictly follow the scope hierarchy. Additionally, the variable namespace is shared between blocks of ECMAScript within `<script>` elements and variables explicitly defined within VoiceXML proper using the `<var>` element. All of the same rules regarding referencing equivalently named variables from a parental scope apply within ECMAScript, as well. Once again, the entire model winds up being fairly intuitive once you start to internalize the basic building blocks of the language's structure.

To provide a detailed example of how ECMAScript can be used within VoiceXML applications to implement significant functionality, here is a complete implementation (provided by Tellme Networks, Inc.) of the classic casino game Blackjack:

```
<!--
Tellme Blackjack (Tellme Studio Code Example 106)
Copyright (C) 1999-2001 Tellme Networks, Inc. All Rights
Reserved.

THIS CODE IS MADE AVAILABLE SOLELY ON AN "AS IS" BASIS,
WITHOUT WARRANTY OF ANY KIND, EITHER EXPRESSED OR IMPLIED,
INCLUDING, WITHOUT LIMITATION, WARRANTIES THAT THE CODE IS
FREE OF DEFECTS, MERCHANTABLE, FIT FOR A PARTICULAR PURPOSE
OR NON-INFRINGING.
-->

<!-- THIS EXAMPLE CAN BE FOUND IN ITS ENTIRETY AT:
     http://studio.tellme.com/library2/code/ex-106/ -->

<vxml version="2.0">

<!-- common field tuning parameters -->
<property name="confidencelevel" value="30"/>
```

```
<property name="timeout" value="5.0"/>
<property name="tellme.endseconds" value="0.25"/>
<property name="tellme.pruning" value="500"/>
<property name="tellme.bargeinlevel" value="12"/>
<property name="tellme.magicword" value="true"/>

<!-- data/state to be shared across dialogs -->
<var name="gsSkinPath"
     expr="'http://studio.tellme.com/library2/code/ex-
106/set2'"/>
<!-- path to the current audio 'skin' -->
<var name="gsNextDialog"/> <!-- navigation state tracking -->
<var name="gsPlayState"/> <!-- game state tracking -->
<var name="gsGameResult" expr="0"/> <!-- win/lose -->
<var name="gsDealerTotal" />
<!-- number of points the dealer ended up with -->
<var name="gsPlayerNewCard"/>
<!-- latest card dealt to the player -->
<var name="gsPlayerTotal"/> <!-- player's current total -->
<var name="gsPlayerCard1"/> <!-- player's 1st card -->
<var name="gsPlayerCard2"/> <!-- player's 2nd card -->
<var name="gsDealerCardShowing"/> <!-- dealer's exposed card
-->

<!-- when the user requests a new dealer,
     stop everything and jump to the change_dealer dialog. -->
<link event="tellme.blackjack.newdealer">
<grammar>
   [new_dealer (change_dealer) dtmf-3]
</grammar>
</link>

<catch event="tellme.blackjack.newdealer">
   <goto next="#change_dealer"/>
</catch>

<!-- when the user says repeat, replay the current dialog -->
<link event="tellme.blackjack.repeat">
<grammar>
   [repeat]
</grammar>
</link>

<catch event="tellme.blackjack.repeat">
   <goto expr="gsPlayState"/>
</catch>

<link event="help">
<grammar>
   [help dtmf-0]
</grammar>
</link>
```

```
<!-- source in the Blackjack class -->
<script src="http://studio.tellme.com/library2/code/ex-
106/bj.js"/>
<script>
    // Instantiate a Blackjack object once, and reuse it
    var oBJ = new Blackjack();
</script>


<form id="PlayBlackJack">
    <block>
        <audio expr="gsSkinPath + '/welcome01.wav'"/>
        <audio expr="gsSkinPath + '/to_exit.wav'"/>
        <audio expr="gsSkinPath + '/play01.wav'"/>
        <goto next="#EvalDeal"/>
    </block>
</form>

<!-- Initialize the player and dealer hands and the array that
     tracks dealt cards. Then deal cards to the caller and dealer.
-->
<form id="EvalDeal">
    <block>
     <script>
     <![CDATA[

        // Initialize the Blackjack object
        oBJ.Init();

        var oPlayerCard1 = oBJ.Hit("caller");
        var oPlayerCard2 = oBJ.Hit("caller");
        gsPlayerCard1 = oPlayerCard1.GetTypeSuit();
        gsPlayerCard2 = oPlayerCard2.GetTypeSuit();
        gsPlayerTotal = oBJ.GetTotalOf("caller").toString();

        // According to http://www.gamblingtimes.com/gtbasbj.html,
        // dealer gets TWO cards initially
        oBJ.Hit("dealer");
        var oDealerCard2 = oBJ.Hit("dealer");
        gsDealerCardShowing = oDealerCard2.GetTypeSuit();

        gsNextDialog = "#AskHit";
        gsPlayState = "#PlayDeal";

     ]]>
     </script>
    <goto next="#PlayDeal"/>
    </block>
</form>


<form id="PlayDeal">
    <block>
        <log>pc1= <value expr="gsPlayerCard1"/>, pc2= <value
```

```
       expr="gsPlayerCard2"/>, dc1= <value
       expr="gsDealerCardShowing"/></log>
              <audio expr="gsSkinPath + '/shuffle.wav'"/>
              <audio expr="gsSkinPath + '/deal01.wav'"/>
              <audio expr="gsSkinPath + '/' + gsPlayerCard1 +'.wav'"/>
              <audio expr="gsSkinPath + '/and.wav'"/>
              <audio expr="gsSkinPath + '/' + gsPlayerCard2 +'.wav'"/>
              <audio expr="gsSkinPath + '/total01.wav'"/>
              <audio expr="gsSkinPath + '/' + gsPlayerTotal +'.wav'"/>
              <audio expr="gsSkinPath + '/showing.wav'"/>
              <audio expr="gsSkinPath + '/' + gsDealerCardShowing +'.wav'"/>
              <goto expr="gsNextDialog"/>
          </block>
       </form>


       <!-- swap skins, and start over -->
       <form id="ChangeDealer">
          <block>
           <script>
           <![CDATA[
             gsSkinPath = ((gsSkinPath == "set2") ? "set4" : "set2");
           ]]>
           </script>
           <goto next="#PlayBlackJack"/>
          </block>
       </form>


       <!-- Ask the user if they want another card -->
       <form id="AskHit">

          <field name="askhit">
             <prompt>
               <audio expr="gsSkinPath + '/another01.wav'"/>
             </prompt>

          <grammar>
          <![CDATA[
          [
             [yes dtmf-1] {<option "yes">}
             [no dtmf-2] {<option "no">}
          ]
          ]]>
          </grammar>

             <noinput>
               <goto expr="gsPlayState"/>
             </noinput>

             <nomatch>
               <reprompt/>
             </nomatch>
```

```
        <help>
          <audio expr="gsSkinPath + '/help-se.wav'"/>
          <audio expr="gsSkinPath + '/to_exit.wav'"/>
          <reprompt/>
        </help>

        <catch event="nomatch noinput">
          <goto expr="gsPlayState"/>
        </catch>

        <filled>
          <if cond="'yes'==askhit">
            <goto next="#EvalHit"/>
          <elseif cond="'no'==askhit"/>
            <goto next="#EvalDone"/>
          </if>
        </filled>

    </field>
</form>

<!-- deal a card to the user -->
<form id="EvalHit">
    <block>
     <script>
     <![CDATA[
       var oPlayerNewCard = oBJ.Hit("caller");
       gsPlayerNewCard = oPlayerNewCard.GetTypeSuit();
       gsPlayerTotal = oBJ.GetTotalOf("caller").toString();
     ]]>
     </script>
     <goto next="#PlayNewCard"/>
    </block>
</form>

<!-- play back the player's new card and total hand value -->
<form id="PlayNewCard">
    <block>
       <audio expr="gsSkinPath + '/deal02.wav'"/>
       <audio expr="gsSkinPath + '/' + gsPlayerNewCard +'.wav'"/>
       <audio expr="gsSkinPath + '/total01.wav'"/>
       <audio expr="gsSkinPath + '/' + gsPlayerTotal +'.wav'"/>
       <goto next="#TestOver"/>
    </block>
</form>

<!-- has the player's hand gone over 21? -->
<form id="TestOver">
    <block>
     <script>
     <![CDATA[
```

```
    // if caller exceeded 21. Pick a random "you lose" audio file.
    if(oBJ.GetTotalOf("caller") > 21)
    {
      /*
      There are 4 winner and 4 loser audio files.
      Use the JS Math object to generate a random number in the
      range of 1..4, and map the result to an audio file of the form
      lose0x.wav where x = [1..4]
      */
      var iRandResult = Math.floor(Math.random()*4) +1;
      gsDealerTotal = oBJ.GetTotalOf("dealer").toString();
      gsGameResult = "lose0" + iRandResult.toString();
      gsNextDialog = "#PlayDone";
    }
    else
    {
      gsPlayState = "#PlayNewCard";
    }
    ]]>
    </script>
  <goto expr="gsNextDialog"/>
  </block>
</form>

<!-- finish up the current hand, and determine the results -->
<form id="EvalDone">
   <block>
    <script>
    <![CDATA[
      // finish up the hand
      oBJ.Finish();

      /* There are 4 winner and 4 loser audio files.
         Use the JS Math object to generate a random number in the
         range of 1..4 and map the result to an audio file of the
         form [win|lose]0x.wav where x = [1..4]. In the case of a
         push, the random number is not appended
      */
      var sRandResult = (Math.floor(Math.random()*4)
                         + 1).toString();
      var aGameResults = new Array("lose0" + sRandResult, "win0" +
                                  sRandResult, "push");
      gsGameResult = aGameResults[oBJ.GetGameResult()];
      gsDealerTotal = oBJ.GetTotalOf("dealer").toString();
      gsNextDialog = "#PlayDone";
    ]]>
    </script>
  <goto expr="gsNextDialog"/>
   </block>
 </form>
```

```
      <!-- play the results, and ask the user to play again -->
    <form id="PlayDone">
      <field name="playagain">

        <prompt>
          <audio expr="gsSkinPath + '/' + gsGameResult + '.wav'"/>
          <audio expr="gsSkinPath + '/dealer01.wav'"/>
          <audio expr="gsSkinPath + '/' + gsDealerTotal + '.wav'"/>
          <break time="500"/>
          <audio expr="gsSkinPath + '/playagain01.wav'"/>
        </prompt>

    <grammar>
    <![CDATA[
    [
        [yes dtmf-1] {<option "yes">}
        [no dtmf-2] {<option "no">}
    ]
    ]]>
    </grammar>

        <help>
          <audio expr="gsSkinPath + '/help-se.wav'"/>
          <audio expr="gsSkinPath + '/to_exit.wav'"/>
          <reprompt/>
        </help>

        <catch event="nomatch noinput">
          <goto expr="gsPlayState"/>
        </catch>

        <filled>
          <if cond="'yes'==playagain">
            <audio expr="gsSkinPath + '/play01.wav'"/>
            <goto next="#EvalDeal"/>
          <elseif cond="'no'==playagain"/>
            <audio expr="gsSkinPath + '/goodbye.wav'"/>
            <goto next="_home"/>
          </if>
        </filled>
      </field>
    </form>
</vxml>

// ECMASCRIPT CODE FOR BLACKJACK EXAMPLE
// THIS IS THE SEPARATE FILE SOURCED IN BY THE VOICEXML DOCUMENT

/*  Encapsulates a game of Blackjack. Can be used anywhere
    ECMAScript is supported - in a Voice application, in a Web
    application, etc.
```

```
      a card object consists of
         num - an absolute number from 1..52
         type - 2..10, j, q, k, a
         value - 2...11
         suit - c (clubs), h (hearts), s (spades), d (diamonds)
*/

function Card(iNum, sType, iValue, sSuit)
{
  this.num = iNum;
  this.type = sType;
  this.value = iValue;
  this.suit = sSuit;
}

// Diagnostic
Card.prototype.Dump = function()
{
  return "num=" + this.num + ", type=" + this.type + ",
value=" + this. value + ", suit=" + this.suit;
}

// return the card's value
Card.prototype.GetValue = function()
{
  return this.value;
}

// return the card's type
Card.prototype.GetType = function()
{
  return this.type;
}

// return the concatenation of cards type and suit (e.g. "as" ==
// "ace of spades")
// the audio files for each card use this naming scheme
Card.prototype.GetTypeSuit = function()
{
  return this.type + this.suit;
}

// a blackjack object
function Blackjack()
{
  /*
  a tuple consisting of card type and its corresponding value
  a card is picked at random from 1 to 52
  the random value is normalized down to 0..12 to determine its
  corresponding tuple
  */
```

```
   this.aCardInfos = new Array(
["a", 11], // 0
["2", 2], // 1
["3", 3], // 2
["4", 4],
["5", 5],
["6", 6],
["7", 7],
["8", 8],
["9", 9],
["10", 10],
["j", 10],
["q", 10],
["k", 10]); // 12
}


// Initialize the array of dealt cards and each player's hand
Blackjack.prototype.Init = function()
{
   this.aDealtCards = new Array();
   // cards dealt to the dealer and player
   this.hPlayers = {
      "caller" : [], // array of cards dealt to the player
      "dealer" : []}; // array of cards dealt to the dealer

   this.iIterations = 0;
   // number of iterations to generate valid card
}


// deal a card to sWho
Blackjack.prototype.Hit = function(sWho)
{
  var aHand = this.hPlayers[sWho];
  if (!aHand)
  {
     return null;
  }

  var oCard = this.GetCard();
  aHand[aHand.length] = oCard;
  this.aDealtCards[this.aDealtCards.length] = oCard;
  return oCard;
}

// return the last card dealt to sWho
Blackjack.prototype.GetLastCardOf = function(sWho)
{
  var aHand = this.hPlayers[sWho];
  if (!aHand)
  {
    return null;
```

```
  }
  return aHand[aHand.length-1];
}


// return the total value of the players hand
Blackjack.prototype.GetTotalOf = function(sWho)
{
  var aHand = this.hPlayers[sWho];
  if (!aHand)
  {
    return 0;
  }

  var iAces = 0, iTotal = 0;
  for(var i=0; i<aHand.length; i++)
  {
    if(aHand[i].value == 11) {
        iAces++;
    }
    iTotal += aHand[i].value;
  }

  // if the players total is above 21, count aces as low (aka 1
  // point instead of 11)
  // but only until the players score is below 21
  while(iTotal > 21 && iAces > 0)
  {
    iAces--;
    iTotal -= 10;
  }

  return iTotal;
}

// manufacture a random card from a deck of 52.
Blackjack.prototype.GetCard = function()
{
  var aDealtCards = this.aDealtCards;
  var sSuit = "d";

  // make a card by picking a number at random from 1..52
  var iNum = Math.floor(Math.random()*52) + 1;

  // make sure the card hasn't already been dealt
  for(var i=0; i<aDealtCards.length; i++)
  {
    ++this.iIterations;
    if(iNum == aDealtCards[i].num)
    {
      i=0;
      iNum = Math.floor(Math.random()*52) + 1;
```

```
      }
   }

   // normalize the card's number from 0 (A) .. 11 (J), 12 (Q), 12
   // (K)
   var iCardInfoIndex = iNum % 13;

   // map the normalized number to a (type,value) tuple
   var aCard = this.aCardInfos[iCardInfoIndex];

   // assign a suit
   if(iNum >= 1 && iNum <= 13) {
      sSuit = 'd';
   }
   else if(iNum >= 14 && iNum <= 26) {
      sSuit = 'c';
   }
   else if(iNum >= 17 && iNum <= 39) {
      sSuit = 'h';
   }
   else if(iNum >= 40 && iNum <= 52) {
      sSuit = 's';
   }

   return new Card(iNum, aCard[0], aCard[1], sSuit);
}

// Finish up the hand
Blackjack.prototype.Finish = function()
{
  var iDealerTotal = this.GetTotalOf("dealer");
  // dealer must take cards until she hits at least 17
  while(iDealerTotal < 17)
  {
     oBJ.Hit("dealer");
     iDealerTotal = oBJ.GetTotalOf("dealer");
  }

  return true;
}

// 0 == lose, 1 == win, 2 == draw/push
Blackjack.prototype.GetGameResult = function()
{
  var iPlayerTotal = this.GetTotalOf("caller");
  var iDealerTotal = this.GetTotalOf("dealer");

  // figure out who won
  if (iPlayerTotal > 21 && iDealerTotal > 21)
  {
     return 0;
```

```
    }
    else if (iPlayerTotal > 21 && iDealerTotal <= 21)
    {
       return 0;
    }
    else if (iPlayerTotal <= 21 && iDealerTotal > 21)
    {
       return 1;
    }
    else // (iPlayerTotal <= 21 && iDealerTotal <= 21)
    {
       if(iDealerTotal == iPlayerTotal)
       {
          return 2;
       }
       else if (iDealerTotal > iPlayerTotal)
       {
          return 0;
       }
       else // (iDealerTotal < iPlayerTotal)
       {
          return 1;
       }
    }
  }
}
```

The combination of the FIA, event handlers, ECMAScript, grammars, etc. makes for quite a powerful language. In the remaining few sections, we'll flesh out a few final points and features and you'll be on your way.

Subdialogs and HTTP Semantics

In this section, we'll cover a bit more about subdialogs, as well as some of the additional features VoiceXML provides for dealing with HTTP semantics like caching.

Subdialogs

So far, we've only tangentially covered subdialogs. To reiterate, subdialogs are a mechanism—similar to but different than "subroutines" in the classic sense—for developers to create reusable "modules" of VoiceXML code that can be leveraged across many applications.

Very simply, subdialogs are invoked as a form item (for example, a child of <form> like <field> or <block>), and when activated they temporarily suspend the current execution context while creating a *completely new execution context from the application scope on down* for the subdialog to execute in. When the subdialog returns, its context is destroyed and execution resumes in the original document as if nothing had happened.

It's important to stress this point—literally, *a completely new execution context is* instantiated when invoking a subdialog. This even applies if the URL for the subdialog is technically in the same document as the invoking dialog. This means that variables, event handlers, etc. are all completely independent for the subdialog—even if the sub-dialog happens to be in the same physical document and "recreate" many of the same variables that were part of the calling dialog's context. Within the subdialog, everything else we've discussed (the FIA, hierarchically scoped event handlers, links and menus, etc.) all behave identically to those in "normal" documents.

When working with subdialogs, here are the key points and techniques to keep in mind:

- **Subdialogs instantiate a new and independent execution context.** Hope-fully we've sufficiently hammered this point home.

- **Use "namelist" to pass data to the server via HTTP.** If you're invoking a subdialog whose URL is a server-side script, you can use the "namelist" and "method" attributes (just like with `<submit>`) to submit a list of variables to the server via HTTP GET or POST along with the request for the subdialog's document. Given this data, the server can dynamically generate the actual subdialog document and provide a customized experience. For example, the main applica-tion may have already collected the caller's name, and is invoking a subdialog to ask them some more questions. The application could use the "namelist" param-eter to send this information to the server, which would embed the information directly in the VoiceXML document it responds with for the subdialog.

```
<!-- main.vxml: this document collects the caller's
     name, and then invokes a subdialog to collect more
     info -->
<vxml version="2.0">
  <form id="do_subd">
    <var name="fname" expr="'Jeff'" />
    <!-- setting a variable directly rather than
         collecting from the user, just to keep this
         example short. -->

    <subdialog name="getmore"
               src="http://myserver/getmore.jsp"
               namelist="fname" method="get">
      <filled>
        <submit next="http://myserver/process.jsp"
                namelist="getmore.dob fname" />
        <!-- when the subdialog returns, any returned
             variables are placed in the subdialog's form
             item variable as an ECMAScript array. -->
      </filled>
    </subdialog>
  </form>
</vxml>

<!-- getmore.jsp: this document is dynamically generated
     to be personalized, collects more info, then returns
     -->
```

```
<vxml version="2.0">
  <form id="dob">
    <block>
      <var name="dob" expr="'19680829'" />
      <audio>Hi Jeff, it's nice to meet you</audio>
      <!-- notice that the first name was seamlessly
           included into the text of the document;
           the Web server dynamically generated this -->
      <audio>I would ask you for more info, but
             for now I'm going to pretend.</audio>
      <return namelist="dob" />
    </block>
  </form>
</vxml>
```

■ **Alternatively, use <param> to pass data within the interpreter context.**
If you're not referencing a dynamically generated subdialog, or if you simply
prefer doing everything within the interpreter context, subdialogs also provide a
way to pass data directly:

```
<!-- main.vxml: this document collects the caller's
     name, and then invokes a subdialog to collect more
     info -->
<vxml version="2.0">
  <form id="do_subd">
    <var name="fname" expr="'Jeff'" />
    <!-- setting a variable directly rather than
         collecting from the user, just to keep this
         example short. -->

    <subdialog name="getmore" src="#form_getmore">
    <!-- this time, we're invoking the subdialog in the
         same document -->
      <param name="the_name" expr="fname" />
      <!-- the param element allows developers to pass
           data directly to the subdialog -->
      <filled>
        <audio><value expr="getmore.dob +
                            getmore.the_name" />
        </audio>
        <submit next="http://myserver/process.jsp"
                namelist="getmore.dob
getmore.the_name" />
      </filled>
    </subdialog>
  </form>

  <form id="form_getmore">
    <var name="the_name" />
    <block>
      <!-- Each variable passed using the param element
           needs to be declared by name within the
```

```
                    subdialog. At runtime, it will be
                    initialized
                    with the value passed in (if any) via the
                    param element -->
        <var name="dob" expr="'19680829'" />
        <audio>Hi <value expr="the_name" />,
                it's nice to meet you</audio>
        <!-- this time, the first name was filled in using
                the variable passed in to the subdialog -->
        <audio>I would ask you for more info, but
                for now I'm going to pretend.</audio>
        <return namelist="dob the_name" />
      </block>
    </form>
</vxml>
```

■ **Use <return> to end the subdialog and return data to the invoking dialog.** As we've shown in the earlier examples, the `<return>` element at the end of a subdialog immediately destroys the subdialog's execution context and resumes execution in the original invoking document. Using the "namelist" element, `<return>` can pass data back to the invoking dialog—the list of variables is placed in the subdialog's form item variable as an ECMAScript array. Alternatively, `<return>` can use the "event" attribute instead, which exits the subdialog and immediately throws the specified event in the original invoking dialog. It is handled as per the normal event handler hierarchy and the FIA.

HTTP Semantics: Caching, Fetching, etc.

VoiceXML applications, like traditional HTML applications, entail a large amount of resource fetching and document retrieval via HTTP. VoiceXML documents, audio files, and externally sourced grammars and ECMAScript documents are all resources that must be repeatedly retrieved while executing VoiceXML applications.

While VoiceXML does provide some specific attributes on various elements for explicitly manipulating the behaviors regarding fetching, caching, and other HTTP semantics, these are (for the most part) merely opportunities for developers to *suggest* particular behaviors to the underlying VoiceXML platform. In reality, most developers tend to rely on the standard characteristics and behaviors implemented by their vendor of choice to optimize performance in their particular deployment scenario.

That said, here are some general comments regarding various HTTP-related behaviors and characteristics that are relevant for VoiceXML applications:

■ **When in doubt, it follows HTTP and works just like a Web browser.** The general implicit rule for all things VoiceXML is "it works just like an ordinary Web browser." Especially from the perspective of HTTP transactions, this is true almost without exception, and in the cases not explicitly covered by the VoiceXML specification, leading platforms tend to implement according to this implicit assumption to maximize interoperability with existing Web infrastructure.

■ **HTTP GET and POST.** VoiceXML platforms are required to support both HTTP GET and POST for submitting data back to the Web server. The "method" attribute on `<subdialog>` and `<submit>` allows developers to select which method they prefer.

■ **Secure Sockets Layer (SSL, HTTPS).** VoiceXML platforms are required to support the HTTP protocol, encouraged to support the secure HTTPS protocol, and may optionally support other URI protocols for document fetching. The VoiceXML 2.0 specification does not explicitly cover whether support for SSL with "client certificates" is recommended. As of August 2001, few VoiceXML platforms support client certificates. (Note that for VoiceXML, the client certificate would be installed on the VoiceXML server, which acts as the "client" from an HTTP perspective.)

■ **Cookies.** The VoiceXML 2.0 specification does not explicitly cover how or whether VoiceXML platforms should support cookies. Leading platforms tend to intrinsically support HTTP "session" cookies identically to traditional Web browsers (for example, if the Web server sets them, then the VoiceXML platform will faithfully send them back to the server on subsequent requests to the appropriate domain/path). The notion of "persistent" cookies on the telephone requires some kind of centrally managed (at least for a given phone number) user authentication system, so that callers can "unlock" their personal private persistent cookie store "on the server" (which again is acting on the caller's behalf as their "client"). Due to the difficulty of offering such a service in a generic way, combined with the fact that once you build an authentication system it's equally easy to retrieve persistent data from back-end systems, most (if not all) VoiceXML platforms avoid support for persistent cookies today. As a final note, some leading VoiceXML platforms further extend the notion of matching existing Web developers' expectations by exposing the de facto Web standard ECMAScript functions *setCookie* and *getCookies* to enable "client-side" manipulation of the cookies collection. For more information on how some platforms implement cookie support in VoiceXML, see http://studio.tellme.com/voicexmlref/ovw/cookies.html.

■ **Fetchtimeout.** All VoiceXML attributes that involve retrieving resources via HTTP support the "fetchtimeout" attribute. If the Web server does not respond in less than the time specified by fetchtimeout (for example, "15s" or "6000ms"), then an "error.badfetch" is thrown.

■ **Fetchaudio.** All VoiceXML attributes that involve retrieving resources via HTTP support the "fetchaudio" attribute. While awaiting a response from the Web server, the audio file (URI) specified by fetchaudio is played to the caller. There are some additional properties (see Chapter 7) that govern the exact behavior of playing the fetchaudio.

■ **Streaming Audio.** VoiceXML 2.0 does not specify whether or when platforms should dynamically stream audio (for example, begin playing it before the complete file has been successfully retrieved). It is left to platforms as an optional optimization at their discretion. A future version of VoiceXML may add a boolean "stream" attribute to the `<audio>` element that allows developers to specify their preference for a particular audio file. That said, in almost all deployment scenarios streaming audio is a very powerful optimization that can dramatically improve application performance. We strongly recommend choosing a VoiceXML platform vendor that implements audio streaming with high performance.

- **User Agent String.** VoiceXML 2.0 does not specify what the user agent string VoiceXML platforms "browsers" should use when they request resources via HTTP. The exact string in use is at this time completely platform-dependent.

- **Caching Behavior.** Generally speaking, VoiceXML platforms are expected to follow the standard HTTP semantics for caching documents and optimizing network traffic. There are a number of attributes and properties (see Chapter 7) that enable developers to *suggest* how the platform should cache specific documents and resources. In general, however, it is up to the underlying platform to choose caching behavior (while respecting the standard HTTP headers) that optimizes performance for the given deployment scenario. See Chapter 7 for complete details on the caching-related attributes.

Telephony Control

At this time, VoiceXML only defines a limited amount of standardized behavior for telephony and call control. Specifically, it provides for two types of call transfers—bridged (that is, "tromboned," "hair-pinned") and blind (that is, "release-link," "transfer-connect," "takeback-and-transfer"). Bridged transfers can additionally support active DTMF and/or speech grammars during the transfer, enabling the caller to "come back" to the VoiceXML application by saying a special keyword or dialing a special set of tones (for example, "To come back to the front desk at any time, just dial star-star").

Call transfers in VoiceXML are initiated with the `<transfer>` element, which is another form item along with `<field>`s, `<block>`s, `<subdialog>`s, and `<record>`s. When the transfer completes (either successfully or not), the transfer's form item variable is populated with a string that explains the result of the call (for example, busy, maximum time exceeded, no answer, etc.). In addition, when the transfer completes successfully, a platform-defined variable "*name*$.duration" (where *name* is the form item variable name) is created at the local anonymous scope containing the length of the transfer in seconds.

Here's a brief example of a bridged call transfer in VoiceXML, where the caller has the option to press "star star" and return immediately to the original application:

```
<vxml version="2.0">
  <var name="phone_number" expr="'8005558355'"/>

  <form id="make_call">
    <var name="call_duration" expr="0" />
    <block>
      <audio>testing call transfer</audio>
      <audio>dialing: <value expr="phone_number"/></audio>
    </block>

    <transfer name="mycall" destexpr="phone_number"
              connecttimeout="30s">
      <prompt>
         <audio>transferring</audio>
         <break size="small"/>
      </prompt>
```

```
        <!-- the call is terminated when the user utters/types
             anything in the following grammar -->
        <grammar type="application/x-gsl" mode="dtmf">
          <![CDATA[
          [(dtmf-star dtmf-star)] {<option "abort">}
          ]]>
        </grammar>
        <!-- enable only the star star combination to abort -->

        <filled>
          <audio>transfer returned: <value
expr="mycall"/></audio>
        <!-- ensure the shadow variable is not NULL -->
          <if cond="(typeof(mycall&) == 'object')">
            <assign name="call_duration"
expr="mycall&.duration" />
          </if>

          <if cond="mycall == 'busy'">
            <audio>The line was busy. Please try again later. </audio>
          <elseif cond="mycall == 'noanswer'" />
            <audio>Noone is answering.</audio>
          <elseif cond="mycall == 'network_busy'" />
            <audio>The network is busy!</audio>
          <elseif cond="mycall == 'near_end_disconnect'" />
            <audio>The call was completed, and you terminated it with
                  dtmf input.</audio>
          <elseif cond="mycall == 'far_end_disconnect'" />
            <audio>The call was completed, and the callee terminated
                  it.</audio>
          <elseif cond="mycall == 'network_disconnect'" />
            <audio>The call was completed, but it was terminated by
                  the network.</audio>
          </if>
        </filled>
      </transfer>

      <block>
        <audio>The call lasted approximately
               <value expr="Math.round(call_duration)"/>
               seconds.</audio>
        <disconnect />
      </block>
    </form>
</vxml>
```

Even though VoiceXML does not have standardized advanced telephony support today, leading VoiceXML platforms have already begun to extend VoiceXML to cover the more common call control scenarios such as CTI (Computer Telephony Integration) support for call centers, outbound notifications, etc. Within the W3C (World Wide Web Consortium), the standards body responsible for the VoiceXML standard, there is a large effort underway (subgroup Chaired by Brad Porter, Tellme Networks, as of August 2001) to extend VoiceXML with more advanced telephony features. For more information on the Call Control Subgroup, or the Voice Browser Working Group in general, please see http://www.w3.org/Voice/.

Miscellaneous Features

Finally, we need to discuss the `<record>` element (the ability to actually record what the caller says and POST it back to the Web server for further processing and/or storage) and the notion of runtime-settable properties. Armed with these final points, the complete mechanics of how to architect and manipulate execution flow within your VoiceXML applications will be at your disposal. While there are still a handful of detailed features (for example, N-best lists) that we haven't explicitly covered in this programming overview, Chapter 7 provides an exhaustive reference guide for all VoiceXML features and capabilities.

The `<record>` Element

Very simply put, the `<record>` element in VoiceXML enables developers to produce applications such as voicemail, e-mail replies, and other services that require actually *recording and storing* the raw audio of what a caller says, rather than attempting to recognize or interpret it at that time.

The `<record>` element is simply another form item, with many of the same attributes, except that when a recording is complete the actual audio data is stored in the form item variable for the record item. Once this has been captured, it can be replayed to the caller using the "expr" attribute on `<audio>`, and/or POSTed back to the Web server for further processing and/or storage using the `<submit>` or `<subdialog>` element. It's important to note that when POSTing the audio data back to the Web server, it's critical to use the POST method (GET doesn't allow enough data), and to use the "multipart/form-data" encoding type via the "enctype" attribute.

Similar to the `<transfer>` element, a successful recording yields a set of anonymous scope "shadow variables" that accompany the form item variable (the recording itself), and provide information on the duration, size, and (if appropriate) DTMF key the caller used to terminate the recording.

Here is a simple example of collecting a recording from the caller, and POSTing it back to the Web server for processing:

```
<vxml version="2.0">
  <form id="record_greeting">
    <!-- the resulting recording is stored in the variable
         message. -->
    <record name="message" maxtime="60s" dtmfterm="true"
beep="true"finalsilence="2s">
      <prompt>
        <audio>
          At the tone, please record your message.
```

```
                    When you're done, press pound.
              </audio>
         </prompt>

         <!-- if the user doesn't say anything before finalsilence,
              catch the noinput -->
         <noinput>
           <audio>Sorry. I didn't hear you. Goodbye.</audio>
           <disconnect />
         </noinput>
         <filled>
           <audio>The size of the recording is
                  <value expr="message$.size"/> bytes.</audio>
           <audio>The recording is <value expr="message$.duration"/>
                  milliseconds long</audio>
           <audio>The caller pressed the <value
    expr="(message$.termchar ? message$.termchar : 'none')" />
              key to finish. </audio>
           <audio>You said:</audio>
           <audio expr="message"> </audio>
           <submit next="http://myserver/message.jsp"
                   enctype="multipart/form-data"
                   namelist="message" method="post" />
         </filled>
       </record>
     </form>
   </vxml>
```

Properties

Scattered throughout VoiceXML there are a large number of behaviors that are governed by implicit attributes and values. Examples of this include the default time to wait in silence before throwing a `<noinput>`, and the default volume level to listen for when determining whether a caller has "barged in" on prompts and should be paid attention to.

VoiceXML provides a flexible and extensible mechanism for handling these properties that fits well with the rest of the language's constructs. The `<property>` element gives developers a way to set—according to the standard hierarchical scope model—values for a significant list of platform-defined properties at any scope in their applications.

There are a significant number of standard properties required by the VoiceXML specification, and in addition an extensible scheme is defined where individual platform vendors can expose an arbitrary set of their own properties. Vendor-defined properties always begin with the vendor's name (e.g., "tellme.field.recordutterance"), and all properties follow the same "object-like" dotted name scheme as VoiceXML events.

Please see Chapter 7 for a complete list of VoiceXML standard properties, but here is a brief example of setting properties within VoiceXML:

```
<vxml version="2.0">
  <property name="timeout" value="10.0"/>
```

```
<!-- give the caller an extraordinarily long time to answer before
        throwing a noinput -->
<form id="get_dob">
  <field name="dob" type="date">
    <prompt>
      <audio>What is your birth date?</audio>
    </prompt>
    <filled>
      <audio>You said <value expr="dob" /> </audio>
      <disconnect />
    </filled>
  </field>
</form>
</vxml>
```

In this chapter we have introduced the VoiceXML programming language and have learned about its various features, elements, etc. In Chapters 7 to 9, we will provide a detailed VoiceXML element and behavior reference and look at the two XML and ABNF forms of the VoiceXML vendor-independent grammar format. In addition, we will look at SSML, the programming language used for controlling elements of speech synthesis such as pitch, rate, pronunciation, and volume across different platforms. More advanced topics, such as generating dynamic voice applications from server-side data, security, the voice application development lifecycle, and a complete application example, are discussed later in this book.

## CHAPTER 7

VoiceXML Reference

In Chapter 6, we took a conceptual, step-by-step approach to build an understanding of how the VoiceXML language is structured and how to utilize its rich set of features and capabilities to build sophisticated voice applications. By contrast, this chapter provides a straightforward reference guide for VoiceXML. It includes brief descriptions and examples for all VoiceXML elements (for example, `<vxml>`), as well as tables listing additional required platform features such as session variables, properties, and events.

VoiceXML Structural Overview

VoiceXML elements and features can be broadly categorized as:

- **Root Elements.** These elements establish VoiceXML documents and any relevant metadata developers wish to provide to explicitly describe them.
  - `<meta>`, `<vxml>`
- **Dialog Definition Elements.** These elements outline the basic structure of VoiceXML conversational interfaces.
  - `<form>`, `<menu>`
- **Form Item Elements.** These elements are "things to do" within a form, such as collecting information from the caller or transferring the caller to another phone number.
  - `<block>`, `<field>`, `<initial>`, `<object>`, `<record>`, `<subdialog>`, `<transfer>`
- **Grammar Elements.** These elements, in their respective places within VoiceXML documents, define the actual lists of things callers are expected/allowed to say (or dial).
  - `<choice>`, `<<example>`, `<<grammar>`, `<item>`, `<link>`, `<option>`

- **Event Management Elements.** These elements trigger and handle various events while VoiceXML applications are running.
  - `<catch>`, `<error>`, `<help>`, `<noinput>`, `<nomatch>`, `<throw>`

- **Transition Elements.** These elements perform explicit transitions between dialogs and documents.
  - `<disconnect>`, `<exit>`, `<goto>`, `<param>`, `<return>`, `<submit>`

- **Field Item Elements.** These elements, used within fields and other form item elements, actually manage collecting and reacting to callers' choices.
  - `<audio>`, `<choice>`, `<enumerate>`, `<filled>`, `<prompt>`, `<reprompt>`

- **Logic Elements.** These elements are used to manage dynamic client-side logic for VoiceXML applications.
  - `<assign>`, `<break>`, `<clear>`, `<data>`*, `<foreach>`*, `<if>`/`<elseif>`/`<else>`, `<script>`, `<value>`, `<var>`

- **Text to Speech Elements.** These elements allow modifying the behavior of synthesized text-to-speech within VoiceXML applications. For more information on these, see Chapter 8.
  - `<emphasis>`, `<p>`, `<paragraph>`, `<phoneme>`, `<prosody>`, `<s>`, `<say-as>`, `<sentence>`, `<voice>`

- **Miscellaneous Elements.** These elements offer additional VoiceXML functionality.
  - `<property>`, `<log>`

- **Platform-defined Variables.** There are a set of read-only variables that are dynamically created by VoiceXML platforms during execution to provide additional information about the call and its execution. Some are at "session" scope (for example, *session.telephone.ani* for the ANI of the caller), and others are local to a particular field or other element (for example, *_event* within an event handler to get the specific name of the event that was thrown). The VoiceXML specification outlines a required set of these variables, and VoiceXML platforms are also free to define additional platform-specific variables.

- **Platform-defined Events.** There are a set of events (for example, *error.badfetch* for an unsuccessful HTTP request, *noinput* for when the caller was silent) that VoiceXML platforms automatically throw and provide default handlers for. The VoiceXML specification outlines a required set of these events, and VoiceXML platforms are also free to define additional, platform-specific events.

- **Platform-defined Properties.** There are a set of properties (for example, *bargein* for whether callers can interrupt prompts while they're playing) that can fine-tune VoiceXML platforms' behavior while running applications. The VoiceXML specification outlines a required set of these properties, and VoiceXML platforms are also free to define additional, platform-specific properties.

> **NOTE** This reference is optimized for VoiceXML 2.0—while some references to VoiceXML 1.0 behavior are provided, the reference's intent is to focus on VoiceXML 2.0.

*These elements are not officially part of VoiceXML 2.0, but are actively under consideration for future versions of the VoiceXML standard. As of August 2001, at least one VoiceXML platform (Tellme Networks, Inc.) provides support for these features.

Summary of Changes from VoiceXML 1.0 to 2.0

While this book focuses almost exclusively on VoiceXML 2.0, here is a summarized list of differences between VoiceXML 1.0 and 2.0. At a high level, the changes are comprised of:

- **Adding Vendor-Independent XML and BNF Grammars.** VoiceXML 2.0 includes mandatory support for at least one of these two representations for a vendor-independent grammar format. See Chapter 8 for details on the new grammar format.

- **Adding Support for "N-best" Lists.** VoiceXML 2.0 includes support for "N-best" lists; these are an advanced speech recognition feature that exposes the full list of possible interpretations for what the caller said, rather than just the "best" one. With this, programmers can take more low-level control of how to respond in ambiguous situations.

- **Enriching and Making TTS Support Consistent.** VoiceXML 2.0 includes more complete and consistently defined support for developers to control/influence the sound and behavior of VoiceXML platforms' underlying text-to-speech engines.

- **Behavior Clarifications.** VoiceXML 2.0 rectifies most of the ambiguously defined behaviors in VoiceXML 1.0. As part of this, the expected behavior for certain situations has changed.

- **Miscellaneous Features.** A few additional features have been added here and there, such as the `<log>` element to write to the debug log.

For a complete list, see the VoiceXML 2.0 specification at www.w3.org/voice.

In the remainder of this chapter, we will provide a complete reference for all of these language capabilities.

VoiceXML 2.0 Element Reference

Before providing detailed information and examples for each element, Table 7.1 provides a complete list of the elements available in VoiceXML.

This section provides detailed information about each VoiceXML element. Entries include:

- **Syntax.** How the element is used.
- **Description.** Description of attributes and other details as applicable.
- **Usage.** Information about parent/child elements.
- **Examples.** Short example to illustrate element usage.

NOTE All examples in this chapter are also available on the CD accompanying this book.

Table 7.1 VoiceXML Elements

ELEMENT	DESCRIPTION	PAGE
`<assign>`	Assigns a value to a variable	148
`<audio>`	Plays an audio file or synthesized speech	149
`<block>`	Specifies a set of other elements to execute in document order	151
`<break>`	Inserts a pause	152
`<catch>`	Catches an event	153
`<choice>`	Defines an option within a menu	154
`<clear>`	Reinitializes variables to *undefined*	156
`<count>`[2]	In XML grammars, specifies an optional or repeated grammar rule	157
`<data>`	Retrieves XML data via HTTP, and provides programmatic access to it	157
`<disconnect>`	Hangs up the telephone call and ends the VoiceXML session	159
`<div>`[1]	In TTS (text-to-speech), marks a sentence or paragraph	
`<dtmf>`[1]	Specifies a strictly touch-tone grammar	
`<else>`	Specifies alternative code as part of a conditional	160
`<elseif>`	Specifies alternative code as part of a conditional	161
`<emp>`[2]	In TTS, emphasizes speech	
`<emphasis>`	In TTS, indicates that the enclosed synthesized speech should be emphasized.	162
`<enumerate>`	Used with <choice> or <option>, provides a mechanism to automatically speak the list of available options to the caller.	163
`<error>`	Shorthand for `<catch event= "error">`	164
`<example>`[2]	In XML grammars, specifies an example phrase	166
`<exit>`	Immediately terminates the current application, and returns control to the interpreter	166
`<field>`	Facilitates a dialog with the caller to collect information	167
`<filled>`	Specifies actions to perform when a given field or fields have been "filled in"	170
`<foreach>`	Iterates through an ECMAScript array of items	171
`<form>`	Plays prompts and interacts with the caller through a series of field items	172
`<goto>`	Explicitly transitions to a specified location	173
`<grammar>`	Specifies the "permissible vocabulary" for a given caller interaction	175

Table 7.1 (*Continued*)

ELEMENT	DESCRIPTION	PAGE
`<help>`	Shorthand for `<catch event= "help">`	178
`<if>`	Specifies conditional logic	180
`<import>`[2]	In XML grammars, specifies an alias name for a grammar rule	182
`<initial>`	Prompts the caller for form-wide information in mixed-initiative forms.	182
`<item>`[2]	In XML grammars, defines an expression the caller can say	185
`<link>`	Specifies a grammar and a transition or event to throw when it's matched	185
`<log>`[2]	Outputs debug messages to the platform-specific debug logs	188
`<menu>`	Provides a simple dialog for making a selection between fixed choices	188
`<meta>`	Specifies arbitrary information to further describe a particular VoiceXML document.	190
`<noinput>`	Shorthand for `<catch event= "noinput">`	191
`<nomatch>`	Shorthand for `<catch event= "nomatch">`	193
`<object>`	Executes a platform-specific extended object	194
`<one-of>`[2]	In XML grammars, specifies a set of rule alternatives	197
`<option>`	Specifies a simple available choice and grammar within a field	196
`<p>`[2]	Shorthand for `<paragraph>`	
`<paragraph>`[2]	In TTS, encloses a paragraph of text	198
`<param>`	Submits data to a `<subdialog>` or `<object>`, without the need for server-side scripting	199
`<phoneme>`[2]	In TTS, specifies exact pronunciation using a phonetic alphabet	201
`<prompt>`	Queues audio files and/or TTS to play as part of conversational dialogue	202
`<property>`	Specifies a platform-defined behavior setting	204
`<pros>`[1]	In TTS, sets the prosody (inflection) of a piece of text.	206
`<prosody>`[2]	In TTS, sets the prosody (inflection) of a piece of text.	207
`<record>`	Records audio from the caller	208
`<reprompt>`	Re-queues the most recent `<prompt>` before listening again for the caller to speak	211
`<return>`	Ends a `<subdialog>`, and returns control to the calling application	213

(continues)

Table 7.1 VoiceXML Elements (*Continued*)

ELEMENT	DESCRIPTION	PAGE
`<rule>`[2]	In XML grammars, defines a grammar rule	214
`<ruleref>`[2]	In XML grammars, references an existing `<rule>`	215
`<s>`[2]	Shorthand for `<sentence>`	215
`<say-as>`[2]	In TTS, provides a template for saying particular kinds of text (e.g. dates)	215
`<sayas>`[1]	In TTS, provides a template for saying particular kinds of text (e.g. dates)	216
`<script>`	Defines and executes a block of ECMAScript client-side code	217
`<sentence>`[2]	In TTS, marks text as being a complete sentence	219
`<subdialog>`	Invokes modularized VoiceXML code in an independent application context	220
`<submit>`	Transitions to a new VoiceXML document via HTTP GET or POST	223
`<throw>`	Triggers an event	226
`<token>`	In XML grammars, specifies an input element	227
`<transfer>`	Transfers the caller to another destination	228
`<value>`	In TTS, evaluates and returns an ECMAScript expression	232
`<var>`	Declares a variable	233
`<voice>`[2]	In TTS, specifies the aural characteristics for the synthesized voice	234
`<vxml>`	Declares a VoiceXML document and is the root document element	235

[1]This element does not exist in VoiceXML 2.0; it is now obsolete. These elements are not officially part of VoiceXML 2.0, but are actively under consideration for future versions of the standard. As of August 2001, at least one VoiceXML platform (Tellme Networks, Inc.) provides support for these elements.

[2]This element is new for VoiceXML 2.0; it did not exist previously.

`<assign>`

Syntax	`<assign`
	`    name "ECMAScript_variable"`
	`    expr= "ECMAScript_Expression">`
	`/>`

Description	Assigns a value to a variable. Before using <assign>, variables must first be declared using <var>. If multiple variables with the same name (from different scopes)

are active at the current scope, then the one with the closest scope (for example, dialog versus document, document versus application, etc.) will be used if not otherwise specified (for example, <assign name="document.foo" expr=" 'bar' " />).

Attribute	Description	Required/Optional
name	Name of the variable	Required
expr	ECMAScript expression that is evaluated and assigned to the variable	Required

Usage	Parents		Children
	`<block>`	`<help>`	None
	`<catch>`	`<if>`	
	`<error>`	`<noinput>`	
	`<filled>`	`<nomatch>`	
	`<foreach>`	`<prompt>`	

Example

```
<vxml version="2.0">
  <var name="status" /> <!-- document scope -->
  <form>
    <block>
      <var name="status" /> <!-- anonymous scope -->
      <assign name="status" expr=" 'local' " />
      <!-- assigns the local one -->
      <assign name="document.status" expr=" 'doc' ">
      <!-- assigns the document one -->
      <audio>
        <value expr="status" />
        <value expr="document.status" />
      </audio>
    </block>
  </form>
</vxml>
```

`<audio>`

Syntax

```
<audio
    src= "URI"
    expr= "ECMAScript_Expression"
    fetchhint= "prefetch | safe | stream"
    fetchtimeout= "string"
    maxage= "integer"
    maxstale= "integer">
    alternate text-to-speech text
</audio>
```

Description   Plays an audio file or synthesized text-to-speech to the caller

src and *expr* are mutually exclusive. If neither are specified, or if the URI requested cannot be found, then any specified TTS is played instead.

VoiceXML platforms are required to support the following types of audio files, and may support others as well:

- Raw (headerless) 8kHz 8-bit mono mu-law [PCM] single channel. (G.711)
- Raw (headerless) 8kHz 8 bit mono A-law [PCM] single channel. (G.711)
- WAV (RIFF header) 8kHz 8-bit mono mu-law [PCM] single channel.
- WAV (RIFF header) 8kHz 8-bit mono A-law [PCM] single channel

Note: As with HTML, the MIME type information returned by HTTP servers when requesting audio documents does not uniquely identify the actual audio and file encoding. As a result, please be sure to verify that your VoiceXML platform specifically supports the encoding that you're using.

Attribute	Description	Required/ Optional
src	URI to a prerecorded audio file. *src* and *expr* are mutually exclusive.	Optional
expr	ECMAScript expression that evaluates to a URI to a prerecorded audio file. *src* and *expr* are mutually exclusive.	Optional
fetchhint	See "HTTP Semantics" later in this chapter.	Optional
fetchtimeout	See "HTTP Semantics" later in this chapter.	Optional
maxage	See "HTTP Semantics" later in this chapter.	Optional
maxstale	See "HTTP Semantics" later in this chapter.	Optional

Usage	Parents		Children
	`<audio>`	`<if>`	`<audio>`
	`<block>`	`<initial>`	`<break>`
	`<catch>`	`<menu>`	`<div>`
	`<choice>`	`<noinput>`	`<emp>`
	`<div>`	`<nomatch>`	`<enumerate>`
	`<emp>`	`<object>`	`<pros>`
	`<enumerate>`	`<prompt>`	`<sayas>`
	`<error>`	`<pros>`	`<value>`
	`<field>`	`<record>`	
	`<filled>`	`<subdialog>`	
	`<foreach>`	`<transfer>`	
	`<help>`		

Example	`<choice`
	`ext="http://www.stargazer.example/voice/astronews.vxml">`
	`<prompt>`

```
                        <audio
           src="http://www.stargazer.example/space.wav">
                            Stargazer<emp>astrophysics</emp> news
                        </audio>
                    </prompt>
                </choice>
```

<block>

Syntax	```<block```
	 ``` name= "ECMAScript_variable"```
	 ``` expr= "ECMAScript_Expression"```
	 ``` cond= "ECMAScript_Expression">```
	 ``` Executable content```
	 ```</block>```

Description	Specifies a set of other elements to execute in document order as a form item

Attribute	Description	Required/ Optional
name	Valid ECMAScript variable name that declares the form item variable for this block.	Optional
expr	ECMAScript expression that supplies an initial value for the form item variable (default is undefined). If a value is provided, then the form item will not be visited until/unless it is first cleared.	Optional
cond	ECMAScript expression that must also evaluate to true for this element to be selected by the FIA	Optional

Usage	**Parents**	**Children**	
	<form>	<assign>	<log>
		<audio>	<prompt>
		<clear>	<reprompt>
		<data>	<return>
		<disconnect>	<script>
		<enumerate>	<submit>
		<exit>	<throw>
		<foreach>	<value>
		<goto>	<var>
		<if>	

Example	```<vxml version="2.0">```
	 ``` <form>```
	 ``` <var name="hours"/>```
	 ``` <var name="minutes"/>```

```
                        <var name="seconds"/>
                        <block>
                             <script> var d = new Date(); hours =
          d.getHours(); minutes = d.getMinutes(); seconds =
          d.getSeconds(); </script>
                        </block>
                        <field name="hear_another"
          type="boolean">
                             <prompt> The time is
                               <value ="hours"/> hours,
                               <value expr="minutes"/> minutes, and
                               <value expr="seconds"/> seconds.
                        </prompt>
                        <prompt>Do you want to hear another
                             time?</prompt>
                        <filled>
                             <if cond="hear_another">
                                 <clear/>
                             </if>
                        </filled>
                   </field>
                 </form>
          </vxml>
```

<break>

Syntax	`<break`
	`        time= "time_interval"`
	`        size= "none ∣ small ∣ medium ∣ large" />`

Description	Inserts a period of silence into synthesized speech. *time* and *size* are mutually exclusive. If neither are specified, then a size="medium" pause is the default.

Attribute	Description	Required/ Optional
time	Duration of the pause in seconds (for example, "2.4s") or milliseconds (for example, "2400ms"), as per the W3C Cascading Stylesheets Level 2 Specification, available at www.w3.org/TR/REC-CSS2/syndata.html#q20. *time* and *size* are mutually exclusive.	Optional
size	Duration of the pause, expressed as: None—no pause, Small—200-ms pause, Medium—500-ms pause, (default), Large—1000-ms-s pause, *time* and *size* are mutually exclusive.	Optional

Usage	Parents		Children
	`<audio>`	`<enumerate>`	None
	`<choice>`	`<prompt>`	
	`<div>`	`<pros>`	
	`<emp>`		
Example	```<vxml version ="2.0">```		

```
<vxml version ="2.0">
  <form>
    <block>
      <prompt> This is computer-generated text.
       <break size="medium"/> Do you like it?
      </audio>
    </prompt>
  </form>
</vxml>
```

`<catch>`

Syntax	
	```<catch```

```
<catch
    event= "event1 event2 event3 ..."
    count= "integer"
    cond= "ECMAScript_Expression" >
    Executable content
</catch>
```

Description

Catches an event and defines an event handler.

In an event handler, the platform-defined variables _event and _message are available at the local anonymous scope. _event is a string specifying the exact name of the event that was caught, and _message is a string specifying any additional information about the event provided by the platform or explicitly set using the message or messageexpr attributes of `<throw>`.

For more information on the VoiceXML event model and the FIA, see Chapter 6.

For more information on platform-defined events, see "Platform-Defined Events" later in this chapter.

Attribute	Description	Required/Optional
event	Name of the event(s) to catch	Required
count	Number that specifies how many times event must be thrown before the FIA selects this particular handler (default is 1).	Optional
cond	ECMAScript expression that must also evaluate to true for this handler to catch a given event (Default is true).	Optional

Usage	Parents		Children	
	`<field>`	`<record>`	`<assign>`	`<phoneme>`
	`<form>`	`<subdialog>`	`<audio>`	`<prompt>`
	`<initial>`	`<transfer>`	`<break>`	`<prosody>`
	`<menu>`	`<vxml>`	`<clear>`	`<reprompt>`
	`<object>`		`<data>`	`<return>`
			`<disconnect>`	`<s>`
			`<emphasis>`	`<say-as>`
			`<enumerate>`	`<script>`
			`<exit>`	`<sentence>`
			`<foreach>`	`<submit>`
			`<goto>`	`<throw>`
			`<if>`	`<value>`
			`<log>`	`<var>`
			`<p>`	`<voice>`
			`<paragraph>`	

Example

```
<vxml version="2.0">
  <form id="launch_missiles">
    <field name="password">
      <prompt>What is the code word?</prompt>
      <grammar>rutabaga</grammar>
      <help>It is the name of an obscure
            vegetable.</help>
      <catch event="nomatch noinput" count="3">
        <!-- this will only catch the third (or
             subsequent) nomatch and the third (or
             subsequent) noinput. The next highest-
             scoped handlers for these will be used
             for the first and second instances. -->
        <audio>Security violation!</audio>
        <submit next="apprehend_felon"
                namelist="user_id"/>
      </catch>
    </field>
    <block>
      <goto next="#get_city"/>
    </block>
  </form>
</vxml>
```

`<choice>`

Syntax

```
<choice
    accept= "exact | approximate"
    dtmf = "dtmf_sequence"
    event= "string"
    expr= "ECMAScript_Expression"
    next= "URI"
    fetchaudio= "URI"
```

```
     fetchhint= "prefetch | safe"
     fetchtimeout= "string"
     maxage="integer"
     maxstale="integer">
  Choice Phrase
</choice>
```

Description	Defines an option within a `<menu>`. The `<choice>` element specifies a "choice phrase" and either an event to throw or a URI to transition to if the caller says something to match the choice phrase. The "choice phrase" is a grammar fragment derived from the PCDATA contained within the `<choice>` element's boundaries. *next, event,* and *expr* are mutually exclusive. Specifying a specific *dtmf* option overrides any sequential ordering provided by the dtmf attribute on the parent `<menu>`.

Attribute	Description	Required/ Optional
accept	States if the caller must say all of the words ("exact") or just a subset ("approximate") of the specified grammar fragment (Default is exact).	Optional
next	URI to transition to when this choice is selected. *next, event,* and *expr* are mutually exclusive.	Required
event	Event to throw when this choice is selected. *next, event,* and *expr* are mutually exclusive.	Required
expr	ECMAScript expression that evaluates to a URI to transition to when this choice is selected. *next, event,* and *expr* are mutually exclusive.	Required
dtmf	A dual-tone multifrequency (DTMF) tone that the caller can use (in lieu of speaking) to select this choice	Optional
fetchaudio	See "HTTP Semantics" later in this chapter.	Optional
fetchhint	See "HTTP Semantics" later in this chapter.	Optional
fetchtimeout	See "HTTP Semantics" later in this chapter.	Optional
maxage	See "HTTP Semantics" later in this chapter.	Optional
maxstale	See "HTTP Semantics" later in this chapter.	Optional

Usage	Parents		Children	
	`<menu>`		`<audio>`	`<grammar>`
			`<enumerate>`	`<value>`

Example	
| | ```
<vxml version="2.0">
  <menu id="main_menu" dtmf="true">
    <prompt>
      <audio>Would you like customer service, technical
            support,
            or the front desk?</audio>
    </prompt>
    <choice next="cust_svc.vxml">customer
    service</choice>
    <choice next="tech_support.vxml">technical
          support</choice>
    <choice next="front_desk.vxml">front desk</choice>
    <choice event="event.myapp.goodbye" dtmf="9">
          goodbye</choice>
    <!-- the "event" attribute throws this event rather
        than transitioning to a particular URL, and the
        "dtmf" attribute overrides the sequential dtmf
        behavior of the menu and explicitly makes "9"
        the touch-tone equivalent for this option -->
    <catch event="noinput nomatch">
      <audio>I'm sorry. I didn't catch that.</audio>
      <reprompt />
    </catch>
  </menu>
</vxml>
``` |

`<clear>`

Syntax	
| | ```
<clear
    namelist= "var1 var2 ... varn" />
``` |

Description	
	Reinitializes variables to *undefined.* Within a form item, also resets the prompt and event counters for that form item.

Attribute	Description	Required/Optional
namelist	Space-delimited list of variables to reset (Default is to reset all form item variables in the current context).	Optional

Usage	Parents		Children
	`<block>`	`<if>`	None
	`<catch>`	`<noinput>`	
	`<error>`	`<nomatch>`	
	`<filled>`	`<prompt>`	
	`<foreach>`		

Example	
| | ```
<vxml version="2.0">
  <catch event="noinput nomatch">
    <audio>I'm sorry, but I didn't get that.</audio>
``` |
```

```
                    <reprompt />
                </catch>

            <form id="pick_band">
              <field name="band">
                <prompt>
                    <audio>Is your favorite band Billy Joel,
                            Green Day, or Slayer?</audio>
                </prompt>
                <grammar type="application/x-gsl">
                <![CDATA[
                [
                    (billy joel) {<band "billy_joel">}
                    [greenday (green day)] {<band
                    "green_day">}
                    [slayer] {<band "slayer">}
                    [repeat] {<band "repeat">}
                ]
                ]]>
                </grammar>
                <filled>
                    <log>Recognized <value expr="band"/></log>
                    <if cond="band == 'repeat' ">
                        <clear namelist="band"/>
                        <!-- this clears the form item variable
                                for this field, causing the FIA to
                                reenter the field and reprompt the
                                caller for another choice, rather
                                than continuing on to the next form -->
                    <else/>
                        <audio>you chose <value expr="band"/></audio>
                        <exit/>
                    </if>
                </filled>
              </field>
            </form>
        </vxml>
```

<count>

In XML grammars, specifies an optional or repeated grammar rule. See Chapter 8 for details regarding XML grammars.

<data>

Syntax

```
<data
    enctype = "application/x-www-form-urlencoded |
    multipart/form-data"
    expr = "ECMAScript_Expression"
    fetchtimeout = "string"
    method = "get | post"
    name = "ECMAScript_variable"
```

```
namelist = "var1 var2 ... varn"
src = "URI" />
```

Description	Extension to Voicexml 2.0; under consideration for future versions.
	Retrieves XML data via HTTP, and provides programmatic access to it. The `<data>` element extends the notion of "XML Data Islands" (introduced by Microsoft into the HTML realm in Internet Explorer 5.0) to VoiceXML.
	The data element allows developers to include arbitrary data in a voice application and to reference that data via script. The data consumed by the data element must be formatted in XML, and the Tellme VoiceXML interpreter exposes that data via a subset of the W3C Document Object Model (DOM).
	Data retrieved via the `<data>` element is available in the scope where it is loaded, just as with any other variable assignment.
	For security reasons, the `<data>` element prohibits retrieving data from a URI domain different than that of the VoiceXML document making the request. To access data across domains, developers can use `<subdialog>` to a VoiceXML document in the domain where the data resides. The subdialog specifies a data element and returns the named variable in the namelist of the return element in the subdialog. For more information on data, see Chapter 9.

Attribute	Description	Required/ Optional
enctype	MIME encoding type of any submitted data-via *namelist* (default is application/x-www-form-urlencoded).	Optional
expr	ECMAScript expression that evaluates to a URI to retrieve the XML data from. *expr* and *src* are mutually exclusive.	Required
fetchtimeout	See "HTTP Semantics" later in this chapter.	Optional
method	The HTTP method to use to send the request; either "get" or "post" (default is "get").	Optional
name	The name of a variable to store the retrieved XML DOM data within.	Required
namelist	A space-separated list of variables to be submitted via HTTP along with the request to the URI specified by *src* or *expr*.	Optional
src	URI to retrieve the XML data from. *expr* and *src* are mutually exclusive.	Required

Usage	Parents		Children
	\<block\>	\<help\>	None
	\<catch\>	\<if\>	
	\<error\>	\<noinput\>	
	\<filled\>	\<nomatch\>	
	\<foreach\>	\<prompt\>	
	\<form\>	\<vxml\>	

Example	See Chapter 9.

\<disconnect\>

Syntax	\<disconnect/\>
Description	Hangs up the telephone call and ends the VoiceXML session. Before ending the session, \<disconnect\> first throws a *telephone.disconnect.hangup* event. Developers can catch this event to perform some level of posthangup processing, such as submitting any remaining data (for example, the duration of the call) back to the Web server for offline processing and storage.
	Note: Be very careful of timing issues when performing posthangup processing; if this code takes too much time, it may degrade overall system performance for other calls that are still in progress. To protect against this case, leading VoiceXML platforms typically impose restrictions (for example, 5 seconds) on the total time posthangup processing can take. Please see your VoiceXML platform vendor's documentation on posthangup processing for more information on platform-specific guidelines and restrictions.

Usage	Parents		Children
	\<block\>	\<help\>	None
	\<catch\>	\<if\>	
	\<error\>	\<noinput\>	
	\<filled\>	\<nomatch\>	
	\<foreach\>	\<prompt\>	

Example

```
<vxml version="2.0">
 <var name="time_start" expr="new Date()" />
  <var name="time_end" />
  <catch event="telephone.disconnect.hangup">
    <assign name="time_end" expr="new Date()" />
    <log>this is post-hangup processing</log>
    <log>time start <value expr="time_start" />
         and time end <value expr="time_end" /></log>
    <submit namelist="time_start time_end"
            next="onhangup.cgi" fetchtimeout="5s" />
  </catch>
  <form>
   <block>
     <audio>Welcome to this application. Did you
            know that this application is being
            used to simply demonstrate post-hangup
```

```
                     call processing?</audio>
            <disconnect />
        </block>
    </form>
</vxml>
```

<else>

Syntax	
	```<if cond = "ECMAScript_Expression">```
	Executable_content
	```<elseif cond = "ECMAScript_Expression">```
	Executable_content
	```<elseif cond = "ECMAScript_Expression">```
	Executable_content
	```<else/>```
	Executable_content
	```</if>```

Description Provides the final logic for an `<if><elseif><else>` conditional construct.

If the *cond* attributes of the containing `<if>` and all preceding `<elseif>` elements evaluate to false, then the content between `<else />` and `</if>` are executed.

Usage

Parents	Children
`<if>`	None

Example

```
<vxml version="2.0">
    <form id="pick_band">
    <field name="band">
        <prompt>
        <audio>Pick a band</audio>
        </prompt>
        <grammar type="application/x-gsl">
        <![CDATA[
        [
            (billy joel) {<band "billy_joel">}
            [slayer] {<band "slayer">}
            (green day) {<band "green_day">}
            (tori amos) {<band "tori amos">}
        ]
        ]]>
        </grammar>
        <filled>
            <if cond=" 'billy_joel' == band">
                <audio>only the good die young</audio>
            <elseif cond=" 'slayer' == band"/>
                <audio>old school glam metal</audio>
            <elseif cond=" 'green_day' == band"/>
                <audio>I knew you loved indie pop</audio>
            <else/>
                <audio>I used to love Tori . . . but I
```

```
                               got tired of her.</audio>
          </if>
          <clear/>
        </filled>
      </field>
    </form>
  </vxml>
```

<elseif>

Syntax	`<if cond = "ECMAScript_Expression">`
	  `Executable_content`
	`<elseif cond = "ECMAScript_Expression">`
	  `Executable_content`
	`<elseif cond = "ECMAScript_Expression">`
	  `Executable_content`
	`<else/>`
	  `Executable_content`
	`</if>`

Description	Provides logic for an additional condition within an `<if><elseif><else>` conditional construct. If the *cond* attributes of the containing `<if>` and all preceding `<elseif>` elements evaluate to false, then the content between this `<elseif>` and the next `<elseif>`, `<else>`, or `</if>` are executed. As per ECMAScript convention, expressions that evaluate to 0, –0, null, false, NaN, undefined, and the empty string are evaluated as false. All other values, including the strings "0" and "false," are equivalent to true. ***Note:*** To use an ECMAScript less-than (<), greater-than (>), or and (&&) condition in VoiceXML (or any XML document), replace the symbols with the < >, or && entities respectively.

Attribute	Description	Required/ Optional
cond	ECMAScript expression that must evaluate to true for the clause to execute.	Required

Usage	**Parents**	**Children**
	`<if>`	None

Example	`<vxml version="2.0">`
	  `<form id="pick_band">`
	  `<field name="band">`
	    `<prompt>`
	    `<audio>Pick a band</audio>`
	    `</prompt>`
	    `<grammar type="application/x-gsl">`
	    `<![CDATA[`
	    `[`
	      `(billy joel) {<band "billy_joel">}`

```
                      [slayer] {<band "slayer">}
                      (green day) {<band "green_day">}
                      (tori amos) {<band "tori amos">}
                  ]
                  ]]>
                  </grammar>
                  <filled>
                      <if cond=" 'billy_joel' == band">
                          <audio>only the good die young</audio>
                      <elseif cond=" 'slayer' == band"/>
                          <audio>old school glam metal</audio>
                      <elseif cond=" 'green_day' == band"/>
                          <audio>I knew you loved indie pop</audio>
                      <else/>
                          <audio>I used to love Tori . . . but I
                                 got tired of her.</audio>
                      </if>
                      <clear/>
                  </filled>
                  </field>
              </form>
          </vxml>
```

<emphasis>

Syntax	`<emphasis` ` level = "strong	moderate	none	reduced">` ` TTS_Text` `</emphasis>`
Description	In TTS, indicates that the enclosed synthesized speech should be emphasized.

Attribute	Description	Required/ Optional
level	Level of emphasis—strong, none, or reduced (default is moderate).	Optional

Usage	Parents		Children	
	`<audio>`	`<noinput>`	`<audio>`	`<prosody>`
	`<block>`	`<nomatch>`	`<break>`	`<say-as>`
	`<catch>`	`<p>`	`<emphasis>`	`<value>`
	`<choice>`	`<paragraph>`	`<enumerate>`	`<voice>`
	`<div>`	`<prompt>`	`<phoneme>`	
	`<emphasis>`	`<prosody>`		
	`<enumerate>`	`<s>`		
	`<error>`	`<sentence>`		
	`<filled>`	`<voice>`		
	`<foreach>`			
	`<help>`			
	`<if>`			

Example
```
<prompt>
    <audio src="welcome.wav">
        <emphasis>Welcome</emphasis> to Jack's house.
    </audio>
</prompt>
```

`<enumerate>`

Syntax
```
<enumerate>
    TTS_Text
</enumerate>
```
OR
```
<enumerate />
```

Description

Used with `<choice>` or `<option>`, provides a mechanism to automatically speak the list of available options to the caller.

`<enumerate>` can be used in one of two ways. Used alone (for example, `<enumerate />`), the VoiceXML interpreter simply speaks the list of available options using TTS speech.

Alternatively, developers can specify any valid set of TTS and audio elements (for example, `<emphasis>`, `<value>`, `<audio>`, etc.) within the `<enumerate>`, as well as one of two special platform-defined variables: _prompt_ and _dtmf_. For each available `<choice>` or `<option>`, the VoiceXML interpreter will execute this block of TTS and/or audio (that is, like a template). For each iteration, _prompt_ refers to the grammar fragment that defines the particular option, and _dtmf_ refers to its DTMF equivalent (if any). It is up to the VoiceXML interpreter to remove any special characters from the relevant `<choice>` or `<option>`'s grammar fragment before speaking it to the caller as TTS.

`<enumerate>` can be used within all relevant event handlers, prompts, etc. where there is a current set of `<choice>` or `<option>`s available. Otherwise, an _error.semantic_ is thrown.

Usage

Parents		Children	
`<audio>`	`<noinput>`	`<audio>`	`<phoneme>`
`<block>`	`<nomatch>`	`<break>`	`<prosody>`
`<catch>`	`<object>`	`<emphasis>`	`<s>`
`<choice>`	`<p>`	`<enumerate>`	`<say-as>`
`<emphasis>`	`<paragraph>`	`<p>`	`<sentence>`
`<error>`	`<prompt>`	`<paragraph>`	`<value>`
`<field>`	`<prosody>`		`<voice>`
`<filled>`	`<record>`		
`<foreach>`	`<s>`		
`<help>`	`<sentence>`		
`<if>`	`<subdialog>`		
`<initial>`	`<transfer>`		
`<menu>`	`<voice>`		

Example

```
<vxml version="2.0">
  <catch event="myapp.menu">
    <audio>Event thrown: <value expr="_event" />
    </audio>
    <!-- generic event handler for purposes of
         this example-->
    <goto next="#top" />
  </catch>
  <menu id="top" dtmf="true">
    <prompt> Welcome home.
      <enumerate> For <value expr="_prompt"/> press
                  <value expr="_dtmf"/>.
      </enumerate>
    </prompt>
    <choice event="myapp.menu.bands">bands</choice>
    <choice event="myapp.menu.fruits">fruits</choice>
    <choice
event="myapp.menu.candies">candies</choice>
    <choice dtmf="9"

event="myapp.menu.special">specials</choice>
  </menu>
</vxml>
```

`<error>`

Syntax

```
<error
    count = "integer"
    cond = "ECMAScript_Expression">
    Executable_content
</error>
```

Description

Shorthand for `<catch event="error">`. Catches platform-defined and user-defined events whose names begin with the string `"error."`

For more information about the VoiceXML event model, see Chapter 6.

For more information about platform-defined errors, see "Platform-Defined Events" later in this chapter.

Attribute	Description	Required/ Optional
count	Number that specifies how many times an error event must be thrown before the FIA selects this particular handler (default is 1).	Optional
cond	ECMAScript expression that must also evaluate to true for this handler to catch a given event (default is true).	Optional

Usage	Parents		Children	
	`<field>`	`<record>`	`<assign>`	`<phoneme>`
	`<form>`	`<subdialog>`	`<audio>`	`<prompt>`
	`<initial>`	`<transfer>`	`<break>`	`<prosody>`
	`<menu>`	`<vxml>`	`<clear>`	`<reprompt>`
	`<object>`		`<disconnect>`	`<return>`
			`<emphasis>`	`<s>`
			`<enumerate>`	`<say-as>`
			`<exit>`	`<script>`
			`<foreach>`	`<sentence>`
			`<goto>`	`<submit>`
			`<if>`	`<throw>`
			`<log>`	`<value>`
			`<p>`	`<var>`
			`<paragraph>`	`<voice>`

Example

```
<vxml version="2.0">
  <var name="flag" expr="false" />
  <error>
    <!-- this is a document scope handler -->
    <audio>this is the document handler.
           the error <value expr="_event" />
           occurred.</audio>
    <assign name="flag" expr="true" />
    <goto next="#top" />
  </error>
  <form id="top">
    <error cond="flag">
      <!-- this is a dialog scope handler,
           that will override on the second
           time once the flag is set to
           true -->
      <audio>this is the dialog handler.
           the error <value expr="_event" />
           occurred.</audio>
      <exit />
    </error>
    <field name="hello" type="boolean">
      <prompt>
        <audio>entering the first field.
               say yes or no.</audio>
      </prompt>
      <filled>
        <throw event="error.myapp.unlucky" />
      </filled>
      <!-- this should always
           throw an error -->
    </field>
  </form>
</vxml>
```

`<example>`

In XML grammars, specifies an example of input that matches a grammar rule. See Chapter 8 for details regarding XML grammars.

`<exit>`

Syntax	```<exit```
	    ```expr = "ECMAScript_Expression"```
	    ```namelist = "var1 var2 ... varn" />```

Description	Immediately terminates the current application, and returns control to the interpreter. Unlike `<return>` (which terminates a `<subdialog>` and returns control to the calling context), `<exit>` immediately ends the entire session. However, the VoiceXML 2.0 specification does not specify what the VoiceXML interpreter must do after an `<exit />`—other than stating that it does not throw an *exit* event. It may implicitly `<disconnect />`, play a platform-defined menu, or perform some other platform-specific behavior. Typically, VoiceXML platforms immediately hang up the telephone, but do not throw the *telephone.disconnect.hangup* event for posthangup processing as with `<disconnect>`. If specified, *expr* and *namelist* provide a mechanism for developers to send particular information to the VoiceXML interpreter upon exiting. What the interpreter does with this information is platform-specific.

Attribute	Description	Required/Optional
expr	ECMAScript expression that evaluates to the value assigned to the variable	Optional
namelist	List of variable names to return (default is return nothing)	Optional

Usage	**Parents**	**Children**	
	`<block>`	`<help>`	None
	`<catch>`	`<if>`	
	`<error>`	`<noinput>`	
	`<filled>`	`<nomatch>`	

Example	

```
<vxml version="2.0">
    <form id="say_goodbye">
        <field name="answer" type="boolean">
        <prompt>Shall we say goodbye?
        </prompt>
        <filled>
            <if cond="answer">
                <exit />
            <else />
                <clear namelist="answer"/>
            </if>
```

```
          </filled>
        </field>
      </form>
    </vxml>
```

<field>

| **Syntax** | ```
    cond = "ECMAScript_Expression"
    expr = "ECMAScript_Expression"
    modal = "true | false"
    name = "ECMAScript_variable"
    skiplist = "ECMAScript_Array"
    slot = "string"
    type = "boolean | date | digits | currency | number |
    phone | time">
    Child_elements
</field>
``` |
| **Description** | Facilitates a dialog with the caller to collect information. |

Once one or more grammars have been matched within a field, the <filled> element contained within it is executed. Within the <filled> element, several platform-defined "shadow variables" (defined below) are available within the local scope to inspect the recognition result.

In addition, key aspects that control the specific behavior of the recognition engine can be controlled using VoiceXML properties. For more information on VoiceXML properties, see the <property> element and "Platform-Defined Properties" later in this chapter.

For more information about VoiceXML dialogs and the FIA, see Chapter 6.

Attribute	Description	Required/Optional
cond	ECMAScript expression that must also evaluate to true for the FIA to select this field (Default is true).	Optional
expr	ECMAScript expression that, if specified, is evaluated and provides an initial value for the field's field item variable *name* (default is undefined).	Optional
	If a value is provided, then the form item will not be visited until/unless it is first cleared.	
modal	Boolean value that, if true, temporarily disables all active grammars from higher scopes for this field (default is false).	Optional
```

Attribute	Description	Required/ Optional
name	Valid ECMAScript variable name that declares the field item variable for this field. A successful recognition within this field will store the recognition result in *name* before executing the field's `<filled>` element.	Required
skiplist	Extension to VoiceXML 2.0. Some VoiceXML platforms provide this attribute.	Optional
	ECMAScript array containing a list of possible recognition results for this field that the recognizer should explicitly ignore and not match against.	
	Developers can initialize an array, prompt the user for information, and then confirm their selection in another field within this form.	
	If the caller says "no" (e.g. the platform misrecognized what they said), then the value of the *name* variable can be added to the *skiplist* array and the caller can be reprompted with the original question. In this way, developers can prevent the recognizer from making the same mistake twice.	
slot	For mixed-initiative dialogs, the name of the grammar slot to use when deciding whether to fill in this field's field item variable.	Optional
	If *slot* is not specified, then it is assumed to be the same as *name*. If the grammar that is matched has only one slot, then *name* is filled with that value regardless of whether *slot* has been specified.	
	For more information on mixed-initiative dialogs, see Chapter 6.	
type	One of several platform-defined grammars. For details on the available list of platform-defined grammars and their syntax, see "Platform-Defined Grammars" later in this chapter.	Optional
	The *type* attribute is mutually exclusive with including `<grammar>` elements within the field.	

Shadow Variable	Description
(shadow variables are only available within the `<filled>` element)	
name$.confidence	The recognizer's confidence that the caller actually said this particular match, expressed on a scale from 0.0 (minimum) to 1.0 (maximum).
name$.utterance	The actual string of words said by the caller. The exact spelling is platform-specific (for example, "five hundred thirty" versus "5 hundred 30" versus "530").
name$.inputmode	Either "dtmf" or "voice," indicating whether the grammar was matched via touch-tone or spoken input.

Usage	Parents	Children	
	`<form>`	`<audio>`	`<link>`
		`<catch>`	`<noinput>`
		`<enumerate>`	`<nomatch>`
		`<error>`	`<option>`
		`<filled>`	`<prompt>`
		`<grammar>`	`<property>`
		`<help>`	`<value>`

Example

```
<vxml version="2.0">
<form>
<field name="dob" type="date">
      <prompt> What is your birthdate? </prompt>
      <filled>
        <audio>I am
               <value expr="dob$.confidence * 100"
               />
               percent sure that you said your
               birthdate is
               <value expr="dob$.utterance" />.
               The grammar actually returned
               the value <value expr="dob" />.
        </audio>
        <clear />
      </filled>
    </field>
  </form>
</vxml>
```

`<filled>`

| **Syntax** | ```
<filled
    mode = "any | all"
    namelist = "var1 var2 . . . varn"
    Executable_contents
</filled>
``` |
Description	Specifies actions to perform when a given field or fields have been "filled in." If used as a child of a specific `<field>` or form item (for example, `<transfer>`), then it is executed when that field's field item variable becomes filled in (either via a successful recognition or explicit assignment of the field item variable). In this case, *mode* and *namelist* are irrelevant and ignored.
	Alternatively, `<filled>` can be used as a child of `<form>` to cover multiple fields, using *mode* and *namelist* to specify which fields to act upon.
	Within a `<filled>` element, the executable content have access to a set of "shadow variables" implicitly created by the parent `<field>`. For information on these shadow variables, see `<field>` earlier in this chapter.
	In addition, key aspects that control the specific behavior of the recognition engine can be controlled using VoiceXML properties. For more information on VoiceXML properties, see the `<property>` element and "Platform-Defined Properties" later in this chapter.
	For more information about VoiceXML dialogs and the FIA, see Chapter 6.

Attribute	Description	Required/Optional
mode	When used as a child of `<form>`, specifies whether "all" or "any" of the fields specified in namelist must be filled in order to execute this `<filled>` element (default is all).	Optional
	When used as a child of `<field>` or another form item, it is invalid to specify *mode*.	
namelist	When used as a child of `<form>`, specifies a space-delimited list of field *names* within this form used in conjunction with *mode* to determine behavior (default is all fields in the form).	Optional
	When used as a child of `<field>` or another form item, it is invalid to specify *namelist*.	
```

Usage	Parents		Children	
	`<field>`	`<record>`	`<assign>`	`<phoneme>`
	`<form>`	`<subdialog>`	`<audio>`	`<prompt>`
	`<object>`	`<transfer>`	`<break>`	`<prosody>`
			`<clear>`	`<reprompt>`
			`<disconnect>`	`<return>`
			`<emphasis>`	`<s>`
			`<enumerate>`	`<say-as>`
			`<exit>`	`<script>`
			`<foreach>`	`<sentence>`
			`<goto>`	`<submit>`
			`<if>`	`<throw>`
			`<log>`	`<value>`
			`<p>`	`<var>`
			`<paragraph>`	`<voice>`

Example

```
<vxml version="2.0">
  <form>
    <field name="dob" type="date">
      <prompt> What is your birthdate? </prompt>
      <filled>
        <audio>I am
               <value expr="dob$.confidence * 100"
               />
               percent sure that you said your
               birthdate is
               <value expr="dob$.utterance" />.
               The grammar actually returned
               the value <value expr="dob" />.
        </audio>
        <clear />
      </filled>
    </field>
  </form>
</vxml>
```

`<foreach>`

Syntax

```
<form
    array = "ECMAScript_Expression"
    item = "ECMAScript_Variable">
    Executable_content
</form>
```

Description Extension to VoiceXML 2.0; under consideration for future versions.

Iterates through an ECMAScript array of items. For each member of the array specified by *array*, temporarily assigns its value to *item* and executes any child content.

	Attribute	Description	Required/ Optional
	array	ECMAScript expression that evaluates to an ECMAScript array.	Required
	item	ECMAScript variable that is declared and used to store the contents of each successive member of *array*.	Required

Usage	Parents	Children	
	`<block>`	`<assign>`	`<phoneme>`
	`<catch>`	`<audio>`	`<prompt>`
	`<error>`	`<break>`	`<prosody>`
	`<filled>`	`<clear>`	`<reprompt>`
	`<help>`	`<data>`	`<return>`
	`<noinput>`	`<disconnect>`	`<s>`
	`<nomatch>`	`<emphasis>`	`<say-as>`
		`<enumerate>`	`<script>`
		`<exit>`	`<sentence>`
		`<foreach>`	`<submit>`
		`<goto>`	`<throw>`
		`<if>`	`<value>`
		`<log>`	`<var>`
		`<p>`	`<voice>`
		`<paragraph>`	

Example

```
<vxml version="2.0">
  <form id="play_games">
    <block>
      <!-- create an array of game names -->
      <var name="aGame" expr="new Array('football',
      'baseball', 'squash', 'rugby')"/>
      <audio>Here's a list of games you can play
      today</audio>
      <!-- iterate through each item in the array -->
      <foreach item="game" array="aGame">
        <audio><value expr="game"/></audio>
      </foreach>
    </block>
  </form>
</vxml>
```

`<form>`

Syntax

```
<form
    id = "string"
    scope = "document | dialog">
    Child_elements
</form>
```

			Required/
	Attribute	**Description**	**Optional**

Description   Plays prompts and interacts with the caller through a series of field items—the primary unit of dialog in VoiceXML applications.

For more information about VoiceXML forms and the FIA, see Chapter 6.

Attribute	Description	Required/Optional
id	Name for the form, so that `<goto>` and other elements can explicitly transition to it using "#" notation (for example, `<goto next="#top" />`). As with HTML anchors, *id*s must be unique within a given VoiceXML document.	Optional
scope	Sets the default scope of the form's grammars: Document—the form's grammars are active throughout the current document Dialog—the form's grammars are active throughout the current form (Default is dialog).	Optional

Usage

Parents	Children	
`<vxml>`	`<block>`	`<noinput>`
	`<catch>`	`<nomatch>`
	`<data>`	`<object>`
	`<error>`	`<property>`
	`<field>`	`<record>`
	`<filled>`	`<script>`
	`<grammar>`	`<subdialog>`
	`<help>`	`<transfer>`
	`<initial>`	`<var>`
	`<link>`	

Example

```
<vxml version="2.0">
  <var name="hi" expr=" 'Hello World!' "/>
  <form>
    <block>
      <value expr="hi"/>
      <goto next="#say_goodbye"/>
    </block>
  </form>
  <form id="say_goodbye">
    <block> Goodbye! </block>
    <exit />
  </form>
</vxml>
```

`<goto>`

Syntax	```<goto``` `expr = "ECMAScript_Expression"` `expritem = "ECMAScript_Expression"` `fetchaudio = "URI"` `fetchhint = "prefetch	safe	stream"`     `fetchtimeout = "string"`     `maxage = "integer"`     `maxstale = "integer"`     `next = "URI"`     `nextitem = "string" />`
Description	Explicitly transitions to a specified location within the same or a different document. *expr, expritem, next,* and *nextitem* are all mutually exclusive— only one may be specified.

Attribute	Description	Required/ Optional
expr	ECMAScript expression that evaluates to the URI of a dialog in the current or a different document (for example, `"http://foo.com/bar.vxml,""#top,"` `"bar.vxml#menu"`). *expr, expritem, next,* and *nextitem* are all mutually exclusive—only one may be specified.	Required
expritem	ECMAScript expression that evaluates to the *name* of another form item (for example, field, transfer, etc.) within the current `<form>` or `<menu>`. *expr, expritem, next,* and *nextitem* are all mutually exclusive—only one may be specified.	Required
fetchaudio	See "HTTP Semantics" later in this chapter.	Optional
fetchhint	See "HTTP Semantics" later in this chapter.	Optional
fetchtimeout	See "HTTP Semantics" later in this chapter.	Optional
maxage	See "HTTP Semantics" later in this chapter.	Optional
maxstale	See "HTTP Semantics" later in this chapter.	Optional
next	URI of a dialog in the current or a different document (for example, `"http://foo.com/bar.vxml,"` `"#top," "bar.vxml#menu"`).	Required

Attribute	Description	Required/Optional
next	*expr, expritem, next,* and *nextitem* are all mutually exclusive—only one may be specified.	
nextitem	*name* of another form item (for example, field, transfer, etc.) within the current `<form>` or `<menu>`. *expr, expritem, next,* and *nextitem* are all mutually exclusive—only one may be specified.	Required

Usage	Parents		Children
	`<block>`	`<help>`	None
	`<catch>`	`<if>`	
	`<error>`	`<noinput>`	
	`<filled>`	`<nomatch>`	
	`<foreach>`	`<prompt>`	

Example

```
<vxml version="2.0">
  <form>
    <block>
      <var name="uri_base" expr=" '#menu' " />
      <audio> Hello world! </audio>
      <goto expr="uri_base + '_2nd' " />
      <!-- goes to '#menu_2nd' -->
    </block>
  </form>
  <form id="menu_top">
    <block>
    <audio>we should never get here</audio>
    </block>
  </form>
  <form id="menu_2nd">
    <block>
      <audio>Here is the second menu.</audio>
    <exit />
  </block>
  </form>
</vxml>
```

`<grammar>`

Syntax

```
<grammar>
      fetchhint = "prefetch | safe | stream"
      fetchtimeout = "string"
      maxage = "integer"
      maxstale = "integer"
      mode = "dtmf | speech"
      root = "string"
      scope = "dialog | document"
```

```
          src = "URI"
          type = "MIME_type"
          version = "string"
          weight = "float"
          xml:lang = "language_locale">
          Inline_grammar (Optional)
</grammar>
```

Description	Specifies the "permissible vocabulary" for a given caller interaction.
	For more information on VoiceXML grammars, grammar formats, and grammar scoping, see Chapters 6 and 8.
	For more information on platform-defined VoiceXML grammars, see "Platform-Defined Grammars" later in this chapter.

Attribute	Description	Required/ Optional
fetchhint	See "HTTP Semantics" later in this chapter.	Optional
fetchtimeout	See "HTTP Semantics" later in this chapter.	Optional
maxage	See "HTTP Semantics" later in this chapter.	Optional
maxstale	See "HTTP Semantics" later in this chapter.	Optional
mode	Either "dtmf" or "voice," indicating whether the grammar is for touch-tone or spoken input. If the specified grammar does not match the specified mode, a *badfetch* event is thrown (default is voice).	Optional
root	For inline XML grammar, defines the public rule which acts as the root rule of the grammar. The root rule is only used when the grammar is inline and must be present when using an inline XML grammar to identify which rule to activate.	Optional
scope	Sets the default scope of the grammar: Document—the form's grammar are active throughout the current document Dialog—the form's grammar are active throughout the current form. If omitted, the grammar scoping is resolved by looking at the parent element.	Optional

Attribute	Description	Required/ Optional
src	URI to a valid grammar document. *src* inline grammar definitions and are mutually exclusive, but one must be specified. This URI may reference one of the platform-defined VoiceXML grammars using the special *"builtin:"* URI namespace. For more information about these grammars, see "Platform-Defined Grammars" later in this chapter.	Required
type	MIME type for the grammar format being used either inline or via *src*. If omitted, the recognizer will attempt to determine the format dynamically. MIME types for commonly used grammar formats include: "application/grammar+xml" W3C XML Grammar Format "application/grammar" W3C Augmented BNF Grammar Format "application/x-gsl" Nuance Grammar Specification Language "application/x-jsjf" —Java Grammar Format	Optional
version	Defines the version of the grammar format specified by *type* being used (default is 1.0).	Optional
weight	Positive floating point (or 0) number that indicates the likelihood that the caller will say something to match this grammar, relative to other active grammars (default is 1.0). `<grammar>` weights are evaluated equivalently to `<item>` definitions within a `<one-of>` construct in the W3C XML grammar format. Please see Chapter 8 for details on the W3C XML grammar format.	Optional
xml:lang	Specifies the language and locale identifier of the contained or referenced grammar according to RFC 1766[1] (for example, "fr-CA" for Canadian French). If omitted, the value is inherited down from the document hierarchy, and ultimately a VoiceXML interpreter default.	Optional

[1]See www.nordu.net/ftp/rfc/rfc1766.txt

Usage	Parents	Children
	`<choice>`	`<link>`	
	`<field>`	`<record>`	*Grammar format-specific*
	`<form>`	`<transfer>`	

| **Example** | ```
<vxml version="2.0">
  <property name="universals" value="all">
  <!-- this sets the universals property, enabling a
  global grammar for "help" -->
  <form id="launch_missiles">
    <field name="password">
        <grammar type="application/grammar+xml">
          <rule id="password" scope="public">
            item tag="rutabega">rutabage</item>
          </rule>
        <grammar>
        <prompt>What is the code word</prompt>
        <help>It is the name of an obscure vegetable.
            <reprompt/>
        </help>
        <noinput count="3">
            Security violation!
            <exit/>
        </noinput>
        <nomatch count="3">
            Security violation!
            <exit/>
        </nomatch>
        <!-- these noinput and nomatch handlers are only
        activated on the third try. Before that, the
        platform-defined defaults are used. -->
      </filled>
        </audio>You got it!</audio>
        <clear />
      </filled>
    </field>
  </form>
</vxml>
``` |

`<help>`

| **Syntax** | ```
<help
    count = "integer"
    cond = "ECMAScript_Expression">
    Executable_content
</help>
``` |
| **Description** | Shorthand for `<catch event="help">`. Catches platform-defined and user-defined events whose names begin with the string `"help."` |
| | By default, there is no active grammar or link for the word `"help."` Setting the *universals* property to *all* will activate a global grammar for "help" on most VoiceXML platforms. |

For more information about the VoiceXML event model, see Chapter 6.

For more information about platform-defined events and properties, see "Platform-Defined Events" and "Platform-Defined Properties" later in this chapter.

Attribute	Description	Required/Optional
count	Number that specifies how many times a help event must be thrown before the FIA selects this particular handler (default is 1).	Optional
cond	ECMAScript expression that must also evaluate to true for this handler to catch a given event (default is true).	Optional

Usage	Parents		Children	
	`<field>`	`<record>`	`<assign>`	`<phoneme>`
	`<form>`	`<subdialog>`	`<audio>`	`<prompt>`
	`<initial>`	`<transfer>`	`<break>`	`<prosody>`
	`<menu>`	`<vxml>`	`<clear>`	`<reprompt>`
	`<object>`		`<disconnect>`	`<return>`
			`<emphasis>`	`<s>`
			`<enumerate>`	`<say-as>`
			`<exit>`	`<script>`
			`<foreach>`	`<sentence>`
			`<goto>`	`<submit>`
			`<if>`	`<throw>`
			`<log>`	`<value>`
			`<p>`	`<var>`
			`<paragraph>`	`<voice>`

Example

```
<vxml version="2.0">
  <property name="universals" value="all" />
  <!-- this sets the universals property, enabling
       a global grammar for "help" -->
  <form id="launch_missiles">
    <field name="password">
        <grammar type="application/grammar+xml">
          <rule id="password" scope="public">
            <item tag="rutabaga">rutabaga</item>
          </rule>
        </grammar>
        <prompt>What is the code word?</prompt>
        <help>It is the name of an obscure
              vegetable.
              <reprompt/>
        </help>
        <noinput count="3">
            Security violation!
            <exit />
```

```
            </noinput>
            <nomatch count="3">
                  Security violation!
                  <exit />
            </nomatch>
            <!-- these noinput and nomatch handlers are
      only activated on the third try. Before that, the
      platform-defined defaults are used. -->
            <filled>
               <audio>You got it!</audio>
               <clear />
            </filled>
         </field>
       </form>
      </vxml>
```

`<if>`

Syntax	`<if cond = "ECMAScript_Expression">`
	  `Executable_content`
	`<elseif cond = "ECMAScript_Expression">`
	  `Executable_content`
	`<elseif cond = "ECMAScript_Expression">`
	  `Executable_content`
	`<else/>`
	  `Executable_content`
	`</if>`

Description	Provides logic for an initial condition within an `<if><elseif><else>` conditional construct. If the *cond* attribute evaluates to true, then the content between this `<if>` and the next `<elseif>`, `<else>`, or `</if>` are executed. As per ECMAScript convention, expressions that evaluate to 0, −0, null, false, NaN, undefined, and the empty string are evaluated as false. All other values, including the strings "0" and "false," are equivalent to true. **Note:** To use an ECMAScript less-than ($<$), greater-than ($>$), or and (&&) condition in VoiceXML (or any XML document), replace the symbols with the < > or && entities respectively.

Attribute	Description	Required/Optional
cond	ECMAScript expression that must evaluate to true for the clause to execute.	Required

Usage	**Parents**		**Children**	
	`<block>`	`<help>`	`<assign>`	
	`<catch>`	`<if>`	`<audio>`	`<paragraph>`
	`<error>`	`<noinput>`	`<break>`	`<phoneme>`

Usage	Parents		Children	
	`<filled>`	`<nomatch>`	`<clear>`	`<prompt>`
			`<data>`	`<prosody>`
			`<disconnect>`	`<reprompt>`
			`<else>`	`<return>`
			`<elseif>`	`<s>`
			`<emphasis>`	`<say-as>`
			`<enumerate>`	`<script>`
			`<exit>`	`<sentence>`
			`<foreach>`	`<submit>`
			`<goto>`	`<throw>`
			`<if>`	`<value>`
			`<log>`	`<var>`
			`<p>`	`<voice>`

Example

```
<vxml version="2.0">
    <form id="pick_band">
    <field name="band">
        <prompt>
        <audio>Pick a band</audio>
        </prompt>
        <grammar type="application/x-gsl">
        <![CDATA[
        [
            (billy joel) {<band "billy_joel">}
            [slayer] {<band "slayer">}
            (green day) {<band "green_day">}
            (tori amos) {<band "tori amos">}
        ]
        ]]>
        </grammar>
        <filled>
            <if cond=" 'billy_joel' == band">
                <audio>only the good die young</audio>
            <elseif cond=" 'slayer' == band"/>
                <audio>old school glam metal</audio>
            <elseif cond=" 'green_day' == band"/>
                <audio>I knew you loved indie
                pop</audio>
            <else/>
                <audio>I used to love Tori... but I
                        got tired of her.</audio>
            </if>
            <clear/>
        </filled>
        </field>
    </form>
</vxml>
```

`<import>`

In XML grammars, specifies an alias name for a grammar rule. See Chapter 8 for details regarding XML grammars.

`<initial>`

Syntax	```<initial` ` name = "ECMAScript_Variable"` ` expr = "ECMAScript_Expression"` ` cond = "ECMAScript_Expression">` ` Child_elements` `</initial>```
Description	Prompts the caller for form-wide information in mixed-initiative forms. To use the initial element, a grammar with form scope must exist that can match caller utterances in response to the initial element's prompts. The initial element behaves like a field in that it can have prompt elements, event handlers, and event counters, but it does not have its own grammar or a filled element. For more information about VoiceXML dialogs and the FIA, please see Chapter 6.

Attribute	Description	Required/Optional
name	Valid ECMAScript variable name that declares the form item variable for this `<initial>`.	Optional
expr	ECMAScript expression that supplies an initial value for the form item variable (default is undefined). If a value is provided, then the form item will not be visited until/unless it is first cleared.	Optional
cond	ECMAScript expression that must also evaluate to true for this element to be selected by the FIA (default is true).	Optional

Usage	**Parents**	**Children**	
	`<form>`	`<audio>`	`<noinput>`
		`<catch>`	`<nomatch>`
		`<enumerate>`	`<prompt>`
		`<error>`	`<property>`
		`<help>`	`<value>`
		`<link>`	

Example	```<vxml version="2.0">` ` <catch event="noinput nomatch" count="1">` ` <audio>I'm sorry, I didn't catch that. </audio>` ` <reprompt />` ` </catch>```

```
    <catch event="noinput nomatch" count="2">
      <audio>I'm having a hard time understanding.
</audio>
      <reprompt />
    </catch>

    <form id="dob_menu">
        <grammar type="application/x-gsl">
          <![CDATA[
          [
          ( ?(i was born on) Dates:x ) { <dob_slot
$x> }
          ( ?(my ssn is) SSNs:x ) { <ssn_slot $x> }
          ( Dates:x ?(and) SSNs:y ) { <dob_slot $x>
          <ssn_slot $y> }
          ( SSNs:x ?(and) Dates:y ) { <ssn_slot $x>
          <dob_slot $y> }
          ]

          SSNs [
              [(one oh one four four four nine three
eight)]
              {return(101444938)}
          ]
          Dates [
              [(june twentieth nineteen fifty eight)]
              {return(19580620)}
          ]
          ]]>
        </grammar>

        <!-- this grammar defines some "sub-grammars".
These are not actually active at this moment because
they're merely defining labels that can be referenced in
other grammars down the line. The built-in platform
grammars cannot be used as sub-grammars, and the vendor-
independent XML Grammar format for VoiceXML does not yet
support sub-grammars, so the Nuance GSL format is being
used instead. While it's technically possible to build
mixed-initiative forms without sub-grammars, it is more
academic than practical. For brevity and clarity, only
one option is being included in each of these grammars.
In reality, you would build the complete grammars using
the various pattern-matching rules available, store them
in a separate file, and include them here by URL
reference rather than inline. -->

        <!-- this also defines the actual top-level
grammar for the form that references the sub-grammars.
This grammar allows the caller to say either their ssn,
their dob, or both, as well as some surrounding
contextual sentence structure. The directed version of
this example could have also included the contextual
sentence structure, if you were building your own
```

```
grammars and sub-grammars rather than referencing the
basic built-in ones. -->
    <initial name="try_both">

    <!-- the "initial" element is the defining
characteristic of a mixed-initiative form. It usually
prompts the caller for the whole top-level grammar at
once, and then the other fields are only used to "fall
back" on directed conversation if the caller fails to
answer all of the questions (also called grammar
"slots") at once. -->
        <prompt>
          <audio>What is your birth date and Social
                Security Number? </audio>
        </prompt>
        <catch event="nomatch noinput" count="2">
          <!-- this overrides the "count=2" event
                handler. -->
          <audio>sorry, i didn't catch that.</audio>
          <assign name="try_both" expr="true"/>
          <!-- this assigns the "init" form variable to
true, causing the FIA to skip it on the next pass and
fall through to the next field in the form. Each of
these in turn check to see if their "slot" has been
"filled" yet, and if not prompt the caller accordingly.
-->
          <reprompt/>
        </catch>
    </initial>

  <field name="dob" slot="dob_slot">
    <!-- the "slot" attribute associates this field
with a particular slot in the form-level grammar. If the
slot has been filled, it populates the field "name"
variable. As introduced above, when the "name" variable
for a given form element (field, block, or initial) is
non-NULL, then the FIA assumes it's been "filled", skips
over that form element, and continues evaluating the
next one in sequential order. -->

    <grammar src="builtin:grammar/date"/>
    <!-- this URL syntax is equivalent to using the
"type" attribute for the field -->

    <prompt>
        <audio>What is your birth date? Please include
the month, day, and year. </audio>
    </prompt>

    <filled>
      <if cond="dob.indexOf('?')+1">
        <audio>You didn't say the full date.</audio>
        <clear namelist="dob" />
        <!-- the date grammar returns question marks
```

```
            in the missing parts of the date if the caller gives an
            incomplete answer. If so, clear the field's variable
            (part of FIA processing) so they'll be reprompted to try
            again. This is *not* good UI design, but a functional
            example. -->
                <else />
                  <audio>Got your date of birth.</audio>
                </if>
              </filled>
            </field>

            <field name="ssn" slot="ssn_slot">
              <grammar src="builtin:grammar/digits"/>

              <prompt>
                <audio>What is your Social Security Number?
</audio>
              </prompt>

              <filled>
                <audio>Got your s s n.</audio>
              </filled>
            </field>

            <block name="process">
              <audio>In summary, you said that you were born on
                        <value expr="dob.slice(4,6)" />,
                        <value expr="dob.slice(6,8)" />,
                        <value expr="dob.slice(0,2)" />,
                        <value expr="dob.slice(2,4)" />,
                    and your social security number is
                        <value expr="ssn" />
              </audio>
              <submit next="process.jsp" namelist="dob ssn"
/>
            </block>
          </form>
        </vxml>
```

<item>

In XML grammars, defines an expression the caller can say. See Chapter 8 for details regarding XML grammars.

<link>

Syntax
```
<link
  dtmf = "dtmf_sequence"
  event = "event"
  expr = "ECMAScript_Expression"
  fetchaudio = "URI"
  fetchhint = "prefetch | safe | stream"
```

```
      fetchtimeout = "string"
      maxage = "integer"
      maxstale = "integer"
      next = "URI">
      Grammar_definition
   </link>
```

Description	Specifies a grammar and a transition or event to throw when it's matched.
	For more information about links, scoping, and the VoiceXML event model, see Chapter 6.

Attribute	Description	Required/Optional
dtmf	DTMF tone that is considered part of the link's grammar; when entered by the caller, it activates the link.	Optional
event	Event to throw when the caller says or enters something to match the link's grammar. *event, expr,* and *next* are mutually exclusive.	Required
expr	ECMAScript expression that evaluates to a URI to transition to when the caller says or enters something to match the link's grammar. *event, expr,* and *next* are mutually exclusive.	Required
fetchaudio	See "HTTP Semantics" later in this chapter.	Optional
fetchhint	See "HTTP Semantics" later in this chapter.	Optional
fetchtimeout	See "HTTP Semantics" later in this chapter.	Optional
maxage	See "HTTP Semantics" later in this chapter.	Optional
maxstale	See "HTTP Semantics" later in this chapter.	Optional
next	URI to transition to when the caller says or enters something to match the link's grammar. *event, expr,* and *next* are mutually exclusive.	Required

Usage	**Parents**		**Children**
	`<field>`	`<initial>`	`<grammar>`
	`<form>`	`<vxml>`	

Example	`<?xml version="1.0"?>`

```
<?xml version="1.0"?>
<vxml version="2.0">

  <link event="event.myapp.chocolate">
    <grammar type="application/x-gsl">
```

```
                [chocolate]
            </grammar>
        </link>

        <catch event="event.myapp.chocolate">
            <audio>You said chocolate!!! Goodbye.</audio>
            <disconnect />
        </catch>
        <!-- this defines a document-scope link for the word
             "chocolate". In any field in this document, if
             the caller says "chocolate" the event will fire,
             and this document-scope event handler will
             execute, unless a local one overrides it. -->

        <catch event="noinput nomatch">
            <audio>I'm sorry, I didn't catch that. </audio>
            <reprompt />
        </catch>

        <form id="dob_menu">
            <field name="dob" type="date">
                <prompt>
                    <audio>What is your birth date? Please include
                            the month, day, and year. </audio>
                </prompt>

                <filled>
                    <if cond="dob.indexOf('?')+1">
                        <audio>You didn't say the full date.</audio>
                        <clear namelist="dob" />
                    <else />
                        <audio>Great. You said
                                <value expr="dob.slice(4,6)" />,
                                <value expr="dob.slice(6,8)" />,
                                <value expr="dob.slice(0,2)" />,
                                <value expr="dob.slice(2,4)" />.
                        </audio>
                    </if>
                </filled>
            </field>

            <field name="ssn" type="digits">
                <prompt>
                    <audio>What is your Social Security Number?
                    </audio>
                </prompt>

                <filled>
                    <audio>Great. You said <value expr="ssn" />
                    </audio>
                    <submit next="process.jsp" namelist="dob ssn" />
                </filled>
            </field>
        </form>
    </vxml>
```

<log>

Syntax	```<log>```
	    Static text and/or <value> statements
	```</log>```

Description	Outputs debug messages to the platform-specific debug logs. Most VoiceXML platforms provide developers with some way of viewing the debug log output of their applications at runtime. ***Note:*** On some platforms, developers can use a platform-specific ECMAScript *vxmllog(expression)* function to write to the debug logs from within a block of ECMAScript in VoiceXML applications.

Usage	**Parents**		**Children**
	`<block>`	`<help>`	`<value>`
	`<catch>`	`<if>`	
	`<error>`	`<noinput>`	
	`<filled>`	`<nomatch>`	
	`<foreach>`	`<prompt>`	

Example	```<vxml version="2.0">```
	  ```<var name="today" expr="new Date()" />```
	  ```<form>```
	    ```<block>```
	      ```<log>Entering the first block. Current time is```
	               ```<value expr="today" /></log>```
	      ```Hello world```
	    ```</block>```
	  ```</form>```
	```</vxml>```

<menu>

Syntax	```<menu```
	    ``accept = "exact
		approximate"```
		    ```dtmf = "boolean"```
		    ```id = "string"```
		    ``scope = "document
			dialog">```
			    Child_elements
			```</menu>```

Description	Provides a simple dialog for making a selection between fixed choices. For more information about VoiceXML forms, scoping, and the FIA, see Chapter 6.

	Attribute	**Description**	**Required/ Optional**
	accept	States if the caller must say all of the words ("exact") or just a subset ("approximate") of the specified grammar fragment (Default is exact).	Optional

Attribute	Description	Required/Optional
dtmf	Enables DTMF selection for all choices in this menu:	Optional
	True—for child `<choice>` elements that do not explicitly specify a DTMF sequence using *dtmf,* the interpreter assigns DTMF selectors of "1", "2",... to those choices in document order.	
	False—the interpreter does not make implicit DTMF assignments to menu choices with no DTMF sequences (default is false).	
id	Name for the menu, so that `<goto>` and other elements can explicitly transition to it using "#" notation (for example, `<goto next="#top" />`). As with HTML anchors, *id*s must be unique within a given VoiceXML document.	Optional
scope	Sets the default scope of the menu's grammars:	Optional
	Document—the menu's grammars are active throughout the current document.	
	Dialog—the menu's grammars are active throughout the current form (default is dialog).	

Usage	Parents	Children	
	`<vxml>`	`<audio>`	`<noinput>`
		`<catch>`	`<nomatch>`
		`<choice>`	`<prompt>`
		`<enumerate>`	`<property>`
		`<error>`	`<script>`
		`<help>`	`<value>`
			`<var>`

Example

```
<vxml version="2.0">
  <catch event="myapp.menu">
    <audio>Event thrown: <value expr="_event" />
    </audio>
    <!-- generic event handler for purposes of
         this example-->
    <goto next="#top" />
  </catch>

  <menu id="top" dtmf="true">
    <prompt> Welcome home.
      <enumerate> For <value expr="_prompt" />, press
```

```
                            <value expr="_dtmf" />.
            </enumerate>
        </prompt>

        <choice event="myapp.menu.bands">bands</choice>
        <choice event="myapp.menu.fruits">fruits</choice>
        <choice event="myapp.menu.candies">
        candies</choice>
        <choice dtmf="9" event="myapp.menu.special">
        specials</choice>
    </menu>
</vxml>
```

<meta>

Syntax	

	```<meta```
	``` content = "string"```
	``` http-equiv = "string" />```
	``` name = "string"```

Description	
	Specifies arbitrary information to further describe a particular VoiceXML document. Just as with HTML, the `<meta>` element in VoiceXML can be used either to specify developer-defined information or to include "client-side" information that would otherwise be returned by a Web server as part of the HTTP response headers.
	As in the HTML world, particular VoiceXML platforms and/or other services are free to use `<meta>` information to perform specific functions, such as indexing applications' subject matter for a search engine.
	Some VoiceXML platforms programmatically expose any data set using the `<meta>` element via a set of read-only session variables, *session.meta.name,* where *name* is the name used in the respective `<meta>` element. If not set, the value remains undefined. This behavior when provided is an extension to VoiceXML 2.0.

Attribute	Description	Required/ Optional
content	String specifying whatever information the developer chooses to provide about the document for metadata property *name,* or the intended value for the HTTP response header *http-equiv.*	Required
http-equiv	String specifying an HTTP response header, such as *Last-Modified.* *http-equiv* and *name* are mutually exclusive.	Required
name	String specifying a label for this meta data. *http-equiv* and *name* are mutually exclusive.	Required

Usage	Parents	Children
	`<vxml>`	None

Example	

```
<vxml version="2.0">
  <meta name="author" content="John Doe"/>
  <meta name="email" content="john@doe.org" />
  <var name="hi" expr=" 'Hello World!' "/>
  <form>
    <block>
      <value expr="hi"/>
      Author is: <value expr="session.meta.author" />
      Comments to: <value expr="session.meta.email" />
      Keyword is: <valueexpr="session.meta.keyword" />
      <!-- Some VoiceXML platforms programmatically
           expose any data set using the <meta> element
           via a set of read-only session variables,
           session.meta.name, where name is the name
           used in the respective <meta> element. If not
           set, the value remains undefined. -->
      <goto next="#say_goodbye"/>
    </block>
  </form>
  <form id="say_goodbye">
    <block> Goodbye! </block>
  </form>
</vxml>
```

`<noinput>`

Syntax	

```
<noinput
    count = "integer"
    cond = "ECMAScript_Expression">
    Executable_content
</noinput>
```

Description

Shorthand for `<catch event="noinput">`. Catches the platform-defined event for when the caller does not respond when they're expected to say or enter something. The properties *termtimeout* and *timeout* govern how long the interpreter waits for caller input before throwing the *noinput* event.

For more information about the VoiceXML event model, see Chapter 6.

For more information about platform-defined properties and events, see "Platform-Defined Events" and "Platform-Defined Properties" later in this chapter.

Attribute	Description	Required/Optional
count	Number that specifies how many times a `noinput` event must be thrown before the FIA selects this particular handler (default is 1).	Optional

Attribute	Description	Required/ Optional
cond	ECMAScript expression that must also evaluate to true for this handler to catch a given event (Default is true).	Optional

Usage	Parents		Children	
	`<field>`	`<record>`	`<assign>`	`<phoneme>`
	`<form>`	`<subdialog>`	`<audio>`	`<prompt>`
	`<initial>`	`<transfer>`	`<break>`	`<prosody>`
	`<menu>`	`<vxml>`	`<clear>`	`<reprompt>`
	`<object>`		`<disconnect>`	`<return>`
			`<emphasis>`	`<s>`
			`<enumerate>`	`<say-as>`
			`<exit>`	`<script>`
			`<foreach>`	`<sentence>`
			`<goto>`	`<submit>`
			`<if>`	`<throw>`
			`<log>`	`<value>`
			`<p>`	`<var>`
			`<paragraph>`	`<voice>`

Example

```
<vxml version="2.0">
  <property name="universals" value="all" />
  <!-- this sets the universals property, enabling
       a global grammar for "help" -->
  <form id="launch_missiles">
    <field name="password">
        <grammar type="application/grammar+xml">
          <rule id="password" scope="public">
            <item tag="rutabaga">rutabage</item>
          </rule>
        </grammar>
        <prompt>What is the code word?</prompt>
        <help>It is the name of an obscure
            vegetable.
            <reprompt/>
        </help>
        <noinput count="3">
            Security violation!
            <exit />
        </noinput>
        <nomatch count="3">
            Security violation!
            <exit />
        </nomatch>
        <!-- these noinput and nomatch handlers are
            only activated on the third try. Before
            that, the platform-defined defaults are
            used. -->
        <filled>
        <audio>You got it!</audio>
```

```
                    <clear />
                </filled>
            </field>
        </form>
    </vxml>
```

<nomatch>

Syntax	<pre><nomatch
	    count = "integer"
	    cond = "ECMAScript_Expression">
	    Executable_content
	</nomatch></pre>

Description	Shorthand for `<catch event="nomatch">`. Catches the platform-defined event for when the caller responds with something that's not in any of the active grammars. Several properties (for example, *termtimeout, interdigittimeout,* etc.) govern exactly how the interpreter decides when to throw the *nomatch* event. For more information about the VoiceXML event model, see Chapter 6. For more information about platform-defined properties and events, see "Platform-Defined Events" and "Platform-Defined Properties" later in this chapter.

Attribute	Description	Required/Optional
count	Number that specifies how many times a noinput event must be thrown before the FIA selects this particular handler (default is 1).	Optional
cond	ECMAScript expression that must also evaluate to true for this handler to catch a given event (default is true).	Optional

Usage	**Parents**		**Children**	
	<field>	<record>	<assign>	<phoneme>
	<form>	<subdialog>	<audio>	<prompt>
	<initial>	<transfer>	<break>	<prosody>
	<menu>	<vxml>	<clear>	<reprompt>
	<object>		<disconnect>	<return>
			<emphasis>	<s>
			<enumerate>	<say-as>
			<exit>	<script>
			<foreach>	<sentence>
			<goto>	<submit>
			<if>	<throw>
			<log>	<value>
			<p>	<var>
			<paragraph>	<voice>

Example

```
<vxml version="2.0">
    <property name="universals" value="all" />
    <!-- this sets the universals property, enabling
         a global grammar for "help" -->
    <form id="launch_missiles">
        <field name="password">
            <grammar type="application/grammar+xml">
              <rule id="password" scope="public">
                <item tag="rutabaga">rutabage</item>
              </rule>
            </grammar>
            <prompt>What is the code word?</prompt>
            <help>It is the name of an obscure
                  vegetable.
                  <reprompt/>
            </help>
            <noinput count="3">
                Security violation!
                <exit />
            </noinput>
            <nomatch count="3">
                Security violation!
                <exit />
            </nomatch>

            <!-- these noinput and nomatch handlers are
                 only activated on the third try. Before
                 that, the platform-defined defaults are
                 used. -->

            <filled>
              <audio>You got it!</audio>
              <clear />
            </filled>
        </field>
    </form>
</vxml>
```

<object>

Syntax

```
<object
    archive = "URI1 URI2 ... URIn"
    classid = "URI"
    codebase = "URI"
    codetype = "MIME_type"
    cond = "ECMAScript_Expression"
    data = "URI"
    expr = "ECMAScript_Expression"
    fetchhint = "prefetch | safe | stream"
    fetchtimeout = "string"
    maxage = "integer"
```

```
        maxstale = "integer"
        name = "ECMAScript_Variable"
        type = "MIME_type">
        Child_elements
    </object>
```

Description   Executes a platform-specific extended object. The `<object>`
element provides a mechanism for platforms to offer runtime
support for external platform-specific objects within VoiceXML
applications, similar to Microsoft ActiveX controls and Netscape
Plug-ins in the HTML world.

As with `<subdialog>`, the `<param>` element can be used to pass
data to the object. Upon returning, the form item variable defined by
name contains a platform- and object-specific ECMAScript object.
Typically, this object will contain status information and/or any data
collected from the caller while the object was being invoked.

VoiceXML platforms are not required to support any platform-
specific objects, but must throw *error.unsupported.object* if an
application attempts to reference a non-supported object.

Attribute	Description	Required/ Optional
archive	Space-separated list of URIs specifying archives that resources required by the object, potentially including the resources specified by *classid* and *data.* If a relative URI is specified, *codebase* is prepended to it before evaluating.	Optional
classid	URI specifying the location of the object's implementation. URI conventions are platform-specific. If a relative URI is specified, *codebase* is prepended to it before evaluating.	Optional
codebase	Base path to use when resolving relative URIs specified in *archive, classid,* and *data.*	Optional
codetype	MIME-type to expect when retrieving the object via *classid.* If not specified, *type* is assumed.	Optional
cond	ECMAScript expression that must also evaluate to true for the FIA to select this form element (default is true).	Optional
data	URI specifying the location of the object's data. URI conventions are platform-specific. If a relative URI is specified, *codebase* is prepended to it before evaluating.	Optional

Attribute	Description	Required/Optional
expr	ECMAScript expression that, if specified, is evaluated and provides an initial value for the object's form item variable *name* (default is undefined). If a value is provided, then the form item will not be visited until/unless it is first cleared.	Optional
fetchhint	See "HTTP Semantics" later in this chapter.	Optional
fetchtimeout	See "HTTP Semantics" later in this chapter.	Optional
maxage	See "HTTP Semantics" later in this chapter.	Optional
maxstale	See "HTTP Semantics" later in this chapter.	Optional
name	Valid ECMAScript variable name that declares the form item variable for this object. Upon returning, this will contain a platform- and object-specific ECMAScript object.	Optional
type	MIME-type of the data specified by *data*.	Optional

Usage	Parents		Children	
	`<form>`		`<audio>`	`<noinput>`
			`<catch>`	`<nomatch>`
			`<enumerate>`	`<param>`
			`<error>`	`<prompt>`
			`<filled>`	`<property>`
			`<help>`	`<value>`

Example

```
<vxml version="2.0">
<form>
  <object name="authenticate"
          classid="method://authenticate"
      data="http://www.myplatform.com/prompts/
      authenticate/data.jar">
      <param name="entry" expr=" 'home' "/>
      <param name="date" expr="new Date()"/>
  </object>
  <block>
    <value expr="authenticate.status" />
    <exit />
  </block>
</form>
</vxml>
```

`<one-of>`

In XML grammars, specifies a set of rule alternatives. See Chapter 8 for details regarding XML grammars.

`<option>`

Syntax	```<option```
	        ```dtmf = "dtmf_sequence"```
	        ```value = "string">```
	        ```Grammar_fragment```
	```</option>```

Description	Specifies a simple available choice and grammar within a field. Similar to how `<choice>` works within the even simpler `<menu>` construct, `<option>` makes it possible to quickly provide a list of simple alternatives within a `<field>`. As with `<choice>`, `<enumerate>` can be used to iterate through the list of available choices for the caller.

Attribute	Description	Required/ Optional
dtmf	DTMF sequence that the caller can enter to select this option.	Optional
value	String to assign to the field's field item variable if the caller selects this option. If not specified, *dtmf* is returned.	Optional

Usage	**Parents**	**Children**
	`<field>`	None

Example

```
<vxml version="2.0">
    <form id="pick_flavor">
        <field name="flavor">
        <prompt>
        Choose one of the seven following flavors
        <!-- list the options -->
        <enumerate/>
        </prompt>
          <option> strawberry </option>
          <option> apple </option>
          <option> pear </option>
          <option> grape </option>
          <option> lemon </option>
          <option> chocolate </option>
          <option> caramel</option>
          <option dtmf="9"value="backdoor">secret
          secret</option>
          <filled>
             <audio>i like <value expr="flavor"/>, too.
                by the way, what you actually said
                   was:
```

```
                              <value expr="flavor$.utterance"/></audio>
                       <exit />
                   </filled>
                 </field>
              </form>
           </vxml>
```

\<p\>

Syntax	`<p`
	`    xml:lang = "language_locale">`
	`  TTS_Text`
	`</p>`

Description	In TTS, encloses a paragraph of text. This may assist the speech synthesizer in determining the prosody and normalization of the text.

Attribute	Description	Required/Optional
xml:lang	Specifies the language and locale identifier of the contained or referenced grammar according to RFC 1766.[2] (for example, "fr-CA" for Canadian French). If omitted, the value is inherited down from the document hierarchy, and ultimately a VoiceXML interpreter default.	Optional

Usage	Parents		Children
	`<audio>`	`<help>`	`<audio>`
	`<block>`	`<if>`	`<break>`
	`<catch>`	`<noinput>`	`<emphasis>`
	`<choice>`	`<nomatch>`	`<enumerate>`
	`<error>`	`<prompt>`	`<phoneme>`
	`<enumerate>`	`<prosody>`	`<prosody>`
	`<filled>`	`<voice>`	`<s>`
	`<foreach>`		`<say-as>`
			`<sentence>`
			`<value>`
			`<voice>`

Example	`<p> Today is going to be sunny </p>`

\<paragraph\>

Syntax	`<paragraph`
	`    xml:lang = "language_locale">`
	`  TTS_Text`
	`</paragraph>`

---

[2]See www.nordu.net/ftp/rfc/rfc1766.txt

Description		Shorthand for `<paragraph>`. In TTS, marks a container for zero more sentences.

Attribute	Description	Required/Optional
xml:lang	Specifies the language and locale identifier of the contained or grammar according to RFC 1766.[3] (for example, "fr-CA" for Canadian French). If omitted, the value is inherited down from the document hierarchy, and ultimately a VoiceXMLinterpreter default.	Optional

Usage	**Parents**		**Children**
	`<audio>`	`<help>`	`<audio>`
	`<block>`	`<if>`	`<break>`
	`<catch>`	`<noinput>`	`<emphasis>`
	`<choice>`	`<nomatch>`	`<enumerate>`
	`<error>`	`<prompt>`	`<phoneme>`
	`<enumerate>`	`<prosody>`	`<prosody>`
	`<filled>`	`<voice>`	`<s>`
	`<foreach>`		`<say-as>`
			`<sentence>`
			`<value>`
			`<voice>`

Example	`<paragraph>` Today is going to be sunny. `</paragraph>`

`<param>`

| **Syntax** | ```<param
    expr = "ECMAScript_Expression"
    name = "ECMAScript_Variable"
    type = "MIME_type"
    value = "string"
valuetype = "data	ref" />```
Description	Submits data to a `<subdialog>` or `<object>`, without the need for server-side scripting. For a `<subdialog>`, all data passed via `<param>` becomes available as a series of variables in the new interpreter context. These variables must be explicitly declared in the document invoked by the `<subdialog>`, at which point they are initialized with the values passed in from the invoking dialog via `<param>`. Any *expr* attribute on the declaring `<var>` elements are ignored.

Attribute	Description	Required/Optional
expr	ECMAScript expression that is used as the value for this parameter. *expr* and *value* are mutually exclusive.	Required

[3]See www.nordu.net/ftp/rfc/rfc1766.txt

Attribute	Description	Required/ Optional
name	Legal ECMAScript variable name to label this parameter. When used with `<subdialog>`, each `<param>` generates a corresponding variable for its *name* in the new application context.	Required
type	Only relevant for use with `<object>`, MIME-type of the URI specified by *expr* or *value* if *valuetype* is set to "ref".	Optional
value	Value that is used for this parameter. *expr* and *value* are mutually exclusive.	Required
valuetype	Only relevant for use with `<object>`, specifies whether the value specified by *value* or *expr* is a URI ("ref") or any other data ("data").	Optional

Usage	Parents		Children
	`<object>`	`<subdialog>`	None

Example

```
<!-- main.vxml: this document collects the caller's
     name, and then invokes a subdialog to collect more
     info -->
<vxml version="2.0">
  <form id="do_subd">
    <var name="fname" expr=" 'Jeff' " />
    <!-- setting a variable directly rather than
         collecting from the user, just to keep this
         example short. -->

    <subdialog name="getmore" src="#form_getmore">
    <!-- invoking the subdialog in the
         same document -->
      <param name="the_name" expr="fname" />
      <filled>
        <audio><value expr="getmore.dob +
                            getmore.the_name" />
        </audio>
        <submit next="http://myserver/process.jsp"
                namelist="getmore.dob getmore.the_name" />
      </filled>
    </subdialog>
  </form>

  <form id="form_getmore">
  <var name="the_name" />
  <block>
    <!-- Each variable passed using the param element
         needs to be declared by name within the
         subdialog. At runtime, it will be initialized
```

```
                              with the value passed in (if any) via the
                              param element -->
                  <var name="dob" expr=" '19680829' " />
                  <audio>Hi <value expr="the_name" />,
                          it's nice to meet you</audio>
                  <!-- the first name was filled in using the
                          variable passed in to the subdialog -->
                  <audio>I would ask you for more info, but for now
                          I'm going to pretend.</audio>
                  <return namelist="dob the_name" />
              </block>
          </form>
      </vxml>
```

<phoneme>

Syntax	
	```<phoneme```
	`` alphabet = "ipa	worldbet	xsampa"```
	``` ph = "string" />```

Description	In TTS, specifies exact pronunciation using a phonetic alphabet.

Attribute	Description	Required/ Optional
alphabet	Phonetic alphabet to use to interpret *ph.* Either:	Required
	"ipa"—the International Phonetic Alphabet (IPA)[4]	
	"worldbet"—the Worldbet[5] phonetic alphabet	
	"xsampa"—the X-SAMPA[6] phonetic alphabet	
ph	String to interpret using *alphabet* and play to the caller as TTS.	Required

Usage	Parents		Children
	```<audio>```	```<prompt>```	None
	```<choice>```	```<prosody>```	
	```<emphasis>```	```<s>```	
	```<enumerate>```	```<sentence>```	
	```<p>```	```<voice>```	
	```<paragraph>```		

Example	
	```<prompt>```
	``` Please say```
	``` <phoneme alphabet="ipa">```
	``` ph="tɒmɑtoʊ">```

[4]See www.arts.gla.ac.uk/IPA/ipachart.html

[5]See http://cslu.cse.ogi.edu/publications/ps/hieronymus_att_worldbet.ps.gz

[6]See www.phon.ucl.ac.uk/home/sampa/x-sampa.htm

```
            tomato
      </phoneme>
   </prompt>
```

<prompt>

Syntax	```<prompt
bargein = "true	false"
bargeintype = "energy	speech	recognition"
cond = "ECMAScript_Expression"
count = "integer"
timeout = "string"
xml:lang = "language_locale"
Child_elements
</prompt>```
Description	Queues audio files and/or TTS to play as part of conversational dialogue. For more information about VoiceXML dialogs and the FIA, see Chapter 6.

Attribute	Description	Required/ Optional
bargein	Boolean specifying whether or not the caller can interrupt (for example, "barge in on") the prompt (default is true).	Optional
bargeintype	Specifies whether the recognition engine should use the "energy," "speech," or "recognition" method to determine whether bargein has taken place (default is platform-specific).	Optional
cond	ECMAScript expression that must also evaluate to true for this prompt to be spoken (default is true).	Optional
count	Number that specifies how many times the caller must have visited the form item containing this prompt before the FIA selects this particular prompt (default is 1).	Optional
timeout	Time to wait in seconds (s) or milliseconds (ms) before throwing a noinput event. If multiple prompt elements specify timeout, the most recent one is used (default is platform-specific).	Optional

[7]See www.nordu.net/ftp/rfc/rfc1766.txt

Attribute	Description	Required/Optional
xml:lang	Specifies the language and locale identifier of the contained or referenced grammar according to RFC 1766.[7] (for example, "fr-CA" for Canadian French).	Optional
	If omitted, the value is inherited down from the document hierarchy, and ultimately a VoiceXML interpreter default.	

Usage	Parents		Children	
	<block>	<menu>	<assign>	<phoneme>
	<catch>	<noinput>	<audio>	<prompt>
	<error>	<nomatch>	<break>	<prosody>
	<field>	<object>	<clear>	<reprompt>
	<filled>	<record>	<data>	<return>
	<help>	<subdialog>	<disconnect>	<s>
	<if>	<transfer>	<emphasis>	<say-as>
	<initial>		<enumerate>	<script>
			<exit>	<sentence>
			<foreach>	<submit>
			<goto>	<throw>
			<if>	<value>
			<log>	<var>
			<p>	<voice>
			<paragraph>	

Example

```
<vxml version="2.0">
<form>
  <field name="want_ice_cream" type="boolean">
     <prompt> time out="4s" Do you want ice cream for
     dessert?</prompt>
     <prompt count="2"> If you want ice cream, say yes.
     If you don't want ice cream, say no. </prompt>
     <noinput> I could not hear you.
          <reprompt/>
     </noinput>
   <filled>
     <audio>thanks</audio>
     <exit />
   </filled>
   </field>
</form>
</vxml>
```

`<property>`

Syntax	```<property```
	    `name = "string"`
	    `value = "string"`
	`</property>`

Description	Specifies a platform-defined behavior setting. Properties impact the specific behavior of the voice recognition process and other platform characteristics. Property settings follow standard VoiceXML scoping rules (for example, local settings with a `<field>` override settings from the parent `<form>`, et al.) VoiceXML platforms are required to support a set of platform-defined properties. In addition, platforms are encouraged to expose additional, platform-specific properties to further enrich their development environment. To maximize cross-platform compatibility, platform vendors are strongly encouraged (but not strictly required) to name any extended properties using "reverse domain name" syntax (for example, "com.acme.recognizer.phoneticpruning") and to ignore any unrecognized properties rather than throwing *error.unsupported*. For a complete list of platform-defined VoiceXML properties, see "Platform-Defined Properties" later in this chapter. For more information about the VoiceXML event model, see Chapter 6. (Some VoiceXML platforms extend the `<property>` element, allowing developers to specify an *expr* ECMAScript expression that evaluates to a value for *value*.

Attribute	Description	Required/ Optional
name	Property name. See "Platform-Defined Properties" later in this chapter for a complete list of platform-defined VoiceXML properties.	Required
value	Property value. See "Platform-Defined Properties" later in this chapter for a complete list of platform-defined VoiceXML properties. (***Note:*** Some VoiceXML platforms extend the `<property>` element, allowing developers to specify an *expr* attribute on `<property>` as a programmatic way of computing *value*.)	Required

Usage	Parents		Children
	`<field>`	`<record>`	None
	`<form>`	`<subdialog>`	
	`<initial>`	`<transfer>`	
	`<menu>`	`<vxml>`	
	`<object>`		

Example

```
<vxml version="2.0">
  <property name="bargein" value="true"/>
  <!-- allow bargein on all fields -->
  <property name="confidence" value="0.75"/>
  <!-- throw <nomatch> on all recognitions unless the
       recognizer is 75% confident that the caller said
       something matching a grammar -->
  <property name="universals" value="all"/>
  <!-- enable all platform-defined grammars and links
       such as "help". -->
  <!-- all of these property settings have document
       scope, so they're active by default throughout
       the document. If this were an application root
       document referenced by other documents, then
       these settings would have application scope
       across all documents. -->
  <help>
    The caller just requested help. It's too bad that we
    don't have anything useful to say. <reprompt />
  </help>
  <catch event="noinput nomatch">
    I'm sorry, but I didn't get that.
    <reprompt />
  </catch>
  <form>
    <field name="q1" type="boolean">
      <prompt>
        This is question one.
        I'm going to ask a long question,
        so that we can test whether bargein
        is in effect. Do you like
        ice cream?
      </prompt>
      <filled>
        I am <value expr="q1$.confidence * 100" />
        percent confident that I heard you say: <value
        expr="q1$.utterance" />.
      </filled>
    </field>
    <field name="q2" type="digits">
      <property name="bargein" value="false"/>
      <!-- now, within this field only, disable
           bargein -->
      <property name="confidence" value="0.25"/>
      <!-- lower the confidence level required to
      achieve a match. -->
      <property name="universals" value="none"/>
      <!-- disable universales like "help" -->
      <prompt>
        This is question two.
        I'm going to ask a long question,
```

```
                    so that we can test whether bargein
                    is in effect. What is your social
                    security number?
                </prompt>
                <filled>
                    I am <value expr="q2$.confidence * 100" />
                    percent confident that I heard you say: <value
                    expr="q2$.utterance" />.
                </filled>
            </field>
        </form>
    </vxml>
```

`<pros>`

Syntax	`<pros` ` rate = "fast	medium	slow	default"` ` vol = "silent	soft	medium	loud	default"` ` pitch = "high	medium	low	default"` ` range = "high	medium	low	default">` ` TTS_Text` `</pros>`
Description	VoiceXML 1.0 only. In TTS, sets the prosody (inflection) of a piece of text.

Attribute	Description	Required/Optional
rate	String indicating the speed at which the enclosed TTS text is spoken.	Optional
vol	String indicating the relative volume at which the enclosed TTS text is spoken.	Optional
pitch	String indicating the relative pitch (frequency) at which the enclosed TTS text is spoken.	Optional
range	String indicating the relative variance in pitch (frequency) to use when the enclosed TTS text is spoken.	Optional

Usage	**Parents**		**Children**	
	`<audio>`	`<enumerate>`	`<audio>`	`<enumerate>`
	`<block>`	`<filled>`	`<break>`	`<p>`
	`<catch>`	`<help>`	`<div>`	`<paragraph>`
	`<choice>`	`<if>`	`<emp>`	`<pros>`
	`<error>`	`<noinput>`		`<sayas>`
	`<div>`	`<nomatch>`		`<value>`
	`<emp>`	`<prompt>`		
		`<pros>`		

| **Example** | ```
<prompt>
    Please listen carefully, the password is
    <pros rate="slow" volume="medium">
        transport
    </pros>
</prompt>
``` |

`<prosody>`

| **Syntax** | ```
<prosody
    contour = "float"
    duration = "string"
    rate = "fast | medium | slow | default"
    vol = "silent | soft | medium | loud | default"
    pitch = "high | medium | low | default"
    range = "high | medium | low | default">
    TTS_Text
</prosody>
``` |
| **Description** | In TTS, sets prosody (inflection) of a piece of text (VoiceXML 2.0 only.) |

Attribute	Description	Required/ Optional
contour	Float indicating the contour level at which the enclosed TTS text is spoken.	Optional
duration	String indicating the desired duration in seconds (s) or milliseconds (ms) to speak the enclosed TTS text (for example, "7s," "2000ms").	Optional
pitch	String indicating the relative pitch (frequency) at which the enclosed TTS text is spoken.	Optional
range	String indicating the relative variance in pitch (frequency) to use when the enclosed TTS text is spoken.	Optional|
rate	String indicating the speed at which the enclosed TTS text is spoken.	Optional
volume	String indicating the relative volume at which the enclosed TTS text is spoken.	Optional

Usage	**Parents**		**Children**	
	`<audio>`	`<if>`	`<audio>`	`<phoneme>`
	`<block>`	`<noinput>`	`<break>`	`<prosody>`
	`<catch>`	`<nomatch>`	`<emphasis>`	`<s>`
	`<choice>`	`<p>`	`<enumerate>`	`<say-as>`
	`<emphasis>`	`<paragraph>`	`<p>`	`<sentence>`
	`<enumerate>`	`<prompt>`	`<paragraph>`	`<value>`
	`<error>`	`<prosody>`		`<voice>`

Usage	Parents	Children
	`<filled>`	`<s>`
	`<foreach>`	`<sentence>`
	`<help>`	`<voice>`

Example	
	`<prompt>`
	`  Please listen carefully, the password is`
	`  <prosody rate="slow" volume="medium">`
	`    transport`
	`  </prosody>`
	`</prompt>`

`<record>`

Syntax	
	`<record`
	` beep = "true	false"`
	`    cond = "ECMAScript_Expression"`
	`    dest = "URI"`
	` dtmfterm = "true	false"`
	`    expr = "ECMAScript_Expression"`
	`    finalsilence = "string"`
	`    maxtime = "string"`
	` modal = "true	false"`
	`    name = "ECMAScript_Variable"`
	`    type = "MIME_type" >`
	`  Child_elements`
	`</record>`

Description

Records audio from the caller. As a form item like `<field>`, the `<record>` element can include prompts, event handlers, and a `<filled>` item for handling a successful recording. If the caller never begins to speak and remains silent for *finalsilence,* then the interpreter throws *noinput.*

Once a successful recording has been made, the `<filled>` element contained within it is executed. Within the `<filled>` element, several platform-defined "shadow variables" are available within the local scope to inspect the recording.

Recordings can be played back to the user and/or POSTed back to a Web server for additional processing and storage. Use the *expr* attribute on `<audio>` to play the recording back to the caller, and the *namelist* attribute of `<submit>`, `<subdialog>`, or `<data>` to POST it to a Web server. When submitting recorded audio, set *method* to "post" and *enctype* to "multipart/form-data".

If the platform supports simultaneous recognition and recording and *modal* is set to false, then a local grammar may be used for termination of the recording. As with fields, the "terminating" speech input is accessible via the *name$.utterance* shadow variable and its confidence via the *name$.confidence.*

Attribute	Description	Required/Optional
beep	If "true," play a recognizable tone to signal the caller that recording is about to begin (default is "false").	Optional
cond	ECMAScript expression that must also evaluate to true for the FIA to select this form item (default is true).	Optional
dest	URI for the destination of the recording, for platforms that may support storage of recording to streaming media or messaging servers. If the recording destination cannot be accessed for audio playback and/or HTTP POST submit, *error. semantic* is thrown when the recording form item variable is referenced. Platforms are not required to support *dest*.	Optional
dtmfterm	If "true," recording is terminated when the caller presses any DTMF (touch-tone) key. Otherwise, DTMF input is ignored and just considered part of the recording. If true, the *name$.termchar* shadow variable contains which key was pressed first (default is "false").	Optional
expr	ECMAScript expression that, if specified, is evaluated and provides an initial value for the record's form item variable *name* (default is undefined). If a value is provided, then the form item will not be visited until/unless it is first cleared.	Optional
finalsilence	Time in seconds (s) or milliseconds (ms) of silence before the recognizer stops recording (for example, "5s", "3200ms") (default is platform-specific). If the caller never begins to speak and remains silent for *finalsilence,* then the interpreter throws *noinput.*	Optional
maxtime	Maximum time allowed for recording in seconds (s) or milliseconds (ms) (default is platform-specific). For security and performance, most platforms will enforce a platform-specific maximum for *maxtime,* as well.	Optional

Attribute	Description	Required/Optional
modal	If "true," disable all active grammars while recording. If "false," leave them active and enable recognition during recording.	Optional
	VoiceXML platforms are not required to support "false" (simultaneous recognition and recording) (default is "true").	
name	Valid ECMAScript variable name that declares the form item variable for this record. A successful recording will store the result in *name* before executing the record's `<filled>` element.	Optional
type	MIME type to use for encoding the recorded data (for example, "audio/wav"). Please see `<audio>` earlier for more information on supported audio formats.	Optional
	If an unsupported format is specified, the interpreter throws *error. unsupported.format* (default is platform-specific).	

Shadow Variable	Description
name$.dest	If *dest* was specified, the URI referencing the recording (for example, if the destination redirects the original request, this variable holds the redirected URI).
name$.duration	Duration of the recording, in milliseconds.
name$.maxtime	Boolean, set to true if the recording was cut off because *maxtime* was reached.
name$.size	Size of the recording, in bytes.
name$.termchar	If *dtmfterm* was true and the caller terminated the recording by pressing a DTMF key, then this is set to the specific key that was pressed (for example, "9", "#"). Otherwise, it is null.

Usage	Parents	Children	
	`<form>`	`<audio>`	`<help>`
		`<catch>`	`<noinput>`
		`<enumerate>`	`<nomatch>`
		`<error>`	`<prompt>`
		`<filled>`	`<property>`
		`<grammar>`	`<value>`

Example	
| | ```
<vxml version="2.0">
    <form>
        <record name="greeting" beep="true"
        maxtime="10s" finalsilence="4000ms"
        dtmfterm="true" type="audio/wav">
            <prompt> At the tone, please say your
            greeting. </prompt>
            <noinput> I didn't hear anything, please
            try again. </noinput>
        </record>
        <field name="confirm" type="boolean">
            <prompt> Your greeting is
                <audio expr="greeting"/>.
            </prompt>
            <prompt> To keep it, say yes. To discard
            it, say no. </prompt>
            <filled>
                <if cond="confirm">
                    <submit next="save_greeting.pl"
                    method="post" namelist=
                    "greeting"/>
                </if>
                <clear/>
            </filled>
        </field>
    </form>
</vxml>
``` |

`<reprompt>`

Syntax	`<reprompt/>`
Description	Requeues the most recent `<prompt>` before listening again for the caller to speak.
	Within an event handler such as *noinput, nomatch,* or *help,* `<reprompt>` increases the prompt counter by 1 and reenters the FIA for the current form item.
	It's important to note that the reprompt element has no effect within a filled element because the field item variable has already been filled and the FIA will not reselect it. To reenter the dialog and get prompts requeued after the form item has been filled, `<clear>` the form item variable.
	For more information about the VoiceXML FIA, see Chapter 6.
```

Usage	Parents		Children
	`<block>`	`<help>`	None
	`<catch>`	`<if>`	
	`<error>`	`<noinput>`	
	`<filled>`	`<nomatch>`	
	`<foreach>`	`<prompt>`	

Example	

```
<vxml version="2.0">
  <property name="universals" value="all" />
  <!-- this sets the universals property, enabling
       a global grammar for "help" -->
  <form id="launch_missiles">
    <field name="password">
        <grammar type="application/grammar+xml">
          <rule id="password" scope="public">
            <item tag="rutabaga">rutabage</item>
          </rule>
        </grammar>
        <prompt>What is the code word?</prompt>
        <prompt count="2">I SAID: What is the
                          code word?</prompt>
        <!-- this second prompt will be selected
             after each <reprompt> -->
        <help>It is the name of an obscure
              vegetable.
                <reprompt/>
        </help>
        <noinput count="3">
            Security violation!
            <exit />
        </noinput>
        <nomatch count="3">
            Security violation!
            <exit />
        </nomatch>
        <!-- these noinput and nomatch handlers are
             only activated on the third try. Before
             that, the platform-defined defaults are
             used. -->
        <filled>
          <audio>You got it!</audio>
          <clear />
        </filled>
    </field>
  </form>
</vxml>
```

`<return>`

Syntax	```<return
	    event = "event"
	    namelist = "var1 var2 ... varn"
	</return>```

Description	Ends a `<subdialog>` and returns control to the calling application. `<return>` can specify either an event to throw (which it throws at the scope of the invoking subdialog and can be handled there locally or by inherited handlers from parent scopes) or a list of variables to return and "fill" the subdialog's form item variable. *event* and *namelist* are mutually exclusive, but neither is required.

Attribute	Description	Required/Optional
event	Event to throw when the `<subdialog>` returns control to the calling application. *event* and *namelist* are mutually exclusive.	Optional
namelist	Space-delimited list of variables to return when the `<subdialog>` returns to the calling application. The original subdialog's `<filled>` element is executed, and all variables are returned as properties of an ECMAScript object that is assigned to the subdialog's *name* form item variable. *event* and *namelist* are mutually exclusive.	Optional

Usage	**Parents**		**Children**
	`<block>`	`<help>`	None
	`<catch>`	`<if>`	
	`<error>`	`<noinput>`	
	`<filled>`	`<nomatch>`	

Example	```<!-- main.vxml: this document collects the caller's
	    name, and then invokes a subdialog to collect more
	    info -->
	<vxml version="2.0">
	  <form id="do_subd">
	    <var name="fname" expr=" 'Jeff' " />
	    <!-- setting a variable directly rather than
	        collecting from the user, just to keep this
	        example short. -->
	
	    <subdialog name="getmore" src="#form_getmore">
	    <!-- invoking the subdialog in the
	        same document -->
	      <param name="the_name" expr="fname" />```

```
                    <filled>
                      <audio>The subdialog returned:
                              <value expr="getmore.dob +
                                          getmore.the_name" />
                      </audio>
                      <exit />
                    </filled>
                    <catch event="event.myapp.flag">
                      <audio>The event got fired instead.</audio>
                      <exit />
                    </catch>
                    <!-- this event handler will get invoked instead
                           of the <filled> element if the subdialog
                           returns with "event" instead of "namelist"
                      -->
                  </subdialog>
                </form>

              <form id="form_getmore">
                <var name="the_name" />
                <block>
                    <!-- Each variable passed using the param element
                           needs to be declared by name within the
                           subdialog. At runtime, it will be initialized
                           with the value passed in (if any) via the
                           param element -->
                    <var name="dob" expr=" '19680829' " />
                    <audio>Hi <value expr="the_name" />,
                           it's nice to meet you</audio>
                    <!-- the first name was filled in using
                            the variable passed in to the subdialog
                      -->
                    <audio>I would ask you for more info, but
                             for now I'm going to pretend.</audio>
                    <if cond="Math.random() &gt; .4"> <!-- random # -->
                      <return namelist="dob the_name" />
                    <else />
                      <return event="event.myapp.flag" />
                    </if>
                    <!-- this demonstrates using <return> both with
                            "event" and "namelist" as ways to return
                            information back to the invoking dialog. -->
                  </block>
                </form>
              </vxml>
```

<rule>

In XML grammars, defines a grammar rule. See Chapter 8 for details regarding XML grammars.

<ruleref>

In XML grammars, references an existing `<rule>`. See Chapter 8 for details regarding XML grammars.

<s>

Syntax	`<s`
	`    xml:lang = "language_locale">`
	`  TTS_Text`
	`</s>`		

Description	Shorthand for `<sentence>`. In TTS, marks a container for a sentence. This may assist the speech synthesizer in determining the prosody and normalization of the text.		

	Attribute	Description	Required/ Optional
	xml:lang	Specifies the language and locale identifier of the contained or referenced grammar according to RFC 1766.[8] (for example, "fr-CA" for Canadian French) If omitted, the value is inherited down from the document hierarchy, and ultimately a VoiceXML interpreter default.	Optional

Usage	Parents		Children
	`<audio>`	`<help>`	`<audio>`
	`<block>`	`<if>`	`<break>`
	`<catch>`	`<noinput>`	`<emphasis>`
	`<choice>`	`<nomatch>`	`<enumerate>`
	`<error>`	`<prompt>`	`<phoneme>`
	`<enumerate>`	`<prosody>`	`<prosody>`
	`<filled>`	`<voice>`	`<s>`
	`<foreach>`		`<say-as>`
			`<sentence>`
			`<value>`
			`<voice>`

Example	`<s> Tomorrow is election day </s>`

<say-as>

Syntax	`<say-as` `    sub = "string"` ` type = "acronym	address	currency	date |` ` date:d	date:dmy	date:m	date:md |`

---

[8]See www.nordu.net/ftp/rfc/rfc1766.txt

```
                            date:mdy | date:my | date:y | date:ym |
                            date:ymd | duration | duration:h |
                            duration:hm | duration:hms | duration:m |
                            duration:ms | duration:s |
                            measure | name | net | number |
                            number:digits | number:ordinal |
                            telephone | time | time:h | time:hm |
                            time:hms">
                    TTS_Text
                </say-as>
```

Description	In TTS, provides a template for saying particular kinds of text (for example, dates). This may assist the speech synthesizer in determining the prosody and normalization of the text.

Attribute	Description	Required/ Optional
sub	Substitute text to be spoken instead of the contained text.	Optional
type	One of several platform-defined labels that identify what kind of data the contained TTS text is, so that the TTS engine can best interpret how to pronounce the text (for example, "duration:hm" signifies that the contained text is an elapsed time formatted as hour followed by minutes).	Required

Usage	Parents		Children
	<audio>	<prompt>	None
	<block>	<prosody>	
	<catch>	<s>	
	<choice>	<sentence>	
	<emphasis>	<voice>	
	<enumerate>	<if>	
	<error>	<noinput>	
	<filled>	<nomatch>	
	<foreach>	<p>	
	<help>	<paragraph>	

Example	`<prompt>You are calling`
	`    <say-as class="phone">312-555-1212</say-as>`
	`</prompt>`

<sayas>

Syntax	`<sayas` `    sub = "string"` ` class = "phone	date	digits	literal |` `currency	number" phon = "string">` ` TTS_Text` `<sayas>`

Description	VoiceXML 1.0 only.	

In TTS, provides a template for saying particular kinds of text (for example, dates). This may assist the speech synthesizer in determining the prosody and normalization of the text.

Attribute	Description	Required/Optional
sub	Substitute text to be spoken instead of enclosed text	Optional
class	Speak enclosed text in a given style: phone date digits literal currency number	Optional
phon	Representation of the Unicode international phonetic alphabet (IPA) characters to be spoken instead of the enclosed text	Optional

Usage	**Parents**		**Children**
	`<audio>`	`<enumerate>`	None
	`<choice>`	`<prompt>`	
	`<div>`	`<pros>`	
	`<emp>`		

Example

```
<prompt>You are calling
    <sayas class="phone">312-555-1212</sayas>
</prompt>
```

`<script>`

Syntax

```
<script
    charset = "string"
    fetchhint = "prefetch | safe | stream"
    fetchtimeout = "string"
    maxage = "integer"
    maxstale = "integer"
    src = "URI">
    Optional_Inline_Script Source
</script>
```

Description

Defines and executes a block of ECMAScript client-side code.

Variables and functions defined using `<script>` have the scope of the containing element (for example, variables and functions declared in a block of script within a `<form>` have dialog scope for that form, and can be referenced in other scripts and *expr* attributes within that form).

The VoiceXML interpreter uses an XML parser to parse a VoiceXML document, so it is necessary to embed a block of inline script within an XML CDATA section to prevent the XML parser from parsing the script. Otherwise, characters such as <, >, and & will generate an error.

Attribute	Description	Required/Optional
charset	If *src* is specified, the character encoding of the script. UTF-8 and UTF-16 encodings of 10646 must be supported (as in XML) and other encodings, as defined in the IANA character set registry,[9] may be supported. The default value is UTF-8.	Optional
fetchhint	See "HTTP Semantics" later in this chapter.	Optional
fetchtimeout	See "HTTP Semantics" later in this chapter.	Optional
maxage	See "HTTP Semantics" later in this chapter.	Optional
maxstale	See "HTTP Semantics" later in this chapter.	Optional
src	URI specifying the location of a valid ECMAScript document. If not specified, an inline script definition must be provided. If both are specified, *src* is used and the inline script is ignored.	Optional

Usage	Parents		Children
	<block>	<if>	None
	<catch>	<menu>	
	<error>	<noinput>	
	<filled>	<nomatch>	
	<foreach>	<prompt>	
	<help>	<vxml>	

Example

```
// myscript.js
// an external script file
   function GetRandomNumber(max)
   {
       // get a number between 0 and and (max-1)
       var iNum = Math.floor(Math.random() * max);
       return iNum;
   }
```

---

[9]See www.iana.org/assignments/character-sets

```
<!-- main.vxml
     A VoiceXML document that references myscript.js
-->
<vxml version="2.0">
  <script src="myscript.js" />
  <!-- this document scope use of script makes
       the GetRandomNumber function accessible
       anywhere in the document -->

  <form>
    <block>
      A random number from 0 to 9 is:
      <value expr="GetRandomNumber(10)" />
    </block>
    <block>
      <var name="hours"/>
      <var name="minutes"/>
      <var name="seconds"/>
      <script>
      <![CDATA[
        // this inline script is enclosed in a CDATA
        // section.
        var d = new Date();
        hours = d.getHours();
        minutes = d.getMinutes();
        seconds = d.getSeconds();
       ]]>
      </script>
      The current time is:
      <value expr="hours + ' ' + minutes
                   + ' and ' + seconds
                   + ' seconds.' " />
      <!-- this references the variables
           that were defined in VoiceXML,
           assigned within the script,
           and are now used in an ECMAScript
           expression within VoiceXML again. -->
    </block>
  </form>
</vxml>
```

<sentence>

Syntax	

	``
	<sentence>
	    xml:lang = "language_locale">
	  TTS_Text
	</sentence>
	``

Description	In TTS, marks a container for a sentence. This may assist the speech synthesizer in determining the prosody and normalization.

Attribute	Description	Required/Optional
xml:lang	Specifies the language and locale identifier of the contained or referenced grammar according to RFC 1766[10] (for example, "fr-CA" for Canadian French). If omitted, the value is inherited down from the document hierarchy, and ultimately a VoiceXML interpreter default.	Optional

Usage	Parents		Children
	`<audio>`	`<help>`	`<audio>`
	`<block>`	`<if>`	`<break>`
	`<catch>`	`<noinput>`	`<emphasis>`
	`<choice>`	`<nomatch>`	`<enumerate>`
	`<error>`	`<prompt>`	`<phoneme>`
	`<enumerate>`	`<prosody>`	`<prosody>`
	`<filled>`	`<voice>`	`<s>`
	`<foreach>`		`<say-as>`
			`<sentence>`
			`<value>`
			`<voice>`

Example	`<sentence> Tomorrow is election day </sentence>`0

`<subdialog>`

Syntax	

```
<subdialog
    cond = "ECMAScript_Expression"
    enctype = "MIME_type"
    expr = "ECMAScript_Expression"
    fetchaudio = "URI"
    fetchhint = "prefetch | safe | stream"
    fetchtimeout = "string"
    maxage = "integer"
    maxstale = "integer"
    method = "get | post"
    name = "ECMAScript_Variable"
    namelist = "var1 var2 ... varn"
    src = "URI">
    Child_Elements
</subdialog>
</subdialog>
```

Description   Invokes modularized VoiceXML code in an independent application context.

Once a subdialog has been invoked, `<return>` can specify either an event to throw or a list of variables to return. If an event is thrown,

---

[10]See www.nordu.net/ftp/rfc/rfc1766.txt

it is thrown at the scope of the invoking subdialog and can be handled there locally or by inherited handlers from parent scopes. If a list of variables is returned, the *name* form item variable is filled with an ECMAScript object whose properties correspond to the returned variables and the subdialog's `<filled>` element is executed.

enctype, fetchaudio, fetchhint, fetchtimeout, maxage, maxstale, method, and *namelist* are only relevant if *src* references a URI to another document (for example, requires an actual HTTP request to be made to the Web server).

For more information about VoiceXML subdialogs and the FIA, see Chapter 6.

Attribute	Description	Required/ Optional
cond	ECMAScript expression that must also evaluate to true for the FIA to select this form item (default is true).	Optional
enctype	MIME type to use to encode any included data specified by *namelist* (default is "application/ x-www-form-urlencoded." Interpreters must also support "multipart/form-data" and may support additional encoding types).	Optional
expr	ECMAScript expression that, if specified, is evaluated and provides an initial value for the subdialog's form item variable *name* (default is undefined). If a value is provided, then the form item will not be visited until/unless it is first cleared.	Optional
fetchaudio	See "HTTP Semantics" later in this chapter.	Required
fetchhint	See "HTTP Semantics" later in this chapter.	Optional
fetchtimeout	See "HTTP Semantics" later in this chapter.	Optional
maxage	See "HTTP Semantics" later in this chapter.	Optional
maxstale	See "HTTP Semantics" later in this chapter.	Optional
method	The HTTP method to use to send the request; either "get" or "post" (default is "get").	Optional

	Attribute	Description	Required/ Optional
	name	Valid ECMAScript variable name that declares the form item variable for this subdialog.	Required
		If the invoked subdialog uses the `<return>` *namelist* attribute to return data to this dialog, *name* is set to a ECMAScript object whose properties correspond to the list of variables returned via *namelist*.	
	namelist	A space-separated list of variables to be submitted via HTTP along with the request to the URI specified by *src*.	Optional
		namelist is only valid if *src* references a URI to another document (for example, requires an actual HTTP request to be made to the Web server).	
	src	URI to a valid VoiceXML document that will be invoked in a completely independent interpreter context as a subdialog.	Required
		At some point, this document is expected to use `<return>` to return control to the invoking application.	

Usage	Parents	Children	
	`<form>`	`<audio>`	`<noinput>`
		`<catch>`	`<nomatch>`
		`<enumerate>`	`<param>`
		`<error>`	`<prompt>`
		`<filled>`	`<property>`
		`<help>`	`<value>`

Example	

```
<!-- main.vxml: this document collects the caller's
     name, and then invokes a subdialog to collect more
     info -->
<vxml version="2.0">
  <form id="do_subd">
    <var name="fname" expr=" 'Jeff' " />
    <!-- setting a variable directly rather than
         collecting from the user, just to keep this
         example short. -->

    <subdialog name="getmore" src="#form_getmore">
    <!-- invoking the subdialog in the
         same document -->
      <param name="the_name" expr="fname" />
      <filled>
```

```
                    <audio>The subdialog returned:
                        <value expr="getmore.dob +
                                    getmore.the_name" />
                    </audio>
                    <exit />
                </filled>
                <catch event="event.myapp.flag">
                    <audio>The event got fired instead.</audio>
                    <exit />
                </catch>
                <!-- this event handler will get invoked instead
                     of the <filled> element if the subdialog
                     returns with "event" instead of "namelist"
                -->
            </subdialog>
        </form>

        <form id="form_getmore">
            <var name="the_name" />
            <block>
                <!-- Each variable passed using the param element
                     needs to be declared by name within the
                     subdialog. At runtime, it will be initialized
                     with the value passed in (if any) via the
                     param element -->
                <var name="dob" expr=" '19680829' " />
                <audio>Hi <value expr="the_name" />,
                    it's nice to meet you</audio>
                <!-- the first name was filled in using
                     the variable passed in to the subdialog
                -->
                <audio>I would ask you for more info, but
                        for now I'm going to pretend.</audio>
                <if cond="Math.random() &gt; .4"> <!-- random # -->
                    <return namelist="dob the_name" />
                <else />
                    <return event="event.myapp.flag" />
                </if>
                <!-- this demonstrates using <return> both with
                     "event" and "namelist" as ways to return
                     information back to the invoking dialog. -->
            </block>
        </form>
    </vxml>
```

<submit>

Syntax

```
<submit
    enctype = "MIME_type"
    expr = "ECMAScript_Expression"
    fetchaudio = "URI"
```

```
fetchhint = "prefetch | safe | stream"
fetchtimeout = "string"
maxage = "integer"
maxstale = "integer"
method = "get | post"
namelist = "var1 var2 . . . varn"
next = "URI" />
```

Description	Transitions to a new VoiceXML document via HTTP GET or POST.

Attribute	Description	Required/Optional
enctype	MIME type to use to encode any included data specified by *namelist* (default is "application/x-www-form-urlencoded." Interpreters must also support "multipart/form-data" and may support additional encoding types). ***Note***: If a variable containing recorded audio from `<record>` is included in *namelist,* then *enctype* should be set to "multipart/form-data." If it is not, the behavior is unspecified—some platforms may override *enctype* and send as multipart/form-data; others may attempt to send as specified. However, this may severely impact performance.	Optional
expr	ECMAScript expression that evaluates to a URI to explicitly transition to. For `<submit>`, the URI must reference another document; to transition to another dialog within the same document, use `<goto>` or `<subdialog>`. *expr* and *next* are mutually exclusive.	Required
fetchaudio	See "HTTP Semantics" later in this chapter.	Optional
fetchhint	See "HTTP Semantics" later in this chapter.	Optional
fetchtimeout	See "HTTP Semantics" later in this chapter.	Optional
maxage	See "HTTP Semantics" later in this chapter.	
maxstale	See "HTTP Semantics" later in this chapter.	
method	The HTTP method to use to send the request; either "get" or "post" (default is "get").	Optional

Attribute	Description	Required/Optional
namelist	A space-separated list of variables to be submitted via HTTP along with the request to the URI specified by *src*. If an ECMAScript object is included in *namelist*, then all of its fields are submitted using corresponding names (for example, *myobject.a, myobject.b,* etc.)	Optional
next	URI to explicitly transition to. For `<submit>`, the URI must reference another document; to transition to another dialog within the same document, use `<goto>` or `<subdialog>`. *expr* and *next* are mutually exclusive.	Required

Usage	Parents		Children
	`<block>`	`<help>`	None
	`<catch>`	`<if>`	
	`<error>`	`<noinput>`	
	`<filled>`	`<nomatch>`	
	`<foreach>`	`<prompt>`	

Example

```
<vxml version="2.0">
  <form id="launch_missiles">
    <field name="password">
      <prompt>What is the code word?</prompt>
      <grammar>rutabaga</grammar>
      <help>It is the name of an obscure
            vegetable.</help>
      <catch event="nomatch noinput" count="3">
        <!-- this will only catch the third (or
             subsequent) nomatch and the third (or
             subsequent) noinput. The next highest-
             scoped handlers for these will be used
             for the first and second instances. -->
        <audio>Security violation!</audio>
        <submit next="apprehend_felon;sp"
                namelist="user_id"/>
      </catch>
    </field>
    <block>
      <goto next="#get_city"/>
    </block>
  </form>
</vxml>
```

`<throw>`

Syntax	```
	<throw>
	    event = "event"
	    eventexpr = "ECMAScript_Expression"
	    message = "string"
	    messageexpr = "ECMAScript_Expression"
	</throw>
	``

Description	Triggers an event. Either platform-defined events (for example, *"noinput"*) or user-defined events (for example, *"org.jeff.myapp. status"*) can be triggered using `<throw>`. Just as with extended properties, when naming user-defined events, it is recommended to use this "reverse domain name"-style to avoid any possible conflict with current or future platform-defined events. For more information about the VoiceXML event model, see Chapter 6. For more information about platform-defined events and variables, see "Platform-Defined Events" and "Platform-Defined Variables" later in this chapter.

Attribute	Description	Required/ Optional
event	Name of event to throw. The complete event name will be available in the handler that catches this event via the platform-defined variable *_event*. *event* and *eventexpr* are mutually exclusive.	Required
eventexpr	ECMAScript expression that evaluates to a name of an event to throw. The complete event name will be available in the handler that catches this event via the platform-defined variable *_event*. *event* and *eventexpr* are mutually exclusive.	Required
message	String specifying additional contextual information about the event being thrown. The string will be available in the handler that catches this event via the platform-defined variable *_message*. *message* and *messageexpr* are mutually exclusive.	Optional
messageexpr	ECMAScript expression that evaluates to a string specifying additional contextual information about the event being thrown. The string will be available in the handler that catches this event via the platform-defined variable *_message*.	Optional

	Attribute	Description	Required/Optional
		message and *messageexpr* are mutually exclusive.	
Usage	Parents		Children
	`<block>`	`<help>`	None
	`<catch>`	`<if>`	
	`<error>`	`<noinput>`	
	`<filled>`	`<nomatch>`	
	`<foreach>`	`<prompt>`	

Example

```
<vxml version="2.0">
  <var name="flag" expr="false" />
  <error>
    <!-- this is a document scope handler -->
    <audio>this is the document handler.
          the error <value expr="_event" />
          occurred.</audio>
    <assign name="flag" expr="true" />
    <goto next="#top" />
  </error>

  <form id="top">
    <error cond="flag">
      <!-- this is a dialog scope handler,
           that will override on the second
           time once the flag is set to
           true -->
      <audio>this is the dialog handler.
            the error <value expr="_event" />
            occurred.</audio>
      <exit />
    </error>
    <field name="hello" type="boolean">
      <prompt>
        <audio>entering the first field.
              say yes or no.</audio>
      </prompt>
      <filled>
        <throw event="error.myapp.unlucky" />
      </filled>
      <!-- this should always
           throw an error -->
    </field>
  </form>
</vxml>
```

`<token>`

In XML grammars, specifies an input element. See Chapter 8 for details regarding XML grammars.

`<transfer>`

| **Syntax** | ```
<transfer
      bridge = "true | false"
      cond = "ECMAScript_Expression"
      connecttimeout = "string"
      dest = "string"
      destexpr = "ECMAScript_Expression"
      expr = "ECMAScript_Expression"
      maxtime = "integer"
      name = "ECMAScript_Variable"
      transferaudio = "URI" >
      Child_Elements
</transfer>
``` |

Transfers the call to another destination.

Once the transfer completes, the `<filled>` element contained within it is executed. Within the `<filled>` element, platform-defined "shadow variables" are available within the local scope to provide additional information about the transfer.

DTMF and/or speech grammars may be explicitly specified within a `<transfer>` (only when *bridging* is "true"), enabling the caller to proactively end the transferred call and return to the application by saying or keying in something. However, transfers are always modal in that all other active grammars from parent scopes are explicitly disabled.

NOTE For performance reasons, it is valuable to avoid using speech grammars during transfers except when explicitly necessary or desired (for example, use `<grammar mode="dtmf">`).

When a transfer completes, the *name* form item variable may contain any of the following values:

- **busy.** The endpoint refused the call.
- **noanswer.** No one answered before *connecttimeout*.
- **network_busy.** Some intermediate network refused the call.
- **near_end_disconnect.** The call completed and was terminated by the caller (for example, *bridge* was "true" and they triggered an active grammar).
- **far_end_disconnect.** The call completed and was terminated by the callee (for example, they hung up).
- **network_disconnect.** The call completed and was terminated by the network.
- **maxtime_disconnect.** The call completed, but the duration exceeded *maxtime* and was terminated by the platform.
- **unknown.** The transfer completed or failed for some unknown reason
```

In addition, the transfer may throw an event. Some of the events that may be thrown are listed here, but particular platforms may throw additional events. To be safe, it's best to provide handlers for the generic *telephone.* and *error.* event spaces.

- **telephone.disconnect.hangup.** If the caller hangs up during a bridged transfer.

- **telephone.disconnect.transfer.** Immediately thrown when a non-bridged transfer is connected.

- **error.telephone.noauthorization.** If the caller is not allowed to call *dest/destexpr.*

- **error.telephone.baddestination.** If *dest/destexpr* is malformed.

- **error.telephone.noroute.** If the platform is not able to place a call to *dest/destexpr.*

- **error.telephone.noresource.** If the platform cannot allocate resources to place the call.

- **error.telephone.*protocol.nnn.*** If the underlying telephony infrastructure raised a specific exception.

For more information about the VoiceXML FIA, see Chapter 6.

For more information about platform-defined events, please see "Platform-Defined Events" later in this chapter.

Attribute	Description	Required/ Optional
bridge	Boolean that determines behavior once the call is connected. If "true," the underlying platform "stays on the line" (for example, bridges, trombones, hairpins) while the transfer is under way.	Optional
	When the transfer ends (either because of a disconnection or because the caller says or some DTMF tones to match an active grammar), execution resumes with the transfer's `<filled>` element.	
	Alternatively, certain conditions may throw an event (see earlier section). If "false," then the interpreter throws *telephone.disconnect.transfer* immediately after connecting the transfer.	
	Failed transfers throw appropriate error events (default is "false").	
cond	ECMAScript expression that must also evaluate to true for the FIA to select this form item (default is true).	Optional

Attribute	Description	Required/Optional
connecttimeout	Number of seconds (s) or milliseconds (ms) to wait while trying to connect the call (for example, "15s").	Optional
	If *connecttimeout* passes, then the *name* form item variable is set to "noanswer" and the transfer's `<filled>` element is executed (default is platform-specific).	
dest	String that specifies the destination of the transfer. VoiceXML platforms must support the "tel.//" URI syntax for phone numbers described in RFC 2806,[11] but may support additional platform-defined syntaxes as well. *dest* and *destexpr* are mutually exclusive.	Required
destexpr	ECMAScript expression that evaluates to a string that specifies the destination of the transfer. VoiceXML platforms must support the "tel://" URI syntax for phone numbers described in RFC 2806,[12] but may support additional platform-defined syntaxes as well.	Required
	dest and *destexpr* are mutually exclusive.	
expr	ECMAScript expression that, if specified, is evaluated and provides an initial value for the transfer's form item variable *name* (default is undefined). If a value is provided, then the form item will not be visited until/unless it is first cleared.	Optional
maxtime	If *bridge* is "true," an integer specifying the maximum time, in seconds, that the transfer is allowed to last.	Optional
	After *maxtime* elapses, the call is disconnected, *name* is set to "maxtime_disconnect", and the transfer's `<filled>` element is executed.	

[11]See www.ietf.org/rfc/rfc2806.txt?number=2806

[12]See www.ietf.org/rfc/rfc2806.txt?number=2806

Attribute	Description	Required/ Optional
maxtime	Setting *maxtime* to 0 designates that there is no maximum time allowed (default is 0).	
name	Valid ECMAScript variable name that declares the form item variable for this transfer. In most scenarios, *name* is set to a status value (for example, "busy," "near_end_ disconnect") when the transfer completes and the `<filled>` element is executed.	Required
	Alternatively, some error cases throw an event rather than filling *name*.	
transferaudio	URI to an audio file that is played to the caller while attempting to connect the transfer. Playback is immediately terminated if the callee picks up or if the transfer fails. If playback completes before the callee picks up, then the platform will play through the audio tones (such as ringing, busy signal, etc.) from the far end of the call (default is to play far end audio tones, just like a regular phone call).	Optional

Shadow Variables	Description
name$.duration	Float specifying the duration of the call, in seconds, set to 0 if the transfer was terminated prior to being answered.

Usage	Parents	Children	
	`<form>`	`<audio>`	`<help>`
		`<catch>`	`<noinput>`
		`<enumerate>`	`<nomatch>`
		`<error>`	`<prompt>`
		`<filled>`	`<property>`
		`<grammar>`	`<value>`

Example

```
<?xml version="1.0"?>
<vxml version="2.0">
<form id="call_number">

<transfer name="theCall" connecttimeout="30s"
dest="2065555555">
  <transferaudio="http://resources.tellme.com/audio/
  earcons/intellipause.wav">
```

```
                    <filled>

                      if cond="theCall =='busy'">
                        <audio>The line was busy. Please try again
                        later.</audio>
                      <elseif cond="theCall =='noanswer'"/>
                        <audio>Noone is answering.</audio>
                      <elseif cond="theCall =='network_busy'"/>
                        <audio>The network is busy!</audio>
                      <elseif cond="theCall =='network_disconnect'"/>
                        <audio>The call was completed, but it was
                        terminated by the network.</audio>
                      </if>?

                    </filled>
                  </transfer>

                </form>
              </vxml>
```

`<value>`

Syntax	`<value`
	`    expr = "ECMAScript_Expression"`
	`/>`

Description	In TTS, evaluates and returns an ECMAScript expression.

Attribute	Description	Required/Optional
expr	ECMAScript expression that evaluates to a string, which will be spoken as TTS to the caller.	Required

Usage	Parents		Children
	`<audio>`	`<noinput>`	None
	`<block>`	`<nomatch>`	
	`<catch>`	`<object>`	
	`<choice>`	`<p>`	
	`<emphasis>`	`<paragraph>`	
	`<enumerate>`	`<prompt>`	
	`<error>`	`<prosody>`	
	`<field>`	`<record>`	
	`<filled>`	`<s>`	
	`<foreach>`	`<sentence>`	
	`<help>`	`<subdialog>`	
	`<if>`	`<transfer>`	
	`<initial>`	`<voice>`	
	`<log>`		
	`<menu>`		

Example	`<vxml version="2.0">` `  <script>`

```
<![CDATA[
  function factorial(n)
  { return (n <= 1)? 1 : n * factorial(n–1); }
]]>
</script>
<form id="form">
  <field name="fact" type="number">
    <prompt> Tell me a number and I'll tell you its
             factorial. </prompt>
    <filled>
      <audio>
        <value expr="fact"/> factorial is
        <value expr="factorial(fact)"/>
      </audio>
    </filled>
  </field>
</form>
</vxml>
```

`<var>`

Syntax	`<var`
	`    expr = "ECMAScript_Expression"`
	`    name = "ECMAScript_Variable"`
	`/>`

Description	Declares a variable. The *var* element declares a variable within the scope defined by its container. A variable is accessible to all children of that container. In addition, the variable context is shared between VoiceXML elements, *expr* expressions within VoiceXML elements, and `<script>` blocks. Variables defined in VoiceXML using `<var>` are accessible from any `<script>` block or *expr* expression within the same scope or a child scope of where they are declared. Similarly, variables defined in `<script>` blocks are given the scope of the `<script>` block in which they occur, and are accessible within VoiceXML elements and *expr* expressions accordingly. `<var>` is also used at the beginning of a called subdialog to declare any variables that it expects to be passed via `<param>` from the invoking `<subdialog>`. For more information on this use of `<var>`, see `<param>`, `<subdialog>`, and `<return>` earlier in this chapter. For more information on VoiceXML scoping, please see Chapter 6. For more information on platform-defined variables, see "Platform-defined Variables" later in this chapter.

Attribute	Description	Required/ Optional
expr	ECMAScript expression that is evaluated and assigned to the variable *name* (default is undefined for new variables or the current value if already declared).	Optional

	Attribute	Description	Required/Optional
	name	Valid ECMAScript name for a variable—it can contain letters, digits, underscores "_", and dollar signs "$", but the first character must be a letter or a dollar sign.	Required

Usage	Parents		Children
	`<block>`	`<help>`	None
	`<catch>`	`<if>`	
	`<error>`	`<noinput>`	
	`<filled>`	`<nomatch>`	
	`<foreach>`	`<prompt>`	
	`<form>`	`<vxml>`	

Example

```
<vxml version="2.0">
  <var name="status" /> <!-- document scope -->
  <form>
    <block>
      <var name="status" /> <!-- anonymous scope -->
      <assign name="status" expr=" 'local' " />
      <!-- assigns the local one -->
      <assign name="document.status" expr=" 'doc' ">
      <!-- assigns the document one -->
      <audio>
        <value expr="status" />
        <value expr="document.status" />
      </audio>
    </block>
  </form>
</vxml>
```

`<voice>`

Syntax

```
<voice
    age = "integer"
    category = "adult | child | elder | teenager"
    gender = "male | female | neutral"
    name = "name1 name2 ... namen"
    variant = "integer">
    TTS_Text
</voice>
```

Description	In TTS, specifies the aural characteristics for the synthesized voice. This may assist the speech synthesizer in determining the prosody and normalization of the text.

	Attribute	Description	Required/Optional
	age	Integer specifying the preferred age for the TTS voice to "sound like."	Optional

Attribute	Description	Required/Optional
category	Label specifying the preferred age category for the TTS voice to "sound like."	Optional
gender	Label specifying the preferred gender for the TTS voice to "sound like."	Optional
name	Space-delimited list of platform-specific labels specifying the preferred specific voice or personality for the TTS engine to use. If more than one label is specified, they are assumed to be in decreasing preference order.	Optional
variant	Integer specifying a platform-specific variant on the exact TTS voice used.	Optional

Usage	Parents		Children	
	`<audio>`	`<if>`	`<audio>`	`<phoneme>`
	`<block>`	`<noinput>`	`<break>`	`<prosody>`
	`<catch>`	`<nomatch>`	`<emphasis>`	`<s>`
	`<choice>`	`<p>`	`<enumerate>`	`<say-as>`
	`<error>`	`<paragraph>`	`<p>`	`<sentence>`
	`<emphasis>`	`<prompt>`	`<paragraph>`	`<value>`
	`<enumerate>`	`<prosody>`		`<voice>`
	`<filled>`	`<s>`		
	`<foreach>`	`<sentence>`		
	`<help>`	`<voice>`		

Example

```
<prompt>
  <voice age="6" gender="female">
  Once upon a time there were three bears.
  </voice>
</prompt>
```

`<vxml>`

Syntax

```
<vxml
  application = "URI"
  base = "URI"
  version = "string"
  xml:lang = "language_locale">
  Child_Elements
</vxml>
```

Description

Declares a VoiceXML document and is the root document element.

For more information about application root documents, the VoiceXML FIA, and scoping, see Chapter 6.

Attribute	Description	Required/Optional
application	URI specifying the application root document for this VoiceXML document. If specified, the application root document is loaded. Grammars, links, event handlers, scripts, and variables that are declared at document scope within the application root document itself become available at application scope within this document and any other documents visited during the session that specify the same application root document (default is none).	Optional
base	A URI that, if specified, causes the interpreter to prepend *base* to all relative URIs in the document before evaluating them.	Optional
version	VoiceXML version number. The current version number is "2.0."	Required
xml:lang	Specifies the language and locale identifier of the contained or referenced grammar according to RFC 1766[13] (for example, "fr-CA" for Canadian French). If omitted, the value is inherited down from the document hierarchy, and ultimately a VoiceXML interpreter default.	Optional

Usage	Parents	Children	
	None	`<catch>`	`<meta>`
		`<data>`	`<noinput>`
		`<error>`	`<nomatch>`
		`<form>`	`<property>`
		`<help>`	`<script>`
		`<link>`	`<var>`
		`<menu>`	

Example

```
<!-- myapproot.vxml
     this is an application root document
-->
<vxml version="2.0">
  <link event="myapp.eggplant">
    <grammar type="application/x-gsl">
      [eggplant]
```

---

[13]See www.nordu.net/ftp/rfc/rfc1766.txt

```
        </grammar>
      </link>
      <catch event="myapp.eggplant">
        You said eggplant! I love eggplant!
        <clear />
        <reprompt />
      </catch>
      <!-- this defines a global link and event handler for
           the word "eggplant", which will play a
           fun message and then clear the relevant field
           so the caller will be reprompted -->
      <noinput>
        I really really really didn't hear you.
        <reprompt />
      </noinput>
      <nomatch>
        I really really really didn't understand.
      </nomatch>
    </vxml>


    <!-- first.vxml
         This is the first VoiceXML document
         that is part of this application.
         There could be many others, as well.
    -->
    <vxml version="2.0" application="myapproot.vxml">
      <form>
        <block>
          Hello world!
        </block>
        <field name="dob" type="date">
          <prompt>What is your birthdate?</prompt>
          <!-- try saying eggplant, too! -->
          <filled>
            You said <value expr="dob$.utterance" />
            <clear />
          </filled>
        </field>
      </form>
    </vxml>
```

Platform-Defined Behaviors and Semantics

In addition to the set of elements and attributes, VoiceXML specifies a series of platform-defined variables, events, grammars, and properties that developers can use when building applications. In addition, all of the VoiceXML elements that retrieve content via HTTP include several attributes that govern and/or influence the interpreter's behavior when it executes them. In this section, we'll provide a complete reference for these aspects of VoiceXML.

Platform-Defined Variables

VoiceXML provides a set of platform-defined variables that are available at various scopes and during certain specific situations.

Session Variables

Session variables are read-only platform-defined variables that are available at session scope (for example, in any scope in any document in any application). VoiceXML 2.0 defines a set of required session variables, and platforms are free to provide additional variables as extensions.

VARIABLE	DESCRIPTION	NOTES
session.meta.*name*	String containing the *content* of the *name* `<meta>` element in the current document.	Extension to VoiceXML 2.0 Some VoiceXML platforms provide these variables.
session.telephone.ani	String containing the Automatic Number Identification (ANI) information for the caller, if available. Otherwise undefined. ANI is typically available from toll-free phone numbers in North America, and provides the receiver of a telephone call with the number of the calling phone.	May be deprecated in future versions in favor of *session .connection.** naming convention
session.telephone.dnis	String containing the Dialed Number Information Service (DNIS) information for the current call, if available. Otherwise undefined. DNIS is typically available on all phone calls, and provides the receiver of a telephone call with the exact number the caller dialed to reach them.	""
session.telephone .iidigits	String containing the Information Indicator Digits information for the current call, if available. Otherwise undefined. II digits provide information about theoriginating line (for example,pay phone, cellular service, special operator handling, prison) of the caller. Telecordia publishes the complete list of II digits in Section 1 of each volume of the "Local Exchange Routing Guide"	""

VARIABLE	DESCRIPTION	NOTES
session.telephone.uui	String containing the User-to-User Information (UUI) supplementary information provided as part of an ISDN call set-up from a calling party, if available. Otherwise undefined.	""
session.telephone.rdnis	String containing the Redirect Dialed Number Information Service (RDNIS) information for the current phone call, if available. Otherwise undefined.	""
	RDNIS provides the number from which a call diversion or transfer was invoked.	
	For example, suppose person X subscribes to a messaging service and forwards all calls to an automated system.	
	Person Y then calls X and is redirected to the automated system. A VoiceXML application on the automated system would see RDNIS as X's number, DNIS as the number of the automated system, and ANI as Y's number.	
session.telephone. redirect_reason	If *session.telephone.rdnis* is not undefined, then a string that indicates the reason the call was redirected to this server. Otherwise undefined.	""
	Potential values are "unknown | user-busy | no-answer | unavailable | unconditional | time-of-day | do-not-disturb | deflection | follow-me | out-of-service | away".	

Application Variables

Application variables are read-only platform-defined variables that are available at application scope (for example, in any scope in any document in any application). VoiceXML 2.0 defines a set of required application variables, and platforms are free to provide additional variables as extensions.

VARIABLE	DESCRIPTION
application.lastresult$	Array of elements containing information about the last recognition to occur in the current application. As discussed throughout this book, voice recognition engines work by comparing what the caller said to the list of active grammars, and deciding how confident it is that the caller said a particular matching value. The recognizer actually computes this confidence interval for several of the most likely possibilities, and then selects the one with the highest confidence value as a match (if it's more confident than the current setting of the *confidence* property).
	For richer programmatic control, the read-only *application.lastresult$* array is always available at application scope. Each element of the array contains information about one of the highest-confidence possible matches for the last attempted recognition. If no recognition has happened yet in the application or when inside of an application root document, its value is ECMAScript undefined.

VARIABLE	DESCRIPTION
application.lastresult$ [i].confidence	Float specifying the recognizer's confidence that the caller actually said this particular match, expressed on a scale from 0.0 (minimum) to 1.0 (maximum).
application.lastresult$ [i].utterance	String of words actually said by the caller. The exact spelling is platform-specific (for example, "five hundred fifty" versus "5 hundred 30" versus "530").
application.lastresult$ [i].inputmode	String either "dtmf" or "voice," indicating whether the grammar was matched via touch-tone or spoken input.
application.lastresult$ [i].interpretation	ECMAScript representation of the recognizer's interpretation of the utterance as matched by the relevant grammar, including slot information.
	Note: As of October 2001, the exact method for representing interpretation results in VoiceXML remains a matter of annotated discussion within the various specifications under the auspices of the W3C Voice Browser Working Group. For detailed information on how to use interpretation results within VoiceXML, see *www.w3.org/voice* and your vendor's system documentation.

Shadow and Local Variables

In various specific places within VoiceXML, other platform-defined variables are available. All of these are referenced directly in the appropriate places in the VoiceXML element reference earlier in this chapter, but they are summarized again here for convenience.

VARIABLE	AVAILABLE LOCATION	DESCRIPTION
name$.confidence	`<filled>` after a successful recognition in `<field>`	The recognizer's confidence that the caller actually said this particular match, expressed on a scale from 0.0 (minimum) to 1.0 (maximum).
name$.utterance	""	The actual string of words said by the caller. The exact spelling is platform-specific (for example, "five hundred fifty" versus "5 hundred 30" versus "530").
name$.inputmode	""	Either "dtmf" or "voice," indicating whether the grammar was matched via touch-tone or spoken input.
name$.dest	`<filled>` after successful `<record>`	If *dest* was specified, the URI referencing the recording (for example, if the destination redirects the original request, this variable holds the redirected URI).
name$.duration	""	Duration of the recording, in milliseconds.
name$.maxtime	""	Boolean, set to true if the recording was cut off because *maxtime* was reached.
name$.size	""	Size of the recording in bytes.
name$.termchar	""	If *dtmfterm* was true and the caller terminated the recording by pressing a DTMF key, then this is set to the specific key that was pressed (for example, "9", "#"). Otherwise, it is null.
name$.duration	`<filled>` after successful `<transfer>`	Float specifying the duration of the call, in seconds, set to 0 if the transfer was terminated prior to being answered.
_prompt	`<enumerate>`	String specifying the TTS representation of the grammar fragment for the current `<choice>` or `<option>` being iterated through.
_dtmf	""	String specifying the DTMF equivalent for the current `<choice>` or `<option>` being iterated through.

VARIABLE	AVAILABLE LOCATION	DESCRIPTION
_event	`<catch>`, `<noinput>`, `<nomatch>`, `<help>`, `<error>`	String specifying the exact name of the event that was caught.
_message	""	String specifying any additional information about the event provided by the platform or explicitly set using the *message* or *messageexpr* attributes of `<throw>`.

Platform-Defined Events

VoiceXML provides a set of platform-defined events that are thrown at various appropriate times, and a corresponding set of default event handlers. Using the flexible VoiceXML event model, it's easy for developers to override the platform-defined behavior when they want, without being forced to include extra lines of code for event handlers that they don't need or want specialized behavior for.

Default Event Handlers

VoiceXML platforms are expected to provide default handlers for the following events. Note that when a default audio message is played to the caller, the exact wording, language, sound (for example, TTS versus recorded audio), etc. are platform-specific.

EVENT	THROWN WHEN	DEFAULT BEHAVIOR
cancel	The *universals* property is set to "all" (see "Platform-Defined Grammars" and "Platform-defined Properties" later) and the caller says "stop" or "cancel" or the developer explicitly throws the "cancel" event.	Platform stops playing prompts and listens for the caller to respond (that is, empty `<catch>` handler with no audio and no `<reprompt>`).
error	Any runtime error occurs (see later for more detailed errors) When transitioning to a new document, errors encountered while retrieving and parsing the document throw the relevant error event in the calling document's context; all errors after successful parsing are raised in the new document.	Platform plays a default message to the caller (for example, "I'm sorry, but an error occurred.") and exits.

EVENT	THROWN WHEN	DEFAULT BEHAVIOR
exit	The *universals* property is set to "all" (see "Platform-Defined Grammars" and "Platform-Defined Properties" later) and the caller says "exit" or developer explicitly throws "exit" event.	Platform exits.
help	The *universals* property is set to "all" (see "Platform-Defined Grammars" and "Platform-Defined Properties" later) and the caller says "help" or the developer explicitly throws the "help" event.	Platform plays a default message to the caller (for example, "I'm sorry, but there is no help available right now.") and \<reprompt\>s.
maxspeechtimeout	The caller (or background noise) speaks for longer than the *maxspeechtimeout* property.	Platform plays a default message to the caller (for example, "I'm sorry, but your response was too long.") and \<reprompt\>s.
noinput	The caller is expected to provide input and remains silent.	Platform plays a default message to the caller (for example, "I'm sorry, but I didn't hear you.") and \<reprompt\>s.
nomatch	The caller says something unexpected that doesn't match any active grammar.	Platform plays a default message to the caller (for example, "I'm sorry, but I didn't get that.") and \<reprompt\>s.
telephone .disconnect.hangup	The caller hangs up the phone.	Platform exits.
telephone .disconnect.transfer	A nonbridging transfer is connected.	Platform exits.

Specific Platform-Defined Events

In addition to the general events and handlers described earlier, a number of specific events are thrown by VoiceXML platforms in particular circumstances. In all cases, platforms may throw even more specific event names and/or pass additional information using *_message* to provide developers with more details about what has happened.

EVENT	THROWN WHEN
error.badfetch error.badfetch.http *.response_code* error.badfetch.*protocol* *.response_code*	Platform fails to retrieve a document and the interpreter context has reached a place in document execution where the fetch result is required. Failures can occur for many reasons, including but not limited to missing documents, malformed URIs, timeouts, security violations, or malformed documents.

EVENT	THROWN WHEN
	error.badfetch is not thrown if the interpreter context does not actually need to use a particular document, such as when speculatively prefetching a grammar that is never activated or an audio file when there is alternate TTS text available.
	Platforms are required to throw the most detailed event name possible, denoting the appropriate response codes for the relevant URI protocol being used to fetch the document (for example, *error.badfetch.http.404* for "document not found").
error.semantic	Runtime error while executing the VoiceXML document (for example, divide by 0, referencing an undefined variable, etc.).
error.noauthorization	Application is not authorized to perform the requested operation; attempting to access a service that the application is not provisioned for (for example, transferring to international numbers, using non-bridged transfer, etc.).
error.unsupported.format	Requested resource has a format not supported by the platform (for example, audio file, grammar definition, etc.).
error.unsupported.language	Platform does not support the requested language for either TTS or speech recognition.
error.unsupported.element	Platform does not support a given VoiceXML element.

Platform-Defined Grammars

VoiceXML platforms must provide support for a set of special built-in grammars that developers can use within their applications, as well as a very limited number of "universals" or global grammars.

Built-in Grammars

VoiceXML platforms are required to provide built-in support for several common grammars, and return the results of those grammars in a standard format.

Developers can access all of these built-in grammars can be referenced in one of two ways:

- Using the *type* attribute on `<field>` (for example, `<field type="boolean">`). When using the built-in grammars in this way, they accept *both* dtmf and speech input.

- Using the *"builtin:"* URI namespace for a `<grammar>` *src*. For example, `<grammar src="builtin:grammar/boolean">`, `<grammar src="builtin:dtmf/digits">`. When using the built-in grammars in this way, developers must specify whether they want the dtmf of voice version of the grammar. Of course, they can specify both by having two <grammar> elements in succession.

GRAMMAR	DESCRIPTION / RETURN VALUE
boolean	Accepts "yes," "no," and/or additional locale- and platform-specific phrases signifying the same. DTMF 1 is yes and 2 is no. The result is "true" for "yes" and "false" for "no."
	Developers can additionally specify a different DTMF key for the yes and/or no answer, using the format *boolean?y=a;n=b,* where *a* and *b* are the desired DTMF characters. This is only applicable for the DTMF grammar (for example, in <field> *type* or via *builtin:dtmf/boolean*). If the values conflict, the platform throws *error.badfetch.*
date	Accepts various locale- and platform-specific phrases that specify a date (month, day, and/or year). DTMF inputs are: four digits for the year, followed by two digits for the month, and two digits for the day.
	The result is a fixed-length string in the format *yyyymmdd* (for example, "19740426"), and any missing information is returned as question marks (?) within the string. For example, if the caller said "April tenth," it would return "????0410."
digits	Accepts various locale- and platform-specific phrases that specify a series of one or more DTMF or spoken numeric digits. For example, the caller can say "two five five," but not "two hundred twenty five." Some platforms may support constructs such as "two double five." The result is a string of digits.
	Developers can additionally specify a minimum, maximum, and/or specific length for the number of accepted digits, using the format *digits?length=x;minlength=y;maxlength=z,* where *x, y,* and *z* are the desired values. Any conflicts between values throws *error.badfetch.*
currency	Accepts various locale- and platform-specific phrases that specify a currency amount. For DTMF input, the "*" key acts as the decimal point.
	The result is a string in the format *UUUmm.nn,* where *UUU* is the three character currency indicator according to ISO standard 4217:1995, or *mm.nn* if the currency is not spoken by the user or if the currency cannot be reliably determined (for example, "dollar" and "peso" are ambiguous).
number	Accepts various locale- and platform-specific phrases that specify a number. For example, the caller can say "five hundred and five" or "negative two point seven five." Only positive numbers can be entered via DTMF, and "*" acts as the decimal point.
	The result is a string of digits from 0 to 9, as well as the decimal point (".") and/or the minus sign ("–") if appropriate (e.g. "235," "–84.23"). The intrinsic ECMAScript *parseFloat* function can be used to convert this string to a numeric format.

GRAMMAR	DESCRIPTION / RETURN VALUE
phone	Accepts various locale- and platform-specific phrases that specify a phone number. In DTMF input, "*" represents "x" for an extension. The result is a string of digits, as well as the "x" character if necessary to signify an extension (for example, "8005551212," "5165552039x23").
	Leading platforms will specifically tune and optimize this grammar to best recognize the characteristic prosody and phrasing that people tend to use when speaking phone numbers [for example, (five-one-oh), (six-two-five), (two-three) (one-oh)].
time	Accepts various locale- and platform-specific phrases that specify a time, including hours and minutes. The result is a five character string in the format *hhmmx*, where x is either "a" for a.m., "p" for p.m., "h" to indicate a time specified using 24 hour clock time, or "?" to indicate an ambiguous time.
	For DTMF input, the final digit will always be "?" or "h" because there is no way to signify AM or PM using DTMF.

In addition, VoiceXML platforms are free to provide additional built-in grammars using the same conventions. It is recommended that platforms prepend "x-" (for example, "*x-ssn*") on the name of any platform-specific grammars, to avoid potential conflicts with future versions of VoiceXML.

Universals—Global Grammars

Universals are essentially `<link>` elements at session scope (see Chapter 6 for more information about scoping and the VoiceXML event model). By default, these grammars are inactive. Developers can enable them using the *universals* property. Note that the exact grammar used (for example, the exact set of words/phrases callers can say to activate the grammar) is platform-specific. VoiceXML platforms are expected to provide support for the following universals, and may also provide additional universals by default that are controllable via the *universals* property.

UNIVERSAL	EVENT THROWN
"cancel," "stop"	cancel
"exit"	exit
"help"	help

Platform-Defined Properties

The `<property>` element provides programmatic control over a wide range of specific behaviors for recognition and other aspects of the VoiceXML interpreter. VoiceXML platforms must support the following sets of platform-defined properties, and are free to expose additional platform-specific properties.

General Speech Recognizer Properties

PROPERTY	DESCRIPTION
completetimeout	Float specifying time, in seconds, to wait for additional input after the platform has recognized speech matching one of the active grammars. After *completetimeout* seconds of silence, either the utterance will be accepted or *nomatch* will be thrown (default is platform-specific).
confidencelevel	Float specifying the confidence threshold required for the platform to decide if the input speech matches the grammar, expressed on a scale from 0.0 (minimum) to 1.0 (maximum).
incompletetimeout	Float-specifying time, in seconds, to wait for additional input after the caller has spoken something and paused, but the platform has not yet recognized anything matching one of the active grammars. After *incompletetimeout* seconds of silence, either the utterance will be accepted or *nomatch* will be thrown (default is platform-specific).
maxspeechtimeout	Float specifying the maximum duration of user speech. If this time elapsed before the user stops speaking, the event *maxspeechtimeout* is thrown (Default is platform-specific).
sensitivity	Float specifying the sensitivity of the speech recognition engine to quiet input, expressed on a scale from 0.0 (least sensitive) to 1.0 (most sensitive) (default is 0.5).
speecvsaccuracy	Float specifying the desired balance between speed and accuracy for the recognition process, expressed on a scale from 0.0 (fastest) to 1.0 (most accurate) (default is 0.5).

DTMF Recognition Properties

PROPERTY	DESCRIPTION
interdigittimeout	Float specifying the time, in seconds, to wait for another DTMF digit (once at least one has been entered) before it decides that the caller has finished entering digits and returns a recognition or *nomatch* (default is platform-specific).
termchar	String specifying the single DTMF character that signifies the end of DTMF recognition (default is "#").
termtimeout	If *termchar* is not empty, float specifying the time, in seconds, to wait for the *termchar* to be entered, once the maximum amount of digits allowed by the relevant DTMF grammar have already been entered. If silence or only the *termchar* are entered before *termtimeout* elapses, then the grammar is matched and the recognition result is returned. If other additional DTMF digits are entered, then *nomatch* is thrown because the caller has now entered a DTMF string that does not match the active grammar (default is 0).

Prompt and Response Properties

PROPERTY	DESCRIPTION
bargein	Boolean specifying whether or not the caller can interrupt ("barge in on") prompts with their response (default is true).
bargeintype	Label specifying whether the recognizer should use the "energy," "speech," or "recognition" method to detect bargein (default is platform-specific).
timeout	Float specifying the time, in seconds, to wait for any speech or dtmf input to begin, after which *noinput* is thrown (default is platform-specific).

Resource Control and Document Fetching Properties

PROPERTY	DESCRIPTION
audiofetchhint	Label specifying whether the platform can attempt to optimize performance by prefetching audio files before they're explicitly needed. "safe" indicates that files must be fetched only when needed and not before; "prefetch" indicates that the platform may (but is not required to) prefetch files (default is "prefetch"). **Note:** Platforms are free to stream audio files as an additional performance optimization, regardless of the *audiofetchint* value.
audiomaxage	Float specifying the maximum acceptable age, in seconds, for cached audio resources. Resources older than *audiomaxage* must be rerequested from the Web server (default is platform-specific).
audiomaxstale	Float specifying the maximum acceptable age, in seconds, for cached audio resources that are expired (as per HTTP headers). Resources staler than *audiomaxstale* must be rerequested from the Web server (Default is platform-specific).
documentfetchhint	Same as *audiofetchhint,* but for VoiceXML documents.
documentmaxage	Same as *audiomaxage,* but for VoiceXML documents.
documentmaxstale	Same as *audiomaxstale,* but for VoiceXML documents.
fetchaudio	URI specifying audio to play to the caller while waiting for a new VoiceXML document to be fetched. If NULL, or if the audio completes playing before the fetch is complete, then the caller hears silence (default is platform-specific).

PROPERTY	DESCRIPTION
	The fetching of this audio clip is governed by the *audiofetchhint, audiomaxage, audiomaxstale,* and *fetchtimeout* properties in effect at the time of the fetch. The playing of the audio clip is governed by the *fetchaudiodelay* and *fetchaudiominimum* properties in effect at the time of the fetch.
	fetchaudio does not play when retrieving audio, grammars, objects, and/or scripts—only when transitioning to a new VoiceXML document.
fetchaudiodelay	String specifying the time, in seconds (s) or milliseconds (ms), to wait before beginning to play *fetchaudio* during a document transition. The idea is that when a new document is fetched very quickly, then it may be better to have a brief silence rather than a bit of *fetchaudio* that is immediately cut off (Default is platform-specific).
fetchaudiominimum	String specifying the minimum time, in seconds (s) or milliseconds (ms), to play *fetchaudio* (once it's started)— even if the new document arrives in the meantime. The idea is that once the caller does begin to hear *fetchaudio,* it should not be cut off too quickly (default is platform-specific).
fetchtimeout	String specifying the maximum time, in seconds (s) or milliseconds (ms), to wait while attempting to fetch any resource. If *fetchtimeout* elapses without a response from the Web server, *error.badfetch* is thrown.
grammarfetchhint	Same as *audiofetchhint,* but for grammars.
grammarmaxage	Same as *audiomaxage,* but for grammars.
grammarmaxstale	Same as *audiomaxstale,* but for grammars.
objectfetchhint	Same as *audiofetchhint,* but for objects.
objectmaxage	Same as *audiomaxage,* but for objects.
objectmaxstale	Same as *audiomaxstale,* but for objects.
scriptfetchhint	Same as *audiofetchhint,* but for scripts.
scriptmaxage	Same as *audiomaxage,* but for scripts.
scriptmaxstale	Same as *audiomaxstale,* but for scripts.

Miscellaneous Properties

PROPERTY	DESCRIPTION
inputmodes	Space-delimited list of labels specifying which kinds of caller input are enabled. Available labels are "voice," which designates speech input, and "dtmf," which designates DTMF input. One common use of *inputmodes* is to temporarily disable speech input when the caller is known to be in an especially noisy environment (default is "dtmf voice").

PROPERTY	DESCRIPTION
universals	Space-delimited list of labels specifying which platform-defined grammars (see "Platform-Defined Grammars" earlier) should be active.
	Available labels are "all,, which activates all platform-defined grammars; "none," which disables all of them; or a list of specific grammars (for example, "help exit").
	Platforms must support the "cancel," "exit," and "help" grammars, and may provide additional platform-specific ones (default is "none").
maxnbest	Integer (>= 1) specifying the maximum size of the *application.lastresult$* array (default is 1).

HTTP Semantics

The fundamental premise of VoiceXML is to bring the Internet architecture to the telephone. As a result, VoiceXML applications make extensive use of the HTTP protocol. VoiceXML applications use HTTP to retrieve VoiceXML, grammar, script, and audio documents.

As a result, the specific mechanisms and properties governing how VoiceXML platforms behave when the request and process documents via HTTP are critical for performance, reliability, and robustness.

The three governing principles of how VoiceXML interacts with HTTP are:

1. **"When in doubt, it works just like the Web!".** Of course, this is because VoiceXML *is* the Web.

2. **"Specifically, support and follow all relevant HTTP conventions."** Most VoiceXML platforms take this to at least mean HTTP response codes like redirects; leading VoiceXML platforms tend to extend this principle as far as possible to include support for things like cookies, SSL, and completely following the HTTP response headers for directing caching behavior.

3. **"Developers can specify a preference for behavior, but platforms are generally free to bypass these preferences in favor of alternative behavior that is known to better optimize performance without disturbing functionality."** Performance and reliability are ultimately what matter most, and since applications can run on multiple platforms/networks, it's critical that platforms be free to make appropriate local optimization decisions.

Specifically, VoiceXML platforms follow certain prescribed (and some optional) behaviors for requesting, retrieving, processing, and caching documents via HTTP. In addition, some of these behaviors are programmatically controllable.

Fetching and Initializing New Documents

Several VoiceXML elements (for example, <link>, <submit>, etc.) specify transitions to a new VoiceXML dialog via a URI. If that URI refers to another dialog in the same document (for example, "#top"), then a new HTTP fetch is not required and the transition proceeds immediately.

Transitions to another document trigger a new HTTP request. This request can trigger an actual HTTP request to the originating Web server, or can be fulfilled from the platform's internal cache (see "Caching Policies" later in this chapter).

Regardless of whether the document was cached or not, the newly retrieved document is processed in the following manner:

1. If specified, the application root document is fetched and initialized.

2. Any document scope variables are initialized.

3. Any document scope scripts are executed.

4. The requested dialog (or the first dialog if none is specified) is initialized and execution of the dialog begins.

Caching Policies

One of the fundamental benefits of the VoiceXML architecture is the ability to cleanly separate where the application lives (the Web server) from where the interpreter/platform lives. In practice, this means that smart and effective caching policies can dramatically impact the performance of commercially deployed VoiceXML applications. This condition is further exacerbated by the fact that VoiceXML tends to reference very large documents such as long audio files and complex grammars.

VoiceXML platforms are required to adhere to the cache correctness rules of HTTP 1.1, as specified in RFC2616.[14] In particular, the "expires" and "cache-control" response headers must be honored. Generally speaking, this means the following:

- IF (resource is not in the cache), THEN (fetch it from the server using GET).
- ELSE
    - IF (*maxage* is specified), THEN
        - IF (age of cached resource <= *maxage*), THEN
            - IF (age of cached resource >= Expires header), THEN
                - IF (*maxstale* is specified) AND ((age of cached resource – Expires header) <= *maxstale*), THEN (use the cached copy)
                - ELSE (fetch from the server using GET)
            - ELSE (use the cached copy)
        - ELSE (fetch from the server using GET)
    - ELSEIF (age of cached resource >= Expires header), THEN
        - IF (*maxstale* is specified) AND ((age of cached resource – Expires header) <= *maxstale*), THEN (use the cached copy)
        - ELSE (fetch from the server using GET)
    - ELSE (use the cached copy)

[14]See www.ietf.org/rfc/rfc2616.txt?number=2616

NOTE Platforms may perform an additional optimization and perform a "GET if modified" on a cached document when the policy requires a fetch from the server, particularly for long files.

NOTE For documents requested using protocols other than HTTP that do not support the notion of age or staleness, platforms must compute a resource's age from the time it was received and assume that resources expire immediately upon receipt.

Streaming Audio

VoiceXML 2.0 does not explicitly specify or require any behaviors for streaming audio. However, for the aforementioned reasons streaming audio can be an extremely beneficial performance optimization in practice for commercially deployed applications.

VoiceXML 2.0 specifies that platforms may at their discretion stream any audio resource as a performance optimization.

Future versions of VoiceXML are likely to include a *streaming* attribute and/or property that will enable developers to indicate their preference for streaming behavior.

HTTP Fetching Attributes

All elements that retrieve documents via HTTP support the following attributes to provide programmatic control for these behaviors:

ATTRIBUTE	DESCRIPTION
fetchaudio	Same as *fetchaudio* property, except only impacts the element where it is specified. Unlike the other attributes listed here, *fetchaudio* is only available on elements that retrieve VoiceXML documents; not grammar, audio, or script documents.
fetchhint	Same as *audiofetchhint* property, except only impacts the element where it is specified.
fetchtimeout	Same as *audiofetchtimeout* property, except only impacts the element where it is specified.
maxage	Same as *audiomaxage* property, except only impacts the element where it is specified.
maxstale	Same as *audiomaxstale* property, except only impacts the element where it is specified.

Conclusions

In this chapter, we've presented a comprehensive reference for the core elements and behaviors of the VoiceXML language. In the following three chapters, we'll explore some further details and techniques for maximizing the results you can achieve with VoiceXML programming.

VoiceXML Grammars and Speech Synthesis Markup Language (SSML)

VoiceXML Grammars

In speech applications, grammars define acceptable user utterances at various prompts and states of an application or service. Further, depending on the user utterance, a pre-defined action or task, such as providing the user with information, may be performed. You can define valid expressions for your application within a single grammar, but we recommend that you categorize expressions into separate grammars that have limited scopes. For example, a typical voice application provides instructions for:

- Navigating through menus and choosing an option
- Obtaining more information about an option
- Asking for help

To simplify your application, you should divide the commands for each type of action into a separate grammar. In addition to making your application easier to maintain, this approach enables you to control the scope of each grammar.

The grammar formats must meet two key VoiceXML requirements:

- VoiceXML platforms must support at least one common format, the Extensible Markup Language (XML) form of the World Wide Web Consortium (W3C) Speech Recognition Grammar Format (SRGF).

- VoiceXML platforms may support the Augmented Backus-Naur Form (ABNF) of the W3C SRGF. VoiceXML 2.0 browsers are required to support SRGF. Additionally, VoiceXML platforms may support other grammar formats such as JSGF, Nuance Grammar Specifications Language (GSL), or other proprietary formats. Platforms such as Tellme, BeVocal, and Nuance have implemented GSL, while platforms such as IBM have chosen JSGF.

The SRGF specification is available at www.w3.org/TR/speech-grammar. As just mentioned, the two grammar formats are:

1. **XML form:** The XML form represents a grammar as an XML document with the logical structure of the grammar captured by XML elements. This format is ideal for computer-to-computer communication of grammars because widely available XML technology (parsers, Extensible Style Language Transformation (XSLT), etc.) can be used to produce and accept the grammar format.

2. **ABNF form:** The logical structure of the grammar is captured by a combination of traditional Backus-Naur Form (BNF) and a regular expression language. This format is familiar to many current speech application developers, is similar to the proprietary grammar formats of most current speech recognizers, and is a more compact representation than XML. However, a special parser is required to accept this format. ABNF is different than extended BNF, which is used in document type definitions (DTDs) for XML and Standard Generalized Markup Language (SGML).

In this chapter we will review both grammar formats with examples and explanations.

MIME Types and File Extensions

Table 8.1 lists the Multipurpose Internet Mail Extensions (MIME) types and file extensions for grammar files for the various grammar formats.

The body of the grammar is basically a set of rules. Each rule has a unique name within the grammar and its scope can be public or private. A public rule may be activated for recognition. A public rule may also be imported into other grammars. All non-public rules are private. Private rules can be referenced only by other rules within the same grammar, but they can reference public rules imported from other grammars. Most importantly, a rule defines an expansion that declares how the rule is expanded into words, references to other rules, and patterns of words and references.

```
<grammar type="application|grammar+xml">
    <rule_id="consulting">
        <one-of>
            <item>creative</item>
            <item>technology</item>
            <item>strategy</item>
        </one-of>
</grammar>
```

Table 8.1 MIME Types and File Extensions for VoiceXML Grammar Files

GRAMMAR FORMAT	MIME TYPES	FILENAME EXTENSION
XML form	Application/grammar+xml	.grxml
ABNF form	Application/grammar	.grm
JSGF	Application/x-jsgf	.gram
GSL	Application/x-gsl	.grammar

Later, this rule can be referenced as:

```
<ruleref uri="#consulting"/>
```

We will look at other ways to reference grammars in more detail later in the chapter. Now, let's look at the various building blocks of grammar design: tokens, rule references, sequences, tags, choices, counts, and precedences.

Tokens

A token is the basic unit of grammar, which is basically the words the user can say. For example:

```
VoiceXML book
"New Delhi"
2
Travel
Tourist place
Help
```

are all tokens. If there is white space or special symbols (= * & ^ % $ # {} [] ( ) ,) between the words of a token, the token should appear within quotes (e.g., "New Delhi" or "Harry Smith"). Instead of using quotes, such tokens can also appear within the `<token></token>` elements:

```
<token>
     New Delhi
</token>
```

Optionally, one can also specify the language for appropriate speech synthesis with the `xml:lang` attribute. For example, schedule is pronounced differently in American and U.K. English, so the pronunciation can be differentiated by:

```
<token xml:lang="en-US">
     schedule
</token>
```

and

```
<token xml:lang="en-GB"
     schedule
</token>
```

Rules can specify multiple tokens, each with a different language/locale, and they can even specify tokens which, themselves, reference multiple languages at the same time.

NOTE Most platforms do not support simultaneous recognition in multiple languages. For example:

```
$welcome = bonjour|fr-FR |welcome|en-US
```

in ABNF form and

```
<rule Id="welcome">
    <one-of>
            <Item xml:lang="fr-FR">bonjour</Item>
            <Item xml:lang="en-US">welcome</Item>
    </one-of>
</rule>
```

in XML form.

You can also attach multiple languages to a token:

```
Herb|en-US, en-GB
```

in ABNF form, and

```
<rule Id="plants">
    <token lexicon="en-US, en-GB">Herb</token>
</rule>
```

Rule Reference

Table 8.2 summarizes the rule reference notation for ABNF and XML forms.

If a grammar is composed of multiple rule definitions at the top level, the grammar behaves as if they were a set of choices. It's important to be clear about sequence and choices and their usage. Multiple rule definitions can be overridden by specifying the root attribute of the `<grammar>` element. Root attribute forces the grammar to be treated as if it contained one rule reference to the given rule. For example,

```
<grammar root="country">
    <rule id="asia" scope "public">
    ...
    </rule>
    <rule id="Africa" scope "public">
    ...
    </rule>
</grammar>
```

The root rule must be public in scope.

Sequence

A sequence of tokens implies the order in which they must be spoken by the user and detected by the speech recognition engine. For example, for the grammar:

```
<grammar>
    San Francisco
</grammar>
```

Table 8.2 Rule Reference Notation for ABNF and XML Forms

REFERENCE TYPE	ABNF FORM	XML FORM
Local rule reference	`$rulename`, **e.g.,** `$state`, `$country`	`<ruleref uri="rulename"/>`, **e.g.,** `<ruleref uri="#state"/>`, `<ruleref uri="#country"/>`
Reference to a named rule of a grammar identified by a Uniform Resource Locator (URI)	`$(grammarURI#rulename)` **e.g.** `$` `$(http://www.VoiceXML.org/us.gram#state)`	`<rulerefuri="grammarURI# rulename;>`, **e.g.,**`>ruleref uri= http://www.VoiceXML.org/ us.gram#state/>`
Reference to the root rule of a grammar identified by a URI	`$(grammarURI)`, **e.g.,** `$(../state.gram)`	`<ruleref uri="grammarURI"/>`, **e.g.,** `<ruleref uri="../state.gram"/>`
Reference to a named rule of a grammar identified by an import alias (alias for a URI)	`$$alias#rulename`, **e.g.,** `$$us#state`	`<ruleref import="alias#rule name"/>`, **e.g.,** `<ruleref import="us#state"/>`
Reference to the root rule of a grammar identified by an import alias (alias for a URI)	`$$alias`, **e.g.,** `$$us`	`<ruleref import="alias"/>`, **e.g.,** `<ruleref import="us"/>`
Special rule definitions	`$NULL, $VOID, $GARBAGE`, **e.g.,** `$location = $country $GARBAGE $state`	`<ruleref special="#NULL"/>,` `<ruleref special="#VOID"/>,` `<ruleref special="#GARBAGE"/>,` **e.g.,** `<ruleid="us_state">,` `<ruleref uri="#country"/>,` `<ruleref special="GARBAGE"/>,` `<ruleref uri="#state"/>, </rule>`

San Francisco will be matched, but not Francisco San.

A sequence can also be a series of rule references or tokens or both combined; for instance, in ABNF format:

```
Rose is red
$flower is $color
$flower $color
(Rose is $color)
```

are all valid. In the last example parentheses are used for explicit boundaries.

In XML format, a sequence of XML rule expansion elements like `<ruleref>`, `<item>`, `<one-of>`, `<count>`, `<token>` and CDATA sections containing space separated tokens must be recognized in temporal sequence:

```
Rose is red
<ruleref uri="#flower"/> is <ruleref uri="#color"/>
<ruleref uri="#flower"/> <ruleref uri="#color"/>
<item>rose is <ruleref uri="#color"/> </item>
```

Tags

A tag is an arbitrary string that is utilized primarily for postprocessing of speech recognition results.

ABNF Form

A tag is delimited by curly braces and is a postfix attachment to a rule expansion. The number of opening curly braces matches the number of closing curly braces. This is useful when the enclosed text contains curly braces—for example, when the enclosed text is a scripting language. Alternatively, enclosed closing braces may be escaped with a backslash. A backslash must also be escaped with a backslash.

```
this is a test {tag attached to "test"}
open {action=open;} | close {action=shut;}
```

XML Form

A `<tag>` element may be attached to any of the rule expansion elements: `<ruleref>`, `<one-of>`, `<item>`, or `<count>`.

```
this is a <item tag='tag attached to "test"'>test</item>
<one-of>
     <item tag="action=open;"> open </item>
     <item tag="action=shut;"> close </item>
</one-of>
```

Choices

A choice or alternative is a set of options from which the user can choose (defined within the grammar). In ABNF form, the alternatives are separated by vertical bars (|) and optionally can be contained within parentheses, for example:

```
Washington | California | Oregon | $otherenergycrisisstates
(icecream | soda | coffee | tea)
```

Another option is to be able to apply weights to different alternatives indicating the likelihood of them being chosen by the user. Weights should be greater than zero and are floating point numbers, for example:

```
/23/ chevy | /34/ ford | /4/ impala
```

In XML form the choices are identified by `<one-of>` tag and then each choice is contained with `<item></item>` elements. Optionally, weights can be indicated by the weight attribute of the `<item>` element.

```
<grammar>
    <one-of>
         <item>Washington</item>
```

```
            <item>California</item>
            <item>Oregon</item>
            <ruleref uri="#otherenergycrisisstates"/></item>
      </one-of>
</grammar>

<grammar>
      <one-of>
            <item weight="23">chevy</item>
            <item weight="34">ford</item>
            <item weight="4"impala</item>
      </one-of>
</grammar>
```

Counts

The `<count>` tag provides a way to say that its contents are optional or may be repeated several times (specified by the number attribute). In XML form, the value of the number attribute could be set to ? or optional (the contents may be present 0 or 1 time in the utterance), 0+ (contents may be present 0, 1, or more times in the utterance), or 1+ (contents may be present one or more times in the utterance). For example,

```
<count number="0+">
    <count number="optional">
        <one-of>
            <item>half</item>
            <item>full</item>
        </one-of>
    </count>
day
<count number="optional">
    <count number="optional">boat</count>
    excursions
</count>
<count number="1+"><ruleref uri="#digit"/></count>
```

In ABNF, the optional expansions are delimited by square braces []. The operator * is attached to the choices that are to be repeated 0 or more times and + to the choices that are repeated 1 or more times. For example,

```
([half | full]) * day [ [boat] excursions ]
$digit +
```

Precedence

The precedence of rule expansion syntax is defined by some rules. This applies only to the ABNF format, as XML document structure is explicit. The following is the ordering of precedence of rule expansions. Parentheses are used when necessary to explicitly control rule structure:

1. Rulename denoted by $, and a quoted or unquoted token

2. Parentheses for grouping and square brackets for optional grouping

3. Unary operators such as +, *, and tag attachment, which apply to the tightest immediate preceding rule expansion

4. Sequence of rule expansions

5. Set of alternative rule expansions separated by vertical bars

Rule Definitions

A rule definition associates a legal rule expansion with a rulename and is responsible for defining the scope of the rule definition (whether it is local to the grammar in which it is defined or whether it may be imported into and referenced within other grammars). The rule definition may additionally include documentation comments and other pragmatics.

One important thing to keep in mind is that the rulename must be unique within a grammar. The same rulename may be used in multiple grammars, with the rulename resolution specification defining how to uniquely identify each rule definition.

ABNF Form

In ABNF form, the rule definition consists of an optional scoping declaration followed by a legal rule name, an equal sign, a legal rule expansion, and a closing semicolon. The rule definition has one of the following legal forms:

```
$ruleName = ruleExpansion;
public $ruleName = ruleExpansion;
private $ruleName = ruleExpansion;
```

For example:

```
private $city = Seattle | "New Delhi" | Sydney;
public $command = $action $object;
```

XML Form

A rule definition is represented by the `<rule>` element. The id attribute of the element indicates the name of the rule and must be unique within the grammar (this is enforced by XML). The contents of the `<rule>` element may be any legal rule expansion defined in Rule Reference section "

```
<rule id="city" scope="private">
    <one-of>
        <item>Seattle</item>
        <item>"New Delhi"</item>
        <item>Sydney</item>
    </one-of>
</rule>
```

```
<rule id="command" scope="public">
    <ruleref uri="#action"/>
    <ruleref uri="#object"/>
</rule>
```

A rule definition may be defined as local to a grammar or may be referenceable within other grammars. Rules with local scope are private and rules that may be referenced from other grammars are public. The default scope is private. Rules with public scope may be activated for recognition. That is, they may define the top-level syntax of spoken input. For instance, VoiceXML grammar activation may explicitly reference a single public rule or multiple public rules.

Grammar Documents

A grammar document specifies a set of associated rules. All rules defined within the grammar are scoped within the grammar's namespace. Each rule defined within the grammar must have a unique name. In the XML format the grammar name is an XML ID and must be a unique ID within the complete XML document. The character encoding indicates the symbol set used in the document. For example, for U.S. applications it would be common to use ASCII or the superset of ISO8859. For Japanese grammars, character sets such as Japan Industry Standard (JIS) and Unicode could be used. For both the ABNF and XML forms, the omission of the character encoding passes responsibility for determining encoding to the recognizer or host platform.

ABNF Form

The ABNF form defines the character encoding in the opening line of the grammar. A legal grammar must start with the pound symbol (#), and the characters leading to the first newline symbol are of the style:

```
#ABNF version-number optional-char-encoding;
#ABNF 1.0;
#ABNF 1.0 ISO8859-5;
#ABNF 1.0 JIS;
```

XML Form

XML defines character encodings as part of the document's XML declaration on the first line of the document. (Note that the version number in this declaration refers to the XML version and not the version of the grammar specification.)

```
<?xml version="1.0" ?>
<?xml version="1.0" encoding="ISO8859-5" ?>
<?xml version="1.0" encoding="JIS" ?>
```

The mode of a grammar indicates the type of input that the speech recognizer should be detecting. The default mode is voice. An alternative is dual-tone multifrequency (DTMF) input.

Grammar Mode

Grammar Mode indicates the type of input from the user. It could be voice (default) or dtmf input.

ABNF Form

```
mode voice;
mode dtmf;
```

XML Form

The mode declaration is provided as an optional mode attribute on the root `<grammar>` element. Legal values are voice (the default) and dtmf. Other values are permitted but should be considered vendor-specific.

```
<grammar mode="voice" version="1.0" xml:lang="en-US">
... imports
... rule definitions
</grammar>
```

Root Rule Declaration

The grammar specification permits rule references to target either a specific public rule definition of an external grammar or the implicit or explicit root rule defined within the grammar.

- **Explicit root rule:** Both the XML and ABNF forms permit the grammar header to declare a single rule to be the root rule of the grammar. The rule must be a public rule. The specified rule is the rule that is referenced when a `<ruleref>` element references the grammar without a rulename identifier (applies to both URI references and import references).

- **Implicit root rule:** For both the XML and ABNF forms, if there is not an explicit definition of the root rule, the speech recognizer should generate a root rule by the conjunction of all the public rules defined within the grammar. In effect, this is equivalent to defining a rule with all the public rules as alternatives. In other respects the implicit root rule is equivalent to explicit definition.

Although a grammar is not required to declare a root rule, it is good practice to declare the root rule of any grammar.

ABNF Form

An optional root rule declaration should follow the language and mode declarations (if present) or otherwise be the first noncomment declaration of an ABNF grammar file following the self-identifying header. The root declaration must identify one public rule defined elsewhere within the same grammar.

```
root rulename;
```

XML Form

The root rulename declaration is provided as an optional root attribute on the `<grammar>` element. The root declaration must identify one public rule defined elsewhere within the same grammar.

```
<grammar root="rulename" ...>
... imports
... rule definitions
</grammar>
```

DTMF Grammars

In addition to supporting speech recognition, the grammar format can be used to define patterns of DTMF input to a telephony browser. The following is a simple DTMF grammar that accepts a 10-digit Social Security number followed by a pound sign and allows * for invoking help.

ABNF Form

```
#ABNF 1.0 ISO8859-1;
mode dtmf;

$digit = 0 | 1 | 2 | 3 | 4 | 5 | 6 | 7 | 8 | 9;
public $ssn= $digit $digit $digit $digit $digit $digit $digit
$digit $digit $digit "#" | "*";
```

XML Form

```
<?xml version="1.0"?>
<grammar mode="dtmf" version="1.0">

<rule id="digit">
    <one-of>
        <item> 0 </item>
        <item> 1 </item>
        <item> 2 </item>
        <item> 3 </item>
        <item> 4 </item>
        <item> 5 </item>
        <item> 6 </item>
        <item> 7 </item>
```

```
                <item> 8 </item>
                <item> 9 </item>
        </one-of>
    </rule>

    <rule id="ssn" scope="public">
        <one-of>
            <item>
                <ruleref uri="#digit"/> <ruleref uri="#digit"/>
                <ruleref uri="#digit"/> <ruleref uri="#digit"/>
                <ruleref uri="#digit"/> <ruleref uri="#digit"/>
                <ruleref uri="#digit"/> <ruleref uri="#digit"/>
                <ruleref uri="#digit"/> <ruleref uri="#digit"/>
                #
            </item>
            <item>
            *
            </item>
        </one-of>
    </rule>

</grammar>
```

Grammar Scope

Grammars can be active for the entire application, a document, a form, or a field. Multiple grammars can be active at the same time so that if a caller is in a form and speaks a word in a higher-level grammar, the caller is taken to the document or form where that grammar was defined, unless an event is defined that throws the caller to an event. If there is an event, execution resumes at the point where the match occurred in the current form, after the event is handled. The default scope for a grammar is the element in which it is defined. Therefore, a field grammar is active for that field, a form grammar is active for that form, etc. See Chapters 6 and 7 for details on scoping.

Precedence Order

Precedence order is used when input matches more than one active grammar. If the input matches more than one active grammar with the same precedence, precedence is determined by document order.

If input matches grammar in a form or menu other than the current form or menu, control passes to the other form or menu. In transition to another form, all current form data is lost.

Grammar Elements

Table 8.4 summarizes the elements of the `<grammar>` element.

Table 8.3 Grammar Scopes

ELEMENT	SCOPE IS	GRAMMAR IS ACTIVE
`<form>`	Dialog (default) Document Document in the root document	Only in the form in which it is defined During any dialog in the same document During any dialog in any document of this application
`<menu>`	Dialog (default) Document Menu in the application root document	Only when the user transitions into the menu Over the whole document In any loaded document in the application
`<grammar>`	Dialog (default)	Throughout the current form
	Document	In all dialogs of the current document (and relevant application leaf documents)
	Grammar in the application root document	In any loaded document in the application
`<link>`	Element containing the link	For the entire application (if defined directly under the `<vxml>` element)

Grammar Examples

In the following example, a rule (rule id= "country") is defined that specifies a list of valid choices from a list of cities. The `<one of>` element specifies that the rule is met when one of the words in the list of `<items>` is matched.

The next rule (rule id="medals") is defined as a choice among a list of medals; a rule with id= 'medal_tally' is defined as a typical restaurant search request that uses the other two rules.

The country rule is public, so a match can be made by saying either the country from the country rule, a medal type from the medals rule, or a phrase for a country, as defined by medal_tally. Also, phrases such as total medals won by France would match all three rules. If the medal_tally rule were not public, saying total medals won by France would not work.

```
<?xml version="1.0"?>

<grammar xml:lang="en-US">

  <rule id="country" scope="public">
     <one-of>
       <item>united states</item>
       <item>france</item>
       <item>england</item>
       <item>nigeria</item>
```

Table 8.4 `<grammar>` Element

Syntax	

Syntax	```<grammar>```
	```scope="dialog"```
	```src="URL"```
	```type="mime_types"```
	```mode="dtmf"|"voice"```
	```root="text"```
	```version="1.0"|"2.0"```
	```xml:lang="text"```
	```caching="safe"|"fast"```
	```fetchhint="prefetch"|"safe"|"stream"```
	```fetchtimeout="time_interval"```
	```fetchaudio="URL">```
	```Optional inline grammar```
	```</grammar>```

Description	Specifies a speech recognition grammar

Attribute	Description	Required/ Optional
scope	Sets the scope of grammar: Document—the form's grammar is active throughout the current document Dialogue—the form's grammar is active throughout the current form Default is set by parent element	Optional
src	Uniform Resource Locator (URL) of the grammar specification (external file)	Optional
type	MIME type of the grammar, e.g.: Nuance GSL—application/x-gsl JSGF—application/x-jsgf Grammar XML—application/grammar+xml	Optional
mode	Mode of input: dtmf/voice	Optional
root	Name of the root grammar rule	Optional
version	Version of grammar	Optional
xml:lang	Language and country identifier, for example, en-US for US English	Optional
caching	"safe" forces a resource fetch every time the resource is used "fast" enables use of a cache	Optional
fetchhint	Specifies when a resource may be fetched and when to begin using it Options are: "prefetch": fetch the resource at any time after the page is loaded	Optional

continues

266

Table 8.4   *(Continued)*

Attribute	Description	Required/Optional
fetchhint	"safe":-fetch the resource at the time it is referenced "stream": fetch the resource at the time it is referenced and should begin using it while the resource is being fetched without waiting for the fetch to complete	
fetchtimeout	The length of time to wait before throwing an error.badfetch event. Value is in seconds (s) or the default milliseconds (ms)	Optional
fetchaudio	Specifies the URL of an audio clip to play while the VoiceXML document is being fetched	Optional

Usage	Parents	Children
`<choice>`	`<link>`	`<import>`
`<field>`	`<record>`	`<rule>`
`<form>`	`<transfer>`	

Example

```
<vxml version="2.0">
 <property name="universals" value="all" />
 <!-- this sets the universals property, enabling
     a global grammar for "help" -->
 <form id="launch_missiles">
   <field name="password">
       <grammar type="application/grammar+xml">
        <rule id="password" scope="public">
         <item tag="rutabaga">rutabage</item>
        </rule>
       </grammar>
       <prompt>What is the code word?</prompt>
       <help>It is the name of an obscure
          vegetable.
           <reprompt/>
       </help>
       <noinput count="3">
          Security violation!
          <exit />
       </noinput>
       <nomatch count="3">
          Security violation!
          <exit />
       </nomatch>
       <!-- these noinput and nomatch handlers are
          only activated on the third try. Before
          that, the platform-defined defaults are
          used. -->
```

continues

Table 8.4 *(Continued)*

Attribute	Description	Required/Optional

```
        <filled>
          <audio>You got it!</audio>
          <clear />
        </filled>
      </field>
    </form>
    </vxml>
```

```
      <item>australia</item>
    </one-of>
  </rule>

  <rule id="medals" scope="public">
    <one-of>
      <item>gold</item>
      <item>silver</item>
      <item>bronze</item>
      <item>total</item>
    </one-of>
  </rule>

  <rule id="medal_tally" scope="public">
    <example>total medals won by france</example>
    <ruleref uri="#medals"/> medals won by <ruleref
uri="#country"/>
  </rule>

</grammar>
```

The <example> element allows examples of words or phrases that match the rule definition to be included for a rule. The <example> element has no attributes and cannot have any other child elements. An example is similar to a comment. By including examples, automated tools can use them to test a rule definition or generate documentation or as examples to help users in voice applications.

There is no limit to the number of examples that can be included in a definition.

```
<!-- This rule defines a restaurant request -->
  <rule id="restaurant_request" scope="public">
    <example>chinese restaurant in chicago</example>
    <ruleref uri="#cuisine"/> restaurant in <ruleref
uri="#city"/>
  </rule>
</grammar>

<?xml version="1.0"?>
```

```
<grammar xml:lang="en" version="1.0" root="basicCommand">

<import name="polite"
        uri="http://www.sayplease.com/politeness.xml"/>

<rule id="basicCommand" scope="public">
  <example>please move the window</example>
  <example>open a file</example>

  <!-- A sequence of 3 rule references -->
  <ruleref import="polite#startPolite"/>
  <ruleref uri="#command"/>
  <ruleref import="polite#endPolite"/>
</rule>

<rule id="command">
  <example>move the window</example>
  <!-- A sequence of 2 rule references -->
  <ruleref uri="#action"/> <ruleref uri="#object"/>
</rule>

<rule id="action">
  <one-of>
    <item>open</item>
    <item>close</item>
    <item>delete</item>
    <item>move</item>
  </one-of>
</rule>

<rule id="object">
  <count number="optional">
    <one-of>
      <item>the</item>
      <item>a</item>
    </one-of>
  </count>
  <one-of>
    <item>window</item>
    <item>file</item>
    <item>menu</item>
  </one-of>
</rule>
</grammar>
```

Internationalization

Both the ABNF and XML grammar formats permit the use of a wide range of character encodings. For example, Shift-JIS can be used for the Japanese character sets (kanji, katakana, and hiragana). The grammar format also allows the mixing of more than one language in a grammar—or even in a single utterance.

Imports

The <import> element allows local aliases to be assigned to an external grammar. An alias is used in a local rule to refer to a grammar defined in an external URI. The <import> element should be declared as a child of the <grammar> element. It must be declared before the first <rule> element. The <import> element cannot contain any text or a child element. The reference must include both the grammar name and the name of a rule defined within that grammar. The syntax for an imported rule is the imported alias followed by the hash separator # and the rulename within the imported grammar. A name attribute is used to assign an alias to the imported grammar. Alias names must be unique.

```
<?xml version="1.0"?>
<grammar xml:lang= "en">
<import uri="http://my_server/states.gram" name="states"/>

    <rule id="state_Info" scope="public">
    <item>What's the capital of <ruleref
            import="drinks#hawaii"/></item>
    </rule>
</grammar>
```

Referencing Internal Grammars

References to internal grammar descriptions must be placed inside the <grammar> elements in the VoiceXML code. CDATA escapes are used in the description to include any special characters, which the VoiceXML code cannot recognize. XML rules for < , >, and & do not have to be followed if you place them within the CDATA escapes.

```
<vxml version="2.0">
<form>
    <grammar>
    <![CDATA[
        Inline Grammar
        ]]>
    </grammar>
```

Mixed-Initiative Grammars

The previous section talked about forms implementing rigid, computer-directed conversations. To make a form mixed-initiative (i.e., both the computer and the human direct the conversation), there must be one or more <initial> form items and one or more form-level grammars.

If a form has form-level grammars:

■ Its fields can be filled in any order.

■ More than one field can be filled as a result of a single user utterance.

Also, the form's grammars can be active when the user is in other dialogues. If a document has two forms on it—say a car rental form and a hotel reservation form—and both forms have grammars that are active for that document, a user could respond to a request for hotel reservation information with information about the car rental, and thus direct the computer to talk about the car rental instead. The user can speak to any active grammar and have fields set and actions taken in response.

```
<vxml 2.0>
<form id="seattle_traffic_info">

<grammar src="seattletrafficinfo.grxml"
type="application/grammar+xml"/>

 <!-- Caller can't barge in on today's advertisement. -->
 <block>
  <prompt bargein="false">
     Welcome to AT&T's traffic info center
     <audio src="http://www.online-ads.example/wis.wav"/>
  </prompt>
 </block>

 <initial name="start">
  <prompt>
     Please say the highway for which you would like traffic reports
  </prompt>
  <help>
    Please say the name of the highway and direction
     For example, Highway I-5 North
  </help>

  <!-- If user is silent, reprompt once, then
    try directed prompts. -->
  <noinput count="1"> <reprompt/></noinput>
  <noinput count="2"> <reprompt/>
     <assign name="start" expr="true"/></noinput>
 </initial>

<var name="hours"/>

<block>
 <script>
  var d = new Date();
  hours = d.getHours();
 </script>
</block>

<field name="highway">
 <prompt>What's the highway?<prompt>
 <help>
  Please say the highway for which you would like traffic reports
 </help>
</field>
```

```
<field name="direction">
 <prompt>Please say highway direction <value expr="highway"/>
       </prompt>
 <help>
       Please say the direction of the highway for which you would like
       to hear the traffic reports
</help>

<filled>
 <!-- In the mornings, folks generally ask for South and in the
afternoon and evening, North -->
 <if cond="highway == 'I-5' && hours < 12 && direction == undefined">
  <assign name="direction" expr="'South'"/>
 else
  <assign name="direction" expr="'North'"/>

  </if>
 </filled>
</field>

<field name="go_ahead" type="boolean" modal="true">
 <prompt>Do you want to hear the traffic reports for
   <value expr="highway"/>, <value expr="direction"/>?
 </prompt>
 <filled>
    <if cond="go_ahead">
      <prompt bargein="false">
        <audio src="http://www.online-ads.example/wis2.wav"/>
      </prompt>
      <submit next="/servlet/seattletrafficinfo" namelist="highway
direction"/>
    </if>
    <clear namelist="start highway direction go_ahead"/>
 </filled>
 </field>
</form>
</vxml>
```

The human-computer Interaction might go as follows:

C: Welcome to AT&T's traffic Info center. Joe's Pizza Shop brings this
traffic report to you. Please say the highway for which you would
like traffic reports.

H: (Silence)

C: Please say the name of the highway and direction. For example,
Highway I-5 North.

H: I-5.

C: Do you want to hear traffic reports for I-5 North?

H: No.

C: Please say the highway for which you would like traffic reports.

H: I-5 South.

```
C:   For mouth-watering pizza, don't forget Joe. There is one accident
     reported near Northgate on I-5 South, two left lanes are blocked,
     heavy traffic.
```

The go_ahead field has its modal attribute set to true. This causes all grammars to be disabled except the ones defined in the current form item, so that the only grammar active during this field is the built-in grammar for boolean.

An experienced user can get things done much faster (but is still forced to listen to the ads):

```
C:   Welcome to AT&T's traffic Info center. Joe's Pizza Shop brings this
     traffic report to you.
H:   Yeah, yeah . . .
C:   Please say the highway . . .
H (barging in):  I-5 North.
C:   Do you . . .
H (barging in):  Yes.
C:   For mouth-watering pizza, don't forget Joe. There is one accident
     reported near Northgate on I-5 South, two left lanes are blocked,
     heavy traffic.
```

For more information on mixed initiative, see Chapter 6.

SSML

Speech synthesis markup language (SSML) based on the Java Speech Markup Language (JSML) specification is part of the W3C framework. Its goal is to provide developers with a standard way to control elements of speech synthesis such as pitch, rate, pronunciation, and volume across different platforms. In this section we will briefly review some of the SSML elements and how they can be used to enhance user experience of text-to-speech (TTS) environments. The latest W3C document on SSML can be found at www.w3.org/TR/speech-synthesis.

Figure 8.1 shows an overview of SSML.

The elements and attributes of SSML can be broadly represented as follows:

- Document structure, text processing, and pronunciation

- Prosody and style

- Miscellaneous

Let's discuss them one at a time.

Document Structure, Text Processing, and Pronunciation

In this section we discuss the <speak>, <xml:lang>, <paragraph>, <sentence>, <say-as>, and <phoneme> elements.

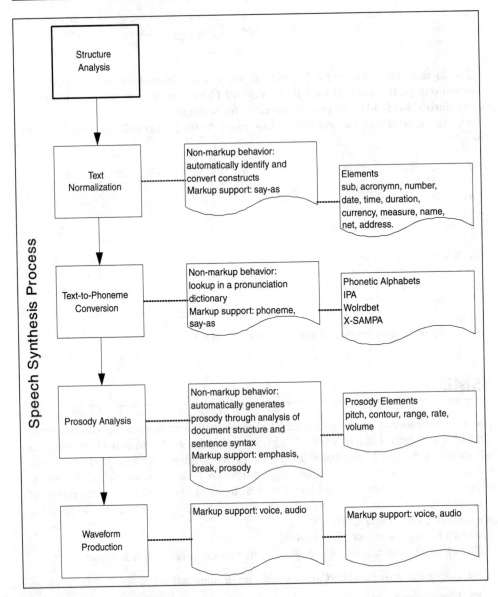

Figure 8.1 Overview of SSML.

`<speak>`

The root element `<speak>` is required when the document type is synthesis only.

```
<?xml version="1.0"?>
<speak>
SSML body ...
</speak>
```

SSML fragments are denoted by `<prompt>` containers when imbedded in a VoiceXML dialog:

```
<prompt>Please say your city.</prompt>
```

The `<prompt>` element controls the output of synthesized speech and prerecorded audio within a dialogue instance. The `<prompt>...</prompt>` container is not required in cases where there is no need to specify a prompt attribute, and the prompt further contains no speech markups or consists of just an `<audio>` element:

```
<audio src="say_your_city.wav"/>
```

xml:lang

The xml:lang attribute is derived from the XML language and is used to indicate language associated with the application document. The speech output platform determines behavior in the case where a document requires speech output in a language not supported by the speech output platform according to common text formatting patterns of the language.

```
<speak xml:lang="en-US">
    <paragraph>I don't speak Japanese.</paragraph>
    <paragraph xml:lang="ja">Nihongo-ga wakarimasen.
    </paragraph>
</speak>
```

The format for the language code is specified by ISO 639 (language) and ISO 3166 (country). Some examples are given in Table 8.5.

The browser specifies the default if xml:language is not specified. The child elements inherit language information.

Table 8.5 Language and Country Codes

ISO 639 CODES	ISO 3166 CODES
AR = Arabic	AU = Australia
DA = Danish	AU = Australia
EN = English	CN = China
ES = Spanish	FR = France
FR = French	GB = United Kingdom
JP = Japanese	HK = Hong Kong
RU = Russian	JP = Japan
VI = Vietnamese	RU = Russia
ZH = Chinese	US = United States

`<paragraph>` *and* `<sentence>`

`<paragraph>` and `<sentence>` elements are used to delimit sentences and paragraphs explicitly. The `<paragraph>` element represents the paragraph structure in text. A `<sentence>` element represents the sentence structure in text. A paragraph contains zero or more sentences.

```
<prompt>
     <paragraph>
      <sentence>
        This is the first sentence of the paragraph.
   </sentence>
   <sentence>
        Here's another sentence.
        </sentence>
   </paragraph>
   </prompt>
```

The use of `<paragraph>` and `<sentence>` elements is optional. Where text occurs without an enclosing `<paragraph>` or `<sentence>` element, the SSML processor should attempt to determine the structure. These elements are used by the speech synthesizer to inflect speech (depending on the language) by including pauses and emphasis at the starting and ending of paragraphs and sentences.

`<say-as>`

The `<say-as>` element indicates the type of text construct contained within the element. This information is used to help disambiguate the pronunciation of the contained text. In any case, it is assumed that pronunciations generated through the use of explicit text markup always take precedence over pronunciations produced by a lexicon.

The type attribute is a required attribute that indicates the contained text construct. The base set of enumerated type values includes spell-out (contained text is pronounced as individual characters), acronym (contained text is an acronym), number, date, time (time of day), duration (temporal duration), currency, measure (measurement), telephone (telephone number), name, net (Internet identifier), and address (indicates a postal address).

Some examples are as follows:

Acronym

```
<say-as type="spell-out">
    USA </say-as>
<!-- U. S. A. -->

<say-as type="acronym">
    IBM </say-as>
<!-- I. B. M. ‡
```

Numerical Digits

```
Rocky <say-as type="number">XIII</say-as>
<!-- Rocky thirteen -->

My name is John Stevens
<say-as type="number:ordinal">VI</say-as>
<!-- Pope John the sixth -->

Deliver to
<say-as type="number:digits">123 </say-as>
Brookwood.
<!-- Deliver to one two three Brookwood-->
```

Date, Time, and Measure Types

```
<say-as type="date:ymd"> 2000/1/20 </say-as>
<!-- January 20th two thousand -->

Proposals are due in
<say-as type="date:my"> 5/2001 </say-as>
<!-- Proposals are due in May two thousand and one -->
```

Currency, Measure, Telephone

```
The total is <say-as type="currency">&20.45</say-as>
<!-- The total is twenty dollars and forty-five cents -->
```

Address, Name, Net Types

```
<say-as type="net:email">
road.runner@acme.com
</say-as>
```

Substitution

```
<say-as sub="World Wide Web Consortium">
W3C </say-as>
<!-- World Wide Web Consortium -->
```

<phoneme>

The <phoneme> element provides a phonetic pronunciation for the contained text. The <phoneme> element may be empty. However, it is recommended that the element contain human-readable text that can be used for nonspoken rendering of the document. The ph attribute is a required attribute that specifies the phoneme string itself. The alphabet attribute is an optional attribute that specifies the phonetic alphabet. Phoneme alphabets currently supported by SSML include the International Phonetic Alphabet (IPA), WorldBet, and Extension of Speech Assessment Methods Phonetic Alphabet www.phon.ucl.ac.uk/home/sampa/x-sampa.htm (X-SAMPA).

```
Well
<phoneme alphabet="worldbet" ph="h;&amp;l;ou>
hello
</phoneme>
there!
```

Prosody and Style

In this section we discuss the `<voice>`, `<emphasis>`, `<break>`, and `<prosody>` elements.

`<voice>`

The `<voice>` element is a production element that requests a change in speaking voice. Optional attributes include:

- **gender**—gender of the voice to speak the contained text, with enumerated values male, female, neutral.
- **age**—age of the voice; takes on integer values.
- **category**—preferred age category of the voice, with enumerated values child, teenager, adult, elderly.
- **variant**—preferred variant of the other voice; takes on integer values.
- **name**—a platform-specific voice name. The value may be a space-separated list of names ordered from top preference down.

```
<voice gender="female" category="child">
    There comes Santa
</voice>

<voice gender="female" category="child" variant="2">
    and my presents
</voice>

<!-- platform-specific voice selection -->
<voice name="Mike">I want to be like Mike.</voice>
```

When there is no voice available that exactly matches the attributes specified in the document, a conforming SSML processor should throw an error event. Subsequent behavior of the application after the error event may be platform-specific. Voice attributes are inherited down the tree, including elements that change the language:

```
<voice gender="female">
 any female voice
   <voice category="child">
     female child voice
       <paragraph xml:lang="ja">
```

```
        <!-- A female child voice in Japanese. -->
      </paragraph>
    </voice>
  </voice>
```

A change in voice resets the prosodic parameters because different voices have different natural pitches and speaking rates. The xml:lang attribute may also be used to request usage of a voice with a specific dialect or other variant of the enclosing language.

`<emphasis>`

The `<emphasis>` element requests that the contained text be spoken with emphasis (also referred to as prominence or stress). The synthesizer essentially determines how to render emphasis, since the nature of emphasis differs between languages, dialects, or even voices. The optional level attribute indicates the strength of emphasis to be applied.

```
Today I got a <emphasis> big </emphasis> raise.
I am <emphasis level="strong">
so
</emphasis>happy.
```

`<break>`

The `<break>` element is an empty element that controls the pausing or other prosodic boundaries between words. If the element is not defined, the speech synthesizer is expected to automatically determine a break based on the linguistic context. Optional attributes include size and time.

```
First go right <break/> then take a left
Once you find the red brick building <break time="1s"/>
Stop.
```

In practice, the `<break>` element is most often used to override the typical automatic behavior of a speech synthesizer.

`<prosody>`

The `<prosody>` element permits control of the pitch, speaking rate, and volume of the speech output. The attributes include:

- **pitch**—the baseline pitch for the contained text in Hertz.
- **contour**—the actual pitch contour for the contained text.
- **rate**—the speaking rate for the contained text.
- **duration**—the time to take to read the element contents.
- **volume**—the volume for the contained text in the range 0.0 to 100.0. Relative changes for any of these attributes above are specified as floating point values.

For the pitch and range attributes, relative changes in semitones are permitted: "+5st", "–2st". Since speech synthesizers are not able to apply arbitrary prosodic values, conforming speech synthesis processors may set platform-specific limits on the values.

```
The price of the package is
<prosody rate="-10%">
   <say-as type="currency">$45
     </say-as>
</prosody>
```

The contour attribute is used to define a set of pitch targets at specified intervals in the speech output. The algorithm for interpolating between the targets is platform-specific. In each pair of the form (interval,target), the first value is a percentage of the period of the contained text and the second value is the value of the pitch attribute.

```
<prosody contour="(0%,+20) (10%,+30%) (40%,+10)">
 good morning
</prosody>
```

Miscellaneous Elements

In this section we discuss the <audio> element.

<audio>

The <audio> element supports the insertion of recorded audio files and the insertion of other audio formats in conjunction with synthesized speech output. The <audio> element may be empty. If the <audio> element is not empty, the contents correspond to the marked-up text to be spoken if the audio document is not available. The required attribute is src, which is the URI of a document with an appropriate MIME type.

```
<!-- Empty element -->
Please say your name after the tone.
<audio src="beep.wav"/>

<!-- Container element with alternative text -->
<audio src="prompt.au">
What city do you want to fly from?</audio>
```

The <audio> element is not intended to be a complete mechanism for synchronizing synthetic speech output with other audio output or other output media (video, etc.).

SSML provides developers with the flexibility of controlling the synthesis and speech aspects of the voice applications. The standard will continue to evolve to support even richer features and functionality.

Referencing N-Gram Documents

The Voice Browser Working Group is developing the Speech Recognition N-Gram Grammar Specification in parallel with VoiceXML specification. N-gram SGML defines syntax for representing N-Gram (Markovian) stochastic grammars within the W3C Voice Browser Markup Language. An N-Gram grammar is a representation of an Nth-order Markov language model in which the probability of occurrence of a symbol is conditioned upon the prior occurrence of $N - 1$ other symbols. N-Gram grammars are typically constructed from statistics obtained from a large corpus of text using the co-occurrences of words in the corpus to determine word sequence probabilities. N-Gram grammars have the advantage of being able to cover a much larger language than would normally be derived directly from a corpus. Open vocabulary applications are easily supported with N-Gram grammars.

These two specifications represent different and complementary ways of informing a speech recognizer about which words and patterns of words to listen for. A speech recognizer may choose to support the Speech Recognition N-Gram Grammar Specification in addition to the Speech Recognition Grammar Specification defined in this document. If a speech recognizer supports both grammar representations, it may optionally support references between the two formats. Grammars defined in the ABNF or XML formats may reference start symbols of N-Gram documents and vice versa.

The syntax for referencing an N-Gram document is the same as that for referencing externally defined ABNF or XML grammar documents. Both URI references and import referencing methods are permitted in the ABNF and XML forms. The fragment identifier (a rulename when referencing ABNF and XML grammars) identifies a start symbol as defined by the N-Gram specification. If the start symbol is absent, the N-Gram as a whole is referenced as defined in the N-Gram specification.

ABNF Form

The URI references and import references to N-Gram documents follow the same syntax as references to other ABNF/XML grammar documents. The following are examples of a URI reference and an import reference, each with an explicit rule reference and a reference to the root rule.

```
$(http://voicexml.com/ngram.xml#StartSymbol)
$(http://voicexml.com/ngram.xml)

$$ngram#StartSymbol
$$ngram
```

XML Form

URI references and import references to N-Gram documents follow the same syntax as references to other ABNF/XML grammar documents. The following are examples of a URI reference and an import reference, each with an explicit rule reference and a reference to the root rule.

```
<ruleref uri="http://voicexml.com/ngram.xml#StartSymbol"/>
<ruleref uri="http://voicexml.com/ngram.xml"/>

<ruleref import="ngram#StartSymbol"/>
<ruleref import="ngram"/>
```

In this chapter we have reviewed the details of SRGF and SSML. This completes our introduction to VoiceXML. We will be applying the basics learned in the next few chapters, where we discuss advanced and practical aspects of voice application development such as security, voice user interface design, and using Extensible Style Language (XSL) to create dynamic VoiceXML applications. In the next chapter we will learn about creating dynamic VoiceXML applications from server-side data using some examples.

Dynamic VoiceXML: Generating Voice Applications from Server-Side Data

As discussed in previous chapters, the true power of VoiceXML goes far beyond the details of the language itself; rather, it is in the ability of VoiceXML to extend the Web paradigm for application development to the phone. VoiceXML provides a simple, text-based markup language to express the user interface—the presentation layer—for voice-activated telephone applications. Because VoiceXML is an Extensible Markup Language (XML)-based language, everything about it inherits from and fits within the technologies, architectures, and development strategies for building and deploying Internet-powered applications for any device.

In this chapter, we will briefly recap how traditional Web applications are built using server-side logic to dynamically generate Hypertext Markup Language (HTML) markup; then we will walk through a series of simple examples that demonstrate using analogous techniques to create powerful VoiceXML applications that fully inherit any existing Web-based infrastructure you may have in place.

Dynamic Web Applications Overview

Some Web sites consist of purely static content—they are a simple series of static HTML documents stored on one or more Web servers. This, of course, was the original goal of the creation of HTML and the Web—a basic mechanism to allow the seamless interchange of documents across the Internet without the need to mail individual copies to all intended recipients and without requiring readers to have a particular high-end, proprietary word processing program to open and view the documents.

However, few Web sites and Web applications today are purely made up of static content. They are almost invariably produced from a combination of server- and client-side logic dynamically accessing and then processing at least one back-end data source to produce custom HTML documents that are generated on the fly. Figure 9.1 illustrates at a high level the components used to produce most sophisticated Web applications today. Generally speaking, the process works as follows:

1. The user launches the Web browser software (e.g., Microsoft Internet Explorer 5.1) on his or her personal computer (PC).

2. The user types the Uniform Resource Locator (URL) for a particular Web site (e.g., http://studio.tellme.com) into the browser.

3. The browser initiates a Hypertext Transfer Protocol (HTTP) request for that URL to the appropriate Web server on the Internet, based upon a Domain Naming System (DNS) lookup to find the Internet Protocol (IP) address corresponding with the domain and server name within the URL (e.g., 64.41.140.79).

4. The Web server receives the request, and it begins to be processed by application server software (e.g., Microsoft Active Server Pages, IBM Websphere, BEA WebLogic).

5. The application server maps the requested URL to some number of scripts that contain business rules and user interface logic (e.g., business objects, authentication/authorization code, global navigation).

6. These scripts execute, often communicating with back-end systems to retrieve data specific to this request, such as a personalized user profile or a search result (e.g., Oracle databases, Inktomi index engines).

7. When complete, the user interface (UI) scripts format whatever data has been collected into a specific HTML document and respond to the original request.

8. The browser receives the HTML document, repeats steps 1 through 7 to retrieve any images or other related files referenced within it, and then ultimately displays it on the user's screen.

The amount and sophistication of work that must be done on the server in steps 4 through 7—and in fact whether there are distinct application server, business rules, and UI scripts layers at all—vary enormously from site to site and are completely dependent on the nature of the application or service being provided. However, in principle, all of these logical steps compose the anatomy of how a dynamic Web page is delivered.

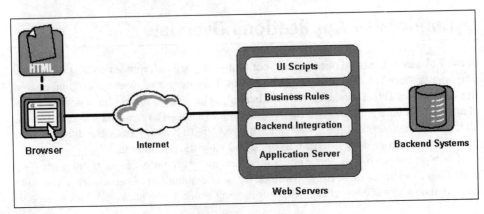

Figure 9.1 Conceptual overview of dynamic Web sites.

Some common examples of using dynamic data to generate HTML and Web applications are as follows:

■ **Simple computation.** The simplest form of dynamic data does not involve communication with back-end systems at all, but rather takes a simple set of inputs from the user as part of the HTTP request (using the URL query string or an HTTP POST) and performs some basic manipulation to modify what would otherwise be a static HTML page before responding to the request. Examples of this would be a simple tip calculator (e.g., www.gseis.ucla.edu/etu/training/materials/php_basics/tips.html) or "Mad Libs" (e.g., http://hammer.ne.mediaone.net/madlibs/madlib.html).

■ **UI templates/database lookup.** Online encyclopedias, newspapers, schedules, dictionaries, and other reference materials are extremely common on the Web. These sites typically involve vast databases of content in the same basic format, such as movie reviews, magazine articles, word definitions, etc. Even though the content varies from entry to entry, the basic form—and hence the format in which it will be displayed—remains almost identical. Rather than creating thousands or millions of static HTML pages for each entry and duplicating all of the UI/formatting code every time, it's much more efficient and manageable to store the content in its raw form (e.g., plaintext) in a database, and then have a single page on the Web site. This page is really a script that takes input parameters (again, using the query string, etc.), then dynamically looks up the appropriate entry in the database and formats it into the standard HTML template before responding to the user's original request. The result is that site administrators can easily maintain a content database, and adding or changing new entries is simply a matter of updating the one record in the database. Similarly, updating the UI simply requires changing the one template script, rather than having to modify thousands or millions of individual pages. For some examples of this kind of site, see http://www.transitinfo.org/cgi-bin/map_sched/CT and http://us.imdb.com/search.

■ **Real-time data.** Following the same concepts as UI templates, real-time data sites dynamically connect to continually changing data sources in addition to or instead of relatively static content databases. Examples include currency calculators, such as www.xe.com/ucc/, and any financial site that provides stock quotes and other up-to-the-minute information.

■ **Transactions.** Transactions and e-commerce have become one of the cornerstones of Internet-powered applications. Once again, the basic moving parts of HTML markup, business rules, UI scripts, and back-end data access remain the same. However, in this case the back-end systems are being written to in addition to simple information retrieval. Amazon.com, home banking sites, and thousands of other Web services exist that power sophisticated transactions.

Developers use an extremely wide variety of technologies on and off the Web Server to build dynamic Web applications. While this book does not go into detail on any of them, there are a staggering range of resources available online and in print for learning about the features and distinguishing characteristics of various approaches. Tables 9.1 and 9.2 summarize some of the leading technologies in common use today. Table 9.3 lists some advanced application server platforms.

Table 9.1 Web Servers

VENDOR	PRODUCT	OPERATING SYSTEMS	PRODUCT INFORMATION
Apache Software Foundation	Apache	Windows, UNIX	www.apache.org
Microsoft	Internet Information Server (IIS)	Windows	www.microsoft.com
Netscape	iPlanet Web Server	Windows, UNIX	www.iplanet.com

Table 9.2 Scripting Languages and Basic Platforms

LANGUAGE	PLATFORMS	PRODUCT INFORMATION
ECMAScript (JavaScript)	All	www.ecma.ch/ecma1/stand/ecma-262.htm
VBScript	Windows	msdn.microsoft.com/scripting/default.htm?/scripting/vbscript/default.htm
Practical Extraction Report Language (Perl)	All	www.perl.org/
PHP	All	www.php.net/
Active Server Pages (ASP)	All	msdn.microsoft.com/library/default.asp?URL=/library/psdk/iisref/aspguide.htm
Java Server Pages (JSP)	All	java.sun.com/products/jsp/

Table 9.3 Advanced Application Server Platforms

VENDOR	PRODUCT	OPERATING SYSTEMS	PRODUCT INFORMATION
Microsoft	BizTalk server	Windows	www.microsoft.com/biztalk
Netscape	IPlanet application server	Windows, UNIX	www.iplanet.com/products
BEA	WebLogic	Windows, UNIX	www.bea.com
IBM	Websphere application server	Windows, UNIX	www-4.ibm.com/software/webservers/appserv/
Allaire	ColdFusion	Windows, UNIX	www.macromedia.com/software/coldfusion
Allaire	Jrun	Windows, UNIX	www.allaire.com/Products/JRun/

Given this brief foundation, let's begin to explore how to apply these industry standard techniques and technologies to dynamically generating voice applications using VoiceXML. All of the examples discussed in this chapter are purposefully simple: By demonstrating a high-level overview of several common techniques as applied to VoiceXML, we aim to provide sufficient context for the experienced Web developer to make the transition to developing VoiceXML.

NOTE Many of the code examples included are reproduced with permission from Tellme Networks, Inc. and Tellme Studio (http://studio.tellme.com).

Starting Simple: Query String Parameters

Query string parameters are the simplest way of passing information that represents user choice (or other dynamically derived information) to a Web server in order to drive dynamic HTML or VoiceXML generation. The query string is a standard component of valid URLs, and supports sending a series of zero or more name-value pairs (like function parameters). URLs with query strings use the following syntax:

```
http://server.domain/path/document?name_1=value_1&name_2=value_2&name_n=
value_n
```

All names and values must follow standard Uniform Resource Indicator (URI) encoding. For detailed information on the syntax of properly formatted URIs, see IETF RFC 1630 at www.w3.org/Addressing/URL/URI_Overview.html.

Figure 9.2 provides an extremely simple dynamic VoiceXML application, written in the Perl scripting language, that implements the classic children's game Mad Libs. Query string parameters can be set to specify several nouns, verbs, and adjectives. The output is a valid VoiceXML document that inserts these customized choices into an otherwise static story that is read back to the caller using computer-generated text to speech. For any parameters not explicitly specified on the query string, reasonable defaults are used instead.

Assuming that this file was installed on a Web server at myserver.com and called madlibs.cgi, some valid URLs for accessing a customized version of the application would be:

- http://myserver.com/madlibs.cgi
- http://myserver.com/madlibs.cgi?n1=cat&a1=happy
- http://myserver.com/madlibs.cgi?n1=dog&n2=bird&n3=camel&n4=impala&n5=moose

Screen Scraping: Rapid Prototypes for Extending Any Web Site to the Phone

Particularly when traditional Web developers are first beginning to explore VoiceXML programming and building voice applications, a common first desire is to take existing

```perl
#!/usr/local/bin/perl

# simple "madlib" dynamic VoiceXML example using PERL
# created 6/7/2001 by Jeff Kunins (jeff@tellme.com)

use CGI;

# Get all query string parameters
# This application expects that someone will call it using a
URL of the form
# http://server/madlib.cgi?n1=dog&a1=green

# Initialize to default values if not present
$query = new CGI;
$n1 = $query->param('n1') or $n1 = "cat" ;
$n2 = $query->param('n2') or $n2 = "cat" ;
$n3 = $query->param('n3') or $n3 = "cat" ;
$n4 = $query->param('n4') or $n4 = "cat" ;
$n5 = $query->param('n5') or $n5 = "cat" ;
$a1 = $query->param('a1') or $a1 = "blue" ;
$a2 = $query->param('a2') or $a2 = "blue" ;
$a3 = $query->param('a3') or $a3 = "blue" ;
$a4 = $query->param('a4') or $a4 = "blue" ;
$a5 = $query->param('a5') or $a5 = "blue" ;
$v1 = $query->param('v1') or $v1 = "jump" ;
$v2 = $query->param('v2') or $v2 = "jump" ;
$v3 = $query->param('v3') or &v3 = "jump" ;

# Print the VoiceXML document, based on the query string parameters
# Print till the EOF marker, and identify the document as XML print
<<"EOF";
Content-type: text/xml

<?xml version="1.0" ?>
<vxml version = "2.0">
 <form>
  <block>
    Listen to this madlib...
    Once upon a time there was a $a1 $n1. Every Saturday, the $n1
    would $v1 and $v2 very quickly,
    and then $v3 three times on a $a2 and $a3 $n2. This was usually fun,
    but sometimes it was kind of $a4.

    Oh, well. I guess it all comes down to $a5 $n3 and $a2 $n4.

    Bye!
  </block>
 </form>
</vxml>

EOF
```

Figure 9.2 Simple query strings: Mad Libs.

Web pages and Web applications and make them available via the phone. With a little bit of server code, it's possible to do this extremely quickly by essentially treating existing HTML pages as a back-end data source, filtering out all of the extraneous HTML markup to get at just the data, and then reformatting this data as VoiceXML.

This technique, commonly called *screen scraping*, is a venerable method from the early days of computing still in use today to make legacy 3270 and other mainframe applications available via client-server and Web interfaces without having to disturb or reauthor the original application.

Because the UI paradigm for the telephone is so fundamentally different from that for visual applications, screen scraping is generally not an effective technique for developing true production-quality applications. It's much more appropriate to write a voice-specific UI layer that runs on top of shared business logic and back-end integration. However, screen scraping can be a great tool to use for rapid prototyping and for getting familiar with the VoiceXML language and identifying the kinds of features you may already have implemented on the Web that make sense to extend to the phone through the power of VoiceXML and voice recognition.

Figures 9.3 through 9.5 present a working example of screen scraping that can easily be modified to work with other Web sites. The particular example creates a voice-based interface to the Cal Train schedule times for the San Francisco Bay Area (www .transitinfo.org/). The code is organized into the following files:

- **index.vxml.** This static document prompts the caller to choose a starting station and ending station that he or she would like schedule information for. After collecting this information, the program sends this information (using the query string) to a dynamically generated VoiceXML document called cal.cgi.

- **cal.cgi.** This Perl script uses the inputs provided on the query string to initiate its own HTTP request to the Cal Train Web site, just as if it were an ordinary Web browser. It then extracts the relevant information from the HTML that gets returned from the Cal Train Web site and formats it as VoiceXML. The result is a dynamically generated VoiceXML document with the results the caller is looking for. Note: This script makes use of the HTML:Parser Perl module available from http://search.cpan.org/doc/GAAS/HTML-Parser-3.25/Parser.pm.

- **stations.gsl.** A grammar file (here written in Nuance Grammar Specification Language [GSL]) that specifies the names of all available Cal Train stations.

Database Access and Full-Scale Development

As you get familiar with VoiceXML and are ready to begin developing feature-rich production applications, you most likely will begin to use whatever application server and back-end infrastructure you already have in place to write "native" voice applications that are built from the ground up to reuse your back-end and business rules while specifying the unique voice UI in new scripts, Java servlets, etc.

In the next example we will explore a very simplified drink recipe application that accesses a simple flat file database to dynamically look up ingredient and mixing

```
<?xml version="1.0"?>
<!--
 INDEX.VXML. COPIED WITH PERMISSION FROM TELLME STUDIO

 This static document prompts the caller to choose a starting station
 and ending station they would like schedule information for. After
 collecting this information, it sends this information (using the query
 string) to a dynamically generated VoiceXML document called cal.cgi
 (implemented here in PERL).
-->

<vxml version="2.0">
<var name="train_from"/>
<var name="train_to"/>
<var name="train_day"/>

<!--
- CalTrainScheduler
-
- Ask the user for what stations they want to travel to and populate
- document.to and document.from
-->
<form id="CalTrainScheduler">

 <block>
 <audio> Welcome to the Bay Area Cal Train Scheduler </audio>
 </block>

 <field name="from">
 <grammar src="stations.gsl"/>

 <prompt>
 <audio> Which station are you leaving from? </audio>
 </prompt>

 <nomatch>
 <audio> I'm sorry, I didn't get that.
 Please say the name of a Cal Train station. </audio>
 <reprompt/>
 </nomatch>

 <noinput>
 <audio> Please say the name of a Cal Train station</audio>
 <reprompt/>
 </noinput>

 <help>
 <audio> Please say the name of a Cal Train station location. </audio>
 <reprompt/>
```

Figure 9.3   Screen scraping example 1: Cal Train index.vxml.

```
  </help>

  <filled>
  <assign name="train_from" expr="from"/>
  <log> got a from: <value expr="train_from"/> </log>
  </filled>
  </field>

  <field name="to">
  <grammar src="stations.gsl"/>

  <prompt>
  <audio> What station are you going to? </audio>
  </prompt>

  <nomatch>
  <audio> I'm sorry, I didn't get that. Please say the name of a Cal
  Train station. </audio>
  <reprompt/>
  </nomatch>

  <noinput>
  <audio> Please say the name of a Cal Train station</audio>
  <reprompt/>
  </noinput>

  <help>
  <audio> Please say the name of a Cal Train station location. </audio>
  <reprompt/>
  </help>

  <filled>
  <assign name="train_to" expr="to"/>
  <log> got a to: <value expr="train_to"/> </log>
  </filled>
  </field>

  <block>
  <goto next="#call_cgi" />
  </block>
</form>

<!--
- call_cgi
-
- Use goto to call perl code to generate VoiceXML response
-->
<form id="call_cgi">
   <block>
```

Figure 9.3 Continued.

continues

```
    <script>
      <! [CDATA[
    /* decide if weekday or weekend */
    var day = new Date();

    train_day = "WD" /* assume week day */
    if (day.getDay() == 0)
    {
    train_day = "SU";
    }
    else if (day.getDay() == 6)
    {
    train_day = "SA";
    }

    /* generate Query String */
    var par = "cal.cgi?C=CT&amp;FromStation=" + train_from +
"$amp;ToStation=" + train_to + "$amp;D=" + train_day + "$amp;ALL=Y";
    ]]>
    </script>
    <log> goto: <value expr="par"/> </log>
<!-- SERVER -->
   <goto expr="par"/>
<!-- SERVER -->
   </block>
  </form>

</vxml>
```

Figure 9.3 *Continued.*

```
#!/usr/local/bin/perl

#COPIED WITH PERMISSION FROM TELLME STUDIO

# Packages to retrieve the URL using HTTP
use LWP::Simple;
use CGI;

# Used to parse HTML from the web server
use HTML::Parser ();
use strict;
```

Figure 9.4 Screen scraping example 2: Cal Train cal.cgi.

```perl
# buffer of train data parsed from the web page
my $buffer;
# flag used to indicate whether the parse is within a html tag
my $pre_flag=0;


###############################################################
#
#
# Checkline ($line)
#
# Params: Line of text to parse
#
# Checkline parses out train id and times from a line of HTML
#


###############################################################
#
sub checkLine {
    my $text = shift;
    if ($pre_flag) {
        if ($text) {
    $text =~ s/\n\n/\n/g;
    $text =~ s/(.*)TRAIN(.*)\n//g;
    $buffer .= $text;
        }
    }
}


###############################################################
#
#
# start_handler ($HTML::Parser->instance)
#
# PARAMS: A parser instance object
#
# Specific to this web page, start_handler looks for the <pre>
# tag indicating the start of train data. Once within the <pre>
# block, it calls &checkLine to parse each line.
#
# See The Perl Journal Issue, Spring 2000, Issue #17, for a good
# article on HTML::Parser by Ken MacFarlane
###############################################################
#
sub start_handler {
    return if shift ne "pre";
    my $self = shift;
    $pre_flag=1;
    $self->handler(text => \&checkLine, "dtext");
```

Figure 9.4 *Continued*

continues

```
    $self->handler(end => sub { $pre_flag=0 if shift eq "pre";
},
"tagname,self");
}


###############################################################
#
#
# process ($buffer)
#
# Params: Takes a buffer with a train schedule on each line
#
# process ($buffer) goes through the buffer of train listings
# parsing out train number, time train is leaving, and the
# time the train is arriving.
# Returns:
# $buffer - original buffer
# $trains - array of train ids
# %data - hash of train information keys on the train id
#      LTIME, ATIME - leave, arrival time
#      LTIME_AM, LTIME_PM - am/pr for leaving and arrival time
#
###############################################################
#
sub process {
    my $buffer = shift;

    # list of trains in chronological order
    my @trains;

    #info hash, keys on id of train

    my %data;

    my @lines = split /^/m, $buffer;

    foreach my $line (@lines) {
unless ($line =~ /.\W./) {
    next;
}
$line =~ s/^\s+//; #trim leading whitespace
$line =~ s/\s+$//; #trim tailing whitespace
$line =~ s/[\s;,]+/,/g;

my %entry;
my ($train_id, $1_time, $a_time, $trash) = split /,/, $line;
@trains = (@trains, $train_id);
if ( $1_time =~ /^(\d+:\d+) (\D+)/ ) {
```

```perl
        if ($2 eq 'a') {
 $entry{"LTIME_AM}"} = "1";
 $entry{"LTIME_PM}"} = "0";
        } elsif ($2 eq 'p') {
 $entry{"LTIME_AM}"} = "0";
 $entry{"LTIME_PM}"} = "1";
        }
 $entry{"LTIME"} = $1;
        }

 if ( $a_time =~ /^(\d+:\d+) (\D+)/ ) {
        if ($2 eq 'a') {
 $entry{"ATIME_AM}"} = "1";
 $entry{"ATIME_PM}"} = "0";
        } elsif ($2 eq 'p') {
 $entry{"ATIME_AM}"} = "0";
 $entry{"ATIME_PM}"} = "1";
        }
 $entry{"ATIME"} = $1;
 }
        $data{$train_id} = \%entry;
        }

        return ($buffer, \@trains, \%data);
 }


 ##################################################################
 #
 #
 # Begin in-line code
 #
 ##################################################################
 #

 # build url using the parameters passed into cal.cgi
 # url: www.transitinfo.org/cgi-bin/all_times
 # params: C=CT
 #    FromStation: Abbreviation for station(ex. SF)
 #    ToStation: Abbreviation for station (ex. MView)
 #    D: Code for what day you are leavingon (ex. WD weekday)
 #    ALL: Where you want all train times (Y/N)
 #    TIME: Time after which you are leaving (hour%3Aminutes)
 #web server to get schedules from
 my $url = qq(www.transitinfo.org/cgi-bin/all_times);

 my $q = new CGI;

 $url .= qq(?C=) . $q->param('C');
```

Figure 9.4 *Continued.*

continues

```perl
$url .= qq(&FromStation=) . $q->param('FromStation');
$url .= qq(&ToStation=) . $q->param('ToStation');
$url .= qq(&D=) . $q->param('D');
$url .= qq(&ALL=) . $q->param('ALL');
$url .= qq(&TIME=) . $q->param('TIME');

# Fetch the content using CGI package
my $content = get($url);
unless (defined ($content)) {
 die "cound not get $url";
}

# Parse the buffer for train times using HTML::Parser
my $p = HTML::Parser->new(api_version => 3);
$p->handler( start => \&start_handler, "tagname,self");
$p->parse($content) || die $!;

# Process train data into datastructures
my $trains_ref;
my $data_ref;
($buffer, $trains_ref, $data_ref) = process($buffer);

# print VoiceXML header
print "Content-type: text/xml\n\n";
print "<?xml version=\"1.0\"?>\n";
print "<vxml version=\"2.0\"> \n <form id=\"answer\"><block>";
print qq(\n <log> starting audio </log> \n);

# print audio for each entry
foreach my $train_id (@$trains_ref) {
    my $info = $data_ref->{$train_id};
    print qq(<audio>) . " train $train_id is leaving at " .
$info->{"LTIME"} . qq(</audio>);
    print "\n";
    print qq(<audio> and arrives at $info->{"ATIME"}
</audio>\n);
}

# print trailer for vxml
print qq(<log> ending audio </log>);
print qq(<goto next="_home"/>);
print qq(\n </block> \n </form> </vxml> \n \n);
```

Figure 9.4 *Continued.*

```
###############################################################
#
# End inline code block
#
###############################################################
#
[
 [dtmf-1 san_francisco (fourth and king) (fourth)] {<option "SF">}
 [dtmf-2 (22nd ?(street)) (twenty second ?(street))] {<option "22nd">}
 [dtmf-3 paul_ave paul (paul avenue)] {<option "Paul">}
 [dtmf-4 bay_shore (bay shore)] {<option "Baysh">}
 [dtmf-5 san_bruno (san bruno)] {<option "SBruno">}
 [dtmf-6 millbrae mill_bray] {<option "Millbr">}
 [dtmf-7 broadway] {<option "Bway">}
 [dtmf-8 burlingame burling_game] {<option "Burling">}
 [san_mateo (san mateo)] {<option "SMateo">}
 [howard_park (howard park)] {<option "HaywrdP">}
 [hillsdale] {<option "Hillsd">}
 [belmont] {<option "Belmont">}
 [san_carlos (san carlos)] {<option "SCarlos">}
 [redwood_city (redwood city)] {<option "Redwood">}
 [atherton] {<option "Athertn">}
 [menlo_park (menlo park)] {<option "Menlo">}
 [palo_alto (palo alto)] {<option "PA">}
 [(california ?avenue)] {<option "Calif">}
 [san_antonio (san antonio)] {<option "SAnton">}
 [dtmf-9 mountain_view (mountain view)] {<option "MView">}
 [sunnyvale] {<option "Sunny">}
 [lawrence] {<option "Lawrenc">}
 [santa_clara (santa clara)] {<option "SClara">}
 [college] {<option "college">}
 [san_jose (san jose)] {<option "SanJose">}
 [tamien] {<option "Tamien">}
 [capital] {<option "Capital">}
 [blossom_hill blossom (blossom hill)] {<option "Blossom">}
 [morgan_hill morgan (morgan hill)] {<option "Morgan">}
 [san_martin (san martin)] {<option "SMartin">}
 [gilroy] {<option "Gilroy">}
]
```

Figure 9.5 Screen scraping example 3: Cal Train stations.gsl.

instructions for a given beverage and present the results over the phone using VoiceXML. For the sake of brevity, the list of drinks presented here is extremely short. Figures 9.6 through 9.9 present the code, organized into the following files:

- **drinks.vxml.** This static document prompts callers to choose the drink they want to hear, uses a subdialog to call drinks.cgi to look up the requested bever-

```xml
<?xml version="1.0"?>

<!--
DRINKS.VXML-COPIED WITH PERMISSION FROM TELLME STUDIO
This static document prompts the caller to choose a drink they want to
hear, uses a <subdialog> to call drinks.cgi to look up the requested
beverage, and (if it's in the database) reads the ingredients and mixing
instructions to the caller.
-->

<vxml version="2.0">

  <form id="Main">

    <var name="id" />
    <field name="drinkchoice">
      <grammar>
        <![CDATA[
        [
        [(mint julep) mint_julep] {<option "0028">}
        [(singapore sling) singapore_sling] {<option "0148">}
        [(fuzzy navel) fuzzy_navel] {<option "0190">}
        ]
        ]]>
      </grammar>

      <prompt>Which drink do you wanna make? Say the name.</prompt>

      <catch event="nomatch noinput">
        <audio>sorry, i didn't catch that.</audio>
        <reprompt/>
      </catch>

      <filled>
        <assign name="id" expr="drinkchoice" />
        <goto nextitem="get_drink"/>
      </filled>

    </field>

    <subdialog name="get_drink" src="drinks.cgi" namelist="id"
               method="get">
      <filled>
        <audio><value expr="get_drink.drinknames"/></audio>
        <break time="500ms" />
        <audio>The ingredients are</audio>
        <break time="500ms" />
```

Figure 9.6 Database access example 1: Drink Recipes Index.vxml.

```
        <!-- NOTE: The FOREACH element is *not* an official part of the
        VoiceXML 2.0. It is listed in the VoiceXML 2.0 specification
        as one of several elements under active consideration for
        inclusion in VoiceXML 2.1. As of June 2001, the FOREACH element
is supported by the Tellme Networks VoiceXML implementation.
        -->
        <foreach item="item" array="get_drink.drinkingrs">
          <audio><value expr="item"/></audio>
          <break time="300ms" />
        </foreach>

        <audio><value expr="get_drink.drinkdescs"/></audio>
        <break time="1000ms" />
        <goto next="#Main"/>
      </filled>
      <catch event="event.failure">
        <audio>Oops. I forgot how to make that one.</audio>
        <clear namelist="drinkchoice" />
        <goto next="#Main"/>
      </catch>
    </subdialog>
  </form>
</vxml>
```

Figure 9.6 *Continued.*

```perl
#!/usr/local/bin/perl -w
use CGI qw/:standard/;

#COPIED WITH PERMISSION FROM TELLME STUDIO

$query = new CGI;
$id_in = $query->param('id');
$event = "event.failure";

$id = "0000";
$name = "unknown";
$type = "unknown";
$desc = "unknown";
$ingr = "unknown";
$order = 0;
$DBROOT = "./";
$DBFILE_NAME = "names.db";
$DBFILE_INGR = "ingredients.db";
%ingrlist = ();

open FNAME, "$DBROOT/&DBFILE_NAME";
while (<FNAME>)
```

Figure 9.7 Database access example 2: Drink Recipes drinks.cgi.   *continues*

```
{
   if ($_ =~ /^$id_in\;/)
   {
     ($id, $name, $type, $desc) = split /\;/, $_;
     chomp $desc;
     last;
   }
}
close FNAME;

open FINGR, "$DBROOT/$DBFILE_INGR";
while (<FINGR>)
{
   if ($_ =~ /^$id_in\;/)
    {
       ($id, $order, $ingr) = split /\;/, $_;
      chomp $ingr;
      $ingrlist{$order} = $ingr;
    }
}
close FINGR;

if ($name && $type && $desc)
{
   if (defined $ingrlist{'1'})
   {
    $event = "event.success";
   }
}

print "Content-type: text/xml\n\n";

if ($event eq "event.success")
{
 &PrintSuccess;
}
else
{
    &PrintFailure;
}

#
# subroutines here
#
sub PrintSuccess
{
```

Figure 9.7 *Continued.*

```
 print <<EOF1;
 <?xml version="1.0"?>
 <vxml version="2.0">
   <form id="main">
    <var name="drinknames"/>
    <var name="drinkdescs"/>
    <var name="drinkingrs" expr="new Array"/>

    <script>
    <![CDATA[
     drinknames="$name";
     drinkdescs="$desc";

 EOF1

 foreach $_ (sort keys %ingrlist)
 {
   if ($_ eq "1")
   {
   print " drinkingrs[drinkingrs.length]=\"$ingrlist{$_}\"\;\n";
   }
   else
   {
   print " drinkingrs[drinkingrs.length]=\"$ingrlist{$_}\"\;\n";
 }
 }

print <<EOF2;
  ]]>
  </script>
  <block>
  <foreach item="stuff" array="drinkingrs">
  <log>***** ingredient is : <value expr="stuff"/></log>
  </foreach>
  <log>***** drinknamescs is <value expr="drinknames"/></log>
  <log>***** drinkdescs is <value expr="drinkdescs"/></log>
  <return namelist="drinkingrs drinknames drinkdescs"/>
  </block>
 </form>
</vxml>
EOF2
}

sub PrintFailure
{
print <<EOF;
<?xml version="1.0"?>
<vxml version="2.0">
```

Figure 9.7 *Continued.*

continues.

```
  <form id="main">
   <block>
   <return event="event.failure"/>
   </block>
  </form>
 </vxml>
EOF
}
```

Figure 9.7 *Continued.*

```
0028;Mint Julep;bourbon;In silver julep cup, silver mug, or collins
glass, muddle mint leaves, powdered sugar, and water. Fill glass or mug
with shaved or crushed ice and add bourbon. Top with more ice and
garnish with a mint spring and straws. 0148;Singapore sling;brandy;Shake
lemon, sugar, and gin with ice and strain into collins glass. Add ice
cubes and fill with club soda. Float cherry-flavored brandy on top.
Decorate with fruits in season and serve with straws.
0190;Fuzzy navel;cordials;Pour over ice into highball glass and stir.
Garnish with an orange slice and a cherry.
```

Figure 9.8 Database access example 3: Drink Recipes names.db.

```
0028;1;4 sprigs mint
0028;2;1 teaspoon powdered sugar
0028;3;2 teaspoon water
0028;4;2 1/2 oz bourbon
0148;1;Juice of 1/2 lemon
0148;2;1 teaspoon powdered sugar
0148;3;2 oz gin
0148;4;Club soda
0148;5;1/2 oz cherry-flavored brandy
0190;1;3 oz 48-proof peach schnapps
0190;2;3 oz orange juice
```

Figure 9.9 Database access example 3: Drink Recipes ingredients.db.

age, and (if the drink is in the database) reads the ingredients and mixing instructions to the caller.

■ **drinks.cgi.** This Perl script uses the inputs provided on the query string to initiate a database lookup. In this case, a simple relational database is implemented as two flat files—names.db and ingredients.db.

■ **names.db and ingredients.db.** These simple text files contain the database tables.

Using Cookies with VoiceXML

Cookies are a technology frequently used in traditional Web applications to set local session state and manage personalization, authentication, and other features. Just as with all of the other similarities between VoiceXML and traditional Web development, most VoiceXML platform implementations support at least session cookies. Persistent cookies are more complex on the phone because there's simply no notion of persistent state built into the phone, or any mechanism on individual telephone handsets to store cookies for the future. Some VoiceXML platform vendors provide a server-side mechanism for user authentication that provides a platform-specific persistent cookie store for registered users. For the purposes of this book, we will only demonstrate an example of session cookies.

Working with session cookies and VoiceXML is the same as doing so from HTML. In most cases, cookies are not manipulated directly within the HTML markup itself, but rather are gotten and set by the dynamic script code running on the server. The job of the browser in the case of cookies is simply to remember cookies that have been set as incoming headers on the responses to some HTTP requests, and to faithfully send those cookies as headers on all future HTTP requests to URLs within the appropriate domain. For detailed information on how cookies work, regardless of whether you're developing in HTML or VoiceXML, see www.cookiecentral.com/faq.

In the following example, a simple application allows the caller to selectively set, retrieve, and delete a cookie that is manipulated on the server and maintained faithfully within the VoiceXML browser. Figures 9.10 and 9.11 are organized into the following files:

- **cookies.vxml.** This static document prompts the caller to choose whether to get, set, or delete a cookie. Given that choice, it uses a subdialog to call setcookie.cgi and take the appropriate action.

- **setcookie.cgi.** This Perl script expects a particular action as a parameter, and examines the appropriate HTTP headers to either set a new cookie or determine whether the VoiceXML browser has in fact passed it an existing cookie.

XSL Stylesheets: Multiple Devices from the Same Back End

XML and Extensible Style Language (XSL) are powerful and practical tools developers can use today to begin delivering on the promise of pervasive computing, where cleanly abstracted data and presentation layers deliver an appropriate interface to a given application on a comprehensive suite of devices, all of which are dynamically generated from a shared back-end infrastructure.

XML is typically used for two purposes today—pure representation of data and interface specification. VoiceXML itself is an example of the latter, while many business-to-business (B2B) exchanges or internal data formats (e.g., next generation Electronic Data Interchange [EDI], etc.) use the former.

XSL is an accompanying standard for XML that specifies template-like constructs that enable developers to transform raw XML data into a particular XML-based inter-

```
<?xml version="1.0"?>
<!--
COOKIES.VXML COPIED WITH PERMISSION FROM TELLME STUDIO
This static document prompts the caller to choose whether to get, set,
or delete their cookie. Given that choice, it uses a <subdialog> to call
setcookie.cgi and take the appropriate action.-->

<vxml version="2.0">
 <!-- Giving choices on whether to set, get, or delete a cookie
-->
 <var name="cookie_command" />
 <form id="main">
   <field name="choice">
   <grammar>
   <![CDATA[
     [
     [(set ?cookie)]{<option "set">}
     [(get ?cookie)]{<option "get">}
     [(delete ?cookie)]{<option "delete">}
     ]
   ]]>
   </grammar>

   <prompt>say set, get, or delete cookie</prompt>

   <catch event="nomatch noinput">
     <audio> I'm sorry...I didn't catch that </audio>
     <reprompt />
   </catch>

   <filled>
     <assign name="cookie_command" expr="choice" />
     <goto next="#cookie_action"/>
   </filled>
   </field>
 </form>

 <!-- Retrieving cookie -->
 <form id="cookie_action">
   <subdialog name="cookie_sub" src="setcookie.cgi"
              namelist="cookie_command" method="get">

   <catch event="state.setcookie">
     <audio> Your cookie was set </audio>
     <goto next="#main"/>
   </catch>

    <catch event="state.notgotcookie">
```

Figure 9.10 Cookies example 1: Cookie Access cookies.vxml.

```
      <audio> I'm sorry...I was unable to retrieve your cookie.</audio>
      <goto next="#main"/>
    </catch>
    <catch event="state.deletecookie">
      <audio> Your cookie was deleted </audio>
      <goto next="#main"/>
    </catch>

    <catch event="state.nothappy">
      <audio> I'm sorry...there was an unexpected
problem...goodbye.</audio>
      <disconnect />
 </catch>

    <filled>
      <audio> Your cookie is <value expr="cookie_sub.value"/>
</audio>
      <goto next="#main"/>
    </filled>
  </subdialog>
 </form>
</vxml>
```

Figure 9.10   *Continued.*

```
#!/usr/local/bin/perl

#COPIED WITH PERMISSION FROM TELLME STUDIO

use CGI qw/:standard/;
use CGI::Cookie;

#using CGI Cookie module,
#see
www.perl.com/pub/doc/manual/html/lib/CGI/Cookie.html

$query= new CGI;
$cookie_command=$query->param('cookie_command');
$good_cookie_value="chocolate_chip";

# If cookie command is set a cookie
if ($cookie_command eq "set")
{
 $cookie = new CGI::Cookie(-name =>'good_cookie',
    -value =>$good_cookie_value,
    -expires =>'+20d',
    -path =>'/');
```

Figure 9.11   Cookies example 2: Cookie Access setcookie.cgi.   *continues*

```perl
 print "Set-Cookie: $cookie\n";
 print "Content-type: text/xml\n\n";
 print <<WRITECOOKIE;
<?xml version="1.0"?>
<vxml version="2.0">
  <form id="set_cook">
    <block>
      <log> status is: state.setcookie</log>
    <return event="state.setcookie"/>
  </block>
 </form>
</vxml>
WRITECOOKIE

#If cookie command is get a cookie
} elsif ($cookie_command eq "get")
{
   %cookies = fetch CGI::Cookie;
   if (defined $cookies{"good_cookie"}){
   $mycookie = $cookies{"good_cookie"}->value;

   print "Content-Type: text/xml\n\n";
   print <<"READCOOKIE";
<?xml version="1.0"?>
<vxml version="2.0">
   <form id="got_cook">
     <var name="value" expr="'$mycookie'"/>
     <block>
       <log> status is: state.gotcookie </log>
       <log> got cookie is : <value expr="value"/></log>
       <return namelist="value"/>
     </block>
   </form>
</vxml>
READCOOKIE
}else {
print "Content-Type: text/xml\n\n";
print <<NOTGOTCOOKIE;
<?xml version="1.0"?>
<vxml version="2.0">
  <form id="not_got_cook">
    <block>
      <log> status is: state.notgotcookie </log>
      <return event="state.notgotcookie"/>
    </block>
  </form>
</vxml>
```

Figure 9.11 *Continued.*

```
NOTGOTCOOKIE
}

#If cookie command is delete a cookie
} elsif ($cookie_command eq "delete"){

$cookie = new CGI::Cookie (-name =>'good_cookie',
        -value =>$good_cookie_value,
        -expires =>'-1d',
        -path =>'/');
print "Set-Cookie: $cookie\n";
print "Content-Type: text/xml\n\n";
print <<DELETECOOKIE;
<?xml version="1.0"?>
<vxml version="2.0">
   <form id="delete_cook">
     <var name="status" expr="'state.deletecookie'"/>
     <block>
       <log> status is: state.deletecookie </log>
       <return event="state.deletecookie"/>
     </block>
   </form>
</vxml>
DELETECOOKIE

#Else something went wrong.
} else {
print "Content-Type: text/xml\n\n";
print <<NOTHAPPY;
<?xml version="1.0"?>
<vxml version="2.0">
   <form id="wrong">
     <block>
       <log> status is: state.nohappy </log>
       <return event="state.nohappy"/>
     </block>
   </form>
</vxml>
NOTHAPPY
}
```

Figure 9.11 *Continued.*

face specification, such as HTML[1] or VoiceXML. For example, it has constructs to search for and then iterate through various data sets within an XML document (e.g., a set of available airline flights), printing out various pieces of VoiceXML or HTML interspersed within the data along the way.

---

[1]HTML is not technically XML, but for the practical purposes of this example can be considered as such. For more information on XHTML, the new "pure" XML variant of HTML, see www.w3.org.

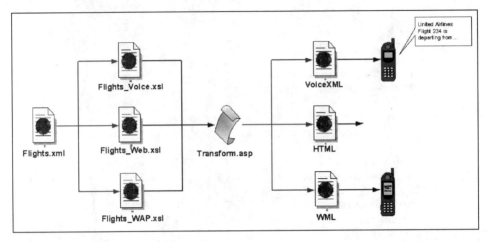

Figure 9.12   XSL and VoiceXML.

The result is that developers can architect their Web infrastructure such that one set of server code (JSP, ASP, Cold Fusion, etc.) manages connecting to back-end databases, triggering transactions, and exposing the results as XML data, while another set (running on the same or a different server) essentially grabs that data through simple URL calls and then applies a device-specific XSL stylesheet, ultimately responding with a single document in the proper XML-based markup language for a given user's device of choice. Figure 9.12 depicts the conceptual relationship between XML, XSL, HTML, and VoiceXML.

XML and XSL are powerful tools for developers looking to efficiently deliver applications across multiple devices. However, there are some key issues to watch out for:

- **XSL is not transcoding.** XML and XSL do not automatically transform or transcode an application from one device to another, such as from a Web page to VoiceXML. Rather, they are simply a technological tool developers can use to cleanly author device-specific interfaces in the appropriate markup language for that device (e.g., VoiceXML, WML, HTML) with maximal code reuse. Developers still must explicitly design and author the interface for each device they wish to support.

- **Careful voice UI design is vital.** Particularly for VoiceXML, excellent interface design is absolutely critical to usability and application success. While even the worst visual interfaces are essentially usable, all but the best voice interfaces are confusing and frustrating to callers. XML and XSL in no way eliminate the need for expert application design.

- **Code length efficiency is important.** XSL can easily produce code that is particularly long and repetitive. While this shouldn't be a major concern, it is worth spending some time and attention to ensure that the resulting application code is as efficient and streamlined as possible.

Figures 9.13 through 9.16 provide some brief examples of XML data, XSL stylesheets for both HTML and VoiceXML, and the resulting markup. For this particular example, we'll look at a subset of the information that an airline might store to deliver a flight status application across multiple devices.

```
<?xml version="1.0">
<flights>
    <flight>
        <carrier>United Airlines</carrier>
        <flightnum>1224</flightnum>
        <origin>
            <airport>Seattle</airport>
            <time>April 4, 2001, 2:34pm</time>
        </origin>
        <dest>
            <airport>San Francisco</airport>
            <time>April 4, 2001, 4:34pm</time>
        </dest>
        <price>167</price>
    </flight>
</flights>
```

Figure 9.13 XML data for flight information.

```
<?xml version="1.0">
<xsl:stylesheet xmlns:xsl="www.w3.org/TR/WD-xsl">
<xsl:template match="flights">

<HTML><BODY>
<xsl:for-each select="flight">
    <xsl:value-of select="carrier"/>
    <xsl:value-of select="flightnum"/><BR/>
    Departing <xsl:value-of select="origin/airport"/> on
    <xsl:value-of select="origin/time"/><BR/>
    Arriving <xsl:value-of select="dest/airport"/> on
    <xsl:value-of select="dest/time"/><BR/>
    $<xsl:value-of select="price"/><BR/>
    </xsl:for-each>
</BODY></HTML>

</xsl:template>
</xsl:stylesheet>
```

Figure 9.14 XSL stylesheet for producing HTML flight information.

There are many rich and complex possibilities for interacting with XML and XSL stylesheets. For more information and resources about XML, XSL, and VoiceXML, see:

■ Tellme Studio—http://studio.tellme.com

■ World Wide Web Consortium (W3C)—www.w3.org

■ Microsoft XML Developer Center—http://msdn.microsoft.com/xml

■ XML.COM—www.xml.com

```
<HTML><BODY>
United Airlines
     1224<BR>
     Departing Seattle on April 4, 2001, 2:34pm
     <BR>
     Arriving San Francisco on April 4, 2001, 4:34pm
     <BR>
     $167
     <BR>
</BODY></HTML>
```

Figure 9.15   HTML result of processing XSL stylesheet.

```
<?xml version="1.0">
<xsl:stylesheet xmlns:xsl="www.w3.org/TR/WD-xsl">
<xsl:template match="flights">

<xsl:pi name="xml">version='1.0'</xsl:pi>
<vxml><form><block><audio>
<xsl:for-each select="flight">
     For <xsl:value-of select="price"/> dollars,
     <xsl:value-of select="carrier"/> flight
     <xsl:value-of select="flightnum"/> is departing from
 <xsl:value-of select="origin/airport"/> at
 <xsl:value-of select="origin/time"/>, and arrives at
 <xsl:value-of select="dest/airport"/> at
 <xsl:value-of select="dest/time"/>.
</xsl:for-each>
</audio></block></form></vxml>
</xsl:template>
</xsl:stylesheet>

<?xml version="1.0">
<vxml><form><block><audio>
     For 167 dollars,
     United Airlines flight 1224
     is departing from Seattle at
     April 4, 2001, 2:34pm,
     and arrives at San Francisco at
     April 4, 2001, 4:34pm
</audio></block></form></vxml>
```

Figure 9.16   VoiceXML stylesheet for flight information.

XML Data Islands: Another Powerful Data Abstraction Tool

Not only is data abstraction useful for cleanly building applications that work across multiple devices, but it can also greatly aid in doing shared development between members of the same team and even across companies.

Particularly with voice-enabled applications and VoiceXML, companies often find themselves wanting to work with a partner that has specific expertise in the design of effective voice user interfaces, while they continue to own all of the back-end integration code and business rules.

In the HTML world, Microsoft debuted a feature called XML Data Islands in 1999 with the release of Microsoft Internet Explorer 5.0, which was the result of a note entitled "XML in HTML Meeting Report," promulgated by the W3C (the standards body responsible for HTML, XML, and VoiceXML).

The feature allows HTML developers to dynamically include references to XML data within HTML documents and manipulate them through scripting and the XML Document Object Model (DOM) on the client to efficiently produce dynamic content on the fly. Because this XML data can be retrieved from any URL (e.g., any server), the result is that developers can begin to put most or all of their business rules and transaction management behind clean XML-based interfaces on the server and strictly use HTML documents for UI presentation. For more information on using XML data islands in HTML, please see http://msdn.microsoft.com/library/default.asp?URL=/library/psdk/xmlsdk/xmlp2n03.htm.

In May 2001, several leading VoiceXML platform vendors including Tellme Networks and BeVocal proposed to the W3C Voice Brower Working Group (the group within the W3C responsible for the VoiceXML standard) that an equivalent feature should be added to VoiceXML. As mentioned earlier, this is particularly useful in the world of voice applications because it would allow, for example, a third-party partner to author voice user interface templates for an application. These templates could be (from a programmatic perspective) simple, static VoiceXML documents that use XML data island functionality to dynamically request live data from the server. Because the XML data is requested via URLs (with query strings, etc.), all of the expressiveness and back-end integration discussed throughout this chapter are still possible, with the added benefit that the logic sits behind a clean XML data interface that can be reused across devices and—more importantly—can be maintained and improved over time independently of the underlying interface design portion of the application.

XML data islands in VoiceXML have been proposed to the W3C as a new `<data>` element. The `<data>` element allows VoiceXML applications to dynamically retrieve XML documents from any URL, placing the result in an ECMAScript object that can be iterated through using an appropriate subset of the W3C XML DOM (see www.w3.org/TR/2000/REC-DOM-Level-2-Core-20001113/Overview.html).

The `<data>` element is not included in the VoiceXML 2.0 specification, but is officially under consideration for inclusion in VoiceXML 2.1. As of June 2001, Tellme Networks' VoiceXML implementation supports the `<data>` element, and at least two other compatible platform implementations are expected to be publicly available by Fall 2001.

Figures 9.17 and 9.18 present a brief example of using XML data islands within VoiceXML, organized into the following files:

```
<?xml version="1.0" ?>
<vxml version="2.0">
  <catch event="error.badfetch">
   <!--COPIED WITH PERMISSION FROM TELLME STUDIO
     In this example, the data tag is the only resource that could have
caused this error. In a real application, however, failure to fetch
other resources such as scripts and grammars may have caused the fetch
error, so either bail out as demonstrated here or check the named
variable for null before accessing it.
    -->
     <log>An HTTP fetch error occurred. Terminating...</log>
     <audio>Sorry, but I could not retrieve the list.
Goodbye.</audio>
    <disconnect />
  </catch>

  <!-- This is the data element, fetching the local data and placing
    the result in a variable -->
  <data src="fruits.xml" name="oFruits" />

  <script>
  <![CDATA[
  // accept a DOM reference and return an array of (tts, wav)
tuples
  function GetFruits(oData)
  {
    var aFruits = [];

    try {
        var oRoot = oData.documentElement;
        var oFruits = oRoot.getElementsByTagName("fruit");
        for (var i = 0; i < oFruits.length; i++)
        {
          var oFruit = oFruits.item(i);
          var fID = oFruit.getAttribute("id");
          var fName =
oFruit.getElementsByTagName("name").item(0).firstChild.data;
          aFruits.push({'tts' : fName, 'wav' : fID + '.wav'});
      }
  }
  catch(e)
  {
    Log("GetFruits exception: " + e);
  }

    return aFruits;
  }
```

Figure 9.17 XML data islands: Fruits.vxml.

```
function Log(s) { vxmllog(s); } /* vxmllog is a proposed mechanism for
being able to write to the log from ECMA script, like the log element */
]]>
</script>
<form>
   <!-- retrieve a list of fruits -->
      <var name="aFruits" expr="GetFruits(oFruits)"/>
      <block>
        <log>Fruit count=<value expr="aFruits.length"/></log>
        <if cond="aFruits.length &gt; 0">
          <audio>Here's the list of fruits</audio>
          <!-- since we have fruits, play them back to the user -->
          <foreach item="oFruit" array="aFruits">
            <audio expr="oFruit.wav">
          <value expr="oFruit.tts"/></audio>
            <break size="small"/>
          </foreach>
        <else/>
          <audio>There are no fruits.</audio>
        </if>
      </block>
   </form>
</vxml>
```

Figure 9.17 *Continued.*

```
<?xml version="1.0" ?>
<fruits>
  <fruit id="APP"><name>apples</name></fruit>
  <fruit id="PEA"><name>pears</name></fruit>
  <fruit id="BAN"><name>bananas</name></fruit>
  <fruit id="GUA"><name>guavas</name></fruit>
</fruits>
```

Figure 9.18 XML data islands: Fruits.xml.

- **fruits.vxml.** This static document retrieves XML data listing a set of fruits available for sale and simply reads the list to the caller.

- **fruits.xml.** This static XML document contains the list of available fruits. Of course, this document could be generated dynamically using any of the techniques previously discussed in this chapter (e.g., by querying a database, etc.)

In this chapter, we've reiterated how directly analogous VoiceXML development is to HTML and traditional Web development, including all of the common ways that have evolved to dynamically render rich, powerful, and transaction-enabled applications using clean, well-abstracted business rules and back-end integration on the Web server to produce device-specific user interfaces via simple markup languages.

While designing effective voice applications (see Chapters 3, 4, and 10 through 12) is extremely different and significantly harder than designing visual applications, the technical architecture on the Web server is virtually identical. Particularly when deploying VoiceXML applications through a Voice Application Network (see Chapter 4), this has the substantial benefit of allowing businesses to produce tightly integrated applications across devices from a unified code base with a single architecture, a single set of underlying business rules, and a unified development and testing team. The end result is a much more efficient development process that maximizes customer service quality (through integrated personalization) while simultaneously minimizing expenses and team overhead.

In the next chapter, we'll further explore the natural extension of traditional Web methods to voice applications through VoiceXML by investigating the critical security issues that are relevant for building and deploying production-quality VoiceXML applications.

VoiceXML Security

No one will disagree that security is a critical component for evaluating any technology investment or decision. The specific parameters defining what level of security is warranted or required vary widely across applications and deployment scenarios, yet in this world of almost unilateral business and societal dependence on mission-critical services of one kind or another, prudent developers and project managers must painstakingly identify and execute against the appropriate security measures necessary for the systems they own.

As has been stated and demonstrated throughout this book, one of the primary advantages of developing voice applications using VoiceXML is that expertise, infrastructure, tools, and solutions can be directly inherited from traditional Web development. Security is no exception—while there are a few security areas unique to voice applications (most notably the telephone network itself), by and large the number one takeaway is that VoiceXML security works just like Web security, and that companies that have taken the necessary steps to make secure transactions ranging from online commerce to online stock trading available via the Web should be extremely confident that they can safely extend these services to the phone. Several of the largest financial institutions in the world have already begun replacing their traditional interactive voice response (IVR) systems with VoiceXML solutions powered by both Voice Application Networks and premises-based infrastructure.

NOTE This chapter is not intended to be an exhaustive or authoritative guide to what is required to adequately secure a company's Web or VoiceXML infrastructure. Rather, it is intended to illustrate the key relevant factors that must be considered and how they naturally extend from the same industry best practices used to secure traditional Web applications. Companies and

developers are strongly encouraged to collaborate with security professionals when designing Web solutions of any kind (including VoiceXML) and when evaluating vendors.

A Brief Word About the Phone Itself

Security and privacy issues are often as heavily influenced by public perception as by technical reality. Generally speaking, the everyday public switched telephone network (PSTN) is substantially less secure than any of the common techniques used to secure Web sites, Web transactions, and other Internet-connected computer systems. For example, it is far easier (though still relatively difficult) for someone to bug the phone lines coming into or going out of a particular person's home or business office than it is to successfully crack a Secure Socket Layer (SSL)-enabled Web site. Similarly, people routinely leave paper receipts with their credit card numbers on restaurant tables and in gas station garbage cans. However, for a variety of reasons including the simple newness of Internet technology and inflammatory examples of specific security violations, public scrutiny and awareness of, and concern about, Internet security continues to play an enormous role in determining the rate at which the general public becomes comfortable with conducting important transactions over the Web.

By contrast, U.S. consumers performed over $430 billion in commerce transactions over the telephone in 1999, more than 10 times the value of global Web purchases. People comfortably share their most confidential information (e.g., health history, stock trades) with live agents over the public telephone network. More than anything, this dichotomy is a function of convenience and time. With each new technology revolution, popular security concerns dominate and are ultimately tempered by a combination of better education/popular understanding and the irresistible urge of convenience.

That said, through a combination of proven industry best-practices security measures for applications and back-end systems, automated voice applications powered by VoiceXML can easily be made to be equivalent to or better than talking to live customer service agents—who of course may be anywhere and whose discretion is not guaranteed.

Primary Security Components to Consider

Businesses looking to deploy VoiceXML applications have to separately consider the security of their Web infrastructure (where the application lives/is generated) and their VoiceXML platform/telephony infrastructure. Similar factors must be evaluated for both areas—companies that intend to deploy their VoiceXML strategy entirely through on-premises infrastructure must carefully evaluate each component they're purchasing to assemble their data centers, while companies looking to deploy through a Voice Application Network must apply the same level of scrutiny to the vendors they're considering.

For companies that are already adept at deploying and managing secure Web infrastructure but are newer to telecom, IVR, and/or VoiceXML, one particular advantage of working with a Voice Application Network is that information technology (IT) managers can continue to focus on securing their existing infrastructure using known techniques and staff while depending upon a trusted and market-proven vendor that provides strong service level agreements (SLAs) with appropriate contractual recourse for violations for the new pieces of the overall solution.

This, ultimately, is why most companies do not run private internet service providers (ISPs) or phone networks, or nationwide networks of points of presence (POPs), in order to enable their customers to access their Web sites or telephone customer service agents: such techniques simply aren't cost-effective or necessary. Rather, companies typically manage and run their Web sites and call centers locally, while relying on shared network resources from trusted partners (e.g., telecom carriers, ISPs, etc.) to ultimately make their services available to the general public.

When considering security measures and evaluating component and service vendors, it is critical to consider all of the following areas:

- **Physical security.** All data centers and other buildings where any hardware, software, log data, or other components that interact with the applications are located must enforce strict physical security to avoid unauthorized access. The greatest risk to all systems is, ultimately, unauthorized physical access.

- **Employee policies.** Given physical security, access to key systems must be tightly restricted to specific personnel who are legally bound and deeply trusted to manage and administer sensitive data. Permissions must be sufficiently granular to grant the minimum possible authorization required by each employee to get his or her job done.

- **Network security—production.** Production networks must be designed using industry best practices to protect against intrusion, denial of service, data theft, and other common attacks.

- **Network security—corporate.** Corporate intranets are often the least well-secured piece of a company's network infrastructure. Because a system's security is determined by that of its weakest link, it is critical to tightly control corporate network policies. In particular, the interface points between corporate and production networks whereby employees exchange data and applications must be well examined.

- **VoiceXML platform security.** Because the VoiceXML platform/interpreter simultaneously plays the same role as the Web browser client in traditional Web applications and acts as a server that is simultaneously processing many phone calls from different people potentially to different applications, a significant amount of attention must be paid to the internal security features of the VoiceXML platform itself. Proper sandboxing and other features must be present to prevent unique denial of service and data theft attacks.

- **Data policies.** Applications are often used to collect, disseminate, and manage massive amounts of personal information on behalf of end users. Strong privacy policies regarding data collection, storage, and reuse must be designed and enforced to protect the rights and interests of users.

■ **Extranet security.** Specifically when working with a Voice Application Network, it is additionally critical to ensure that appropriate measures are being taken to secure log/traffic/billing data and the means by which companies can access that data for their own analysis. Leading Voice Application Network providers make traffic logs and other statistics available via a Web-based "Extranet." It's critical that this Web site be secured similarly to any brokerage or other financial data site.

Physical Security

The greatest risk to all systems is ultimately unauthorized physical access. All data centers and other buildings where any hardware, software, log data, or other components that interact with the applications are located must enforce strict physical security to avoid unauthorized access. Whether your infrastructure is hosted through collocation facilities (e.g., Exodus Communications, etc.), in dedicated private data centers, through a Voice Application Network, or through a combination thereof, it is critical to consider each of the following mechanisms:

■ **Geographic redundancy.** Having multiple redundant data centers is typically mentioned as a requirement for reliability and scalability. However, it is also a critical security factor—if, for whatever reason, a catastrophic security breach results in the temporary or permanent disruption of a data center, then this is ultimately akin to experiencing a physical disaster such as an earthquake or flood. Geographical redundancy can help provide additional options to network administrators in the event of the worst possible failures.

■ **Disaster tolerance/redundant systems.** All facilities should be equipped with the highest available degree of disaster tolerance to resist physical disruptions both from people and from nature. For example, facilities should always have preprovisioned redundant power, air conditioning, network, telecom, and other systems with hot backups in the event of a failure. Similarly, it is critical to select facilities that have enough spare power, cooling, connectivity, and floor space to accommodate even the most aggressive estimates of future growth for your systems.

■ **24/7 physical surveillance.** Personnel should be on site at all times, monitoring physical access to the building through a combination of audio/video monitoring and physical surveillance of the premises.

■ **Presence tracking/cardkeys.** Data center facilities should always use cardkeys or other mechanisms to permanently log all entrances and exits by authorized personnel through all areas of each building.

■ **Photo identification and biometric scanning.** At a minimum, manually verified photo identification should always be required for all entrances to and exits from data center facilities. In addition, various biometric authentication devices including fingerprint and retinal scanners can only further improve security.

Employee Policies

Employees can be the greatest risk to all systems—ultimately they have the greatest physical access to systems and data, necessarily have the largest amount of knowledge about how to circumvent other security measures, and can potentially become antagonistic and/or hostile in the event of unfortunate human events such as being fired. By contrast, they are also the most vital tools companies have to build and enforce effective security policies. Obviously, people have to be trusted and have to be empowered to do their jobs with reasonable autonomy and freedom.

To balance these concerns, companies (and the vendors they elect to work with) must place reasonable and effective controls on which employees have access to data center and other facilities. Top-level issues to consider include:

- **Employee confidentiality agreements.** All employees should sign employee confidentiality agreements that protect the intellectual and physical property rights of the company, its customers, and its partners.

- **Strict data center access restrictions.** The absolute minimum possible number of employees should have rights to physically enter and access data center and other critical system facilities. These employees should all have the specialized training required to properly handle critical infrastructure; all employees should be personally evaluated for trustworthiness by company security staff, and only employees who truly must have such access to complete their work should have it granted. For example, even senior product managers and executives likely do not need such access.

- **Strict database/data warehouse access restrictions.** No production user or log data should be directly accessible directly from the corporate network. Rather, explicitly authorized employees should be required to use strongly encrypted connections (e.g., Secure Shell (SSH) with 128-bit public key and strong symmetric key encryption) from the corporate network to access log databases, data warehouse systems, and other related resources. In addition, of course, access should be granted only to critical personnel who strictly require such access for their day-to-day job functions.

- **Transcription personnel management.** Specifically for voice applications, one of the key tasks that must be performed to optimize voice recognition accuracy is manual human transcription of the utterances (people actually talking on the phone using the application) from a statistically significant number of real phone calls. The utterance logs (the actual recordings and accompanying metadata) from wherever your voice infrastructure is running (either on-premises or with a Voice Application Network) must be properly secured as described throughout this chapter, and in addition to this, the specific personnel who perform transcription must be carefully managed and given very specific parcels of reasonably anonymized (e.g., randomized) utterance data to transcribe, rather than being granted carte blanche access to logs.

Network Security—Production

Production networks must be designed using industry best practices to protect against intrusion, denial of service, data theft, and other common attacks. To reiterate, VoiceXML applications will typically extend a customer's existing Internet infrastructure to support telephone-based customers, in most cases reusing the same business logic and support infrastructure found on corresponding or related Web sites. From the perspective of the Web server, all VoiceXML-specific infrastructure is effectively acting as a Web browser and all security tactics remain applicable. This is especially true when deploying with a Voice Application Network, where companies retain full control of their VoiceXML applications hosted on their own Web servers and partner with an established vendor to securely run the VoiceXML and telephony infrastructure on their behalf.

Particularly in the Voice Application Network model, the primary mechanism used to secure application code and data itself across the network is the established SSL encryption technology. SSL is used to secure almost all of the $30+ billion in consumer transactions that take place over the Web each year. The SSL 3.0 spec can be found at http://home.netscape.com/eng/ssl3/draft302.txt, and a good overview of how SSL works can be found at http://developer.netscape.com/docs/manuals/security/sslin/contents.htm. Figure 10.1 depicts how SSL fits in to a VoiceXML deployment.

Regardless of deployment method, it is of paramount importance to maintain the security, integrity, and availability of the Web infrastructure on which you choose to host your voice application. Companies must consider the following network security factors for all of the servers, both under their control and under the control of vendors they choose to work with:

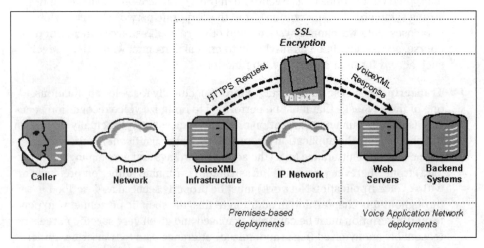

Figure 10.1 SSL and voice applications.

- **Isolated networks.** Wherever possible, all back-end systems traffic should take place over industry standard nonroutable (RFC1918) networks, and traffic on public routable networks should be protected by firewalls. Only absolute minimum access should be allowed. For more information about RFC 1918, see www.cis.ohio-state.edu/cgi-bin/rfc/rfc1918.html.

- **Firewalls.** Industry best practices with regard to installing and properly configuring multiple firewalls must be employed, including when designing interface points between corporate networks and production networks.

- **Host security.** All hosts (physical machines) should be configured for maximum security, including minimal system installations with only the necessary software. Companies should ensure that they and their vendors always install the most recent security patches, tightly administer network settings and file permissions, and run only the minimum number of necessary services. For example, a Windows NT Web server should never enable file uploading and/or Microsoft Front Page Server Extensions unless such services are absolutely necessary for the functioning of the applications being delivered, and only then after extremely tight review of configuration details by security professionals.

- **SSL.** SSL should always be used for sensitive Hypertext Transfer Protocol (HTTP) traffic whenever it takes place outside of the boundary of the data center (e.g., with a Voice Application Network, redundant data centers, etc.). Alternatively, dedicated virtual private networks (VPNs), frame relay, or other secure Internet Protocol (IP) connectivity channels can be employed.

- **IP filters.** Although most public Web sites are made fully open to all HTTP traffic, so that anyone with Internet access can access their services, the primary intended usage of voice applications is of course through the telephone. Even though the VoiceXML application code and audio files play the same role as Hypertext Markup Language (HTML) and images, some companies may wish to strictly restrict the access available to these documents via HTTP or HTTPS (Secure HTTP).

For companies deploying on-premises infrastructure, this can be done through IETF RFC 1918 (Internet Engineering Task Force Request for Comments) nonroutable networks. Companies deploying through Voice Application Networks can further restrict access to their Web servers via IP filters on their router hardware to restrict who may initiate HTTPS connections, and can further require HTTPS and signed client certificates to provide even further assurances. Client certificates with SSL use 128-bit public key encryption to securely assert that agents initiating the HTTPS request are assuredly who they say they are.

For an example, Figure 10.2 depicts a summarized illustration of secure network infrastructure for the VoiceXML infrastructure component. As per the note at the beginning of this chapter, this diagram and the rest of the information presented here is in no way intended to be a how-to guide to delivering secure Web or VoiceXML infrastructure,

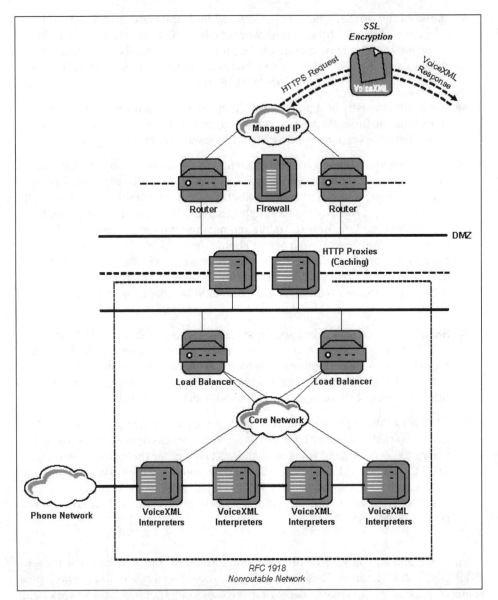

Figure 10.2 VoiceXML infrastructure network security.

but rather to highlight the key issues and factors companies must consider when deploying such systems, and to reiterate the parallels between making traditional Web applications and VoiceXML applications appropriately secure.

Balancing security concerns with performance, it is also important to use the HTTPS protocol wisely, as with traditional Web applications. In conformance with traditional Web design methods, HTTPS connections should be used to fetch sensitive data only, rather than for all audio and voice application files. Performance and bandwidth requirements can be significantly improved while retaining extremely solid security by making smart and appropriate design decisions in this area.

Network Security—Corporate

Corporate networks must serve a much broader range of functions than production networks, and by definition they must support a large number of people who necessarily require a significant level of access to corporate systems and data. This must be tightly balanced against the needs of security for public applications and services, particularly where personnel on the corporate network must access data or services from production applications.

Companies should ensure that they, and all vendors they partner with, consider and enforce the following types of policies:

- **Personal computer (PC) use policy.** Companies should have a PC use policy for employees and should regularly conduct employee education regarding security requirements to ensure compliance. Employee network accounts should be tightly tracked (created at the request of Human Resources upon start of employment and immediately disabled upon termination). Employee network passwords should be checked at creation to ensure sufficient security and adherence to strict corporate password protocols, and should be regularly expired with no less than the eight most recent passwords prohibited for reuse. For a Windows environment, domain authentication requests should be logged and periodically checked for the presence of any anomalies. All employee desktop and laptop machines—regardless of operating system—should be have all core system software installed via a standard ghosted image; virus protection software should be meticulously updated; and all machines should be configured to activate a password-protected screen saver after more than a few minutes of inactivity. It is perfectly fine to allow unrestricted employee access to the Web, though all access should take place through well-configured proxy servers and employees should be required to run desktop browsers and productivity applications with medium or high security settings in place. For example, employees should never download unsigned, untrusted ActiveX controls or allow macros on untrusted Microsoft Office documents to run.

- **Secure corporate network design.** Similar to production networks, corporate networks must be secured through a combination of routers and firewalls with features such as complete IP header-based logging, antispoofing rules, and Network Address Translation enabled. Mail servers should employ automatically updated antivirus protection, and geographically disparate offices should route internal e-mail through dedicated secure connectivity such as an Internet Protocol Security (IPSEC) VPN tunnel (for more information on IPSEC, see www.cs.umass.edu/~lmccarth/ipsec.html). In addition to general security of the corporate network, wherever possible companies should take further steps to segregate network access and limit the ability of unauthorized personnel to inadvertently or purposefully compromise critical system data and/or internal services that interact with production servers (e.g., content management systems, etc.). For example, a company could implement a segregated corporate network that isolates its finance department on its own local area network (LAN) and provides yet another layer of security for the production network. The production network would be accessible only from within the Network Operations Center network, to which only specific users are granted access. Most developers are isolated on the development network, while all other employees are restricted to the general corporate network. Finally, badge readers further secure the network operations center from unauthorized physical access, even further protecting access to the production network. Figure 10.3 depicts the logical orientation of the various interlocking corporate networks at a company employing these strategies.

- **Wireless networking encryption.** 802.11b wireless local area networks (see www.manta.ieee.org/groups/802/11/) are increasingly in use in corporate environments. Companies that employ this technology should be sure to use at least 104-bit encryption for their WiFi networks and to bolster the built-in encryption by authenticating wireless cards using Mandatory Access Control (MAC) addresses. Further, they should segregate wireless access on its own private network with access to the rest of the corporate network through a VPN only. This further protects sensitive systems and data from interlopers by requiring explicit domain authentication to the corporate network, even in the unlikely event that wireless cards and encryption keys to the wireless network are compromised.

- **Secure modem policies.** If modems are used within the corporate environment at all (such as for Private Branch Exchanges [PBXs] or corporate alarm

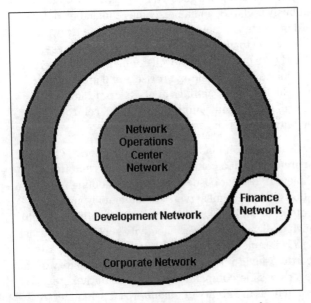

Figure 10.3 Corporate intranet security example.

systems), then they should be strictly configured for outbound, secured dial-back access only and not accept incoming calls.

VoiceXML Platform Security

Because the VoiceXML platform/interpreter simultaneously plays the same role as the Web browser client in traditional Web applications and acts as a server that is simultaneously processing many phone calls from different people potentially to different applications, a significant amount of attention must be paid to the internal security features of the VoiceXML platform itself. Proper sandboxing and other features must be present to prevent unique denial of service and data theft attacks. Key features to pay attention to include:

- **Caller session isolation.** VoiceXML servers should be written so that one caller session cannot access another session running on the same or a different physical machine. The session state object of the VoiceXML interpreter should not be available to other sessions, and all sessions should be sandboxed in distinct memory space.

- **Malicious JavaScript controls.** JavaScript engines should use separate monitoring threads to ensure that the total execution time of a given block of Java-Script code cannot exceed a particular threshold, and the JavaScript Document Object Model should be carefully authored so as not to allow unauthorized control of local resources (e.g., local file manipulation, etc.)

- **Variable-context sandboxing.** VoiceXML variables set within an application should be tightly sandboxed so that they cannot leak across applications and be accessed by another session—even in the event of an unanticipated buffer overrun or similar attack.

- **Excellent garbage collection.** All application states—including cookies and recorded audio files—should be immediately destroyed as soon as they are completely out of scope and no longer needed.

- **Cookies and cookie security.** VoiceXML platform implementations should all support cookies, just like their HTML counterparts, to enable application developers to use this extremely useful feature for session management. For example, most Web sites use secure encrypted cookies to handle authentication and authorization during each user session. It is critical that cookie implementations within VoiceXML platforms be complete—including support for secure (HTTPS only) cookies and proper access restrictions so that requests to documents in one domain cannot access cookies issued by another domain.

- **Utterance-level log control.** As discussed earlier, one of the key by-products of VoiceXML applications in a production environment are utterance files—the raw recordings of callers actually interacting with the applications. These files are critical for performing orthographic transcription so that accuracy reports can be generated and studied. However, it is not always the case that developers want to log the utterances for all grammars in an application; in particular, sensitive grammars like passwords or personal identification numbers (PINs) should typically never be recorded. VoiceXML platforms should provide developers with a mechanism (e.g., via a special `<property>` or similar technique) to indicate grammars within an application whose utterances should explicitly never be logged.

Data Policies

Applications are often used to collect, disseminate, and manage massive amounts of personal information on behalf of end users. Just as with Web sites, strong privacy policies regarding data collection, storage, and reuse must be designed and enforced to protect the rights and interests of users. (For more information on Internet privacy and governmental efforts to help protect consumer privacy, see www.ftc.gov/privacy/.) Companies should consider the following issues when formulating their privacy policies.

NOTE The following statements include one of the authors' opinions regarding privacy ethics.

- **Have a publicly published privacy policy.** Regardless of the details of your company's (and your vendors' companies') policies with regard to privacy and data management, these policies should be clearly available from your corporate Web site. For a great example of a common Web privacy policy, see www.expedia.com/daily/service/privacy.asp.

- **Never sell personally identifying information.** Personally identifying information is any data that, of its own accord by linking with other available data sources, can specifically identify an individual human being (e.g., a full name or phone number). While it is certainly common to buy and sell lists of personally identifying information without the specific consent of the individuals involved, it is the opinion of the authors (and the strong recommendation of the Federal Trade Commission) that this practice should cease. If your company does buy or sell personally identifying information, then this should at minimum be explicitly called out in your published privacy policy.

- **Only use personal information in the collected context.** When people provide personal information for the purposes of receiving certain services, it is only ethically appropriate to use such data in the same context/pretenses under which it was collected. A company that wishes to use personal information to provide additional and substantively different services should explicitly ask its customers for consent. For example, historical purchase data at commerce sites should not be automatically retained and used to offer customized recommendations of future shopping choices via e-mail without first obtaining explicit permission from customers to do so.

- **Do not collect personal information from children under 13.** By law, it is illegal to collect personally identifying information from children under 13. For more information on how to protect kids' privacy while still delivering valuable services, see www.ftc.gov/bcp/conline/edcams/kidzprivacy/index.html.

Extranet Security

Specifically when working with a Voice Application Network, it is additionally critical to ensure that appropriate measures are being taken to secure log/traffic/billing data and the means by which companies can access that data for their own analysis. Leading Voice Application Network providers make traffic logs and other statistics available via a Web-based "Extranet." It's critical that this Web site be secured similarly to any brokerage or other financial data site.

Customers should be able to view usage information on how their voice applications are executed on a Voice Application Network via a series of secure Web-based extranet reporting tools. This usage information typically consists of recognition logs and statistics kept in a data warehouse, as well as recorded end user utterances saved as sound files. All of this information should be made available only to the customer, and contractual assurances should be made to delete this data upon termination of any business relationship.

With regard to utterance data, customers should be able to request that their vendors delete all utterance and log data immediately or selectively delete categories of data (e.g., account numbers and personal identification numbers). For any remaining data, customers should be contractually assured that all log and utterance files are stored and secured in a manner consistent with the rest of the guidelines detailed in this chapter.

All database log entries should be tagged with an identifier that designates the customer application from which they originated, allowing for segregation of data by customer and further segregation by employees or groups within a customer's organization. A vendor's data warehouse should use securely administered access control lists (e.g., via Lightweight Directory Access Protocol [LDAP]) to control extranet availability of sensitive resources, such as reporting data. Once signed in via an SSL connection, the extranet Web applications should obtain the specific access level and security token for the given end user and use it in all subsequent log database queries.

Finally, any Voice Application Network provider should be willing to allow your security personnel to conduct an on-site audit of its infrastructure, people, and policies to ensure that they are able to meet and exceed the claims warranted in their SLAs.

Summary

In this chapter we have reviewed the key areas and factors that companies must consider when evaluating the security of VoiceXML applications. Most notably, we have illustrated yet again the clean parallels between traditional Web development and VoiceXML applications, and have made it clear that it is absolutely possible to deliver VoiceXML applications—either through on-premises or Voice Application Network deployments—in a secure fashion that meets the needs of even the most demanding companies, such as financial and governmental institutions. With strong, experienced vendors, VoiceXML solutions can easily be as secure as or more secure than any traditional IVR or live agent-powered call center. In the next few chapters, we will begin to look much more closely at the most unique thing about VoiceXML applications—voice user interface design and the voice application development life cycle.

The Voice Application Life Cycle

A s with any programming language, learning to write VoiceXML code is just one of the many components that are essential to designing, developing, deploying, and operating a successful world-class application. All successful software development projects, whether they are customer-facing services or shrink-wrapped packaged products, are the result of carefully executing against all states of a detailed development life cycle. Voice applications are anything but an exception to this—and while several of the high-level stages of the voice application life cycle are similar to those for other kinds of services, there are many critical details that are unique to doing voice well.

Roles and Responsibilities

Before delving into the stages and process aspects of the voice application life cycle, it is important to discuss the distinct skill sets and roles that are typically required to develop successful commercial-grade voice applications. As with Web development, it is certainly possible to develop VoiceXML applications without many of the specific skill sets being represented on your team—one of the primary advantages of working with VoiceXML is how easy it is to get started (particularly when working with a Voice Application Network where there's no need to provision or manage voice- or telephony-specific infrastructure). However, the unique challenges of doing voice well—and the unique penalties of doing voice poorly—make it particularly important to carefully consider the scope and purpose of your project, as well as the people (both internally and through partners) you have available to make you successful.

The "Steep Cliff" of Voice Application Quality

As discussed in Chapter 4, there are some specific challenges that must be overcome to achieve optimal voice recognition performance. These challenges include design issues such as audio production and the differences between visual and voice-based interfaces, as well as underlying platform factors such as tuning the acoustic models of voice recognition engines. Understanding these concepts is very important, but at the end of the day what most project managers fundamentally care about are the automation rate and customer satisfaction that the voice application ultimately delivers.

Figure 11.1 depicts the steep cliff of voice application quality. Generally speaking, even the most abominably poorly designed Web site or other visual interface is ultimately OK. This is typically true because (1) people can take their time to exhaustively review all of the options on the screen; (2) there are a finite number of options available, and they're all visible; and (3) when people are using personal computer (PC) software or Web sites, they typically don't have an easy option not to use the application and communicate with a live person instead. By contrast, (1) voice takes place serially in time and people have to remember what they've heard already in their short-term memory; (2) it's not at all clear (especially with poor prompts) what the complete list of available options is; and, most importantly, (3) almost all voice applications are acting as a "front end" to call centers with live operators.

Especially because of the last 20 years of collective negative experiences with touchtone interactive voice response (IVR), people are extremely trigger-happy when it comes to pressing 0 to bail out of an automated application and speak with a live operator. As a consequence, even very small drops in the overall quality of a voice application—be they in UI design, audio production values, or recognition accuracy—tend to

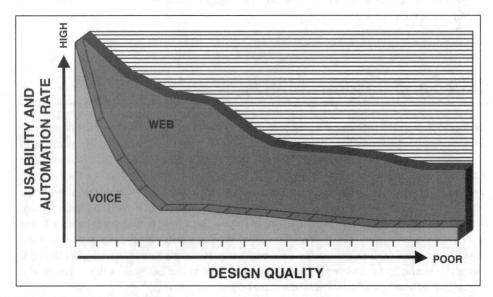

Figure 11.1   The steep cliff of voice application design quality.

rapidly and disproportionately reduce the resulting automation rate and customer satisfaction level for the application.

The Four Primary Skills and Specific Roles

So how does one meet these challenges and embark on a successful voice application development life cycle? Four primary skills are required: design/usability, audio production, recognition quality, and VoiceXML/application development (see Figure 11.2). Throughout the life cycle, different team members with unique skills in each area collaborate to produce the resulting application so that it can be deployed, tuned, and refined over time. While VoiceXML and application development are the ultimate runtime product of the complete process, the other areas actually tend to constitute the vast majority of total time spent on any project.

> **NOTE** Network operations is not being discussed in this chapter. For more on the network operations components required to deploy voice applications in various ways, see Chapters 4 and 10.

Design/Usability

The crux of the application is the voice user interface (VUI) design. The people who fill these roles ultimately determine the answers to key questions such as features, schedule, and dialogue style, as well as the fine-grained specifics of how every prompt, error condition, and potential nonlinear path through the application is handled.

- **Project manager/business owner.** Just as with any software development project, the project manager and/or business owner is ultimately responsible for

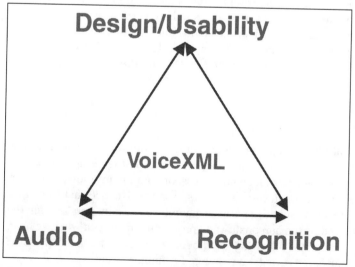

Figure 11.2 The four primary skill set areas for voice development.

the questions, "What are we building?" "Why are we building it?" "How much can we spend?" and, "By when do we need it?"

- **Voice user interface designer.** Voice user interface designers are not the same as traditional visual UI designers. VUI designers are responsible for deeply understanding the unique and specific challenges of communicating over the telephone with automated systems given the current (and ever evolving) state of the underlying technology. This typically requires an excellent background in classic interaction design and human factors (which cut across all media), combined with outstanding written communications skills and specific study of both voice-based systems and speech science topics such as linguistics. Regarding written communications skills, it is critical to have people who are conversant and talented in the differences between the written and spoken language, which are in fact quite extensive (and consistently but distinctly manifested across all human languages). So, for example, a trained interaction designer who is a playwright in her spare time would be in a great position to learn how to become a strong VUI designer. However, to become successful she would also have to become very familiar with the strengths and weaknesses of voice recognition technology and with how to work effectively within those constraints to design the grammars for each interaction in the application. The MIT Media Lab Speech Interface Group (www.media.mit.edu/speech/) offers one of a handful of Ph.D. programs in the world that focuses specifically on voice user interface design.

- **Usability engineer.** Usability testing is a commonly (though not nearly commonly enough) used tool in software application development across media. Usability engineers are experts in human factors and behavioral science who design, execute, and statistically analyze various types of usability studies to help understand how well (and why or why not) systems actually work for their intended audience. For voice applications in particular, the primary (and obvious) distinction from typical usability labs is the requirement to have several types of telephones and a reasonable facsimile of various on-the-phone environments rather than purely an office environment with a desktop or laptop PC. The University of Maryland provides a detailed guide to usability engineering resources on the Internet, including Ph.D. and other programs, at www.otal.umd.edu/guse/.

Audio Production

It is impossible to separate the design and quality of the audio for voice applications from the voice user interface design itself. Imagine Martin Luther King's "I Have a Dream" speech being recited deadpan and emotionless, or your favorite song being performed by a bad cover band through tinny speakers, and you will see that the entire experience of how we react to sound, and even people (especially people over the phone), is greatly influenced by the personality and production quality of what we hear. For all of the roles discussed in the following list, the American Federation of Television and Radio Artists (www.aftra.org) is a great resource for finding talent.

- **Creative directors.** The creative director on a project is responsible for working together with the voice user interface designer to craft the appropriate sound and feel for the application based on the business requirements. This includes making decisions about what actor/voice talent (or combination of actors) to use, what type and level of sound effects and background music to include, and how to craft the prompt language and actors' delivery of those prompts so that the pacing, personality, brand, and overall emotional feel of the application are consistent and deliberate. Creative directors are also responsible for working with the voice user interface designer to determine how exactly to use concatenative speech within the application to balance quality and cost. While there are many unique aspects to producing the experience of telephone-based voice applications versus other media, talented creative directors (particularly those with experience in radio and music) can often make the crossover fairly easily.

- **Voice talent (actors).** Voice talent is a multi-billion-dollar industry in its own right. Many actors (the term *actors* typically refers both to male and female artists) specialize in voice talent work. While the majority of this work is traditionally for radio, movie previews, books on tape, and other entertainment properties, an increasing amount is for telephone-based systems such as voice mail and voice applications. Sophisticated voice applications present unique challenges to voice talent because they typically involve recording vast amounts of fragments used for concatenative speech (e.g., recording all 30,000 cities and states in the U.S.). Actors must deliver these fragments extremely consistently to make the recording process timely and cost-effective.

- **Recording engineers.** Recording engineers are expert at operating the equipment and facilities in a professional recording studio. They appropriately place actors next to the right microphone in the right physical orientation, configure signal processing equipment to achieve the proper Equalization (EQ), minimize noise levels, and operate the digital and/or analog recording equipment while the actor(s) is speaking. Particularly for the unique (terrible) acoustics of the telephone, even minutely subtle shifts in the way prompts and sound effects are recorded can have a dramatic impact on how the resulting files actually sound over the phone.

- **Editors.** Once all of the audio has been recorded, recording editors go through the painstaking process of properly assembling the final audio files from all of the raw material produced during the recording sessions. Considering that many large voice applications may entail thousands or even hundreds of thousands of audio files, a staff of diligent and extremely efficient editors who are trained in the specifics of producing audio for the phone (and concatenative speech in particular) is critically important.

Recognition Quality

Tuning the underlying voice recognition engines and related technologies invariably makes a huge difference in the ultimate recognition accuracy that can be achieved. For example, some leading-edge providers today can demonstrably double the accuracy (which means cutting the error rate in half) for common recognition tasks such as U.S. cities and states relative to using leading recognition engines out of the box. This is similar to enterprise database systems like Oracle, where the difference between having a great Oracle database administrator (DBA) and not having one can easily be a factor of 1,000 in performance. Voice recognition engines are incredibly impressive erector sets—but they are erector sets, and the results you achieve with them depend heavily on the quality of people you have using them. M.I.T.'s Speech Interface Group (www.media.mit.edu/speech/) is once again a great resource for learning more about the people who can best play these roles, as is Carnegie Mellon University's speech group (www.speech.cs.cmu.edu/) and the Center for Spoken Language Understanding at the Oregon Graduate Institute (http://cslu.cse.ogi.edu/).

- **Speech recognition scientists.** Speech recognition scientists are expert in the underlying mechanics of speech recognition technology. They are intimately familiar with the relevant pieces from computer science, computational linguistics, phonetics, and other disciplines that make it possible to optimally configure the underlying recognition engines for each application. In addition, they work with voice user interface designers to analyze the results of accuracy reports for applications to help tune the performance of specific grammars and the UI design itself.

- **Phoneticians.** As discussed in Chapter 2, phonetic dictionaries are one of the primary components used during the recognition process. While all leading recognition engines ship with fairly extensive phonetic dictionaries in the box, in practice it is often valuable or necessary to refine and add to these dictionaries based on the vocabulary and/or user base diversity for your application. Voice-activated dialing and retail catalogs with product names are examples of cases in which new words need to be continually added to phonetic dictionaries. Even for applications that have what one might expect are common vocabularies, phoneticians can often discover during the accuracy tuning process that the specific pronunciation variations used by a given user base are not accurately covered or weighted in the base dictionaries.

- **Transcriptionists.** Orthographic transcription is the process of having human beings listen to actual recordings of callers using the application and write down what the callers actually said so that it can be compared with what the recognizer thought they said. This manual process is the basis for doing accuracy reports. While it is possible to do a lot of interesting analysis of voice application performance without transcription, it is impossible to get a true sense of how accurate the system is without it. This is fundamentally true because voice recognition doesn't know when it's wrong. We'll discuss this further when we talk about tuning the life cycle. Transcriptionists are typically contractor, clerical-level employees who are trustworthy, reliable, and fast. A reasonably proficient transcriptionist can easily transcribe 800 to 1,000 utterances per day.

VoiceXML and Application Development

Finally, VoiceXML and application development complete the picture. Once functional requirements have been set, dialogue flows have been designed, audio files have been scripted and planned, etc., the programmers can set to work and implement the application. The primary message of this book is, of course, that the skills required to complete this piece of the puzzle are virtually identical to those used for any other Web-based development. VoiceXML is easy for Web developers to learn and become proficient in, and the back-end integration pieces are the same as for any other Web-based application. Any of the common job sites such as Monster.com (www.monster.com) and BrassRing.com (www.brassring.com) are easy places to begin the search for qualified developers.

- **VoiceXML developers.** In many companies, different developers actually author the script-level and business rules code for Hypertext Markup Language (HTML)-based Web sites than author the back-end integration components. If appropriate, exactly the same distinction can be applied in the VoiceXML realm. Whichever staff members typically author HTML code, server-side script logic such as Active Server Pages (ASP) or Java Server Pages (JSP) (if you use that), etc., can be trained to learn and write VoiceXML applications based on the input from the design team. Once again, this is almost identical to the situation in developing Web sites.

- **Back-end developers.** If necessary, separate developers may be brought in to build new or extended integration with back-end systems such as Enterprise Resource Planning (ERP), Customer-Relationship Management (CRM), Sales Force Automation (SFA), and legacy systems. Because VoiceXML is built on the Web paradigm, this piece is the same as for any other Web-based system.

The Six Life Cycle Stages

While terminology and specifics may vary, the voice application life cycle can be effectively broken down into six primary stages: (1) planning, (2) prototyping and iteration, (3) development, (4) quality assurance (QA) and alpha release, (5) beta release and tuning, and (6) launch and maintenance. At each step in this life cycle, the team members assuming each role play a different part in assuring that the project is a success. Figure 11.3 is a simple depiction of the voice application life cycle.

Stage 1: Planning

As with all software development projects, the initial planning stage is ultimately the most critical for determining whether a project will succeed. It is at this stage that initial business requirements are fleshed out and approved, feasibility and scope are established, and the high-level creative and interface design concepts for the application are conceived and ratified. Organizations that take the time to prudently establish all of these pieces up front will encounter the fewest surprises along the way toward completion. Key areas that must be addressed during the planning stage include:

- **Business requirements and budget.** Without great requirements definition up front, people are almost guaranteed to be disappointed. High-level statements like "We want voice-activated stock trading" are far from sufficient. Significant

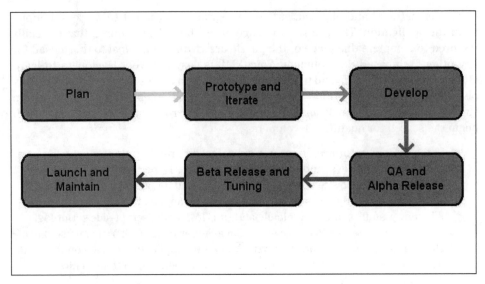

Figure 11.3 Voice application life cycle.

effort must be expended to carefully craft the business case ("Why are we doing this?"), business model ("What are the economics of doing this?"), and product requirements ("For specifically whom are we going to build specifically what?"). The more detailed this information is, the easier all other pieces become.

- **User scenarios and task analyses.** Given the general concept of what's required, user interface designers should spend time developing significantly comprehensive user scenarios and task analyses. User scenarios are simple (usually about a paragraph long) but specific descriptions of a real-world situation where some specific person would potentially use the application. User scenarios are helpful because they aid designers in thinking creatively and comprehensively about all the different ways real people may use the application they're building—making them specific means by which interesting details often emerge that directly map to how certain features should be built. Task analyses are a further extension of user scenarios—given a particular user scenario, they are a step-by-step examination of what the person would do in order to get what he or she wants from the application. This can include things like, "While driving, Barbara reaches over to the glove compartment and fishes for the piece of paper where she wrote down Jim's address." Once again, these can really help designers to discover interesting things about the application they're building that they wouldn't have otherwise noticed until after they started doing usability tests (or worse, until after the app had launched).

- **Feasibility analysis.** As discussed in Chapters 3 and 4, voice recognition technology isn't perfect. It can work fantastically (>97 percent automation rates) for many very sophisticated applications, but there are certain things that it simply isn't good for yet. For example, spelling arbitrary words or e-mail addresses is just not feasible yet. So it's critical early on for speech scientists and voice user interface designers to think deeply about the application and make sure that all of the features and recognition tasks under consideration are feasible and can be made to perform well.

■ **Application scope and feature details.** As a continuation of the business requirements, a detailed specification for the exact scope and features of the application should be prepared. Scope is particularly important—just as it is for all software projects—because of scheduling and resourcing issues. Which features are explicitly must-have versus nice to have? If problems occur, at what point is it right to cut features versus slip the schedule? Once again, making sure that everyone (including senior management) is completely bought in can save a lot of potential pain down the road.

■ **Creative brief.** Creative briefs are fairly unique to voice applications, though some Web sites and creativity-heavy software applications (e.g., multimedia encyclopedias) have typically used them as well. For voice applications, the creative brief is a high-level document detailing the brand, personality, and other creative elements that apply to the application. For example, how much use of background music and sound effects should there be? What is the general sound and feel of these sounds? Should the voice talent be male or female? What age? Any particular accent? The creative director, project manager, and voice user interface designer collaborate to produce this document, which will heavily influence the details of both prompt language and audio production.

Stage 2: Prototyping and Iteration

The merits of iterative design and the value of prototyping in product development are extremely well known and have been written about extensively. Particularly for voice applications, iteratively testing detailed call flows with real potential callers is extremely valuable. There are many assumptions that must be made by voice user interface designers about how people will choose to interact with a given application, and the aforementioned differences between spoken and written dialogue remain challenging even for seasoned designers. Taking the time to iteratively design your applications, including formal usability studies, will almost invariably deliver healthy customer satisfaction and application performance dividends. Key tasks during this stage include:

■ **Initial prototyping (with reasonable data).** Just as with visual applications, there are several different types of prototyping that can be done for voice applications. At the low end, simple "Wizard of Oz" interactions have two people role-play the caller and the automated system given a tightly scripted prompt (and grammar) sequence for the automated system. At the high end, fully functional prototypes including full data integration with a live system provide the most realistic assessment of how people will interact with the application. Depending on time, budget, and the specific application, you should choose a reasonable combination of approaches. It is important to note that there are significant differences between how people interact over the phone and in person, so be sure to include at least some level of prototyping that actually happens over the phone.

■ **Usability testing.** The companion to prototyping is usability testing. Ideally, you will have access (either your own or through a vendor you're collaborating with) to a formal usability lab equipped with a hidden observation room, video camera, telephone(s), etc. Similarly, it is important to have access to a stream of appropriate usability test subjects for the audience of your application. Leading Voice Application Network and other professional services firms will tend to have these services available and include them by default in solutions packages.

■ **Iterative prototyping.** Given the usability lab and the initial prototype, the key task is to simply conduct several tests and iteratively improve/tweak/change the prototype based on the insights gathered during each test. As with any laboratory work, it isn't guaranteed to model the real world exactly, but is proven to be an invaluable tool for discovering 80+ percent of the major usability issues that would otherwise remain unaddressed until the application was already in the hands of real customers.

■ **Detailed call flows and audio scripts.** These are the meat of the application design. The voice user interface designer must produce the detailed call flows (typically expressed as Visio flowchart diagrams or the equivalent) and audio scripts (literally, the printed scripts that actors will read from in the recording studio) for every single prompt in the application. For areas that involve concatenative speech, this can be significantly time-consuming—but it is critical. Companies that produce many voice applications will tend to have established standards for authoring call flows and audio scripts, and in fact will have long-standing relationships with many recording studios and actors who become comfortable with the specific format they use. In an arena where thousands or tens of thousands of prompts are routinely recorded in a single day, this familiarity can rapidly translate to enormous cost and time savings, both in terms of recording everything faster and in reducing the need to do pick-up sessions to fix mistakes.

■ **Initial grammar design.** The basic idea for every grammar is inherently part of the call flows, because they explicitly track out the application behavior for every allowed state. However, effective grammar design often goes far beyond just putting the specific words in a list. At this stage, speech scientists collaborate with voice user interface designers to take the first cut at every grammar in the application. For example, an application may ask someone to say *yes* or *no*. The designer must decide whether to specifically (and only) listen for *yes* and *no*, or to also listen for related phrases like *yep*, *yeah*, *nope*, etc. While this appears simple, doing it well (and arriving at the unique combination of how the UI prompts pair up with the grammars that follow them) is at the heart of making effective voice applications.

Stage 3: Development

Once a very clear plan for the application has been established, and all of the detailed work necessary to craft the specific behavior, prompting, and audio file/concatenative speech functionality has been solidified after an iterative series of usability tests and design revisions, then all is clear to actually develop the complete application. The actual VoiceXML (and how it's dynamically rendered from back-end data as per Chapter 8) and back-end integration gets developed alongside a comprehensive QA plan. In parallel, the (often extremely intensive) bulk of audio gets recorded and the recognition tuning process begins. Key tasks during this stage include:

- **VoiceXML development and back-end integration.** At this point, actual application development can proceed as expected. VoiceXML is written with all appropriate back-end integration.

- **QA planning.** A great QA plan and a great QA team have saved many software projects; the opposite has killed many more. QA for voice applications needs to include functional testing (to ensure all paths through the application behave as expected, including error recovery), UI testing (to ensure all prompts were recorded properly, no missing audio, etc.), and operational/stress testing (to ensure that the platform the application is running on can actually handle the expected traffic). Contrary to the case for typical Web or PC applications, great off-the-shelf tools do not exist yet for performing automated functional and stress testing of voice applications. Leading vendors tend to have in-house solutions (including stress testing arrays that can make many simultaneous phone calls) that can help their customers do this well.

- **Recording all audio.** Given the audio scripts, all of the voice talent and studio time must be scheduled, recorded, and then edited into all of the discrete audio files that will actually be placed on your Web server at run time. It is important not to underestimate the challenge or cost of this step, particularly with regard to application maintenance down the road. Having a good formal process in place (or working with a partner) to manage the storage, source control, and deployment of audio files over time is critical.

- **Initial grammar tuning.** At this stage, even before there is a significant amount of call traffic, it is possible to begin making significant a priori improvements/refinements to all of the grammars in the application. For example, relative weightings can be applied to the various options in particular grammars (e.g., people are more likely to say *New York, New York* than *Mallorck, New York*). This is also the stage when speech scientists and phoneticians begin to seriously look at all of the recognition tasks in the application, the expected caller base, etc. and to set the appropriate recognizer parameters (e.g., confidence thresholds, UI timeouts) and create a plan for adding/updating necessary pronunciations to the phonetic dictionaries.

- **Usability testing.** One more usability test at the end of this phase is useful to ensure that, once the entire application has been developed, previous issues haven't crept back in and any new feature areas that weren't tested in the original prototypes work well. In particular, this is a good time to explicitly test scenarios where callers have to move around between different areas of the application (which may not have been able to be tested before, especially with live data).

Stage 4: QA and Alpha Release

In this stage, testing of the (now complete) application with live callers is almost ready to begin. After comprehensive QA testing to ensure that all reasonable (and unreasonable) paths through the application behave as expected, bugs are fixed and the application is made available to a limited set of initial callers. Speech scientists and voice user interface designers (and of course the project manager) produce and carefully analyze the recordings of live phone calls and initial accuracy reports to determine how well the application is actually performing—both from a raw accuracy perspective and from a caller experience/satisfaction perspective. Key tasks during this stage include:

- **Full QA pass with regression testing.** Very simply, given the QA plan, a systematic and comprehensive QA pass of the entire application is performed, including regression tests to ensure that old bugs have not resurfaced.

- **Deployment to initial live callers.** For the first time, the live application is made available to a constrained set of callers that is representative of the production user base. The callers should be aware that this is an early release of the new application, and should be encouraged to send feedback.

- **Establishment of a transcription plan.** Speech scientists and voice user interface designers collaborate to identify the specific transcription plan. Depending on the size and scope of the application, this could be as simple as transcribing every call for a two-week-long alpha test, or it could be a much more sophisticated and targeted subset. Transcription typically requires a large amount of manual work to collect all of the utterance files stored on all of the VoiceXML servers, sort them, divide them up among different transcribers, and collect/store/manage all of the transcriptions. Traditionally, most companies that have deployed voice applications have relied entirely on their speech recognition engine vendors to do transcription for them, but have still had to take the step of collecting all of the utterance files and delivering them (e.g., via secure File Transfer Protocol [FTP]) to the vendor. With Voice Application Networks, this happens seamlessly because the utterances are already at the vendor and leading vendors already have sophisticated Web-based tools in place that greatly simplify the process of dividing transcription work across large teams while strictly enforcing security.

- **Analysis of accuracy and usability.** Given transcribed utterances and the logs from the recognition servers, it becomes possible to segment and query the resulting data warehouse in many different ways to discover insights about how well the application is performing. At the simplest level, the raw accuracy performance of each grammar can be computed. Accuracy for grammars is measured on four fronts, just as for vaccines or pregnancy tests. Each time the recognizer tries to understand something, the result can be:

Correct accept (CA)—The application said "Yes or no?", the caller said "Yes," and the recognizer returned *yes*.

Correct reject (CR)—The application said "Yes or no?", the caller said "Huckleberry pizza," and the recognizer returned `<nomatch>` (e.g., *I didn't understand that.*)

False accept (FA)—The application said "Yes or no?", the caller said "Huckleberry pizza," and the recognizer returned *yes*.

False reject (FR)—The application said "Yes or no?", the caller said "Yes," and the recognizer returned `<nomatch>` (e.g., *I didn't understand that.*)

Using this information across a large number of calls, speech scientists and designers can discover two particularly interesting things: (1) how well the recognizer is actually performing when people are saying things that are in grammar (CA and FR), and (2) how often people are saying things that are out of grammar (CR and FA). Further tuning of the grammars themselves and the recognition engine can improve the former, while adjustments to the UI can potentially help the latter. In addition to this quantitative analysis, qualitative analysis can be performed of the softer factors, such as personal feedback from users and just listening to the emotional state of callers actually using the application, particularly when they're stuck or in an error recovery state. Questions such as, "How well is our error handling? Is there anything we can do to make it easier to recover from an error?" can be explored and hopefully addressed.

Stage 5: Beta Release and Tuning

Once necessary changes have been made to the application, it is ready for the real production launch. This is called a *beta release* more because the final (and critical) recognition tuning process still has to happen than because the release should literally be called a beta to end users. To them, the application will simply begin to perform better and better over time as the intricate data from accuracy reports and targeted transcription helps speech scientists and voice user interface designers to achieve every last possible percentage point of accuracy and customer satisfaction. Key tasks during this stage include:

- **Deployment to production.** Very simply, the application is launched. Even though this is the beta test, it is the official launch to all callers. It is only a beta because the first few weeks of production usage by real-world traffic are required to collect much more granular data for final accuracy tuning and UI tweaks.

- **Transcription and analysis.** This involves much more of the analysis and tuning performed in Stage 4, but with a larger call set from a more diverse audience.

- **Tuning grammars, UI, audio, and/or pronunciations.** Everything that has been learned along the way is now finally implemented.

Stage 6: Launch and Maintenance

Though the work is never truly done, the final stage marks a major milestone for the application. After a few weeks of intense analysis during the tuning phase, a final round of tweaks is applied. At that point, the application is considered officially launched and enters maintenance mode. Any new audio (e.g., new product names) is scheduled for periodic recording incorporation, and a plan is put in place to periodically (e.g., every few months) reexamine current accuracy reports and determine if more changes need to be made as the audience for the application matures (e.g., isn't all novice users) and/or grows. Of course, significant new features or entirely new applications have to start all over again at Stage 1. Key tasks during this stage include:

- **Scheduling ongoing audio and/or pronunciation updates.** This is very straightforward—for dynamically changing content like product lists, new audio and pronunciations will always have to be added.

- **Periodically tuning performance.** Every few months, a new tuning session should be scheduled to ensure that no new performance and usability issues have come up as a result of the application being in the market over time. For example, as the user base grows and matures and there is a significant number of expert users, new issues may come up and/or it may become obvious that additional verbal shortcuts or features could be simply added to deliver great improvements in customer satisfaction.

Summary

In this chapter we've reviewed the key skill sets, roles, and responsibilities required to successfully implement sophisticated voice applications, and a simple six-stage process to follow during the voice application development life cycle. While the specific amount of time and relative importance of these roles and stages will of course vary widely depending on the sophistication, scope, and mission-criticality of the application at hand, we have also discussed how critical it is to optimize the quality of voice applications due to the unique nature of how people interact with voice interfaces. In the next chapter we will spend more time discussing what high-level concepts and techniques comprise great voice user interface design.

CHAPTER 12

Designing an Effective Voice User Interface (VUI)

In the last chapter, we looked at the life cycle of voice application development. As emphasized in the discussion, voice user interface (VUI) design is the most critical element of the development process, and it needs to be taken into account right at the start of the project. Emphasis on and attention to the VUI need to persist throughout the length of the project, even long after the application or service is officially launched. In this chapter we will discuss the guiding principles and best practices of voice user interface design.

NOTE Design is such a critical aspect of voice application development that companies looking to build commercially deployed, customer-facing applications are strongly encouraged to either hire staff with all of the relevant expertise discussed in Chapter 11 or to partner with a leading vendor that has this expertise in-house.

Before we get into the details of voice interface design, let's spend some time discussing what applications and services are most suited for voice interfaces and in what situations voice automation might not make sense. For more business-centric considerations regarding investments in voice applications, see Chapters 3 and 4.

Voice is best suited for applications and services if:

■ Voice is the most convenient mode of device input (for example, while driving a car).

■ Users are motivated to use voice-enabled applications and services because it saves them time, money, and gets the task accomplished quickly.

■ Corporations or call centers can minimize operator-assisted help, thereby driving costs down.

- Navigation of the application is complex and commands are embedded deep into the menu structure.

- Users have physical disabilities.

By contrast, voice might not be suited for applications and services if:

- The work environment is extremely noisy and it is very difficult to understand what a user is saying (e.g., in a shop floor environment in manufacturing situations).

- The user is in a situation of talking with devices and people at the same time. (This will lead to speech recognition problems.)

- It is easier to accomplish the task using another means of device input—keyboard, mouse, etc. (However, it is possible that the scenario might change when the user is mobile and speech might be the only way to access the applications and services.)

- The application content is large and visually complex.

- The task requires users to compare large numbers of data items (for example, long product comparison lists).

Now let's look at some of the design principles for voice user interface design. VUI design needs to be guided by the following key principles:

Focus Application Design On User Needs and Business Goals

This is true for any application or service, but is extremely critical for voice applications, primarily because users don't have the patience to interact with voice applications—they want to dial in, get their task accomplished, and hang up. If the application is confusing and makes users look inept, they might never use it again. So this rule needs to be the focus of all application development through each phase of the development cycle.

Perform Extensive User Testing Throughout the Lifecycle

It's very important to conduct focus groups with actual users to determine what works for the people who will actually depend on the application. This must be done early and often throughout the voice application development lifecycle, as outlined in Chapter 11. Follow a Rigorous Process to Prevent Mistakes and Minimize Cleanup Work Later.

As in any other application development project, the more thorough you are with the requirements gathering and analysis phase, the more quickly your development and testing phases of work will be completed.

Although these principles apply for Web and wireless applications as well, we can't emphasize enough the importance of these rules for voice application development.

In the following sections, we will discuss the various stages of VUI design and implementation in more detail, using a field services application as a case study. A user-centric VUI methodology can be outlined into four main categories:

1. Requirements definition
2. High-level design
3. Detailed design
4. Validation and tuning

Requirements Definition

Requirements definition is the stage where you collect information about the users, create user and usage profiles, understand the business issues and demands regarding the application or service, and get a good grasp of the functionality of the application. It's also the stage where the critical success factors are set, so that on completion the application or service can be evaluated against these criteria. Also, the quality assurance (QA) test plans should be formulated based on the user and business requirements.

Understanding the Caller

Like any other requirements definition projects, voice projects begin with a thorough understanding of the users, their usage profiles, and what kind of functionality they are looking for in an application or service.

Caller Profile

It is very important to get a good grasp on the user profile of your voice application. Some of the questions that need to be answered are:

- What types of users are going to be calling?
- What are their demographics (sex, age, education, etc.)?
- Are they experienced with and receptive to automated voice services?
- How much help will they need?
- Will they need to talk to a human operator?
- What is their motivation for calling in?
- What is the spoken language that is most convenient to them?
- Does the dialog design need to be multilingual?
- Do the users have experience with similar applications?

Usage Profile

To help determine the system and hardware requirements, you need to have a good idea of the usage profiles of the users. Some of the questions that need to be answered during this phase are:

- How many users are going to be calling in and how often?

- What are the concurrency requirements? What is the probability of users calling in at the exact same instant?

- What kind of noise environment are users going to be in during calls (for example, office versus home versus car versus airports)?

- Does the application need to be available 24/7?

What Users Want/Need

You need to understand users' motivations to call in to an automated voice application. It's important to understand the tasks they are interested in completing and the information they want to get out of the system. You also want to understand user expectations based on the user profile so that you can personalize the application to suit the needs and demands of your user population.

Though doing so is tedious, it is recommended that you collect user information through a series of one-on-one or group interviews so that you are able to gather as much information as possible from users directly. Once you have collected and analyzed the information, revisit the findings of the interview session with the users to make sure their expectations and goals are in alignment with your understanding.

Field Services Application

Let's apply this methodology to our field services application. In this application, our users are the field services personnel (FSP) of ACME Corporation. On a daily basis, they are assigned a task list to be completed by the end of the day. Their job list is dynamic in nature: Depending on different scenarios (for example, a new customer request coming in, reassignment of tasks, or rescheduling of tasks and routes), the administrator can change it. FSP are required to update the status of a task as soon as it changes state (from accepted, rejected, canceled, etc., to finished). This allows the administrator of the operations to assess and manage progress throughout the day, increasing efficiency and eventually customer satisfaction at lower operational cost. Currently, FSP can either update their tasks manually by going back to their networked computers at the end of the day or by calling back to the operations center and updating their task statuses with the assistance of a human operator. Most of the time the users are outside of wireless data coverage, so providing any kind of wireless wide area network application to access their task information does not always make sense. They can use a thick-client application setup that can cache their updates on the device and then, when they synchronize the device with the network, apply the updates against the task list. But this doesn't allow the operations administrator to monitor the status of the tasks dynamically and optimize operation efficiency. FSP from ACME are task-oriented trained professionals who know about their tasks and are familiar with the functionality of the application. They are on the run and often call back to the operations center to update job status from their cell phones in their trucks or cars. In the morning they want to listen to their job list for the day, and as they move from task to task throughout the day, they want to update the status as soon as it changes. They typically call the operations center 5 to 10 times a day depending on their task list.

These users (approximately 200 spread over four states) are also receptive to automated services and are obviously time-conscious (their bonuses are based on number of tasks completed, so they want to get to the maximum number of tasks in a day). They are all English-speaking, ages 18 to 25, divided evenly between males and females, and are mostly college graduates. They have all interacted with automated voice applications before, though never at ACME.

Next, let's look at the business aspects of the application.

Understanding the Business Goals and Context

Each application or service needs to have a well-understood business goal(s). Why is it important to roll out this application right now? What objectives is it going to satisfy? What's the return on investment (ROI)? Are you going to gain competitive advantage due to this? How does this impact your bottom line? How can you make sure this application or service adheres to your corporate image and branding? What is the roll-out plan going to look like, and how can you make sure to stay on track? These are all the questions that you generally need to answer to make a case for your business plan.

The Business Case

To make the case for a voice application, the project sponsor needs to justify the reason for investing in the project for the given project duration and functionality. This aids in understanding the key reasons for building service, clarifying how the proposed project is going to impact the corporation financially, and determining the metrics by which the success or failure of the initiative is going to be measured.

Corporate Image Branding

Corporations need consistency in their corporate image identity and branding, especially if they provide a consumer application or service such as a travel reservation system from a major airline or hotel chain or a customer support line for a credit card company. It's important to use your corporate image and branding principles and apply them in your voice applications to convey value, reliability, and efficiency so that consumers or end users get a similar experience irrespective of their mode of interaction (Web, wireless, cable, voice, etc.).

The Business Environment

Extending the thought process of your business case analysis, you also need to see how your competitors are doing in the area of voice applications. Are they planning on rolling out a similar application or service, or do they already have something out? How is the consumer or end user going to react to your application? Does this change the requirements of your application? Do you want to scale back your efforts or add more funding to provide more functionality to your application? How are your competition and market going to react to this? Will this lead to some competitive advantage, or are you just playing catch-up? Answering all these questions will help you decide on the scale and urgency of the project rollout.

The Rollout Plan

Once you have finalized your business plan and have gathered user requirements, you need to decide on your rollout strategy. Is it going to be a phased rollout? At what stages of the project do you need to do user testing? How are you going to promote your service? Are you going to be providing any classroom training or marketing and sales collateral along with the project rollout? All this will help you to decide the scope of your application and thus aid in the design, testing, and launch of the project.

Field Services Application

In our field services example, the business motivations for considering an automated voice application are as follows.

Making Application Access Pervasive and Efficient

Currently users can access the application only when they are connected to the network (which is rare because of the nature of their job) or if they call back into the operations center and get help from a system operator. Even though there is a team of 15 operators to assist the field services personnel, a good percentage of the users have to wait their turn before they can update the status of their tasks. Field services personnel lose time, sometimes get frustrated, and as result often choose to just call at the end of the day or update their status when they get back to their desks.

Reducing the Cost and Use of Live Agents

Since agents cost the business in salary and benefits, ACME Corporation is always looking for ways to decrease costs and increase productivity. The field services voice application will allow for the business unit to do both—decrease costs by eliminating some agent positions and increase productivity by getting more real-time updates from the field services personnel. Personnel can also use this application to set an example and attract new hires.

Improving Customer Satisfaction

Due to increased productivity, more tasks will be completed in a timely fashion, thus enhancing customer satisfaction and retention. The application needs to be 100 percent reliable during work hours (8:00 A.M. to 5:00 P.M.) and the operations need to have a backup plan using human operators if something goes wrong. All the system maintenance tasks need to be performed after hours or on weekends. The application will use voices similar to those in other automated voice applications at ACME.

Ensuring the Application Is Secure, Fast, and Dependable

To encourage field services personnel to use the automated service, incentives will be provided, so that in six months after the launch, all field services personnel can be transitioned over to the new service. Adequate user and system training will be provided ahead of the rollout.

After finalizing the business requirements, it is time to evaluate and understand the application requirements.

Understanding the Application

At this stage, we are set to capture the functional requirements for the project. Details regarding the application environment also need to be understood, so that the application can be designed under those constraints. Issues such as recognition complexity and naturalness, grammars (size, language, scope, and database and back-end integration), and integration with existing infrastructure also need to be understood.

Functionality

Getting a grasp on functional aspects of the application or service is critical from two points of view. The first has to do with the design aspects of the application. Second, the QA test plans need to be based on these functional requirements so that a success metric can be defined to test application design at various stages of the development cycle.

Application Environment

For the majority of voice applications, there is some level of system integration with existing infrastructure so that past investment can be leveraged and application environment can be streamlined. Development, integration, and deployment aspects of the application need to be well understood at this point.

Field Services Application

Let's take a look at the functional and application environment requirements of the field services application.

Functionality

The functionality of the field services application can be summarized as follows:

- Task/job lists need to be personalized by the field personnel.
- Users should be able to access all jobs assigned to them—past, present, and future.

- Users should be able to get detailed information about their tasks.
- Users should be able to update the status of their tasks.
- Users should be able to get help at any point in time.
- Users should be able to transfer to a live agent at any point in time.
- Expert users should be able to take shortcuts.

Application Environment

The task/job data already resides in the DB2 database. The Web-based interface for this application uses an IBM Websphere application server. The operator and administrator both use this back-end setup to monitor the system, run reports, and help field services personnel on a real-time basis. ACME's current on-premises IVR infrastructure does not support voice recognition or VoiceXML, and they have no staff with expertise in managing voice recognition platforms. As a result, ACME believes that using a network-based Voice Application Network is the optimal and most cost-effective way to deploy their application once it's built.

In this section, we have reviewed the steps required to gain a thorough understanding of the requirements for building a robust voice application. In the next section, we will see how this information can be used to create a high-level design.

High-Level Design

During the high-level design phase, a consistent character of the application needs to be defined. More often than not, when interacting with a voice application, users do feel that they are interacting with a personality and get used to that personality; hence it is important to consider character design and voice talent creative direction in your application (once again, see Chapter 11 for details on the skill sets required to optimally execute in this area). Also, constructing a design metaphor for your application may help users to form a consistent mental model of the application and interact with it more easily. For examples, metaphors such as *shopping cart* have helped users of Web-based e-commerce applications to visualize the transaction flow and access services more seamlessly.

Defining the Consistent Character of the Application

The voice of an application gives a character to the application or service whether it is designed or not. Research shows that people can tell a lot about a person from his or her voice—age, gender, education, personality characteristics, background, etc.—and that this voice personality is associated with the company and its brand. So it is important that design of the persona or character be considered up front.

Using Metaphor and Persona

As discussed before, giving a personality to your voice applications helps users to relate to your application or service. Metaphors are used to convey context and meaning to conversations; they can be effectively used for voice applications as well. To create a metaphor, you must first understand and define the service (or application) and understand the relationship between caller and service. To help define a personality for your application, try answering the following questions:

- What are the signature qualities of the application or service?
- What is the user expecting from this service?
- Who is the user or customer base?
- What is the role of the system? Is it going to be used 24/7? What is the typical user scenario?
- What is the mind-set of the caller? What is the mental state of the caller?
- What are the demographics?

A variety of attention-retaining words or phrases can be used for application personae, such as standard or proper names (Bob, Tim, Sue), acronyms (WTA, NBA), product names or nicknames (ViaVoice, Wildfire), or fictional names (Maya, TerriWhatever) might suit your requirements and design needs, it should be emphasized that it must remain consistent from marketing and advertising through implementation.

NOTE The value/effectiveness of explicitly anthropomorphic interfaces like "Bob" is a matter of great debate—not only for voice applications, but in all interactive media.

Building a Mental Model

A mental model is a user's perception of what an application does and how it works. Users form a mental model of a VoiceXML application as they listen to its prompts and messages, provide input, navigate among the application's functions, and encounter errors. A task-oriented design will help you understand users' mental models for the current work flow, and you can leverage that knowledge by cuing users to similarities between your application and the old task model.

A mental model is based on the tasks an application supports. The task analysis step identifies tasks and task dependencies that should be represented in the application and by the mental model. You can create a mental model by:

- Using terms in the application that match users' terms
- Maintaining the expected sequence of events that represents task dependencies during prompt design
- Respecting observed error recovery processes or resources in help and error recovery routines
- Respecting appropriate accent, speaking patterns, or culture-specific slang to match the target user population

Creating a mental model overlaps work performed in user and task analysis, application design, and prompt design. Implement the mental model in the form of requirements or goals for:

- Prompt and message design
- Voice and speaking style selection
- Grammar terms
- Tasks supported by the application

High-Level Call Flow

The high-level call flow design is useful for recognizing the impact of usability requirements, and helps in laying the framework for early prototypes and focus group assessments and testing. Based on early feedback, high-level design can be tweaked and fine-tuned before transitioning into the detailed design phase. It also helps in designing future focus group experiments and test cases.

Field Services Application

In the "Requirements Definition" section we discussed the usage model, application, and functional requirements of the field services application. In this section we will create a high-level usage model. Figure 12.1 shows a high-level VUI design for our field services application. The tasks are divided into the following functional areas:

- Provide an introduction
- Validate user ID and password
- List the job type options: new, open, all
- Depending on the user's choice, list jobs in a category
- Allow navigation between various jobs in a category
- Help users get more details about a job

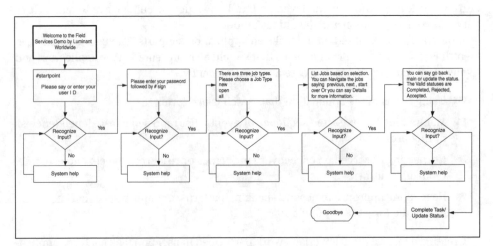

Figure 12.1 High-level design of field services application.

- Help users update status of a given job
- Provide an exit from the application
- Provide help and error recovery at each level
- Allow users to barge in

This basic usage model can be tested with focus groups to see if the prompts are self-explanatory or not or if more levels of help need to be provided at a particular stage or all stages of the application.

Detailed Design

Once you have reviewed the results from high-level field testing, it is time for detailed design. During this phase, you will also have to decide on some key design issues, such as:

- Should barge-in be allowed?
- Should recorded prompts or synthesized speech be used?
- Should audio formatting be used?
- Should simple or mixed-initiative grammars be used?
- Should mixed-mode interfaces or dual-tone multifrequency (DTMF)-only interfaces be used?
- How much customization and personalization is needed?
- Which universal (always-active) navigation commands should be provided?
- How should consistency and seamless error recovery be provided?

Let's discuss these issues in more detail.

Allowing Barge-in

Barge-in allows users to interrupt text-to-speech prompts and dialogs and interact with the system at the same time. With barge-in disabled, the system and the user must speak one at a time without having the ability to interrupt. Most of the time, applications that enable barge-in are preferable because they allow users to navigate through the menu structure quickly, especially after users have become accustomed to the application. However, there are certain situations where it makes sense to temporarily disable barge-in; for instance, sign-in or other authentication processes require users to provide necessary information before they can navigate around in the application. In other instances, if there are advertisements or some legal statements that have to be presented, users might be required to listen to the complete information before continuing.

There are two ways of allowing barge-in. The recognition system can be set up such that the system only stops when the user utterance is valid in a currently active grammar. Alternatively, the system can stop as soon as the recognition system detects sound (energy). The advantage of using the former method is that the dialog/application will become resistant to accidental interruptions or background noise; however, it does lead to a stuttering effect. The advantage of the latter is that the stuttering effect is minimized; however, the system becomes susceptible to background noise and other accidental interruptions.

The stuttering effect may occur when a prompt keeps playing for more than about 300 ms after the user begins speaking. In some cases, users might interpret this as the system's inability to hear or understand them. This may lead users to stop and start their utterances, leading to their utterances being classed as out of grammar even though they might actually be in grammar. To control the stuttering effect when using recognition barge-in detection, a reasonable guideline is that prompts should stop within 300ms after the user begins talking. If you are allowing barge-in, it is advisable to promote short user responses.

If there is a lot of background noise and if the echo cancellation on the telephony environment is not good enough, it might be necessary to (at least temporarily) disable barge-in.

Barge-in has cultural implications as well. In some cultures, it is considered impolite to interrupt during conversations. In those situations, you can insert pauses (around 70 ms) to give users a chance to interrupt. Also, if your prompts are long, try placing important information at the start of your dialog, so users can barge-in quickly. For shorter dialogs, place important information toward the end of the dialog.

Recorded Prompts versus Synthesized Speech

Consumers expect professional audio quality completely from commercial voice applications, although it is difficult to prerecord audio for unbounded content such as e-mail, news, employee directories, etc. It is recommended that professional recorded audio be used whenever possible. One of the key advantages of Voice Application Network providers is that they provide customers with the requisite expertise and production facilities to include optimally crafted audio in their applications.

Text-to-speech (TTS) prompts are easy to maintain and convenient to use. The quality of TTS prompts and dialogs can be improved by taking advantage of tags specified in Speech Synthesis Markup Language (SSML). (See Chapter 8 for more details on SSML.) Elements such as `<speak>`, `<xml:lang>`, `<paragraph>`, `<sentence>`, `<say-as>`, `<phoneme>`, `<voice>`, `<emphasis>`, `<break>`, `<prosody>`, and `<audio>`, can be used to control elements of speech synthesis such as pitch, rate, pronunciation, and volume across different platforms. For nonnative speakers, consider slowing down the speed of synthesized speech.

As a rule of thumb, try to remain consistent in pitch, rate, and volume across your voice application. This helps the user become familiar and remain engaged with the application dialogs and prompts.

Audio Formatting

One of the issues with voice applications is that voice is invisible—you cannot touch and feel the menu structure, and there are no graphics, no tables, etc. to structure the

Table 12.1 Guidelines for Audio Formatting

PURPOSE	RECOMMENDATION
Prompting tone	If the users are getting confused about when they have provide input to the application/service, prompting tones could be used to indicate to the user that it is their turn to speak or provide input
Turn-taking tones	Unique tones to indicate that it's the user's turn to speak/interact
Disabled barge-in	During messages such as legal notices when barge-in is temporarily disabled, it is useful to play a unique tone/prompt in the background
System busy audio	When application is busy fetching content/documents
Logo/earcon	Unique tones can be used for branding purposes or as auditory cues to identify with an application or portion of an application
Confirmation tone	Short tones to convey to the user that the input is valid and has been accepted
Error tone	In case of errors
Help tone	Unique tone used when about to present help messages (global vs. local help could also be differentiated by unique tones)
Emphasis tone	Consider changing volume or pitch
Miscellaneous	Unique tones to indicate secure transactions (just like displaying locks in the PC and wireless world)

content. Developers and designers use elements of font, indentation, color, etc. to provide layout cues in designing visual and graphical user interfaces and content. This helps the user remain connected to the context and content. Similarly, speech and non-speech cues can be used to provide structural and contextual cues for voice applications and services. As discussed in Chapter 11, audio designers should be consulted for designing audio tones (or earcons), tunes, beeps, chimes, blips, and formatting. Shorter tones 0.5 to 1.0 seconds in duration are recommended so that they do not become distracting and obtrusive. Tones should be used to enhance user experience and should not be overused. Consider following the guidelines in Table 12.1 for audio formatting, but once again be sure to consult with audio design professionals who specialize in producing audio for automated voice applications.

Simple versus Mixed Initiative Grammars

Simple grammars use basic words and phrases that any user is expected to say in response to system prompts. These work well with directed-dialog kinds of applications where the user is guided to say words from a designed grammar/dialog setup. This helps in increasing recognition accuracy and is easy to code and maintain, but does restrict the user and makes the system unnatural for power users.

Mixed-initiative or Natural Language Understanding (NLU)-like grammars, on the other hand, are lexically flexible, allowing users to respond to free-form and open dialogs menu structure. This enhances users' ability to interact with the system in a more conversational style, but it does raise user expectations for better system performance and understanding; hence the design of the grammar becomes much more complex, uses more resources, takes more time, and is difficult to maintain.

SIMPLE GRAMMAR

```
System:  Please say the departure city. For example, Seattle.
User:    Boston.
System:  Please say the arrival city.
User:    Dallas.
```

MIXED-INITIATIVE GRAMMAR

```
System:  Welcome to travel services. What can I do for you?
User:    I would like to go from Boston to Dallas tomorrow.
```

Due to the complexity of NLU-like grammars and raised user expectations, it is preferable to start application design with simple and more directed grammar and allow NLU-like grammar to be considered as an enhancement phase. This will allow you to capture user reaction and interactions with the system and will help guide future design of your application. Also, once again, it is critical to work with speech scientists, voice application designers, and usability engineers to carefully craft the optimal design for your applications. As discussed in earlier chapters, voice user interface design is deceptively simple, and very subtle differences can have dramatic effects on the actual automation rates and user satisfaction that result. For more information on implementing mixed-initiative dialogs, see Chapter 6.

Speech vs. DTMF Interfaces

As discussed in Chapters 6 and 8, you can design the following types of interfaces: speech only, DTMF only, or mixed-mode (speech and DTMF). Even though mixed-mode interfaces are more time-consuming and expensive to build, they take advantage of both technologies. If the application or service requires users to input passwords, personal identification numbers (PINs), Social Security numbers, or other sensitive information, it is important to provide DTMF entry capability along with speech input capability as a backup for users of mobile phones and for phones with no keypad. If your focus groups are indicating a lot of speech recognition errors, you might want to consider DTMF interface as a backup so that if there are repeated speech recognition errors, the user can be switched to a DTMF-only navigation interface.

Whenever possible, try avoiding using DTMF and speech in the same prompt. For instance, instead of using

```
System: For health insurance, say health or press 1.
```

use

```
System: For health insurance, say health.
```

or

```
System: For health insurance, press 1.
```

Universal Navigation Commands

Sometimes users get lost in the menu and dialog hierarchy (typical for novice users), so it is a good idea to provide always-active navigation commands, which can be, as the name suggests, activated from anywhere in the application. Some of the commonly used commands are:

1. **What can I say now**—List all available commands
2. **List commands**—List all available commands
3. **Repeat**—Repeat the dialog or prompt
4. **Start over**—Go to the beginning of the application
5. **Operator**—Transfer to an operator
6. **Cancel**—Cancel playing the prompt and get the previous state
7. **Quiet**—Stop playing the prompt
8. **Help**—Provide help with current prompt or application
9. **Exit**—Exit the application
10. **Goodbye**—Exit the application
11. **Backup**—Go back to the previous prompt

VoiceXML platforms include some simple universal commands such as help and cancel. That said, a primary difficulty with universal commands is *discoverability*—how do the users know that these commands are available? While it's possible to make users aware of these commands up front by playing introductory help at the beginning of the application, this is a slippery slope and can quickly become counter-productive if users (even and especially new users) are bombarded with too much information. That said, once a user becomes accustomed to the application or service, applications can proactively adapt and stop playing various introductory and help messages throughout the application. Information about always-active commands can also be played after a help message or as a part of the error recovery strategy.

Personalization and Customization

Personalization and customization are essential for successful user experience of any application, be it Web, wireless, or voice. However, this issue becomes extremely important for voice applications, as users have absolutely no intent of listening to content that is of no interest or value to them. Hence, every effort should be made to functionally customize and personalize the application or service and thus the content served to the user. This makes the user feel valued and attached to the service. Depending on the application, various elements can be used to customize the functionality of the application:

- Phone number(s)
- User IDs/passwords/PINs
- Voice verification–based identification

At a minimum, users can be classified as novice, new, power, or experienced. This helps in customizing prompt, reprompt, and error recovery strategies.

Graceful Error Recovery

The goal of any error recovery strategy is to help the user to find his or her way out of the error condition. This can be achieved by understanding where the user went wrong and providing helpful prompts and tapered reprompts as needed.

```
C:   Welcome to the insurance company. To choose an insurance, say
     health, auto, travel, or dental.
H:   I don't get it. (out of grammar)
C:   I'm sorry, I didn't get that. Would you like the health, auto,
     travel, or dental insurance department?
H:   (no utterance = silence timeout)
C:   I'm sorry, but I didn't hear you. You can say health, auto, travel,
     or dental.
H:   I just don't get it. (out of grammar)
C:   Sorry for the confusion, I will transfer you to an agent now. Thanks
     for your patience. (transfer)
```

Consistency

Consistency is one of the cornerstones of successful voice applications. It helps in making users familiar with the application and aids them in anticipating prompts and dialogs. Consistency in timing and sounds also helps users mentally picture where they are in the menu structure. As a general rule, there should be consistency across all of the following:

- Sound and feel
- Timing
- Dialogs
- Introductions
- Prompts and menus
- Error recovery

Detailed Call Flow

This is the step where all the prompts and dialogs of the application are designed and depicted in a detailed call flow. This includes design strategies for graduated prompting and caller and context sensitivity. For new users, help is available each step of the way, while experienced users can barge in to the menu items of interest. Depending on the complexity of the application design, these detailed call flows should be broken down into manageable call flows.

Error Handling

Error handling is an important part of voice user interface design. Effective design strategies need to be employed to make sure that users are guided out of any error condition in a user-friendly way. Here are some guidelines to consider:

1. **First tell the user what happened.** "Sorry, I didn't hear that," or "Sorry, I didn't understand," tells the user that there was a recognition problem.

2. **Then tell the user what to do.** "Please say a city and state."

3. **Give the user some more information on what to do next.** "Please say a city and state, for example, Los Angeles and California."

4. **If needed, tell the user about the help items.**

Silence

There are several situations when the user is not able to comprehend the prompt and as a result might be just pause and stay silent. As a standard rule, any pause over 2.25 seconds or so requires attention; you could replay the prompt, provide further detailed reprompting, or replay the help message.

Using Discourse Markers

Discourse markers are used to provide metalinguistic awareness of the dialog's progress and cohesion between contiguous dialog states. Consider the example in Table 12.2.

Table 12.2 Use of Discourse Markers

NO COHESION	COHESION
Please say the date.	First tell me the date.
Please say the start time.	Next I'll need the time it starts.
Please say the duration.	Thanks, now tell me how long it'll last.
Please say the subject.	Last of all, I just need a brief description . . .

Here the use of discourse markers, such as *first*, *next*, *now*, and *last of all*, makes the user aware of the dialog's structure and progress. This helps to provide a more natural, conversational style of exchange. Consider the following examples:

```
System:   Did you want to review your itinerary?
User:     No.
System:   Okay, so how can I help you? (Okay offers acknowledgement.)
System:   That's all I need—we are done getting your voiceprint.
System:   Now, since you are a new user, would you like a tutorial? (Now
          acts as a verbal paragraph changer.)
User:     Call (206) 999-9999.
System:   Calling (206) 999-9999. By the way, when you are done, I will
          reconnect you back to this application. (By the way introduces
          a tangent, often of parenthetical importance.)
System:   Please choose from the following three options: new, old, or
          all.
User:     Several.
System:   Oh! Several is not a valid option. (oh! signals a cognitive
          mismatch.)
```

Depth and Length of Menus

Focus group research shows that humans have short-term memory in regards to the information presented to them via speech interface. Research shows that humans generally remember 7 ± 2 items. For example, in a banking application, instead of listing seven different action items, the system can just say two of the most used items and then allow users to select more. Users shouldn't be expected to learn many new concepts at once (keep the number of concepts small). So, instead of:

```
System:   Welcome. Would you like to check balances, transfer funds,
          change your PIN, change your personal information, receive
          account statements, pay bills, or close an account?
```

the prompt can be designed to say:

```
System:   Welcome. Would you like to check balances, transfer funds, or
          pay bills? For other options, please say tell me more.
```

Additional Design Guidelines

These guidelines are presented as additional information to help you understand the basic principles of voice user interface design and make smart choices when collaborating with experienced voice user interface designers to build your applications. As discussed above, each application scenario is different, so consider your requirements and functional specifications first before applying these guidelines. For more information about why great voice application design is so challenging, see Chapters 3, 4, and 11.

■ The VUI should be immediately obvious and available to the user. If users are not aware of where they can use speech inputs, they are unlikely to discover this on their own. If you also have a graphical user interface (GUI), it is good practice to have a "what can I say?" window open at all times or at least available by speaking the command, "What can I say?"

■ Some VUI designers have also adopted a layered approach to designing dialogs, which is a combination of short conversational prompts with longer prompts that are more directive. This design approach is useful if you are not able to store previous user responses. For example, when a user doesn't respond to a prompt such as "What do you want to order?" in a predetermined amount of time, the system quickly presents a more directive prompt, such as "You can order X, Y, or Z." This approach is very effective for meeting the needs of both new and experienced users. Inexperienced users get instant help about what they can order, while experienced users can make their orders quickly, guided only by the shorter prompts.

■ In a telephony or mobile device application, use prompts that tell users exactly what they can say (e.g., "What type of call would you like to make? You can say collect, calling card, third number, person-to-person, or operator."). This type of prompting has resulted in greater user success with VUIs. Another successful technique, called removable hints, provides a personalized approach where your application keeps track of how many times a user has successfully answered a prompt. At first, hints are supplied on the prompt by suggesting things the user can say in response to the prompt. Once the user has successfully answered the prompt several times, the hints are removed.

■ People should be subtly guided not to speak out of grammar. Consider making your grammar as small as possible for increased accuracy and usability. Trying to design a dialog that is very brief is a real challenge, but keep in mind that VUI designers have learned that humans are extraordinarily flexible in their speech and readily adapt to the speaking style of their conversational partners. This is not a new finding: Think about how easily we adjust our speech depending on whether we are speaking to children or to adults. This flexibility has useful implications for designing voice user interfaces. For example, people might be more likely to use a word that is in the grammar if they have heard the system use the word first. Likewise, people might naturally use shorter phrases if they are responding to prompts that are also short.

■ The command grammar that controls the VUI must also be kept as simple and intuitive as possible. Even if the commands are known to the caller, the speech recognizer may easily confuse them if there are too many similar options for what to say. It is best to keep the interface as straightforward as possible, limiting the active grammar to include only the commands that are needed to control the currently active features of the application.

■ Do planning work up front. Find out how people speak in the application domain. Even if you are adding speech to a graphical application, it's still important to understand how people talk about it. Go from a natural dialog study at the user's workplace to implementation to usability testing. During your usability testing, create lots of iterations. There's nothing like trying your design out with real people to find all the mistakes you made.

■ Detecting errors in a human-computer conversation is a challenge. Various techniques can be used by the system to figure out the intent of the user. One of the techniques is to identify recognition errors using confirmations, for example:

```
System:   What is your zip code?
User:     52325
System:   I heard you say 52325. Is that correct?
User:     Yes.
```

■ Generally speaking, "dead air" (lots of silence) is an absolute enemy of effective voice applications. Callers rapidly associate dead air with a system problem, and are likely to hang up or press "0"—even after only 2 or 3 seconds of silence. That said, there are situations (just as in real human conversations) when well-placed, conscious pausing and pacing are useful or even critical. For example:

```
System:   You can say checking or savings.
Caller:   Savings.
System:   OK, savings. I will get you that information.
System:   I'm sorry, but the system is down.
```

If we don't insert a pause between the last two statements, user might wonder why the system said the first sentence "I will get you the information" if the system was down. If we add latency before the apology, it clarifies the user experience. Similarly, add pauses where they occur naturally (in conversations) like between numbers and sentences.

■ Use confidence scores. Assign confidence measures to recognizing different tasks and design prompts accordingly. For example, in a trading application, completing a trade transaction of buy or sell is more important than providing news information on a stock symbol.

■ As we learn any language, we are taught of correct and incorrect ways of speaking and writing. Most of the times, "conversational" way of speaking or writing are not encouraged as that is deemed to be incorrect; for example, avoid using split infinitives, starting sentences with "But" or "And." However, using conversational dialogs that are used daily across all walks of life are critical to usability of any application as these increase comfort and enhance loyalty. It is essential to use various properties of conversations effectively such as contractions (If you're finished entering your information, please say "I'm done"), nontechnical word choices (smell versus odor, pavement versus sidewalk), information structure (new information towards the end of sentence), pronouns, discourse markers (first, next, finally), and conversational implications involve personalizing this response such as:

```
User:     I want to eat Italian tonight.
System:   How about Terrazzo Carmine?
```

(The restaurant Terrazzo Carmine is located next to where user is calling from, serves Italian food, is open right now, and seating is available.)

■ As mentioned earlier, by effectively using English information structure, prompts and dialogs can be made more user friendly. For example,

```
System:   Please say the date of your departure.
User:     Book it for 29th February.
System:   I'm sorry; this year February has only 28 days (versus there
          are only 28 days in February)
```

■ People pronounce the same words differently. Pronunciations of words and phrases can vary widely across regions of a given country. Proper names further complicate the matter—consider, for example, how to pronounce *Qantas Airways* or *Worcester Court*. Voice recognition engines rely on built-in dictionaries that specify each of the ways callers may say each word and common phrase. If a grammar includes a word that isn't in the dictionary, the recognition engine must guess how it is supposed to be pronounced. While this system can work reasonably well, it's likely to make mistakes or miss common alternative pronunciations. Especially because voice recognition is rapidly being deployed in new industries for new applications, it's critical to ensure that all relevant pronunciations are in the dictionaries—without this, recognition quality and automation rates can suffer significantly.

■ Researchers have found that people respond socially to computer applications. What does this mean for your design? Think about talking to a (human) customer service representative on the telephone. There may be things about the way the representative speaks that make you feel more or less confident in his or her ability to get the job done. Some people argue that we draw conclusions about the underlying competence of computer applications in a way that is similar to how we draw conclusions about humans. Does the system apologize too much when it makes an unimportant error? Do its prompts seem geared to a three-year-old? Does it talk too slowly? These types of things may make users perceive the system as incompetent. Users may also question the validity of the information that the system provides, just as they would if they felt that they were dealing with an incompetent person. These results suggest that the perceived personality of the system is an important component of a usable voice user interface. Having a dialog that creates the impression of an enthusiastic, competent helper is important in creating confidence for the user. Look for this issue during your usability testing and adjust your prompts accordingly.

■ *n*-best lists aid in. This is particularly true with large grammars such as street addresses or company names, as it is difficult or impossible to eliminate choices that sound similar or identical. For example, consider *Cisco* and *Sysco*, or *Northford Street* and *North First Street*. In such cases it is advisable to use *n*-best list algorithms where a number (>1) of results are returned and either the best match is presented to the user first or the user is presented with both choices. For example:

```
System:    Please say the company name.
User:      Cisco.
System:    Cisco Systems or Sysco Foods?
User:      Cisco Systems.
```

In other situations, the application may determine that the response is illogical based on the context, and that perhaps the user has recently refused this choice or perhaps the input does not correlate well with other task-related information. In some cases, it might be worthwhile to present the list to the user for further processing. The application sets the maximum value of n.

■ In most instances, concatenation or clustering of digits helps in creating better user understanding and experience. For instance, instead of saying *six, five, oh, five, five, five, one, two, one, two*, it is better to say *six five oh, five five five, one two, one two*, which is how most people remember and speak phone numbers (see Figure 12.2).

Additionally, it is important to have a clear understanding of intonation patterns, stress, and the way people pronounce conversational language as it helps to make the prompts much smoother when you hear the application in real time. In addition, knowledge of these patterns makes it easier for designers to adjust the grammars for better recognition.

■ For generic applications, include people from different age and major language segments in your usability studies. For certain applications such as health information or insurance, include representative senior citizens, as they will be the majority of users of the system. There are sensory changes that take place with age, and these factors should be accounted for in requirements development and usability testing of such applications. We all exhibit binaural hearing losses

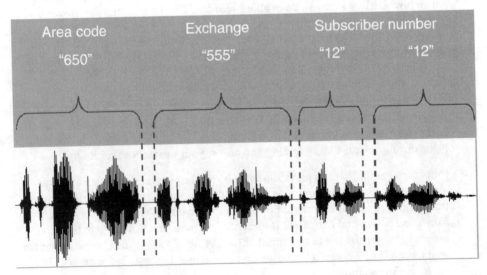

Figure 12.2   Concatenative speech.

of about 2.5 dB/decade until about 55 years of age, after which we lose 8.5 db per decade (source: Davis, Ostri, and Parving, 1991). Both pitch discrimination (source: Cranford & Stream, 1991) and auditory temporal resolution decrease with age, the latter being particularly important to the perception of speech (Kline and Scialfa, 1997). Some cognitive aspects of auditory processing also decline with age. Seniors need more time to switch their processing from one source of auditory input to another (Wickens, Braune, & Stokes, 1987). Some of the suggestions to enhance auditory performance are as follows (source: Bonneau, 2001):

■ During task selection and design, consider the auditory capabilities of older users, and remember that significant variability exists in the population.

■ Avoid the need for high-frequency detection and discrimination.

■ Minimize background noise and reverberation, and allow for volume adjustments.

■ Maximize speech perception by designing messages that are clear, reasonably paced, redundant, and rich in context.

■ Maximize differences in pitch and location to enhance the discrimination of auditory cues.

Field Services Application

Figure 12.3 a–b shows a detailed view of the field services application. Chapter 13 and Appendix A provide the listing of the programming code (code is also available on the companion CD).

Validation and Tuning

The final step consists of validating and optimizing prompts and dialogs based on focus groups and field testing with actual and simulated users and doing analysis based on compilation of actual usage data. It is important to validate whether the metrics put forth in the requirements definition and design criteria step were met or not.

NOTE Once again, optimally tuning voice applications and the underlying VoiceXML platforms that power them requires rare and specialized expertise from qualified speech scientists. While it's certainly possible to build and deploy reasonable voice applications without this expertise, you are unlikely to maximize caller satisfaction, automation rates, and consequently ROI without it. Companies are strongly encouraged to work with their vendors to optimally tune their voice applications for accuracy, performance, and caller satisfaction.

Often, projects don't include enough time for tuning process. It is very important to allocate appropriate time for at least the first phase of the tuning process, as errors and

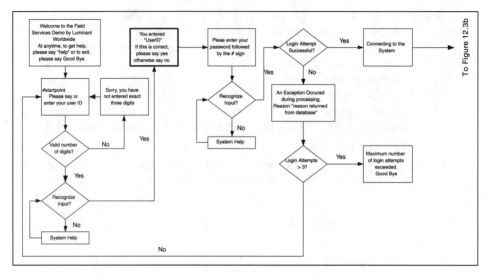

Figure 12.3 a Field services application—detailed design flowchart.

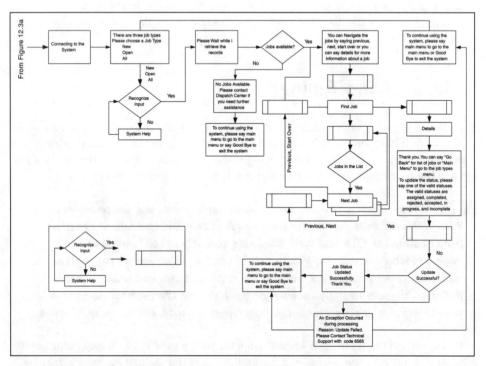

Figure 12.3 b Field services application—detailed design flowchart.

the need for optimization go down after the first iteration (though it is recommended to go through a few such cycles).

The validation and tuning process involves storing the actual user utterances, transcribing them, and comparing them with your prompt and dialog design to determine the rate of success of grammar and speech recognition. This broadly involves tuning of:

- **Parameters**—speech recognition
- **Package**—models, dictionary, and grammar
- **Dialog**—grammar, call flow, and prompts
- **Service**—comparison of results with requirements

Some of the measurement definitions are as follows:

IN-GRAMMAR (IG) RECOGNITION

- **Correct accept**—CA-in
- **False accept**—FA-in
- **False reject**—FR-in

OUT-OF-GRAMMAR (OOG) RECOGNITION

- **OOG rate**
- **Correct reject**—CR-out
- **False accept**—FA-out

Many tuning formulas could be used to fine tune the application, reduce the errors, and enhance performance. The mathematical formula below (source: Nuance Communications) depicts one such relationship between various tuning parameters.

C_{fa} = cost of false accept

C_{fr} = cost of false reject

Total weighted error = $C_{fa} \times (1 - OOG) \times$ FA-in+ $C_{fa} \times OOG \times$ FA-out + $C_{fr} \times (1 - OOG) \times$ FR-in

Assuming,

OOG = 5%

$C_{fa} = C_{fr} = 1$

FA-in = 5%

FA-out = 50%

FR-in = 5%

error would compute to 7.7%. By working with the tuning parameters, error rate can be controlled.

These error rates should be reviewed in reference to the other factors such as first-time errors and reprompting errors, etc.

There are optimizing and tuning tools available from vendors, such as Nuance V-Optimizer (see Figure 12.4 a–b), which go a long way in helping you understand your

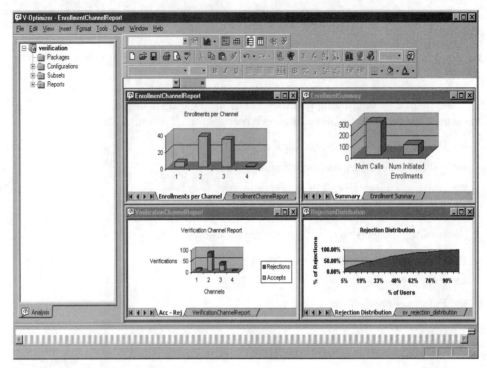

Figure 12.4 a Nuance V-Optimizer.

(Source: Nuance Communications)

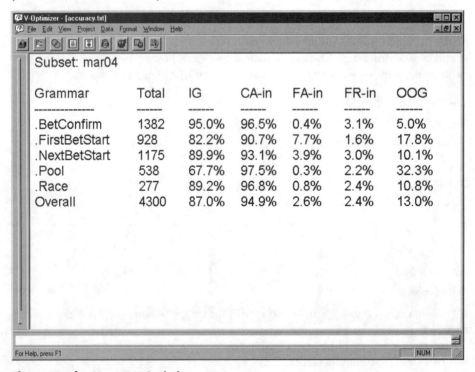

Figure 12.4 b Nuance V-Optimizer.

(Source: Nuance Communications)

logs and fine-tune your application to the next level. Some of the standard analysis reports available are:

- Accuracy
- Rejection Threshold
- Out of Grammar Frequency
- SpeechObject Completion
- Latency Distribution

One can also generate custom reports using the V-Optimizer tool.

As you are working to optimize performance, keep in mind that there is always a balance between accept and reject parameters of a systems. A change in one will affect the other. Figure 12.5 shows a sample "accept vs. reject" graph.

State Transition Diagrams

State transition diagrams (see Figure 12.6) help in visualizing user behavior in voice applications by representing event sequence data as a tree (Suhm, Peterson, 2001). Each dialog/subdialog is defined as a state. The user behavior data is collected and is mapped against the flowchart to provide information at each node. The nodes of the tree correspond to the various states, arcs correspond to state transitions, and leaves correspond to end conditions of the calls. Each node and leaf is marked with the count of calls in the data set and the percentage relative to all calls that reached the parent of the node. Such user path diagrams can help identify usability issues. Parts of the tree that receive little or no caller traffic, or states with high rates of hang-ups or transfers to agents, point to usability issues.

Wizard of Oz Testing

The Wizard of Oz (WoZ) test is a popular test that enables application developers to evaluate a design for an application component before developing the application. The approach uses a trained human tester (the wizard) to simulate the machine side of the dialog. WoZ tests allow the developer to make initial estimates of call duration, vocabulary words, vocabulary size, average utterance length, prompt clarity, and other design attributes. This technique is widely used to design and test speech user interface design.

SUEDE

SUEDE is an Extensible Markup Language (XML)-based/Java speech interface prototyping tool developed by the Group of User Interface Research at the University of California at Berkley. Though it is an elementary tool, using it to test and design prompts can help alleviate the need to constantly conduct focus groups to test hypotheses.

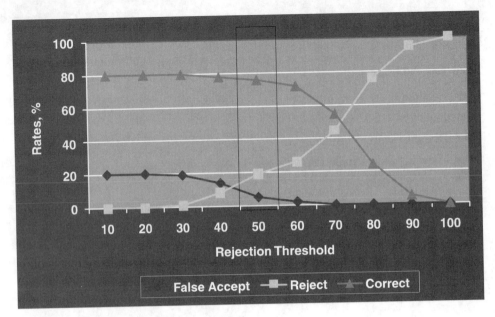

Figure 12.5 Accuracy vs. Rejection tradeoff.
(Source: Nuance Communications).

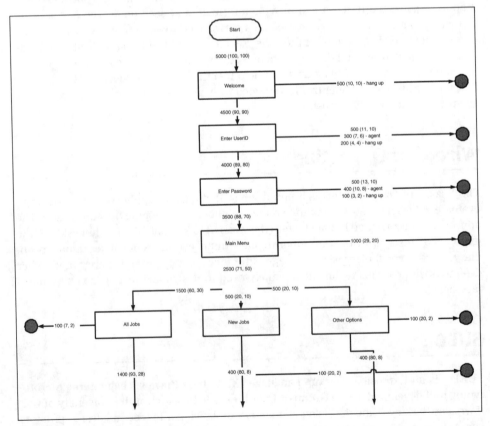

Figure 12.6 State transition diagram.

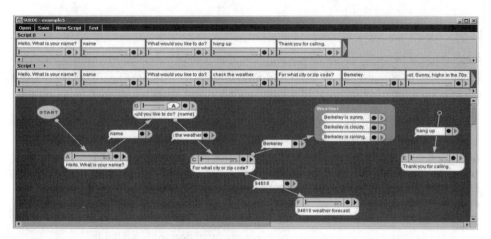

Figure 12.7 SUEDE programming mode.

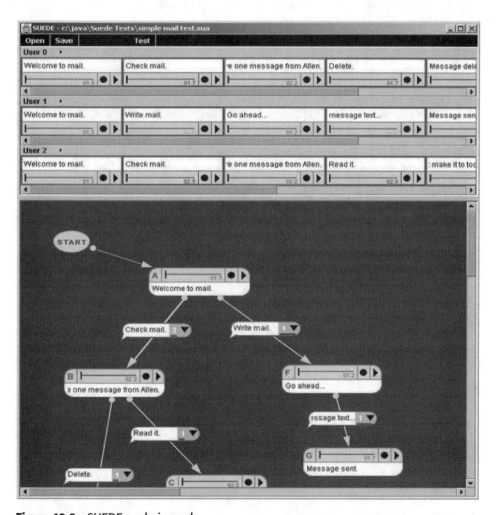

Figure 12.8 SUEDE analysis mode.

SUEDE helps in doing the initial legwork, and once a few cycles of iteration have been accomplished, humans can be used to do the interactive WoZ testing. SUEDE's design mode allows the easy creation of example scripts and speech user interface designs. Once the interface is designed, running the application in a test mode can immediately test the VUI. The analysis mode displays the transcripts from the user sessions as well as an annotated version of the design that summarizes the aggregate test results. The annotated version also provides the ability to hear the set of responses for a particular link.

SUEDE is implemented in Java JDK1.3 using the JavaSound package for audio, and Abstract Window Toolkit (AWT), Swing, and Java 2D packages for graphics. SUEDE software and documentation is provided with the companion CD.

There are two more speech user interface construction tools available:

1. Rapid Application Developer (RAD) from CSLU (http://cslu.cse.ogi.edu/toolkit/)

2. Natural Language Speech Assistant (NLSA) from Unisys
   (www.unisys.com/marketplace/nlu/)

Figures 12.7 through 12.9 show the various programming modes of the SUEDE toolkit.

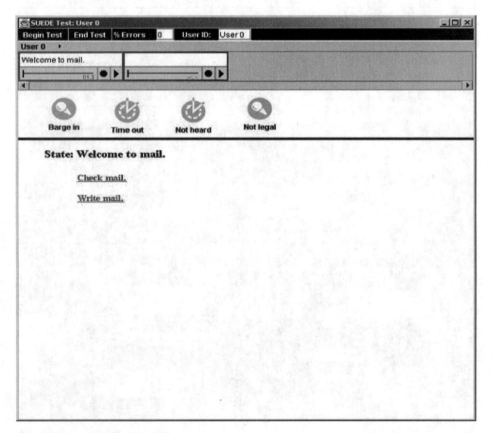

Figure 12.9   SUEDE test mode.

Summary

In this chapter we have looked at the voice user interface design process and principles. Development of the VUI is an extremely important step in voice application design and deployment. It is imperative that good planning and iterative design be included as part of the requirements process and prompt and dialog design process be iterative and flexible. User interactions with the system should be carefully studied during pilot phases and after final launch, so the user interface can be tuned appropriately and effectively. In the next chapter we will build the field services application that we designed in this chapter.

Building an Application: A Case Study

In the preceding chapter we built the requirements for a field services application. In this chapter we will describe the application architecture along with the code listing. Figure 13.1 shows the application architecture. DB2 was used as the database. IBM Websphere 3.5.2 was used as a development environment for writing Java Server Pages (JSP), Beans, Servlets, VoiceXML, and grammar files. The application architecture was completed by using Tellme Studio and runs on the Tellme Voice Application Network platform. Audio for the application (wav files) was recorded using Tellme Studio's "Record by Phone" feature. You can record individual wav files by just dialing 1-800-555-VXML and using the "Record By Phone" feature. The wav files are then sent to the email id associated with your developer id. Tellme debug log was used to troubleshoot the application. The application can also be accessed by dialing 1-866-765-6556 (Courtesy: Tellme Networks). User ID and password for the application are both 123.

The application server architecture is the model-view-controller (MVC) approach with JSP for Wireless Application Protocol (WAP)/Hypertext Markup Language (HTML)/ VoiceXML and the Servlets and Beans for the control and data model.

Architecture Design

Figure 13.1 shows the typical architecture for designing voice applications. Similar architecture can be used for multichannel access design, so WAP phones as well as VoiceXML browsers can access data and logic.

Database Design

The tables and elements created in the database are shown in Figure 13.2 and Table 13.1. It shows the database schema of the design and gives the relationships between tables and fields.

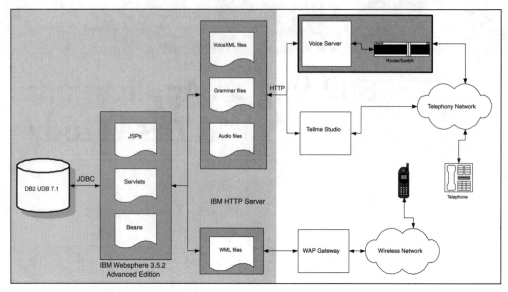

Figure 13.1 Application architecture.

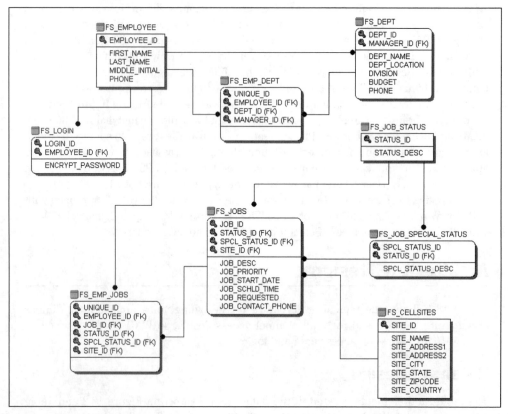

Figure 13.2 Database schema.

Table 13.1 Database Schema.

TABLENAME: FS_EMPLOYEE				
FIELDNAME	DATATYPE	LENGTH	NULLABLE	CONSTRAINT
EMPLOYEE_ID	VARCHAR	20	NO	PRIMARY KEY
FIRST_NAME	VARCHAR	40	NO	
LAST_NAME	VARCHAR	40	NO	
MIDDLE_INITIAL	VARCHAR	1	YES	
PHONE	VARCHAR	20	YES	

TABLENAME: FS_DEPT				
FIELDNAME	DATATYPE	LENGTH	NULLABLE	CONSTRAINT
DEPT_ID	VARCHAR	20	NO	PRIMARY KEY
DEPT_NAME	VARCHAR	50	NO	
DEPT_LOCATION	VARCHAR	10	YES	
DIVISION	VARCHAR	10	YES	
MANAGER_ID	VARCHAR	20	NO	FOREIGN KEY (FS_EMPLOYEE. EMPLOYEE_ID)
BUDGET	DECIMAL	7,2	YES	
PHONE	VARCHAR	20	YES	

TABLENAME: FS_EMP_DEPT				
FIELDNAME	DATATYPE	LENGTH	NULLABLE	CONSTRAINT
UNIQUE_ID	SYSTEM		NO	SYSTEM MAINTAINED PRIMARY KEY
EMPLOYEE_ID	VARCHAR	40	NO	FOREIGN KEY (FS_EMPLOYEE. EMPLOYEE_ID)
DEPT_ID	VARCHAR	20	NO	FOREIGN KEY (FS_DEPT.DEPT_ID)

TABLENAME: FS_LOGIN				
FIELDNAME	DATATYPE	LENGTH	NULLABLE	CONSTRAINT
LOGIN_ID	VARCHAR	20	NO	PRIMARY KEY
EMPLOYEE_ID	VARCHAR	20	NO	FOREIGN KEY (FS_EMPLOYEE. EMPLOYEE_ID)
PASSWORD	VARCHAR	10	YES	

TABLENAME: FS_CELLSITES

FIELDNAME	DATATYPE	LENGTH	NULLABLE	CONSTRAINT
SITE_ID	VARCHAR	20	NO	PRIMARY KEY
SITE_NAME	VARCHAR	50	NO	
SITE_ADDRESS 1	VARCHAR	100	NO	
SITE_ADDRESS 2	VARCHAR	100	YES	
SITE_CITY	VARCHAR	50	NO	
SITE_STATE	VARCHAR	50	NO	
SITE_COUNTRY	VARCHAR	50	NO	
SITE_ZIPCODE	VARCHAR	20	YES	

TABLENAME: FS_JOB_STATUS

FIELDNAME	DATATYPE	LENGTH	NULLABLE	CONSTRAINT
STATUS_ID	INTEGER		NO	PRIMARY KEY
STATUS_DESC	VARCHAR	100	NO	

TABLENAME: FS_JOB_SPECIAL_STATUS

FIELDNAME	DATATYPE	LENGTH	NULLABLE	CONSTRAINT
SPCL_STATUS_ID	INTEGER		NO	PRIMARY KEY
STATUS_ID	INTEGER		NO	FOREIGN KEY (FS_JOB_STATUS. STATUS_ID)
STATUS_DESC	VARCHAR	100	NO	

TABLENAME: FS_JOBS

FIELDNAME	DATATYPE	LENGTH	NULLABLE	CONSTRAINT
JOB_ID	VARCHAR	20	NO	PRIMARY KEY
SITE_ID	VARCHAR	20	NO	FOREIGN KEY (FS_CELLSITES_ID)
STATUS_ID	VARCHAR		NO	FOREIGN KEY (FS_JOB_STATUS. STATUS_ID)
JOB_DESC	VARCHAR	100	YES	
JOB_PRIORITY	SMALLINT		NO	
JOB_START_DATE	DATE		NO	
JOB_SCHLD_TIME	TIME		NO	

TABLENAME: FS_JOBS

FIELDNAME	DATATYPE	LENGTH	NULLABLE	CONSTRAINT
JOB_REQUESTED	BOOLEAN		NO	
JOB_CONTACT_PHONE	VARCHAR	20	YES	
SPCL_STATUS_ID	INTEGER		YES	FOREIGN KEY (FS_JOB_STATUS. STATUS_ID)

TABLENAME: FS_EMP_JOBS

FIELDNAME	DATATYPE	LENGTH	NULLABLE	CONSTRAINT
UNIQUE_ID	SYSTEM		NO	SYSTEM MAINTAINED PRIMARY KEY
EMPLOYEE_ID	VARCHAR	40	NO	FOREIGN KEY (FS_EMPLOYEE. EMPLOYEE_ID)
JOB_ID	VARCHAR	20	NO	FOREIGN KEY (FS_JOBS.JOB_ID)

Code Listing

approot.vxml

This program sets up the properties applicable across the whole application and provides the entry point into the field services application.

```
<?xml version="1.0"?>
<vxml version="2.0">

<var name="logincount" expr="0" />
<!--setting up the property applicable across the whole application-->

<property name="timeout" value="20s" />

<!--the usertype field is to differentiate between the expert user and a
novice. This feature is not used for now-->

<form id="start">
<field name="usertype" type="boolean">
    <property name="timeout" value="1s" />
<prompt><audio src="poweredbytellme.wav"> This application is powered by
Tellme</audio></prompt>
<prompt><audio src="welcome.wav"> Welcome to the Field Services Demo
by Luminant World wide. At anytime, for getting help, please say help or
to exit, please say Good Bye.
        </audio>
```

```
    </prompt>
    <noinput>
        <assign name="usertype" expr="1" />
        <goto next="login.vxml" />
    </noinput>
    <nomatch> The valid commands are help and Good Bye</nomatch>
    <help>
     <audio src="mainhelp.wav">You can return to the main menu by saying
"main menu". There is information available for three types of jobs:
New, Open, and All. At anytime, for getting help, please say help or to
exit, please say Good Bye. To speak to a representative, please contact
Technical Support
     </audio>
    </help>
    <filled>
       <goto next="login.vxml" />
    </filled>
  </field>

  </form>
</vxml>
```

login.vxml

This piece of code is used to validate user ID and password information from the user.

```
<?xml version="1.0"?>
<vxml version="2.0" application="approot.vxml">

<property name="timeout" value="10s" />

<form id="login">
    <field name="userid" type="digits">
        <prompt count="1"> <audio src="login1.wav">Please say or enter
your user I D</audio></prompt>
        <filled>
            <if cond="userid.length != 3">
                <assign name="userid" expr="undefined" />
                <prompt><audio src="login2.wav">Sorry, you have not
entered the exact 3 digits</audio></prompt>
            <else/>
                The user ID entered is <value
expr="userid&.utterance" />.
                <goto nextitem="confirm" />
            </if>
        </filled>
        <help><audio src="login3.wav">Enter the user ID using the
telephone keypad
            </audio>
```

```
                </help>
        </field>


        <field name="password" type="digits">
            <prompt><audio src="login4.wav">Please enter your password
                followed by the pound sign
                </audio>
            </prompt>
            <help> <audio src="login5.wav">Say the PIN number assigned to
you or enter using the keypad
                </audio>
            </help>
            <filled>
                <assign name="logincount" expr="logincount + 1"/>
                <audio src="login9.wav">Connecting to the system
                  </audio>
                <submit next="login" namelist="userid password"
                  method="post"/>
            </filled>
    </field>


    <field name="confirm" type="boolean">
        <prompt><audio src="login6.wav">If this is correct say yes
otherwise say no
                </audio>
        </prompt>
         <filled>
             <if cond="confirm">
             <else/>
                 <clear namelist="userid" />
             </if>
         </filled>
    </field>
    <catch event="noinput">
        <audio src="login7.wav">Sorry, I did not hear any input
        </audio>
    </catch>
    <nomatch><audio src="login8.wav">Sorry, invalid input</audio>
    </nomatch>
  </form>
</vxml>
```

EmpOptions.jsp

This JSP is used to prompt the user with a job type and hand over the control to the
ListJobs Servlet after the user has chosen the job type.

```
<?xml version="1.0"?>
<vxml version="2.0" application="approot.vxml">
```

```
<%//set the content type to vxml %>
<%response.setContentType("text/x-vxml");%>

<!--- Prompts user with a job type and handsover the control to the
'ListJobs' servlet after the user chooses a job type-->

    <form id="jobtypes">
        <field name="select">
            <prompt>
                <audio src="empopt1.wav">There are three job types.
                    Please choose a job type</audio><break size="medium"
/>
                <enumerate/>
            </prompt>
            <option dtmf="1" value="1">new</option>
            <option dtmf="2" value="2">open</option>
            <option dtmf="3" value="3">all</option>
            <filled>
                <prompt>You have said <value expr="select$.utterance"/>.
                    <audio src="empopt2.wav">Please wait while I
retrieve the records.</audio>
                </prompt>
                <submit next="listJobs" method="get" namelist="select"
/>
                <clear namelist="select" />
            </filled>
        </field>
    </form>

<!-- Used to confirm if the user wants to exit the system or continue
using it -->

    <form id="continue">
        <field name="mychoice">
            <grammar type="application/grammar+xml">
                <rule id="back" scope="public">
                  <one-of>
                    <item tag="main">main</item>
                    <item tag="bye">bye</item>
                  </one-of>
                </rule>
            </grammar>
            <prompt><audio src="empopt3.wav">To continue using the
system say main menu or Good Bye to exit the system</audio>
            </prompt>
            <filled>You have said <value expr="mychoice" />
                <if cond="mychoice == 'bye'">
                <prompt><audio src="goodbye.wav">Thank you for using the
application. Good Bye</audio>
                </prompt>
```

```
                    <exit/>
                      <else /><goto next="#jobtypes" />
                 </if>
              </filled>
          </field>
      </form>
 </vxml>
```

ListJobs.jsp

This JSP is used to retrieve the jobs from the JobList Beans. If no jobs are available, the user is prompted with a message to continue or exit the system.

```
<?xml version="1.0"?>
<vxml version="2.0" application="approot.vxml">

<!-This form retrieves the jobs from the "JobList" Beans. If no jobs are
available, it prompts the message and asks the user to continue using
the application or exit the system‡

<!-If the job exists, the application lists the number of jobs and gives
the user the option to navigate forward and backward. The user can
select "details" to listen to more details about the job‡

<% response.setContentType("text/x-vxml"); %>
<jsp:useBean id="jobList" scope="session"
class="com.acme.fs.beans.JobList" type="com.acme.fs.beans.JobList" />
<%@ page import="com.acme.fs.common.*" %>

<meta http-equiv="Expires" content="0" />

  <%
     // Set User Select before getting the result set ( done in
setFsEmployeeId )
     String strUserSelect = (String) session.getValue ("USER_SELECT");
     jobList.setUserSelection ( strUserSelect );
     String strEmpID = (String) session.getValue(
AcmeFSUtil.FS_EMPLOYEE_ID );
     jobList.setEmployeeId( (new Integer(strEmpID)).intValue() ); %>
<var name="count" expr="0"/>
  <form id="ListJobs">
 <link next="EmpOptions.jsp">

     <grammar type="application/grammar+xml">
        <rule id="main" scope="public">
          <one-of>
            <item tag="main">main</item>
          </one-of>
        </rule>
```

```
          </grammar>
    </link>
    <% if ( jobList.getJobsFound() == true ) { %>

        <block> <throw event="header"/></block>
          <% JobDetail jobDetail = null;
             int PrevJob = 0;
             int FirstJob = 0;
             int count = 0;

             while ( jobList.getEndOfList() != true ) {
                jobDetail = jobList.getJobDetail();
                  if (count == 0) {
                  FirstJob = jobDetail.getJobId();
                  PrevJob = FirstJob;
                  }
                  count++;
    %>

    <field name="FLD<%=jobDetail.getJobId()%>">

    <grammar type="application/grammar+xml">
        <rule id="Navg<%=jobDetail.getJobId()%>" scope="public">
            <one-of>
            <item tag="detail">detail</item>
            <item tag="next">next</item>
            <item tag="previous">previous</item>
            <item tag="start">start</item>
            </one-of>
        </rule>
    </grammar>

                   <prompt>The Job I D   <break size="small"/>
    <%=jobDetail.getJobId()%>
                   is at the site <break size="small"/>
    <%=jobDetail.getSiteName()%>
                   and its current status is <break size="small"/>
    <%=jobDetail.getStatus()%>
    </prompt>

    <filled>
        <if cond="FLD<%=jobDetail.getJobId()%>=='detail'">
            <goto next="jobInfo?jobId=<%=jobDetail.getJobId()%>"/>
        <elseif cond="FLD<%=jobDetail.getJobId()%>=='previous'"/>
            <clear namelist="FLD<%=String.valueOf(PrevJob)%>
            FLD<%=jobDetail.getJobId()%>"/>
            <goto nextitem="FLD<%=String.valueOf(PrevJob)%>"/>
        <elseif cond="FLD<%=jobDetail.getJobId()%>=='start'"/>
            <goto next="#ListJobs"/>
        </if>
    </filled>
```

```
</field>
        <%
            PrevJob = jobDetail.getJobId();
            jobList.next();

          }%>

<!-- Last field -->
      <%

          jobDetail = jobList.getJobDetail(); %>

<field name="FLD<%=jobDetail.getJobId()%>">
    <grammar type="application/grammar+xml">
        <rule id="Navg1" scope="public">
          <one-of>
          <item tag="detail">detail</item>
          <item tag="next">next</item>
          <item tag="previous">previous</item>
          <item tag="start">start</item>
          <one-of>
        </rule>
    </grammar>

              <prompt> The Job I D <break size="small"/>
<%=jobDetail.getJobId()%>
              is at the site <break size="small"/>
<%=jobDetail.getSiteName()%>
              and its current status is <break size="small"/>
<%=jobDetail.getStatus()%> </prompt>

<filled>
    <if cond="FLD<%=jobDetail.getJobId()%>=='detail'">
        <goto next="jobInfo?jobId=<%=jobDetail.getJobId()%>"/>
    <elseif cond="FLD<%=jobDetail.getJobId()%>=='previous'"/>
        <clear namelist="FLD<%=String.valueOf(PrevJob)%>
        FLD<%=jobDetail.getJobId()%>"/>
        <goto nextitem="FLD<%=String.valueOf(PrevJob)%>"/>
    <elseif cond="FLD<%=jobDetail.getJobId()%>=='next'"/>
        Last field in the list. To go to the start say begin
        <clear namelist="FLD<%=jobDetail.getJobId()%>"/>
    <elseif cond="FLD<%=jobDetail.getJobId()%>=='start'"/>
        <goto next="#ListJobs"/>
    </if>
</filled>

</field>
<catch event="header">
<prompt>There are <%=String.valueOf(count)%> jobs.</prompt>
<audio src="joblist1.wav">You can Navigate the jobs by saying previous,
next, start over or you can say details for more information about a
```

```
job. </audio>
 <reprompt/>
</catch>
<%} else { %>
    <block>
      <prompt><audio src="joblist2.wav">No Jobs Available.
Please contact the dispatch center if you need further
assistance.</audio></prompt>
    <goto next="EmpOptions.jsp#continue"/>
    </block>
  <% } %>
  </form>
</vxml>
```

ListJobInfo.jsp

This JSP is used to list the job information by job number. If the user wants to update the status of any job, he or she can do so by saying any of the valid job statuses—assigned, accepted, rejected, in progress, completed, and incomplete.

```
<?xml version="1.0"?>
<vxml version="2.0">
<% response.setContentType("text/x-vxml"); %>
<jsp:useBean id="jobList" scope="session"
class="com.acme.fs.beans.JobList" type="com.acme.fs.beans.JobList" />
<%@ page import="com.acme.fs.common.*" %>

<meta http-equiv="Expires" content="0"/>
<form>
<link next="ListJobs.jsp">
    <grammar>
      <rule id="back" scope="public">
        <one-of>
         <item> go back</item>
        </one-of>
        </rule>
    </grammar>
</link>
<link next="EmpOptions.jsp">
    <grammar>
      <rule id="main" scope="public">
        <one-of>
         <item> main</item>
        </one-of>
        </rule>
    </grammar>
</link>
<%
    String strJobId = (String) request.getParameter( "jobId" );
    JobDetail jobDetail = jobList.getJobDetail( (new
Integer(strJobId)).intValue() );
%>
```

```
<field name="jobStatus">
<grammar>
    <rule id="status" scope="public">
        <one-of>
            <item tag="0"> assigned</item>
            <item tag="1"> accepted</item>
            <item tag="4"> completed</item>
            <item tag="2"> rejected</item>
            <item tag="3"> in progress</item>
            <item tag="5"> in complete</item>
            <item tag="bye"> bye</item>
        </one-of>
    </rule>
</grammar>

<prompt> <audio src="jobdetail1.wav">Thank You. You can say "go back"
for list of jobs or "main menu" to go to the job types menu.
</audio></prompt>
<prompt> <audio src="jobdetail2.wav">To update the status, please say
one of the valid statuses. The valid statuses are assigned, completed,
rejected, accepted, in progress and incomplete. </audio></prompt>

<prompt bargein="true">
    Job ID is <%= jobDetail.getJobId() %> <break size="medium"/>
    The status is <%= jobDetail.getStatus() %>  <break
size="medium"/>
    Site is <%= jobDetail.getSiteName() %> <break size="medium"/>
    Job Description is <%= jobDetail.getJobDescription() %> <break
size="medium"/>
    Job Priority is <%= jobDetail.getJobPriority() %> <break
size="medium"/>
    Job Start Date is <%= jobDetail.getStartDate() %> <break
size="medium"/>
    Job Address is <%= jobDetail.getSiteAddress1() %>
       <%= jobDetail.getSiteCity() %>
       <%= jobDetail.getSiteState() %>
       <%= jobDetail.getSiteZipCode() %>
       <%= jobDetail.getSiteCountry() %>
    </prompt>

    <filled>
      <if cond="jobStatus != 'bye'">
     <% session.putValue ( "jobID", strJobId ); %>
     <submit next="/tellme/update" namelist="jobStatus" method="post"/>
     <else/>
    <prompt><audio src="goodbye.wav"> Thank you for using the
application. Good Bye </audio></prompt>
    </if>
    </filled>
</field>
  </form>
</vxml>
```

Update.jsp

This JSP updates the status of the job in the database by invoking the updateStatus method on the JobLIst Bean and then exits the application.

```
<?xml version="1.0"?>
<vxml version="2.0">

<% response.setContentType("text/x-vxml"); %>

<!-This file updates the status of the job in the database by invoking
the updateStatus method on the JobList Bean and exits the application‡

<jsp:useBean id="jobList" scope="session"
class="com.acme.fs.beans.JobList" type="com.acme.fs.beans.JobList" />
<%@ page import="com.acme.fs.common.*" %>
    <meta http-equiv="Expires" content="0"/>
<form>
<block>
    <%
        int updStatus = Integer.parseInt(request.getParameter(
"jobStatus" ));
        if ( jobList.updateJobStatus ( updStatus ) == false ) {
    %>
        <prompt><audio src="update1.wav">
            An exception occurred during processing.
            Reason: "Update failed. Please contact technical support with
code:6565
    </audio>
        </prompt>
    <% } else { %>
    <prompt>
        <audio src="update2.wav">Job status updated successfully. Thank
you.</audio>
    </prompt>
    <% } %>
    <goto next="EmpOptions.jsp#continue"/>
  </block>
  </form>
</vxml>
```

Exception.jsp

This JSP handles the exceptions when the user enters an invalid user ID or password. It also keeps track of unsuccessful log-in attempts.

```
<?xml version="1.0"?>

<% //set the content type to vxml %>
<% response.setContentType("text/x-vxml"); %>
```

```
<!-- handles the exceptions, when the user enters invalid user ID or
password. Also keeps track of unsuccessful log-in attempts-->

<!-- Logs out the user after three unsuccessful attempts. Makes use of
'logincount' application level variable-->

<vxml version="2.0" application="approot.vxml">
    <meta http-equiv="Expires" content="0" />
    <form>
        <%@ page import="com.acme.fs.common.*" %>
        <%
                Exception e = (Exception) session.getValue
(AcmeFSUtil.FS_EXCEPTION );
                String reason = e.getMessage();
            %>
        <block><audio src="exception2.wav">An exception occurred during
processing.</audio> Reason: <%= reason %>
            <if cond="logincount >= 3">
                    <audio src="exception1.wav">Maximum number of
login attempts exceeded. Good Bye </audio><exit />
            </if>
            <goto next="login.vxml" />
        </block>
    </form>
</vxml>
```

Error.jsp

```
<!--
    Simple error page for reporting application errors.
    This error page is called when a servlet throws an Exception, or by
calling response.sendError().  Error pages can use the request-scoped
bean named "ErrorReport" to get more information about the error. --->

<jsp:useBean id="ErrorReport" scope="request"
class="com.ibm.websphere.servlet.error.ServletErrorReport"/> <html>
<head><title>Error <%=ErrorReport.getErrorCode()%></title></head> <body>

    <H1>Error <%= ErrorReport.getErrorCode() %> </H1>
    <% if(ErrorReport.getErrorCode() >= 500 &&
    ErrorReport.getErrorCode() != response.SC_SERVICE_UNAVAILABLE) { %>

    <H4>An error has occurred while processing request: <%=
    HttpUtils.getRequestURL(request) %></H4>
    <B>Message: </B><%= ErrorReport.getMessage() %><BR>
    <B>StackTrace: </B><%= ErrorReport.getStackTrace() %>

    <%}else if(ErrorReport.getErrorCode() == response.SC_NOT_FOUND){ %>
    Document Not Found
    <%}%>
</html>
```

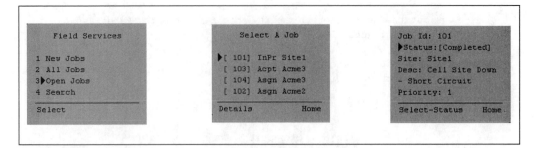

Figure 13.3 WAP access to field services application.

The rest of the code is listed in Appendix A, and the software files are available on the companion CD.

Extending the Architecture to Other Channels

As discussed in the previous chapter, keeping business and data layers separate from the presentation layer helps in leveraging the same/existing architecture to other channels. In this case, our VoiceXML infrastructure and investment can be extended to serve WAP (see Figure 13.3) or other devices so that the same field service functionality can be accessed from a WAP browser on a wireless phone or personal data assistant (PDA).

Making It Work End to End

Since, there aren't that many VoiceXML 2.0 compliant voice application platforms at the time of this writing, we predominately tested the application using Tellme Studio. For building an on-premises voice solution, any web-based voice application platform can be substituted by voice server and necessary network equipment (please see Table 5.3 for more details) to make the application work end-to-end. For example, IBM Websphere Voice Server 1.5 and Cisco 2600 (IOS version 12.1.5 XM) /H.323v2 can be used to run VoiceXML 1.0 version of the field services application.

Summary

In this chapter we have walked through the application building process, the requirements for which were laid out in Chapter 12. In the next chapter, we will take a look at the future of voice and VoiceXML applications and services and discuss the technologies and tools that will further innovation in voice-enabled applications.

The Future of Voice/ VoiceXML Solutions

The past few years have been very instrumental in promoting the role of voice solutions in the computing ecosystem. The improvements in speech technologies and progress with standards such as VoiceXML, Session Initiation Protocol (SIP), etc. have laid the groundwork for future innovation in the design and development of applications and services. Voice is the most commonly used interface modality, and as we continue to get over the hurdles of making user interfaces better, voice-enabled access is going to become more and more pervasive. Further, interaction of voice with other modalities is going to enhance the user experience at both the device and server levels. We will move from simple text to speech (TTS) and speech recognition to multimodal machine translation-based applications and services. Whether used for setting up a conference bridge among participants or accessing a restaurant application in a new neighborhood while driving, voice-based access and task completion are going to become commonplace. There are, no doubt, some serious challenges, but, as in the past, we will continue to develop new ways to accentuate progress through relentless innovation, standardization, and paying attention to the user experience every step of the way.

In the next few sections, we will take a look at some of the work being done that will affect voice solutions of tomorrow in both the near term and the long term:

The second wave—what's on the horizon?

- World Wide Web Consortium (W3C) framework for voice solutions
- Reusable components
- Business models
- Voice verification
- Voice over Internet Protocol (VoIP)
    - Next-generation networks
    - Session Initiation Protocol

- Personalization
- Telematics
- Voice Instant Messaging (VIM)
- True Natural Language Understanding

The third wave—what's down the road?

- Multilingual interaction
- Progress in speech technology
- Multimodal/multichannel access to applications and services
- Wearable computers
- Personal virtual assistants (PVAs)
- Aurora: the distributed speech recognition (DSR) standard

These solutions will affect standalone as well as integrated voice solutions. Whether they function in employing reusable content for a standalone travel application; in providing next-generation call control and management functionality; or in using voice as an interface to other technologies such as wireless Internet, wearable computers, or broadband systems, voice solutions are going become an integral part of the pervasive computing ecosystem.

The W3C Speech Framework

The W3C has taken a very active role in defining a framework for speech-enabled applications. In addition to working with the VoiceXML Forum, the W3C has undertaken several initiatives to drive standardization in programming languages and technologies that allow people to interact with Web content via spoken commands and to listen to prerecorded speech, music, or dynamic speech. Figure 14.1 provides an overview of the W3C speech framework and Table 14.1 lists the status of various speech-related initiatives.

As continuous progress is being made with these initiatives, please check www .w3.org/Voice for the latest updates.

Components of the W3C speech interface framework include the following:

Automatic Speech Recognition (ASR)

ASR converts speech into text and uses a grammar to recognize user utterances. The grammar used could be the one specified by Speech Grammar Markup Language or N-Gram Stochastic Grammar Markup Language. The latter defines syntax for representing N-Gram (Markovian) stochastic grammars within the W3C Voice Browser Framework. An N-Gram grammar is a representation of an Nth-order Markov language model in which the probability of occurrence of a symbol is conditioned upon the prior occurrence of $N - 1$ other symbols. N-Gram grammars are typically constructed from statistics obtained from a large corpus of text using the co-occurrences of words in the corpus to determine word sequence probabilities. N-Gram grammars have the advantage of being

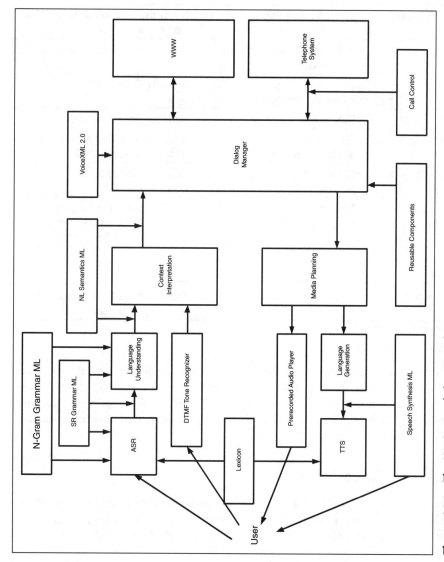

Figure 14.1 The W3C speech framework.
(Source: W3C.)

Table 14.1 W3C Speech Initiatives

REQUIREMENT DOCUMENT	MARKUP LANGUAGE SPECIFICATION	STATUS
VoiceXML 2.0	VoiceXML Specification, version 2.0	Expected to be released in 2001
Speech grammars	Speech recognition grammar	Recommendation estimated to occur in early 2002
	N-Gram Grammar Markup Language	Recommendation Late 2002
	Semantic Interpretation Markup Language	Working Draft 2001
Voice dialogs	Dialog Markup Language	Working Draft Late 2001
Speech synthesis	Speech Synthesis Markup Language	Recommendation estimated to occur in early 2002
Natural language representation	Natural Language Semantics Markup Language	Last call estimated to occur in late 2002
Multimodal systems	Multimodal Dialog Markup Language (MDML)	Working Group to be formed, New SALT Forum consortium formed in October 2001
Pronunciation lexicon		
Call control	Call Control XML (CCXML)	Early draft mid-2001, working draft expected early 2002

Source: www.w3.org/Voice.

able to cover a much larger language than would normally be derived directly from a corpus. What this really means is that N-Gram grammars provide a way to begin representing more truly "natural language" or "how may I help you" voice interfaces in a standardized way. These grammars could then easily be integrated as another standard format in VoiceXML.

DTMF Tone Recognizer

The dual-tone multifrequency (DTMF) tone recognizer accepts touch-tones produced by a telephone when the user presses the keys on the telephone's keypad. Users can either make menu selections or use touch-tones to enter digits per application.

Language Understanding Component

This component extracts semantics from a text string by using a prespecified grammar. The text string may be produced by an ASR or be entered directly by a user via a keyboard. The language understanding component may also use grammars specified using Standard Generalized Markup Language (SGML) or the N-Gram grammar. The output of the language understanding component is expressed using the Natural Language Semantics Markup Language (NLSML). This markup language is intended for use by systems such as voice and Web browsers, as well as applications and services that provide semantic interpretations for a variety of inputs, including but not necessarily limited to speech and natural language text input.

Context Interpreter

The context interpreter enhances the semantics from the language understanding module by obtaining context information from a dialog history. For example, the context interpreter may replace a pronoun with a noun to which the pronoun refers. The input and output of the context interpreter are expressed using NLSML.

Dialog Manager

The dialog manager prompts the user for input, makes sense of the input, and determines what to do next according to instructions in a dialog script specified using VoiceXML 2.0 modeled after VoiceXML 1.0. Depending upon the input received, the dialog manager may invoke application services, download another dialog script from the Web, or cause information to be presented to the user. The dialog manager accepts input specified using NLSML. Dialog scripts may refer to reusable dialog components—portions of another dialog script that can be reused across multiple applications.

Media Planner

The media planner determines whether output from the dialog manager should be presented to the user as synthetic speech or prerecorded audio.

Recorded Audio Player

The recorded audio player replays prerecorded audio files to the user, either in conjunction with or in place of synthesized voices.

Language Generator

The language generator accepts text from the media planner and prepares it for presentation to the user as spoken voice via a TTS synthesizer. The text may contain markup tags expressed using Speech Synthesis Markup Language (SSML), which provides hints and suggestions on how acoustic sounds should be produced. These tags may be produced automatically by the language generator or may be manually inserted by a developer.

TTS Synthesizer

TTS accepts text from the language generator and produces acoustic signals, which the user hears as a humanlike voice according to hints specified using SSML.

The components of any specific voice browser may differ significantly from those shown in Figure 14.1. For example, the context interpretation, language generation, and media planning components may be incorporated into the dialog manager, or the tone recognizer may be incorporated into the context interpretation. However, most voice browser implementations will still be able to use any of the various markup languages defined in the W3C Speech Interface Framework.

Reusable Components

Reusable speech and dialog components help in rapid development of voice solutions because these components are already designed and tested for various error conditions. As discussed in the previous chapter, leading speech vendors such as Nuance, SpeechWorks, and IBM have rolled out several dialog, subdialog, and grammar reusable components. Using these components also helps in maintaining consistency across your application or service. Some of the vendors (e.g., Nuance, SpeechWorks, IBM) have also rolled out or are planning to roll out industry-specific reusable components. As depicted in Figure 14.1, the W3C has taken on the task of standardizing the reusable components specification, so that interoperability among vendors and backward compatibility between versions can be promoted.

As we start to develop and deploy more sophisticated voice solutions, reusable components will become commonplace and will also become more sophisticated to meet the needs and demands of application design. For example, we will see components for initial grammar embedding, call transfers, machine translations, different layers of help, confirmation, collecting data from the user, error and exception handling, etc.

A note of caution: Although reusable components for dialog and grammar design are desirable, it is difficult to standardize flexible components because the usage of components will vary depending on the application and the call flow. Thus, most of

Table 14.2 Reusable Components

	COMPONENT	SPECIFICATION PRIORITY	SPECIFICATION LEVEL	TASK VERSUS TEMPLATE
1	Address	Nice to have	Return only	Task
2	Address, e-mail	Should be present	Return only	Task
3	Alpha string, simple	Should be present	Configure and return	Task
4	Alphanumeric string, nonfixed	Nice to have	Return only	Task
5	Alphanumeric string, sectioned	Should be present	Return only	Task
6	Alphanumeric string, simple	Should be present	Configure and return	Task

Table 14.2   Reusable Components

	COMPONENT	SPECIFICATION PRIORITY	SPECIFICATION LEVEL	TASK VERSUS TEMPLATE
7	Browsable action list	Should be present	Return only	Template
8	Browsable selection list	Should be present	Return only	Template
9	Credit card information	Should be present	Return only	Task
10	Confirmation and correction dialog	Should be present	Return only	Template
11	Currency	Must have	Return only	Task
12	Date, context-compensating	Should be present	Return only	Task
13	Date, fully specified	Must have	Configure and return	Task
14	Date, partially specified	Should be present	Configure and return	Task
15	Digit string, sectioned	Should be present	Return only	Task
16	Digit string, simple	Must have	Configure and return	Task
17	Duration	Should be present	Return only	Task
18	Error recovery dialog, simple	Should be present	Configure and return	Template
19	Menu	Must have	Return only	Template
20	Multiple choice selections	Nice to have	Return only	Template
21	Name, spelled	Should be present	Return only	Task
22	Name, spoken and spelled	Should be present	Return only	Task
23	Natural numbers	Must have	Configure and return	Task
24	Postal code	Should be present	Return only	Task
25	Telephone number	Should be present	Return only	Task
26	Time	Must have	Return only	Task
27	Time range	Should be present	Return only	Task
28	Uniform Resource Locator (URL)	Should be present	Return only	Task
29	Yes/no	Must have	Configure and return	Task

Source: www.w3c.org/TR/reusable-dialog-reqs.

the time, the components will have only the lowest common denominator of functionality and hence be less useful. To preserve implementation flexibility for more complex components, the W3C is considering two categories of components—those requiring only a return semantics specification and those requiring both configuration and return semantics specifications. Table 14.2 lists some of the components under consideration.

The latest information regarding W3C reusable components standardization can be found at www.w3c.org/TR/reusable-dialog-reqs.

Business Models

For any new technology to drive revenue, it has to be supported by a real-life problem-solving business model. If the solution is not packaged to be compelling to the consumer or corporate customer, new technology—however innovative it might be—will not lead to revenues or cost savings. Also, everyone in the value chain needs to have a fair share of revenues flowing to them, or else the business model is not right. It can be argued that sometimes business models drive technology adoption. In the future we will see technology solutions such as wireless and voice being packaged together in development tools, applications, and services to drive maximum benefit to the consumer.

Voice Verification

Voice biometrics combines the physical and behavioral characteristics of an individual. This technology is different from speech recognition. Voice biometrics goes beyond speech and identifies the speaker of the words. Techniques such as measurement of change of frequency between phonemes can be used. Voice-based speaker verification has applications in wireless networks, voice mail, interactive voice response (IVR), calling cards, and so on. As biometric-based authentication is becoming more acceptable in society, voice-based authentication stands to gain the most because it is the most nonintrusive and natural technique of authenticating a user. Instead of remembering their user IDs, passwords, personal identification numbers (PINs), etc., users can be verified by voice as they begin to interact with any back-end applications such as banking, brokerage, and other commerce and enterprise applications. The ease of authentication will promote voice solutions. In addition to voice verification, fingerprint-based authentication is also likely to become popular, especially when authentication needs to be accomplished at the device level. There are already various computing devices (personal computers [PCs], wireless phones, and personal data assistants [PDAs]) that incorporate fingerprint-based authentication and verification. Table 14.3 compares various security methods that can be used for applications. It can be seen that voice verification is by far the most easy to use and efficient.

Voice-based verification can also be used in applications that require nonrepudiation (finance or commerce, for example). Leading vendors such as Nuance and SpeechWorks already have voice verification products that can be integrated with voice applications.

Table 14.3 Comparison of Various Security Methods

	COST OF OWNERSHIP/	EQUIPMENT AT ACCESS POINT	REMOTE IDENTIFICATION	POSSIBLE SECURE	PHYSICALLY INTRUSIVE	POSSIBLE TO LOSE/FORGET
Voice	Lower	No	Yes	Yes	No	No
PIN	Lower	No	Yes	No	No	Yes
Finger/palm prints	Higher	Yes	No	Yes	Yes	No
Smart cards	Higher	Yes	No	No	No	Yes
Iris scan	Higher	Yes	No	Yes	Very	No
Face recognition	Higher	Yes	No	Yes	Very	No

Source: Datamonitor, 2000.

VoIP

With the advances in communication technology, Internet Protocol (IP)-based telephony using VoIP enabling voice services on a data network is becoming commonplace. In general, this means delivery of voice traffic in digital form bundled in discrete IP packets rather than in the traditional circuit switched protocols of the public switched telephone network (PSTN). VoIP voice and data services can be employed to provide a more cost-effective, efficient, and flexible way of building networks. These technologies are based on open standards and provide for the separation of functions such as call control and switching. The distributed nature of VoIP allows innovation and enables service providers to compete for different parts of the network continuum, while at the same time interoperable standards ensure that the overall network model remains consistent. The next-generation converged networks allow many different communications systems to interoperate.

Media gateways are critical internetworking elements that translate between networks having differing standards. This provides conversion of streamed media formats such as voice or video and manages the transfer of information between the different networks. The key element that is used to support VoIP is the set of standards that have evolved over the years to address the various problems associated with voice traffic. Protocols such as H.323, SIP, and Media Gateway Control Protocol (MGCP) are used for call setup and media gateway control by providing an interface for the media path conversion between the legacy circuit network and clients and between the packet network and clients. SIP, as described in Internet Engineering Task Force (IETF) RFC 2543, is a text-based protocol that leverages the power of the Internet by borrowing such common elements as the format of Hypertext Transfer Protocol (HTTP), Domain Naming System (DNS), and e-mail-style addressing. It provides the necessary protocol elements to create services such as call forwarding, call diversion, personal mobility, calling and called party authentication, terminal capabilities negotiation, and multicast conferencing. We will discuss SIP in a bit more detail a little later.

Next-Generation Networks

Next-generation in general is an overused term in the industry. The next generation discussed in this section refers to the convergence of the circuit switched telephone network, the cable-telephony network, the mobile network, and the Internet service provider network using IP technology. This convergence not only allows for easy deployment of existing services in a cost-effective way, but also allows for new applications such as communications services (voice calls, instant messaging, multimedia conferencing), content services (audio/video/graphics/text broadcasts), and transactional services (commerce, Customer-Relationship Management (CRM), etc.) to be built and deployed. Hence the vision of pervasive computing wherein any device/human can talk to any other device/human over any network at any time is becoming a reality. It is the role of this converged network to seamlessly transfer and transition information from one network or content format to another, without the end user having to worry or care about it. Figure 14.2 shows the elements and protocols in the converged network.

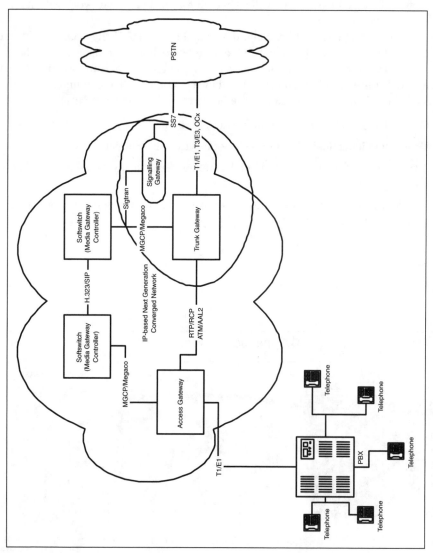

Figure 14.2 Elements and protocols in the converged network.

SIP

SIP, a client server protocol developed by the IETF, is a layered, lightweight protocol that draws from Internet standards like the HTTP and Mbone conferencing protocols. The goal of SIP is to establish, modify, and terminate multimedia, single, or many-party calls. SIP identifies users by an e-mail-like address and reuses some of the infrastructure of Internet e-mail delivery, such as DNS mail forwarding. It can work with its predecessor H.323 as well.

SIP is an open standard that has been developed by the IETF, the organization that standardizes the Internet and e-mail. SIP has also been chosen as the standard for signaling in third-generation mobile networks. This guarantees that investments in SIP solutions are "future-proof" and that an abundance of coming SIP communication applications will be able to work together. Some of the main features of SIP are:

- One single address for all communication (a SIP address, e.g., joe@hotsip.com)

- Terminal independence (computer, phone, wireless terminal, PDA, etc.)

- A free choice of communication media (ranging from instant messages to video conferencing and gaming)

- Simple use and extensive abilities to control and tailor the personal communication environment

- Personal mobility services

- Session independence

- Leveraging of other Internet protocols

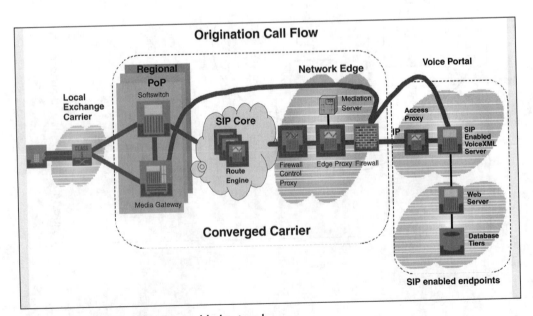

Figure 14.3   Call flow in a SIP-enabled network.

(Copyright © 2001, Dynamicsoft.)

SIP addresses are in the form of URLs. The components are a SIP scheme, username, optional password, hostname, optional port, parameters, and headers and body, for example, sip:joe@yahoo.com:5050;user=host?Subject=temp. Figure 14.3 shows a SIP-enabled network architecture.

Over the past year, SIP has become popular with carriers, network equipment providers, and application developers due to its performance and scalability superiority over its predecessor H.323. SIP offers a time-to-market advantage due to its lower complexity and long-term benefits of extensibility, service flexibility, and ease of interoperability (see Figure 14.4).

In the future, people will tend to belong to multiple communities of interest and will want to project a different image of themselves and their availability to each community. The concept of calling a device such as an office phone or a mobile phone will transform into attempting to contact a specific individual or group of individuals. A person will want to project availability based on a variety of factors:

- Certainly the accessibility of various forms of access will be one factor.

- The actual activities the user is involved in at any instant in time may play an important role.

- The identity of the person attempting to contact someone will clearly be a highly valuable input.

People will want an easy way to set boundaries on how they are contacted and how their availability is projected to different groups of people. Just as important, people will not want to be burdened with constantly having to provide specific input as to what is changing in their personal environment to keep their projections of availability cur-

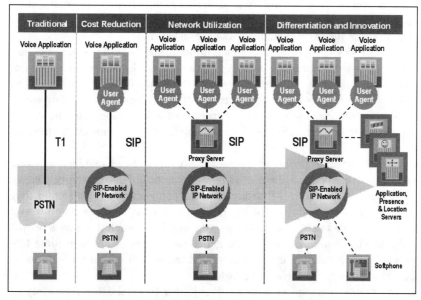

Figure 14.4 Benefits of SIP-enabled architecture.

(Copyright © 2001, Dynamicsoft.)

rent. One of the value propositions of any communications network will be how transparently the information enabling presence projections is managed.

Both large and small changes in the physical location of a person may play an important part in determining desirable availability. Certainly people traveling a long distance from home may want to limit their contact to a small group from home while making themselves readily accessible for contact by people in the area where they are traveling. The fact that someone's mobile access switches to a location significantly away from home should be enough to trigger a different view of availability that is still customizable by the person involved, but without him or her specifically being forced to update anything.

People traveling on business usually want to immediately accept contact from the people they are visiting as well as the airlines, hotels, and other travel-related services they are using. At the same time, their interest in being contacted by their neighbor at home may temporarily be diminished. The various devices that people interact with need to assist in keeping a variety of availability views current. If a user places a cell phone in meeting mode to prevent disrupting a meeting with a distracting ring, there is a good chance that person also would prefer to narrow the set of people he or she is willing to be contacted by. An acknowledged calendar event in a PC or PDA might trigger a different view of availability for the scheduled duration of the event. Inputs can come from many things beyond communications activities. Closing a door or turning off a light are potential sources of transitional information.

The sophistication of services enabling people to be people, and not a collection of devices, will ultimately depend on how easily and efficiently many tidbits of data can be extracted and consolidated. Many people and their associated devices will be generating transitions in their data that may be of limited importance, while other changes are highly relevant. It will be necessary to have some highly effective filtering methods in place as to what actions are meaningful for a particular person to prevent large quantities of meaningless information from congesting multimedia networks just because it is the type of data that can potentially enable some useful service.

Intelligence in edge devices—the cornerstone of the Internet—will play a significant role in session initiation and control in next-generation networks. A network need not control session management. It can be completely in the hands of smart clients, or can be distributed among a few or many cooperating network elements including smart clients. Persistent yet dynamic network-based storage of information mapping device addresses to people's identities will effectively replace number schemes in addressing communications.

Assistance in locating other people to initiate sessions with is a capability someone could easily subscribe to, not a specific access-related function. This capability is easily implemented by something like a SIP proxy server. People simply register and they become reachable. The potential value of any given registration will depend on who it reaches, how easy it makes contacting other people, and how much it exposes people to contact they do not desire. Various media gateways and gateway controllers like SoftSwitches will assist in session interworking with earlier network architectures as well as mitigating various commercial boundaries.

SIP clients or user agents register with a SIP registrar to establish a repository of location information for each user. The caller then places a call by forwarding a SIP invite message to the SIP proxy. The SIP proxy inquires of registrars, redirect servers, or location databases to determine where the called party currently resides. Session establishment functions between SIP clients can now begin, including capabilities exchange, quality of service activities, and establishment of the media path.

SIP's ability to manage presence will enable new applications and services that will make multimode access even more powerful. To get a tast of using SIP and VoiceXML today, see http://Studio.tellme.com/general/voip.html.

Personalization

Personalization is person-specific content. Personalized content may be advertising, items for sale, screen layout, menus, news articles, applications, or anything else we see via the Internet. In addition, personalization also means a customized navigational and interactional experience for the user. Personalization is the result of technology integrated into an application or service that allows the server to modify what is presented to each viewer dynamically. With personalization technology, two individuals accessing the same Web site simultaneously may see two completely different sets of information based on their profiles and preferences.

Personalized voice solutions are similar to personalized Web solutions in the sense that certain key elements such as user ID/password allow the application or service to present personalized content to the user. In the case of voice solutions, the phone number can identify the user by where he or she is dialing from or by voice recognition. Personalized voice solutions are evolving. As tools and standards get more robust, we will see applications taking advantage not only of user profiles and preferences but also their navigational history and context. Integration with position location technology will further enhance the user experience.

Personalization takes a variety of forms, identified here as three major categories. From simplest to most complex, they are:

1. Customization by name
2. Implicit personalization
   a) Configuration
   b) Segmentation and rules-based
3. Explicit personalization

Customized by Name

Name recognition, such as e-mail addressed to John Rivers, is familiar to anyone who receives unsolicited printed material in the mail. This sort of mass personalization is similar to the junk mail entitled "Dear Homeowner at 123 Main Street . . ." but a few years ago it marked a turning point in mass marketing techniques. Name recognition continues to be used because it still has value; most people like to be acknowledged by name.

Implicit Personalization

Implicit personalization uses the personal information provided by the user like name, address, telephone number, personal preferences, hobbies, age, and so on. Based on this personal information, the server dynamically generates user-specific content. Essentially, the whole user population is divided into classes that are defined by some characteristics; for example, a bank could classify it's users as:

1. High-income, low-risk investments

2. High-income, high-risk investments

3. Low-income, low-risk investments

4. Low-income, high-risk investments

Based on which category a user falls into, customized content is displayed to them. Customized content could include news items, stock tips, investment ideas and techniques, portfolio recommendations, and so on. This customization is very useful for consumers as they get targeted information and avoid the hassle of discovering it on their own.

Configuration or Check-Box Personalization

Check box is the short name for user-provided information. Configuration-based personalization comes from questionnaires, surveys, registration forms, and other solicitations in which the user answers specific questions. An example of this would be the registration page for a software purchase. Registration forms often ask for information about the program you just bought as well as additional information, such as store location, whether it's for home or business use, whether you're the head of household, and so on. You check the box beside the appropriate answer. A Web site using check-box personalization presents content based on your answers.

Segmentation and Rules

Segmentation and rules-based personalization uses demographic, geographic, interest profile, or other information to divide or segment large populations into smaller groups. Data such as income level, geographic location, and buying history is aggregated to identify groups of people. Web sites using these types of personalization systems deliver content based on *if this, then that* rules processing.

Explicit Personalization (or Almost Real-Time Personalization)

Explicit personalization refers to the personalization based on click-stream data (for voice applications this will be user traversing through various application states as discussed in State Transition Diagrams in Chapter 12) collected from the user. Click-stream gives information about a user's interaction with services and net content (including advertisements). So, if a user has already read the content, or if the user doesn't read the content even after several iterations of display, the content is either taken off from future displays or recustomized for the next time the user visits the page or the site.

Some preference-based personalization systems are learning systems that allow them to become more precise over time. We have increasingly seen almost all the major net applications and services using personalization to attract and retain customers and partners. As you can imagine, serving personalized content becomes even more important for wireless devices. Future personalization technologies will have to adapt to the need of displaying content onto multiple devices owned by the same user. Personalization essentially amounts to data-mining and business intelligence from the sources of server logs, user preferences, device preferences, click-stream data, and e-commerce history. Business rules need to be applied to the analysis of data to produce personalized content.

These methods can coexist. Each type has a specific purpose, and two or more can be blended to produce a seamless, comprehensive personalized experience of an application or service.

Telematics

As is evident from services like OnStar from General Motors, applications and services are becoming accessible in automobiles. Since voice is the most convenient form of input, voice-enabled applications and services are going to drive the telematics space for years to come. In a recent study by Forrester Research, the revenues from air time, services, and hardware are forecasted to top $19 billion by 2006 (see Figure 14.5). Even

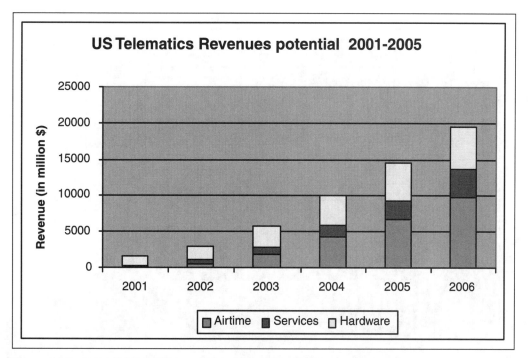

Figure 14.5 U.S. telematics revenues forecast: 2001–2005.

(Source: Forrester Research, Inc.)

though some manufacturers are building touch-screen displays into the dashboard, any access to applications within an automobile or outside is going to be most safely achieved by voice. Several European countries and U.S. states have either already passed or are in the process of passing legislation to enforce hands-free operation of vehicles. (Touch-screen access should in fact be disabled for the driver in a moving vehicle.) As we are building the infrastructure and components, telematics will form the basis of unprecedented access to enterprise and consumer applications via voice.

Since consumers will be able to utilize their time productively, they are willing to pay for compelling telematics services (up to $200 per year, according to Forrester Research). Automakers, wireless carriers, application developers, and telematics service providers are working together to reach the broadest audience as soon as possible.

An automobile is a pretty powerful computing platform. In addition to processing power, features such as the Global Positioning System (GPS) will help personalize content delivery based on user preferences, situations, and needs.

VIM

We are all familiar with the popularity of instant messaging (IM). (See Figure 14.6 and Table 14.4.) Using wired and wireless technologies, consumers of all ages have been communicating and remaining in contact with people and information via instant mes-

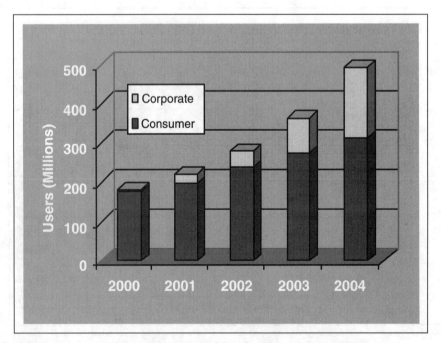

Figure 14.6 Growth in instant messaging subscribers, 2000–2004.
(Source: IDC.)

Table 14.4   Internet Activity by Frequency

US	FRANCE	UK	GERMANY	SPAIN
Web	Web	Web	Web	**IM**
e-mail	**IM**	**IM**	**IM**	Web
IM	News	e-mail	e-mail	e-mail
Downloads	e-mail	News	News	Chat
Games	Games	Games	Downloads	News
News	Downloads	Downloads	Games	Downloads

Source: Netvalue.

saging technology. IM has also become a standard mode of communication in many corporations as well. So, it is only natural for voice instant messaging to gain popularity. With technologies like SIP, it is becoming possible to connect with people using VIM.

Consider the following VIM scenarios:

■ Donna dials into her voice mail and finds that Dave has left an urgent message. While in voice mail, she says, "Is Dave online?" An agent finds Dave and responds, "Yes, he is." Donna says, "Call him," and the system proceeds to connect Dave and Donna.

■ If Dave is not online, the agent takes a message to watch for him. As soon as Dave comes online, a message is sent to Donna and conversation ensues.

Several companies, such as Hotsip (see Figure 14.7) and Odigo, have already come out with VIM products.

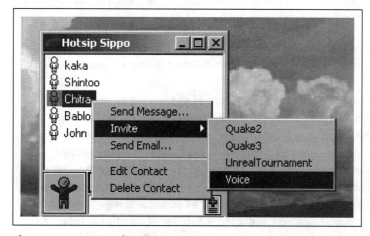

Figure 14.7   IM product from Hotsip.

True Natural Language Recognition

Natural language recognition and understanding is a nirvanic phase for speech recognition where computers and systems can recognize and understand not only the words or phrases but the language itself. It is a very hard goal to achieve. Two perfectly educated (in the same language) and capable individuals can have misunderstandings, so training a computer to understand language is by definition tough. However, by narrowing down the scope of utterances, one can get natural language-like behavior. With progress in speech technology, smarter algorithms, and computing power, it is possible to allow users to say anything within a narrow scope. For example, in a travel application, the system could start with:

System: What can I do for you?

User: Can you please book tickets for my family flying to Boston going out tomorrow for a week?

System: I am buying tickets for Sarah, Joseph, Kimberly, and you from Okinawa to Boston, flying out August 25th and coming back August 31st. Is that correct?

User: No, make that two weeks.

System: OK, you guys are flying out on the 25th and coming back on September 7th. Is that correct?

User: Go for it.

System: The total cost is $5009. I am using your American Express card ending with digits 0007. Let me know if you want to change anything.

User: *That's a steal, dude.*

System: *Excuse me?*

User: *Please go ahead with the booking.*

System: Reservations made. Your confirmation number is 0008. Thanks for using friendly automated services. Goodbye.

In this example, the system is able to capture the meaning of the user's utterances, which would have normally required two or three different dialog exchanges.

NOTE What ultimately matters for the success of automated systems is the automation rate achieved and people's perception of how accurate/easy a system is to use. The underlying technology is completely irrelevant to the caller. Nuance's SayAnything, IBM's natural language understanding (NLU) engine, and other natural language (NL) technologies are still using the same underlying recognition technology, which is still bound by processor power, etc. It is still trying to distinguish between a finite set of possible things the user may say. These NL technologies just add a large number of additional things to what the recognizer is listening for. As soon as you start offering any kind of

NL, people's expectations of what they can or can't say absolutely soar, and they get doubly disappointed and frustrated when things go wrong. So, the right thing to do today is to focus on using voice to put your best foot forward—to optimize the ultimate caller experience by carefully designing prompts, grammars, and applications that set caller expectations and "just work." As technology evolves, you should evolve your techniques—but the worst thing you can do is try to push the technology (and your interfaces) beyond what can practically work across millions of calls from millions of people in different environments day in and day out.

The Next Wave

In this section, we will take a look at some next-generation technologies and concepts.

Multilingual Integration

Multilingual integration refers to the markup language used to support rendering of multilingual documents—i.e., where there is a mixed-language document. For example, English and French speech output and/or input can appear in the same document—a spoken system response can be, "John read the book entitled *Vive La France.*" In counties where there is more than one main language (Europe, Asia), it is advantageous to offer multilingual speech applications to drive better user experience. Today, it is cumbersome to put together a multilingual application or service, but with enhancements in standards and speech recognition technologies, user acceptance of such systems will drive demand.

Another aspect of multilinguism is machine translation of languages. Though the English language is universal, more and more users want information in their native languages—and quickly. Translating spoken language on the fly is much more difficult than translating a few words and phrases of text. There are multiple toolsets available to handle the latter. About 80 to 90 percent of the conversion can be taken care of by automation, the remainder by offline linguists who specialize in this. This is how most Web site content translations are done today. But when it comes to speech, the variables of recognition, culture, context, and of course language come into play, making automatic translation very difficult. A lot of research is being done around the world to improve recognition and translation technology that will help enhance user experience on the fly; however, we have a long way to go.

Progress in Speech Technology

We are continually making tremendous progress in both recognition and synthesis of speech. With further enhancements, using hybrid approach (see Table 14.5), TTS is going to improve to sound more and more natural with options that include emotion as well. Further, with affective computing systems, applications will be able to detect and react to the emotional state of the speaker to enhance the machine-to-human user experience. We might reach a point of sophistication that will make it difficult to distinguish

Table 14.5 Features of Various TTS Techniques

METHOD	INTELLIGIBILITY	NATURALNESS	RESOURCE ECONOMY	FLEXIBILITY	COST TO CREATE A NEW VOICE
Model-based	Medium	Low	High	High	N/A
Concatenation	High	High	Low	Low	Low
Hybrid system	High	High	Medium	High	Low

between human and computer voice. Improvements in speech recognition and verification techniques will also result in a broader acceptance of speech as a popular input means for computing.

Multimodal Access to Applications and Services

Multimodal access to applications and services is difficult with today's networks because it is difficult to create services with simultaneous voice and display characteristics. There are two trends that are encouraging. First, people are building mobile microbrowsers with speech capability; second, 2.5-G and 3-G networks promise to offer greater bandwidth, always-on connections, and simultaneous voice and data channels with reduced latency. Also, as mentioned earlier, the W3C has instantiated work for multimodal market language, which will help in moving applications to the next evolutionary stage. In the meantime, there will be some proprietary technologies coming to the market in this space.

Another dimension of multimodal access is transcoding. Content consists of video, images, text, and audio—this represents the modality dimension of transcoding. The fidelity dimension represents the richness or complexity of the modality. To meet the needs of the devices, content needs to be transformed and reformatted along the dimensions of modality and fidelity. The translation methods could convert content between modalities; for instance, from text to audio or from video to images. Along the same lines, content conversion could be done within the same modality but different fidelity. For example, you could compress images, extract relevant text from a lengthy text document, or extract key video and audio frames and then reanimate them. This Infopyramid framework (Source: Smith, Mohan, Li, 1998), as depicted in Figure 14.8, allows for adapting to environmental needs in an efficient manner.

Microsoft has also been experimenting with speech-centric multimodal interface frameworks. One of the concepts to emerge from Microsoft's speech group is MiPad, which is a wireless PDA that enables users to accomplish many common tasks using a multimodal language interface including speech, pen, and display along with wireless technologies (see Figure 14.9). Experiments with MiPad's tap-and-talk interface prove that pen- and speech-based input modes complement each other. A study has been done to compare task completion times for e-mail transcription for the pen-only interface and the tap-and-talk interface (see Figure 14.10).

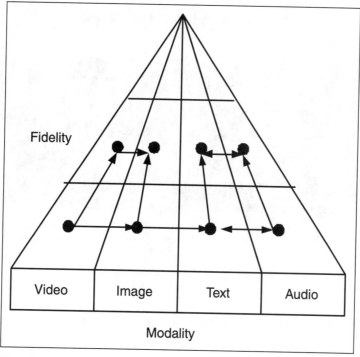

Figure 14.8   Infopyramid framework.

(Copyright © 1998, IEEE. Smith, Mohan, Li, *Transcoding Internet Content for Heterogeneous Client Devices.*)

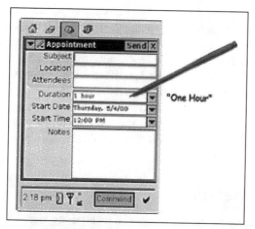

Figure 14.9   Concept design for MiPad's tap-and-talk interface.

(Copyright © 2001, Microsoft.)

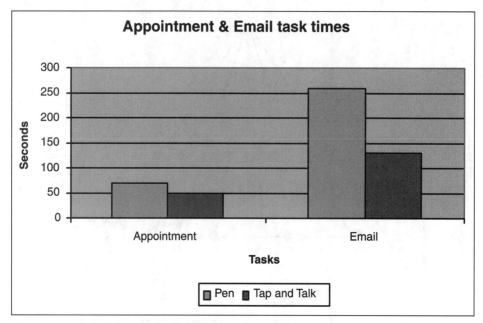

Figure 14.10 Task completion comparisons for pen-only and tap-and-talk interfaces. (Copyright © 2001, HonAVIOS 2001)

So far we have primarily talked about speech, keypad, and stylus input mechanisms. There is a lot of research being done to explore gesture recognition, which essentially processes complex gestural, emotional, and affective input such as face and lip movement. Humans often use gestures, changes in tone, shifting gaze, etc., as cues to direct a conversation. Gesture recognition can help do the same with human-computer interactions. Figure 14.11 shows a multimodal application framework in which various input signals arrive to the application via an intermediary multimodal integration middleware piece in parallel. During recognition, these modality-specific understanding components produce a set of attribute/value meaning representations for each mode. These values generated for an incoming signal provide alternative meaning hypotheses for that signal, each of which is assigned a probability estimate of correctness. The multimodal integration step combines symbolic and statistical information to enhance system response robustness and synchronize interactions.

Though there are still significant challenges in designing perfect multimodal user experiences, considerable energy is being spent integrating technologies and concepts to create devices, markup languages, and technologies to make the dream of multimodal access a reality.

Wearable Computers

In the broad spectrum encompassed by speech technology, wearable computers have to this point quietly moved from their own small niche. That niche, however, is beginning to draw its own share of attention by posting significant growth of its own. These computers, from displayable glasses (see Figure 14.12) to wired jackets (see Figure 14.13) to wireless watches, are designed to be worn and used on the body.

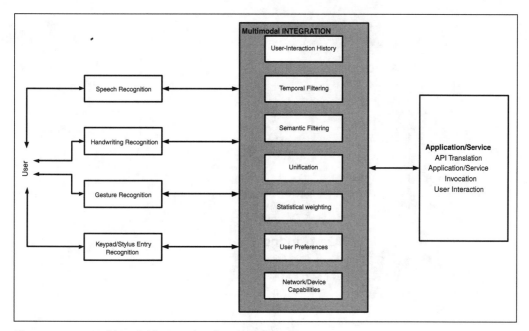

Figure 14.11 Multimodal integration framework.

So far wearable computers have found use mostly in industrial applications, but slowly and steadily they are moving toward consumer applications as well. Industrial applications of wearable computing include systems for warehouse management, automation, performance support, etc. The technology is already being heavily used in industries such as aerospace, law enforcement, aircraft maintenance, field data collection, insurance, emergency services, securities trading, point of sales, etc. International Data Corporation (IDC) expects the worldwide value of wearable computer shipments to grow from $3.5 million in 2000 to $579 million in 2004.

The obstacles for this industry are miniaturization, the cost of specialized parts, user interface, noisy environments, and consumer acceptance. With developments in the areas of wireless, position location, processing, and speech recognition technology,

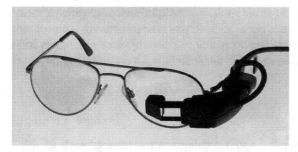

Figure 14.12 Wearable computing glasses.

(Copyright © 2001, Microoptical.)

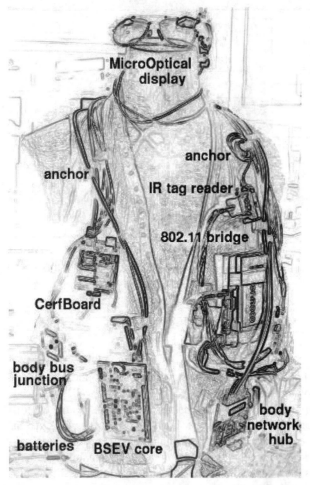

Figure 14.13 Wearable computing prototype—MIThrill from MIT.

(Copyright © 2001, MIT Media labs.)

wearable computing is slowly gathering traction. Even for industrial applications, most of the input is via keypad or stylus, but gradually speech is being integrated as one of the input mechanisms. There are certain situations where users have to use hands-free wearable computers and speech is the only way they can interact with the computer or back-end infrastructure.

PVAs

Our lives rely heavily on communications and communication devices such as telephones, pagers, desktop PCs, etc. to keep us connected and informed. With advances in speech, computing, and networking technology, it has become possible to take machine-human interaction to the next level. Instead of having to dial multiple phone numbers (home, office, wireless, car phone, etc.), PVAs can help in coordinating routing of phone calls and locating individuals. Consider the following:

PVA: Hi there! I am the personal virtual assistant of Jeff Roberts. Your name, please?

Caller: Liz Roberts. Tell him it's urgent.

(Caller on hold. Listens to customized music.)

(PVA locates Jeff—either sends a voice/wireless IM or calls)

PVA: Hey, it's me. Liz is trying to get ahold of you. Sounded urgent. Do you want me to connect or take a message?

Jeff: Hmm. I really want to finish this movie, please take a message.

PVA: Enjoy your movie. I will take the message. Goodbye.

(PVA connects back to Liz)

PVA: Liz, Jeff is currently unavailable. Would you like to leave a message?

Liz: Oh, not again! . . . Sure.

(Liz leaves a message. PVA forwards the .wav file to Jeff.)

PVAs can also help in personalizing messages by individuals or groups of individuals and will help provide a human level of assistance. PVAs will also be integrated with common e-mail and enterprise applications.

Aurora: The DSR Standard

European Telecommunications Standards Institute (ETSI) is working on a standard for the distributed speech recognition DSR front end of speech recognition. In a DSR architecture the recognizer front end is located in the terminal and is connected over a data network to a remote back-end recognition server. DSR provides particular benefits for applications for mobile devices, such as improved recognition performance compared to using the voice channel and ubiquitous access from different networks with a guaranteed level of recognition performance. Because it uses the data channel, DSR facilitates the creation of an exciting new set of applications combining voice and data. To enable all these benefits in a wide market containing a variety of players including terminal manufacturers, operators, server providers, and recognition vendors, a standard for the front end is needed to ensure compatibility between the terminal and the remote recognizer. The Speech Transmission Quality (STQ) Aurora group within ETSI has been actively working on developing this standard.

The main benefits of DSR are (1) improved recognition performance over wireless channels, (2) ease of integration of combined speech and data applications, and (3) ubiquitous access with guaranteed recognition performance levels.

Summary

In this chapter we have reviewed the future of voice/VoiceXML applications, both in the short term and the long term. As the computing and communications industries continue to converge and enhancements in technologies continue to be made, voice applications are going to be an essential part of the pervasive computing landscape for years to come until they become an expected part of our existence. In the next chapter we will summarize our discussions by providing guidelines for your voice strategy, listing some applications, and drawing some conclusions.

The Final Word—Strategy, Applications, and Conclusions

VoiceXML-enabled solutions have started to replace traditional interactive voice response (IVR) systems because they are proving to be more cost-effective and efficient, thus improving the level of customer satisfaction. VoiceXML also improves time to market for voice solutions and increases flexibility in deploying at multiple locations.

VoiceXML poses some challenges as well. There are still inconsistencies in the VoiceXML implementation formulated by different vendors. There is also a lack of standard dialogue components, standard grammar formats, and support for popular audio formats such as RealAudio and Windows Media Player, but hopefully with time the World Wide Web Consortium (W3C) and the VoiceXML forum will address these issues.

In the preceding chapters we have covered a lot. We started by looking at the trends in voice solutions space, got an overview of speech technologies, and reviewed why VoiceXML-enabled solutions are so compelling for any enterprise. Then we looked into development of VoiceXML applications—from setting up the toolkits and the environment to details about the VoiceXML grammar and Speech Synthesis Markup Language (SSML). Next we looked at some advanced VoiceXML topics such as dynamic VoiceXML, security, voice user interfaces (VUIs), and the VoiceXML development life cycle. We also went through the exercise of building a field services application. In Chapter 14 we peeked into the future to see what's coming next. That brings us to this final chapter, in which we will take a look at various elements to consider while implementing a voice strategy, look at some of the players in this emerging field, and review some of the applications and vertical sectors that are adopting voice-enabling technology right now. In addition to the information presented in this book, we have provided a wealth of information in Appendixes B and C for you to explore further. The companion CD contains toolkits, white papers, and other information from leading vendors in VoiceXML and voice solutions space to get you jump-started.

Implementing Your Voice Strategy

In this section we will review the basic steps for building a successful voice strategy, from business requirements to implementation.

Understand Your Business Requirements

As with any other project, start by understanding and defining your business requirements. Consider the following points:

- Why are you considering voice solutions? What are you trying to accomplish? Is it to reduce costs (by replacing live operators and/or touch-tone interactive voice response [IVR]), drive revenue (e.g., automated commerce and/or service), create a marketing differentiator, or something else?

- What is your current investment in Internet technologies? How much of the functionality you want is already on the Web? Will the end users actually be using voice-enabled access?

- What are the user demographics? Is the need internal or external? Does the voice solution need to be multilingual? In what countries?

- What is your current investment in call center technologies? For instance, did you just spend $14 million on thousands of ports of IVR, or is it time to upgrade anyway? How open is your architecture? Are certain elements becoming too cumbersome to maintain and/or obsolete?

- Are you experiencing time-to-market pressure? Are you looking at deploying voice solutions in reaction to your competitor, or are you trying to be the first one in your sector? How is the competition going to react to your offering? Are voice solutions a differentiator or a must-have?

- Have you conducted cost-versus-benefit analysis to determine if now is the time to launch such a solution?

- How much budget is allocated for the voice project?

- How much does branding/personality matter to your company and your users? Can that potentially increase the automation rate and customer satisfaction?

- How much does speech really play into what you're doing? Is your proposed application mostly dual-tone multifrequency (DTMF) with a little speech, or are you doing things that involve a lot of speech and can be helped by getting optimal speech performance?

- How does your voice strategy affect customer retention and relationships? Are you outsourcing any of your CRM strategy today? (More than 80 percent of U.S. companies are—see www.commweb.com/article/COM20010613S0001.)

- Do you want to invest in staffing additional people to specialize in voice user interface design and speech science? Would you require additional application development and system administration resources?

- Do you have an opportunity to consolidate IVR and Web development resources?

- How is voice going to fit in with your overall strategy? Do you have wireless, broadband, and/or online offerings? How are you going to streamline and consolidate content to be delivered to multiple channels and yet maintain your brand and identity and give users a consistent experience?

- What parts of the operation need to be voice-enabled?

Chapters 1 through 4 will help you answer these questions.

Start Small

Once you have identified the business requirements, start to get familiar with VoiceXML design and development tools and with the intricacies of voice user interface design. Begin playing with VoiceXML technology using one of the toolkits discussed in Chapter 5, especially one of the Web-based ones (Tellme, BeVocal, etc.) that require zero download or installation of any software or hardware. As you quickly become familiar with the nuances of the voice solution life cycle (Chapter 11), start building on the requirements for your voice user interface (Chapter 12).

Buy versus Build

One of the decisions you will have to make is whether you want a premises-based solution (i.e., one you build and host yourself) or whether you want to work with a voice application network such as Tellme or Voxeo to manage the development, hosting, and maintenance of your voice solutions. Both strategies have their pros and cons, and they should be evaluated against your business requirements and goals to arrive at the final decision. For more information on how to evaluate your options, see Chapter 9.

Evaluate Vendors

Depending on what buy-versus-build strategy you want to go with, you will need to evaluate vendors and their technology offerings. Most of the vendors work in partnerships, so it might be a good idea to evaluate a joint offering because voice solutions have various parts and pieces. Tables 15.1 through 15.3 list some of the leading players providing cutting-edge voice solutions.

There are two things you should keep in mind: (1) Don't get into a situation where you get locked down by a vendor(s), and (2) choose a vendor(s) that has a good future-proof technology roadmap.

Prototype

Rapid application development is a core requirement in today's world. Solutions and standards are changing at a feverish pace. Long, drawn-out development projects will result in deployment of obsolete technology. Start with a tightly scoped project with clear success criteria and quick time to market. Utilizing an iterative development and

Table 15.1 Voice Technologies Players

TECHNOLOGY	PLAYERS
Recognition engines and TTS (software)	■ Conversay (ASR/TTS/Embedded) ■ Enuncia (TTS) ■ Fonix (ASR/TTS/Embedded) ■ IBM (ASR/TTS/NLU) ■ Inzigo (NLU) ■ L&H (ASR/TTS/NLU) ■ Nuance (ASR/TTS/NLU) ■ Philips Speech Processing (ASR/NLU) ■ Phonetics (ASR) ■ Poly Information (NLU) ■ Speechworks (ASR/TTS) ■ Telelogue (NLU)
Telephony cards (hardware)	■ Aculabs ■ Audiocodes ■ Brooktrout Technology ■ Dialogic (Intel company) ■ Natural Microsystems
VoiceXML platforms	■ BeVocal ■ Cisco ■ Comverse ■ Conversary ■ General Magic ■ IBM DirectTalk ■ Nuance ■ Pipebeach ■ SpeechWorks ■ Telera ■ Tellme Networks ■ Verscape ■ VoiceGenie
Premises-based IVR (hardware)	■ Aspect ■ Avaya ■ BeVocal ■ Comverse ■ Edify ■ IBM ■ InterVoice-Brite ■ Lucent ■ Nortel Periphonics ■ Syntellect ■ Telere
Call-center integration	■ Alcatel Genesys ■ Aspect ■ Avaya ■ Cisco Geotel

Table 15.1 *(Continued)*

TECHNOLOGY	PLAYERS
Voice application networks	■ InterVoice-Brite "Manged IUR" ■ NetbyTel ■ Tellme Networks ■ Voxco
Development tools	■ Alterego ■ Covigo ■ Fonelet ■ Gold Systems ■ IBM ■ IConverse ■ InterVoice-Brite ■ Microsoft ■ Motorola ■ Nuance ■ Philips ■ SpeechWorks ■ Tellme Networks ■ Unisys ■ VoiceGenie ■ Voxeo
Others	■ Dynamicsoft (Session Initiation Protocol) ■ Cisco (Voice over Internet Protocol [VoIP])

ASR: automated speech recognition

TTS: text to speech

NLU: natural language understanding

deployment process supports Rapid Application Developer (RAD) philosophy. Make sure you incorporate focus group and usability testing right up front with requirements definition and prototype development. Anything less will fail user expectations and hence business goals.

Build and Iterate

Based on the feedback from the prototype phase and on incorporating any other requirements changes, you are ready to start the iterative detailed design process. Chapters 11 and 12 provides the guidelines for a successful project implementation.

Stay in Touch

Once the project is launched, evaluate and monitor the system after installation. Tuning is a critical component of deployment that ensures that the system functions effectively and remains optimized for the user group as the service rolls out geographically and as users become more experienced. It is only by thorough capture, transcription, and

Table 15.2 Companies Offering Solutions in the Consumer Applications Space

APPLICATION	COMPANIES
Consumer information	■ AOL by Phone (Quack) ■ Audiopoint ■ BeVocal ■ HeyAnita ■ Lycos ■ MapQuest ■ Sonic Factory ■ Telera ■ Tellme Networks ■ Yahoo! By Phone
Consumer commerce	■ AOL MovieFone ■ NetByTel ■ ShopTalk ■ Tellme Networks ■ Ticketmaster ■ Vicinity
Unified messaging	■ AOL by phone ■ etrieve ■ EVoice ■ Microstrategy ■ Openwave (Phone.com/OneBox) ■ Shoutmail ■ SoundBite ■ Webley ■ Yahoo! By Phone

analysis of live user utterances that the application can be tuned for optimal performance.

Also, it is very important to stay in tune with new developments in the W3C and standard bodies, speech recognition and synthesis quality, call center/VoIP convergence, and multimodal solutions.

Following these steps from start to finish will help you launch successful VoiceXML-based applications and services. In the next section, we briefly review some of the existing and upcoming applications in the voice solutions space.

Applications

Over the course of this book, we have discussed several existing voice applications and services. In addition, we have reviewed some potential scenarios where providing voice access to a solution can be beneficial. Table 15.4 provides a summary list of such applications.

Table 15.3 Companies Offering Solutions in the Enterprise Applications Space

APPLICATION	COMPANIES
Enterprise mobile workforce	■ BeVocal ■ Conita ■ Datria ■ HeyAnita ■ iHello ■ JustTalk ■ Siebel ■ Telcos (in partnership with others) ■ Telera ■ Tellme Networks ■ Webversa
Enterprise Customer-Relationship Management (CRM)	■ Appriss ■ Hanover Communications ■ Interactive Telesys ■ Nextel ■ Placeware ■ ShopTalk ■ Siebel ■ SoundBite ■ Telcos (in partnership with others) ■ Telera ■ Tellme Networks ■ Vail Systems
Enterprise content	■ Net Technologies ■ Telsoft ■ Voicemate

Vertical Sectors

As is the case with any new technology area, some sectors have adopted voice solutions earlier than others. These are primarily customer-facing industries that employ a large customer service workforce to respond to customers' requests and needs. Some of these solutions are:

- **Airline solutions**—enable airlines to offer reservations booking, flight information and notification, baggage tracking, etc.

- **Banking solutions**—enable consumer banks to deliver telephone banking services, automated teller machine (ATM) and branch locators, etc.

- **Brokerage solutions**—enable retail brokerages to bring telephone trading functionality and outbound notifications such as portfolio movements and breaking news to traders anytime, anywhere, from any telephone

- **Insurance solutions**—enable insurance providers to let their customers locate health care providers and insurance agents, manage their accounts, etc.

Table 15.4 Sample Applications

SAMPLE APPLICATIONS—EXISTING AND FUTURE	
Shopping catalogs	Voice command and control of medical instruments
Address book/contact information	Insurance account transactions
Resource management	Store location directions
TV schedules	Voice command and control of home entertainment centers or television sets
Sports results	Banking account data retrieval
Order management	Voice command and control of industrial machinery
Human resource data updates	Prefilling out of information before going to a live operator
Business news	Voice command and control of visual browsers and Web sites
Stock and mutual fund share prices	Stock and mutual fund transactions
Voice mail-to-e-mail conversion-voice recognition	Customer surveys
Voice-controlled directories	General news
Sales force automation	Voice command and control of smartphones
Attachments to e-mail—.wav or MP3 voice mail clips	Knowledge base access (troubleshooting)
Restaurant/hotel location directions	Voice command and control of auto communications, navigation, and entertainment
Voice command and control of scientific equipment	Field force automation
Lottery updates	Financial news
Insurance account data retrieval	Appointment scheduling
Traffic information	Enterprise resource planning
Soap opera news	e-mail-to-voice mail conversion—text to speech
Travel reservations	Travel ticketing
Stock and mutual fund account data retrieval	Multimodal data retrieval—e.g., voice in/Wireless Application Protocol (WAP) out

Table 15.4 *(Continued)*

SAMPLE APPLICATIONS—EXISTING AND FUTURE	
Weather information	Voice command and control of personal data assistants (PDAs)
Shopping transactions	Video messaging—attaching .avi files to e-mail
Network monitoring	Restaurant/hotel reservations
Multimodal full communication—i.e., simultaneous voice and video interaction	Local entertainment schedules (cinema, theater, etc.)
Voice command and control of home appliances	Travel schedules/timetables (trains, planes, etc.)
Reminders	Voice-controlled dialing
Human resource data retrieval	Travel directions
Directory access	Banking account transactions
Horoscope	

- **Retail solutions**—enable retailers to deliver order status, store locators, voice-activated commerce, etc.
- **Service provider solutions**—enable service providers to rapidly add value-added voice services such as stock quotes, weather, directory assistance, voice-activated dialing, e-mail reading, movies, etc.
- **CRM**—replaces traditional IVR applications and services with more interactive and user-friendly VoiceXML applications
- **Field services**—enable field services personal to access enterprise applications from the field, especially when data network coverage is an issue

Summary

It is very clear that voice is going to become a standard and acceptable exchange mode with applications and services, and that the W3C speech framework, which includes VoiceXML, along with several complementary standards, is paving the way to building compelling voice solutions quickly and effectively. Technology advances are enabling machines to speak, hear, and understand. These advances promise to revolutionize telecommunications and the development of applications and services by creating an interface between human and machine based on speech that is natural and intuitive. Toolkits from vendors help you get a jump start.

The key challenges that application developers will face can be summarized as follows:

- Complexity of systems integration
- Low priority of voice projects in the total information technology projects mix
- Lack of resources
- Rapidly changing markets
- Multiple (emerging) standards and interoperability
- Lack of robust development tools
- Security

One person's challenge is another's opportunity. Innovative solution providers look to aggressively develop and deploy useful solutions. The fundamentals for voice solutions for business process reengineering and augmentation are incredibly strong. The technology and solutions infrastructure is already there. It is not wise to sit around till all the bugs are worked out and solutions are hardened: The time for launching voice initiatives is now. This does not mean that any and all applications and services make sense. Each project needs to be evaluated on its own business case merits. If the business case is strong, but you don't want to commit too many resources, then it is worth considering planning and launching the project in a phased approach. Use the early experiences to enhance your company's awareness of other possible voice solutions.

As discussed in early chapters, it is critical to have a sound technology foundation for your voice projects, so that you can leverage your investment on a continuous basis. So, always design and implement solutions with the future in mind. Things are changing very rapidly. The technology components should be selected carefully. There are far too many solution providers today, and not all provide robust and interoperable solutions. So, make sure the solution set you pick is based on open standards and has a roadmap of the future that meets industry needs and demands. Finally, the usability and functionality of their applications define their success.

Design well, partner for success, and embrace VoiceXML.

VoiceXML Tips and Tricks

As with all programming languages, getting started and getting comfortable with VoiceXML are two different things. This appendix lists a small set of commonly helpful tips and tricks for use when working with VoiceXML. All of these examples come from real questions posed by VoiceXML developers through Tellme Studio, at conferences, and via other channels.

Q: My VoiceXML platform consistently complains that my documents must start with `<?xml version='1.0'?>`. My documents do begin this way . . . what is the problem?

A: This is a common problem that VoiceXML developers encounter. To be considered well-formed XML, the very first line of your documents must contain the XML declaration. Initial blank lines or extraneous white space are not permitted. Be sure to remove these, and always check your VoiceXML documents in an XML-compatible Web browser (such as Microsoft Internet Explorer 5.x) before running them on your VoiceXML platform. This will help you make sure that your Web server is delivering syntactically well-formed XML before you delve into any VoiceXML-specific bugs or errors your documents may contain.

Q: Are grammars case-sensitive?

A: Grammars written in the World Wide Web Consortium's (W3C) vendor-independent Speech Grammar Markup Language are not case-sensitive. Grammars written in Nuance Communications' Grammar Speech Language (GSL) grammar format are case-sensitive. To minimize hassles, always use lowercase letters when writing grammars in all formats, except when explicitly referencing subgrammars in Nuance GSL.

Q: **I'm working with VoiceXML and want to know how I can submit recorded sound.**

A: VoiceXML does support recording audio from the caller, such as a personal voice mail message. Once this audio has been recorded, it can be played back and/or posted back to your Web server for offline processing and permanent storage. The `<record>` element in VoiceXML initiates a recording and stores the result in a variable, which can then be used by the `<value>` and `<submit>` elements for further manipulation.

For example:

```
<vxml version="2.0">
  <form id="record_message">

    <record name="message" maxtime="60" dtmfterm="true" beep="true">
      <prompt>At the tone, please leave a message.</prompt>
      <noinput>I didn't hear anything, please try again.</noinput>
    </record>

    <field name="confirm" type="boolean">
      <prompt>You said <audio expr="message"/>
              Would you like to keep this message?
              Say yes or no.
      </prompt>

      <filled>
        <if cond="confirm">
          <submit next="save_message.asp" method="post"
                  namelist="message"/>
        <else/>
          OK. Canceled. Goodbye.
          <disconnect />
        </if>
        <clear/>
      </filled>
    </field>
  </form>
</vxml>
```

In this example, the caller is prompted for a simple voice mail message. The recording is played back to the caller for confirmation, and, on approval, is posted back to the Web server (presumably for storage as the caller's official greeting for this voice mail system).

Q: **How can I play slightly different welcome prompts to liven up the experience my callers get?**

A: This is very easy using a simple JavaScript function and a series of well-named audio files:

```
<vxml version="2.0">
  <script>
```

```
<![CDATA[
function getrandomnumber(seed)
{
   /* returns a random number between 1 and the seed number */
   return (Math.floor(Math.random()*seed) + 1);
}
]]>
</script>

<form name="welcome">
  <block>
    <audio expr="'/prompts/bye' + getrandomnumber(4) + '.wav'">
       Welcome!
    </audio>
  </block>
</form>
</vxml>
```

Q: How can I quickly test and debug my JavaScript expressions?

A: For a quick and dirty way to test JavaScript expressions while developing, you can use the built-in JavaScript evaluation window in Netscape Communicator 4.5 or higher. In the Uniform Resource Locator (URL) address bar, simply type javascript: as the URL. This will launch a new window in which you can enter a series of JavaScript statements and see the evaluated results. This can be very useful for novice JavaScript programmers who are experimenting with client-side logic in their VoiceXML applications.

Q: Does VoiceXML support robust telephony applications or call center integration?

A: The full range of call center applications and IVR tasks in deployment today can be built using a VoiceXML platform. For example, 1-800-555-TELL is a sophisticated voice application built entirely using VoiceXML. More advanced features, such as blind and bridged call transfers, outbound notifications, and intelligent call routing and agent screen pop through integration with computer-telephony integration (CTI) middleware, can all be supported using a combination of VoiceXML and accompanying platform services also built using open Internet standards.

The key lens through which to consider this issue is the analogy of the Web and Hypertext Markup Language (HTML). HTML is explicitly designed to specify the visual presentation of an interactive application via the personal computer. Therefore, it contains appropriate constructs for tasks such as table layout, form input, and embedded images. It does not cover tasks such as database access, credit card processing, or personalization, which are typically handled by code running on the Web server. Products such as Microsoft Passport expose simple application programming interfaces (APIs) to advanced shared services using open standards such as Hypertext Transfer Protocol (HTTP), cookies, and Secure Socket Layer (SSL).

VoiceXML plays exactly the same role in the world of Internet-powered voice applications. VoiceXML has intrinsic constructs for tasks such as dialogue flow, grammars, call transfers, and embedding audio files. It even supports Voice over Internet Protocol-based call transfers through the Session Initiation Protocol. Companies can build upon this foundation to provide additional shared services such as outbound notifications and call center integration through simple URL-based APIs analogous to Microsoft Passport or affiliate programs from Amazon and MapQuest.

Q: **When should I break my VoiceXML application into multiple documents versus keeping it all in one?**

A: If your VoiceXML application exceeds 1,000 lines, it may be time for you to break it down into modules and/or separate documents. Of course, dynamically generated VoiceXML applications that involve many trips back to the Web server to post data and retrieve new instructions automatically are broken up into multiple documents and modules. However, if your application involves navigating large amounts of data with a sophisticated user interface, it can still be very easy for each component of the application to get quite large in its own right.

The question of whether you should split a VoiceXML application into multiple documents hinges on the size of the application. There are advantages to splitting up an application, but these can be outweighed by the costs. For a small application, it is best to keep the number of modules to a minimum. For mid- to large-scale applications, the extra costs can be mitigated.

Clearly, you should have some idea about how the application might grow over time in order to make this call. What appears to be a simple application at first might later turn out to be much more complicated. It is easier to make the decision to go with multiple modules at the outset of a project than to break up an application in the middle of its life cycle. Unless you are certain that the application will remain relatively small, it is best to consider modularization as part of your development process. There is no hard-and-fast metric to deciding what is a small application, but if your VoiceXML code goes beyond 1,000 lines, it's fair to say you no longer have a small application.

To modularize an existing application, begin by breaking out any embedded JavaScript into separate .js modules and modularizing the code using JavaScript functions. You can eliminate the problems created by different tags employing the same JavaScript by creating a JavaScript function and having the application call the function instead. The following example demonstrates how to do this.

```
<!-- Assume we're in a field navigating a list, where user_choice is
the variable holding the result of the grammar -->
<noinput>
  <script>
  <![CDATA[
    onListNextItem();
  ]]>
  </script>
</noinput>

<filled>
  <if cond="user_choice == 'nextitem'">
```

```
    <script>
    <![CDATA[
      onListNextItem();
    ]]>
    </script>
  </if>
</filled>
```

You can either declare the function inside a `<script>` element in the VoiceXML module itself or create an external JavaScript module and declare the function there. The former approach has a quicker load time because the platform only has to load the single VoiceXML document, while the second approach requires the platform to make two HTTP file requests—one for the VoiceXML module and one for the JavaScript module. If you never intend to have more than one VoiceXML module, you might consider embedding the function in the VoiceXML document.

If you have more than one VoiceXML module, you may want to break out your JavaScript into a separate module. A function declared inside one VoiceXML module is not visible by JavaScript in another VoiceXML module. Chances are, once you have VoiceXML living in multiple files, it will call common JavaScript. The only way to make this work is to have your JavaScript in an external module.

(Special thanks to Nick Thomas from Tellme Networks, who originally answered this question.)

Q: **What are dynamic grammars, and why are they interesting?**

A: One of the key benefits of Internet-powered speech applications is the ability to quickly create powerful and integrated services that leverage existing data and systems. Dynamically generated grammars make it possible to create applications that are always current. For example, a voice-activated dialing application could directly integrate with a corporate Lightweight Directory Access Protocol (LDAP) directory, giving callers instant access to the newest names and changes.

It is a fact that grammars must compile when first loaded by any speech recognition platform, and that very large grammars can take several seconds or more to compile. This is absolutely not unique to VoiceXML. The key difference is that VoiceXML makes it extremely easy for developers to intelligently incorporate dynamic grammars in their applications. Developers building speech applications on any platform, including VoiceXML, must carefully plan the usage characteristics of their applications and intelligently design when to use static versus dynamic grammars. For example, a catalog retailer could combine a static grammar for its permanent product line with a dynamic grammar adding in daily or seasonal specials to optimize performance.

Q: **Is it possible to send voice alerts like Wireless Application Protocol alerts? How?**

A: Yes, it is possible. Several companies today (including many of the VoiceXML Forum's member companies) offer voice notification services that support the VoiceXML standard. These services typically operate by allowing application developers to submit a request using a standard HTTP POST (or even by sending an e-mail). The request contains information such as the phone number to call, when to place the call, and the URL of a VoiceXML application to trigger when the call is made. For security and privacy assurance, some level of security-including a company identifier, password, and SSL or S-MIME is also typically required.

Anyone who operates a VoiceXML platform can theoretically build a notification service that provides this functionality. VoiceXML itself does not specify a way to deliver voice notifications, just as HTML and Wireless Markup Language (WML) do not. VoiceXML simply defines the interface for voice applications; how the phone call that initiates the conversation gets generated is a separate issue. That said, it is definitely conceivable that a separate accepted standard that specifies how to use HTTP, e-mail, and other open Internet protocols to trigger alerts across all devices including voice, phones, personal data assistants, and other wireless devices will emerge in the future.

Q: **I'm writing a script using the `<transfer>` tag. I'm trying to place the call dynamically using a number that the user speaks. I'm not having any luck. Any advice?**

A: The attribute destextpr, available on `<transfer>`, lets you use a JavaScript expression to set the destination phone number. For example:

```
<vxml version="2.0">
  <form name="transfer">
    <!-- Set a form-scope variable to be some phone number.
         This could have been collected using a previous form or
         field -->
    <var name="mydest" expr="'8005558355'"/>

    <block>
      <audio>Ready to attempt call transfer</audio>
    </block>

    <!-- Now transfer using the destexpr attribute to use a JS
expression -->

    <transfer destexpr="mydest" />

    <block>
      <!-- The transfer ended somehow, though it may have failed -->
      <audio>welcome back</audio>
    </block>
  </form>
</vxml>
```

Q: **After the caller has hung up, is there any way for me to perform any clean-up to track that back on my Web server?**

A: Yes. There are several reasons why VoiceXML developers may want to perform some kind of post-hangup processing. Most often, it is to post some final information back to the Web server for logging/tracking purposes. For example, a commerce application may want to explicitly note the list of things that were left in a caller's shopping cart when the caller suddenly hung up without buying anything.

VoiceXML specifies the predefined events telephone.disconnect.hangup and telephone.disconnect.transfer, which can be caught to do this kind of post-hangup processing. telephone.disconnect.hangup is thrown when the caller explicitly hangs up the phone, and telephone.disconnect.transfer is thrown when a blind (nonbridging) call transfer is invoked and the caller has been permanently transferred to another line and will not return.

A simple example of using telephone.disconnect.hangup to submit information back to your Web server is as follows:

```
<!-- APPLICATION_ROOT.VXML -->
<vxml version="2.0">
  <!-- some global variables -->
  <var name="last_state" expr="'null'" />
  <var name="usr_id" expr="'null'" />

  <!-- this defines an application-scope event handler for post-
  hangup
      processing -->
  <catch event="telephone.disconnect.hangup">
    <submit namelist="last_state usr_id" src="onhangup.jsp"
         fetchtimeout="5s" />
  </catch>
</vxml>

<!-- MY_APPLICATION.VXML -->
<vxml version="2.0" application="application_root.vxml">
  ...
  ...
  <!-- your whole application that sets last_state and usr_id
  throughout -->

  ...
  ...
</vxml>
```

Note that in this global event handler, fetchtimeout is limited to 5 seconds. This is intentional—it's important to note that post-hangup processing can be very tricky performance-wise. It could be very easy to write applications that accidentally (or intentionally) take a long time to complete this processing, and that would ultimately crash or seriously degrade the performance of your VoiceXML server once enough calls had passed through the system. It is critical to evaluate both your VoiceXML platform and your application's performance and design with regard to this feature.

Acronyms

3G	Third Generation
ABNF	Augmented Backus-Naur Form
ACD	Automatic Call Distribution
AIDC	Automatic Identification and Data Capture
ARPU	Average Revenue per User
ASP	Active Server Pages
ASP	Application Service Provider
ASR	Automatic Speech Recognition
ATVEF	Advanced Television Enhancement Format
BER	Bit Error Rate
BNF	Backus-Naur Form
CHTML	Compact HTML
CLEC	Competitive Local Exchange Carrier
CODEC	Compression/Decompression
CRM	Customer Relationship Management
CSP	Continuous Speech Processing
CTI	Computer Telephony Integration
DES	Data Encryption Standard
DHCP	Dynamic Host Configuration Protocol
DOM	Document Object Model

DSR	Distributed Speech Recognition
DTD	Document Type Definition
DTMF	Dual-Tone Multiple Frequency
EJB	Enterprise Java Beans
ERP	Enterprise Resource Planning
ETSI	European Telecommunications Standards Institute
GIF	Graphics Interchange Format
GSL	Nuance Grammar Specifications Language
HDML	Handheld Device Markup Language
HMM	Hidden Markov Model
HTML	HyperText Markup Language
HTTP	HyperText Transfer Protocol
HTTP-NG	HTTP Next Generation
HTTPS	HTTP Secure
IEEE	Institute of Electrical and Electronics Engineers
IETF	Internet Engineering Task Force
IMT2000	International Mobile Telecommunications 2000
IP	Internet Protocol
IPSec	IP Security
Ipv6	IP Version 6
ISO	International Standards Organization
ITU	International Telecommunications Union
ITV	Interactive Television
IVR	Interactive Voice Response
JPEG	Joint Photographic Experts Group
JSP	Java Server Pages
LAN	Local Area Network
LATA	Local Access and Transport Area
LDAP	Lightweight Directory Access Protocol
MDML	Multimodal Dialog Markup Language
MEO	Medium Earth Orbit
MGCP	Media Gateway Control Protocol
MIPS	Millions of Instructions per Second
MPEG	Motion Picture Experts Group
NLP	Natural Language Processing

NLSML	Natural Language Semantics Markup Language
NLU	Natural Language Understanding
OMC	Operations and Maintenance Center
PDA	Personal Digital Assistant
PGP	Pretty Good Privacy
POP	Point of Presence
PQA	Palm Query Applications
PSTN	Public Switched Telephone Network
QoS	Quality of Service
RAD	Rapid Application Development
RBOC	Regional Bell Operating Company
RF	Radio Frequency
RFC	Request for Comments
SFA	Sales Force Automation
SGML	Standard Generalized Markup Language
SIP	Session Initiation Protocol
SLA	Service-Level Agreement
SMIL	Synchronized Multimedia Markup Language
SMS	Short Message Service
SNR	Signal-to-Noise Ratio
SRGF	Speech Recognition Grammar Format
SSL	Secure Sockets Layer
SSML	Speech Synthesis Markup Language
STQ	Speech Transmission Quality
TLS	Transport Security Layer
TTS	Text to Speech
UIML	User Interface Markup Language
UMTS	Universal Mobile Telecommunications System
URL	Uniform Resource Locator
VIM	Voice Instant Messaging
VoIP	Voice over IP
VPN	Virtual Private Network
VRU	Voice Response Unit
VUI	Voice User Interface
W3C	World Wide Web Consortium

WAE	Wireless Application Environment
WAP	Wireless Application Protocol
WASP	Wireless Application Service Provider
WLAN	Wireless Local Area Network
WML	Wireless Markup Language
WoZ	Wizard of Oz
WSP	Wireless Session Protocol
WTA	Wireless Telephony Applications
WTLS	Wireless Transport Security Layer
WTP	Wireless Transactional Protocol
XML	Extensible Markup Language

APPENDIX C

References and Recommended Readings

Books

1. Arehard, C., et al. 2000. *Professional WAP*. USA: Wrox.

2. Balentine, B. and Morgan D.P. *How to Build a Speech Recognition Application: A Style Guide for Telephony Dialogues*. USA: Enterprise Integration Group, 1999.

3. Bernsen, N.O., Dybkjaer, H., and Dybkjaer, L. *Designing Interactive Speech Systems: From First Ideas to User Testing*. UK: Springer-Verlag, 1998.

4. Bonneau, D.G. *Human Factors and Voice Interactive Systems*. USA: Kluwer Academic Publishers, 1999.

5. Cheswick, W., and Bellovin, S. *Internet Firewalls and Security (2nd edition)*. USA: Addison Wesley Publication, 2001.

6. Garfinkel, S., and Safford, G. 1996. *Practical Unix and Internet Security*. USA: O'Reilly & Associates.

7. Hersent, O., Gurle, D., and Petit, J.P. 2000. *IP Telephony: Packet-based Multimedia Communications Systems*. UK: Addison Wesley.

8. PriceWaterHouseCoopers. 2001. *Technology Forecast: 2001–2003. Mobile Internet: Unleashing the Power of Wireless*. USA: PriceWaterhouseCoopers.

9. Schneier, B. 2000. *Secrets and Lies: Digital Security in Networked World*. USA: John Wiley & Sons.

10. Sharma, C. 2000. *Wireless Internet Enterprise Applications—A Wiley Tech Brief*. USA: John Wiley & Sons.

11. Thomas, S. 2000. *SSL & TLS Essentials*. USA: John Wiley & Sons.

12. Weinschenk, S., and Barker, D.T. 2000. *Designing Effective Speech Interfaces*. USA: John Wiley & Sons.

13. Zwicky, E., et al. 2000. *Building Internet Firewalls (2nd edition)*. USA: O'Reilly & Associates.

Magazine Articles and Whitepapers

14. Andersen, M. 2001. *Strategic News Service*.

15. Codina, E. 2001. *Evaluating the Possibilities to Build a Voice-driven Calendar Interface Using VoiceXML*. PipeBeach AB/Royal Institute of Technology, Sweden.

16. Delaney, B.W. 2001. *Voice User Interface for Wireless Internetworking—A Qualifying Examination Report*. Georgia Institute of Technology, School of Electrical and Computer Engineering.

17. Eluri, E. 2001. *Building Voice Web Applications*. Luminant Worldwide.

18. Hosom, J.P., Cole, R., Fanty, M. 1999. *Speech Recognition Using Neural Networks*. Center for Spoken Language Understanding, Oregon Graduate Institute of Science and Technology.

19. Houlding, D. 2001. *VoiceXML and the Voice-Driven Internet*. Dr. Dobb's Journal, April 2001.

20. *IBM WebSphere Voice Server Software Developers Kit Programmer's Guide*. Version 1.5. 2001.

21. *IBM WebSphere Voice Server with ViaVoice Technology Administrator's Guide*. Version 1.5.

22. *Java Speech API Programmer's Guide Speech User Interface Design*, Chapters 2–3. Sun Microsystems.

23. Klemmer, S. R., Sinha, A.K., et al. 2000. *SUEDE: A Wizard of Oz Prototyping Tool for Speech User Interfaces*. Group for User Interface Research. University of California at Berkley.

24. Kunins, J. *Tellme Voice Advantage*. 2001. Tellme Networks, Inc.

25. Kunins, J. *VoiceXML Facts & Fiction*. 2001. Tellme Networks, Inc.

26. Larson, J. *The W3C Speech Interface Framework*. W3C.

27. Lucente, M. 2000. *Conversational Interfaces for E-Commerce Applications*. September 2000. Vol. 43. No. 9. Communications of the ACM.

28. Mackraz, B. *Tellme DesignMe Design Guidelines (design manual)*. 2000. Tellme Networks, Inc.

29. *Nuance Voice Site Developer's Guide*. Version 1.2. 2001.

30. Oviatt, S., Cohen, P. 2000. *Multimodal Interfaces That Process What Comes Naturally.* March 2000. Vol 43. No. 3, Communications of the ACM.

31. Oviatt, S., Cohen, P., et al. 2000. *Designing the User Interface for Multimodal Speech and Pen-Based Gesture Applications: State-of-the-Art Systems and Future Research Directions.* Human-Computer Interactions. Vol. 15, pp. 263–322.

32. Oviatt. S. 1999. *Ten Myths of Multimodal Interactions.* November 1999. Vol. 42. No. 11, Communications of the ACM.

33. Phillips, M. 2000. *Technology Backgrounder.* SpeechWorks.

34. Rolandi, W. 2001. *The Conita Technologies Personal Virtual Assistant: Just in Time Knowledge, Awareness Transactions for the Mobile Professional.* Conita Technologies, Inc.

35. Sharma, C. *Wireless Internet Applications.* 2000. Luminant Worldwide.

36. Shneiderman, B. *The Limits of Speech Recognition.* Communications of the ACM, Vol. 43, No. 9, September 2000.

37. Sridharan, P. *Tellme Security Policies.* 2001. Tellme Networks, Inc.

38. *Tellme VoiceXML Reference.* 2001.

39. *Tellme VoiceXML Tutorial.* 2001.

40. Theiss, P.F. 2001. *Dialog Designs: Knowing Which Type of Speech Recognition to Use Can Make a Big Difference.* Speech Technology Magazine, May/June 2001.

41. White Paper. 2001. *An Introduction to Speech Recognition.* IBM.

42. White Paper. 2001. *Business Case for Voice Authentication.* Nuance Communications.

43. White Paper. 2001. *How Far Can Speech Recognition Take Your Business?* SpeechWorks.

44. White Paper. 2001. *IBM Voice Systems: Multichannel Access to Information.* IBM.

45. White Paper. 2001. *IBM WebSphere Voice Server with ViaVoice Technology.* IBM.

46. White Paper. 2001. *Next Generation Voice Services.* Dialogic.

47. White Paper. 2001. *Six Quick Steps to Writing Your First Speech User Interface.* IBM.

48. White Paper. 2001. *The Impact of Speech Recognition and Voice Authentication Systems.* Nuance Communications.

49. White Paper. 2001. *The ROI of Speech.* SpeechWorks International.

50. White Paper. *SpeechSite: Bringing the Web Model of Self-service to the Telephone.* SpeechWorks.

51. White Paper. *Voice Portals—The Heart of the Voice Web.* 2001. NMS Communications.

Reports

52. *Annual Review of Communications*. 2001. International Engineering Consortium.

53. *I Hear and Obey: Speech Recognition Applications*. 2000. Dain Rausher Wessels.

54. *The Next 1000 years*. 2001. March 2001. Vol. 44. No. 3. Communications of the ACM.

55. *The Significance of VoiceXML*. 2000. IDC (Tetschner, W. and McClure, S.).

56. *The Voice Ecosystem*. The Kelsey Group, 2001.

57. *Voice Application Networks: The Rise of Network-Based Voice Services*, 2001. IDC (Winther, Mark).

58. *Voice Portals Using VoiceXML Review*. 2001. CT Labs Testing Services.

59. *Wireless Data: Speaking Up. Speaking of the Next Killer Application, Voice Takes Center Stage*. 2001. Robertson Stephens Technology Research.

Conferences

60. *AVIOS 2001*.

61. *V-World*, Nuance Speech Conference. San Diego, May 2001.

Useful URLs

VoiceXML Tools

A list of VoiceXML tools follows.

BeVocal Café	http://developers.bevocal.com
Covigo Studio	www.studio.com
HeyAnita FreeSpeech	http://freespeech.heyanita.com
IBM Speech Tools	www.ibm.com/software/speech
Motorola Mobile ADK	http://mix.motorola.com
Nuance V-Builder	http://developer.nuance.com
Tellme Studio	http://studio.tellme.com
VoiceGenie Developer Workshop	http://developer.voicegenie.com
Voxeo Community	http://community.voxeo.com

Other Tools

A list of other available tools follows.

Apache Web Server	www.apache.org
BEA	www.bea.com
Center for Spoken Language Understanding—Rapid Application Development	http://cslu.cse.ogi.edu/toolkit/

EcmaScript	www.ecma.ch/ecma1/stand/ecma-262.htm
IBM Websphere	www-4.ibm.com/software/webservers/appserv/
IPSec	www.cs.umass.edu/~lmccarth/ipsec.html
Netscape Iplanet	www.iplanet.com/products
PERL	www.perl.org
PHP	www.php.net
SpeechWork's open source VoiceXML interpreter—Open VXI	www.speech.cs.cmu.edu/openvxi
UC Berkley—SUEDE	http://guir.berkeley.edu/projects/suede/
Unisys—Natural Language Speech Assistant	www.unisys.com/marketplace/nlu/
VBScript	http://msdn.microsoft.com/scripting/default.htm?/scripting/vbscript/default.htm

Pervasive Computing

Some information on pervasive computing follows.

Ebiquity.org	http://ebiquity.org/
IBM Pervasive Computing	www.ibm.com/pvc
Pervasive Computing SIG	http://gentoo.cs.umbc.edu/pcsig/about.shtml

Newsletters

A list of newletter URLs follows.

"All Net Devices"	http://devices.internet.com/
"Epaynews.com"	www.epaynews.com/index.cgi
"The Rapidly Changing Face of Computing Journal"	www.harrowtechnologygroup.com
"Strategic News Service"	www.tapsns.com
"Anywhereyougo.com"	www.anywhereyougo.com
"Pervasive Weekly"	www.pervasiveweekly.com
"Fierce Wireless"	www.fiercewireless.com

Organizations

A list of useful organization URLs follows.

Bluetooth	www.bluetooth.com
Internet Engineering Task Force	www.ietf.org
VoiceXML Forum	www.vxmlforum.com
WAP Forum	www.wapforum.com
World Wide Web Consortium (W3C)	www.w3c.org
ETSI	www.etsi.org

Miscellaneous

A list of miscellaneous URLs follows.

Microsoft MiPad	http://research.microsoft.com/srg/mipad.asp
Computer Telephony Lab Report on Voice Portals using VoiceXML	www.commweb.com/article/ COM20010129S003
Carnegie Mellon University's Speech Group	www.speech.cs.cmu.edu

Magazines

A list of magazine URLs follows.

Computational Linguistics	http://mitpress.mit.edu/journal-home .tcl?issn=08912017
Computer Speech and Language	www.academicpress.com/csl
Computer Telephony Magazine	www.computertelephony.com
ELSNews	http://elsnet.org/elsnews.html
IEEE Signal Processing Magazine	www.ieee.org/organizations/pubs/ magazines/sp.htm
IEEE Transactions on Communications	www.comsoc.org/pubs/jrnal/ transcom.html
IEEE Transactions on Signal Processing	www.ieee.org/organizations/society/ sp/tsp.html

IEEE Transactions on Speech and Audio Processing	www.ieee.org/organizations/society/ sp/tsa.html
InSTIL Web Journal	www.speech-technology.org
International Journal for Language and Documentation	www.crux.be/English/english.html
International Journal of Human-Computer Studies	www.academicpress.com/ijhcs
International Journal of Speech Technology	www.kluweronline.nl/journalhome.htm/ 1381-2416
Journal of the Acoustical Society of America	http://asa.aip.org/jasa.html
Speech Communications	www.elsevier.com/inca/publications/ store/5/0/5/5/9/7/
Speech Recognition Update	www.tmaa.com/sru/index.htm
Speech Technology Magazine	www.speechtechmag.com
The Speech Technology Expert	http://epublications.vercomnet.com/speech/
VoiceID Quarterly	www.jmarkowtiz.com/pubs .html#anchor voice
Voice+	www.callvoice.com/publications/voice index.htm
VoiceXML Review	www.voicexmlreview.org
Web Journal of Formal, Computational & Cognitive Linguistics	http://mirror-kcn.unece.org/science/fccl/
WEB-SLS	www.essex.ac.uk/web-sls/

Usability

A List of usability URLs follows.

Use It	www.useit.com
Human-Computer Interaction Virtual Library	http://web.cs.bgsu.edu/hcivl
User Interface Engineering	http://world.std.com/~uieweb/biblio.htm
MIT Media Lab Speech Interface Group	www.media.mit.edu/speech/
University of Maryland	http://otal.umd.edu/guse/

URLs of the Companies Mentioned in This Book

A list of the URLs for the companies mentioned in this book follows.

COMPANY NAME	URL
Aculabs	www.aculabs.com
AirTrac	www.airtrac.com
Alcatel	www.alcatel.com
Allaire	www.allaire.com
AOL	www.aol.com
Appriss	www.appriss.com
AT&T	www.att.com
AT&T Wireless	www.attwns.com
Audiocodes	www.audiocodes.com
Audiopoint	www.audiopoint.com
Audium	www.audium.com
Avaya	www.avaya.com
BEA	www.bea.com
BeVocal	www.bevocal.com
Blue Wireless	www.bluewireless.com
Brooktrout Technology	www.brooktrout.com
Cisco Systems	www.cisco.com
Comverse	www.comverse.com
Conita	www.conita.com
Conversay	www.conversay.com
Covigo	www.covigo.com
Dain Rausher Wessels	www.dainrausher.com
Datria	www.datria.com
Dialogic	www.dialogic.com, www.intel.com
Dynamicsoft	www.dynamicsoft.com
Edify	www.edify.com
Enuncia	www.enuncia.com
Etrieve	www.etrieve.com
Evoice	www.evoice.com

Expedia	www.expedia.com
Fonelet	www.fonelet.com
Fonix	www.fonix.com
Forrester Research	www.forrester.com
General Magic	www.genmagic.com
General Motors	www.gm.com
Gold Systems	www.goldsystems.com
HeyAnita	www.heyanita.com
Hotsip	www.hotsip.com
IBM Corporation	www.ibm.com
IConverse	www.iconverse.com
Informio	www.informio.com
Intel	www.intel.com
International Data Corporation	www.idc.com
InterVoice-Brite	www.intervoicebrite.com
Intovoice	www.intovoice.com
Inzigo	www.inzigo.com
Level3	www.level3.com
Lucent Technologies	www.lucent.com
Luminant Worldwide	www.luminant.com
MCI	www.mci.com
Microoptical	www.microoptical.com
Microsoft	www.microsoft.com
Microstrategy	www.microstrategy.com
Motorola	www.motorola.com
Natural Microsystems	www.nms.com
Net2Phone	www.net2phone.com
Nextel	www.nextel.com
Nortel	www.nortel.com
NTT DoCoMo	www.nttdocomo.com
Nuance Communications	www.nuance.com
OnStar	www.onstar.com
Openwave	www.openwave.com
PipeBeach	www.pipebeach.com
Pipebeach AB	www.pipebeach.com

Placeware	www.placeware.com
Quack	www.quack.com, www.aol.com
Qwest	www.qwest.com
Siebel Systems	www.siebel.com
Soundbite	www.soundbite.com
SpeechWorks International	www.speechworks.com
Sprint	www.sprint.com
Syntellect	www.syntellect.com
Telelogue	www.telelogue.com
Telera	www.telera.com
Tellme Networks, Inc.	www.tellme.com
Telsoft	www.telsoft.com
TelSurf Networks	www.telsurf.com
Unisys	www.unisys.com
Vail Systems	www.vailsystems.com
Verascape	www.verascape.com
Verizon Communications	www.verizon.com
VocalPoint	www.vocalpoint.com
VoiceGenie	www.voicegenie.com
Voicegenie	www.voicegenie.com
Voicemate	www.voicemate.com
Voxeo	www.voxeo.com
Voxeo Corporation	www.voxeo.com
Webley	www.webley.com
Webversa	www.webversa.com
Yahoo	www.yahoo.com

Index

A

accents:
  accounting for, in speech recognition, 19
  selection of, 337, 351
  within words, in speech synthesis, 26
access control lists, 327
acoustic models, 50
acronym list, 437–440
active grammar set, 112–115
Active Server Pages (ASP), 286
actors (voice talent), selection of, 333, 337
age:
  and document expiration, 252
  of usability study participants, 364–365
  of voice, in speech synthesis, 279, 337
airlines, voice applications for, 48, 59, 425
alerts, voice applications for, 433–434
alpha release of voice application, 340–341
American Federation of Television and Radio Artists (AFTRA), 51, 332
anonymous scope, 114
application persona, 350–351

application programming interfaces (APIs), 431, 432
application scope, 113
application server, for dynamic Web applications, 284–286, 289
application service providers, for VoiceXML, 11
application variables, 239–240
architecture:
  for distributed speech recognition, 417
  for field application, 375–379, 390
  for SIP-enabled network, 402
  for Voice Application Networks, 56
  for VoiceXML, 86–87, 93–96, 314
articulation, 24
articulatory speech synthesis, 24
ASCII, in grammar document, 261
`<assign>` element, 146, 148–149
audio:
  listening to/recognizing, 98–111
  playing, 96–98
  production quality of, 51–52, 60, 332–333, 354
  recording from caller, 430
  speaking voice in, 278–279
  surveillance by, 318
`<audio>` element, 146, 149–151, 280

CUSTOMER NOTE: IF THIS BOOK IS ACCOMPANIED BY SOFTWARE, PLEASE READ THE FOLLOWING BEFORE OPENING THE PACKAGE.

This software contains files to help you utilize the models described in the accompanying book. By opening the package, you are agreeing to be bound by the following agreement:

- This software product is protected by copyright and all rights are reserved by the author, John Wiley & Sons, Inc., or their licensors. You are licensed to use this software as described in the software and the accompanying book. Copying the software for any other purpose may be a violation of the U.S. Copyright Law.

- This software product is sold as is without warranty of any kind, either express or implied, including but not limited to the implied warranty of merchantability and fitness for a particular purpose. Neither Wiley nor its dealers or distributors assumes any liability for any alleged or actual damages arising from the use of or the inability to use this software. (Some states do not allow the exclusion of implied warranties, so the exclusion may not apply to you.)

To use this CD-ROM, your system must meet the following requirements:

Platform/Processor/Operating System.

RAM.

Hard Drive Space.

Peripherals.